J. N. HOOK, Ph.D. University of Illinois, is Professor of English and Counselor in the Teaching of English at that institution. He has held both of these positions since 1946. He has been Executive Secretary, National Council of Teachers of English; President, Illinois Association of Teachers of English; and Coordinator, Project English, U.S. Office of Education. Professor Hook is the author of *Hook's Guide to Good Writing: Grammar, Style, Usage* and co-author, with E. G. Mathews, of *Modern American Grammar and Usage* (both published by The Ronald Press Company), as well as a number of high school textbooks.

The Teaching of
High School English

J. N. HOOK

University of Illinois

THIRD EDITION

THE RONALD PRESS COMPANY • NEW YORK

Library of Congress Catalog Card Number: 65–11625
PRINTED IN THE UNITED STATES OF AMERICA

PREFACE

Recent years have witnessed more rapid changes related to the teaching of high school English than has any other quinquennium or decade in the short history of this branch of the profession. Linguistic knowledge has increased; there is talk of a new rhetoric; and theories of literary criticism have been sharpened. Programed instruction has caught the attention of educators and laymen alike; team teaching has become a reality in many schools; and experiments with flexible scheduling are frequent. The National Council of Teachers of English has increased fivefold in membership in ten years; the Commission on English Institutes have focused attention on the importance of excellent preparation of English teachers; Project English has provided federal funds for long needed research and experimentation.

It has been the privilege of the author of this book to have had some kind of role in several of these developments. Service for seven years as Executive Secretary of the National Council of Teachers of English and for a year and a half as the first Coordinator of Project English has made increasingly clear the great responsibilities of secondary English teachers and the constant need to translate research and theory into concrete terms in order to help teachers meet those responsibilities.

The Teaching of High School English is a textbook for students preparing to teach the English language and its literature in junior and senior high schools, and for experienced teachers who wish to keep abreast of the current teaching practices in their profession.

The book stresses application more than theory, presenting a large number of specific suggestions and tested classroom procedures. Some of these have been drawn from the author's years of teaching experience in high school, college, and university, but many more have been derived from the teaching experience of others. Disparate though these suggestions and recommendations are, the author believes that they add up to a coherent theory.

In this edition the Idea Boxes, which combine bibliographical references with a host of tested procedures and suggestions about content, have been retained and expanded. There is also added attention given to linguistics, composition, and literature. Such developments as programed instruction and team teaching are included.

The author's indebtedness is so great that he can again utter only a blanket "Thank you" to the editors of professional magazines, to speakers at professional meetings, to the sometimes inspired and inspiring high school teachers whose classes he has visited, to his own undergraduate and graduate students who are planning to become teachers, and to the hundreds of other teachers who, knowingly or unknowingly, have assisted him. A special "Thank you" goes to two neglected people: a patient woman and a small boy who someday may be in a class taught by a reader of this book.

J. N. Hook

Urbana, Illinois
January, 1965

CONTENTS

The Teaching of
High School English

1

THE TASK

Miss Johnson was arranging books on the shelves of her classroom library. Tomorrow another school year would begin.

She straightened, gave a final pat to a paperbound book that had strayed out of line, and walked to her desk at a pace that denied her usual briskness. She sat down and re-examined her familiar surroundings. Thirty-five movable chairs. Chalkboards. A large bulletin board, still bare, but soon to be decked by students and herself with pictures, clippings, samples of student work, miscellanea. The bookshelves with reference volumes and a constantly to-be-changed array of paperbacks and other books. Literary maps, a tape recorder, a record player. Windows looking out toward a stretch of green grass, a heavily traveled street, rows of houses, and a tall smokestack in the distance.

"My queendom," she thought. "No, my own little chunk of democracy." She recognized the signs. She was going to philosophize again. "Don't be maudlin," she warned herself.

She murmured half-aloud some lines from the prologue of *Henry V:*

> " 'Can this cockpit hold
> The vasty fields of France? Or may we cram
> Within this wooden O the very casques
> That did affright the air at Agincourt?'

It's not France, of course. And it's not an O; it's a rectangle—a plain, unbeautiful rectangle. And five times every day thirty or thirty-five children will file, scramble, saunter, dash into the rectangle and wait

3

for something to happen to them. And I have to see that it does happen. Agincourt, Rome, Raveloe, and Walden Pond have to happen here. People have to happen.

> 'But pardon, gentles all [she looked toward the windows],
> The flat unraised spirits that hath dared
> On this unworthy scaffold to bring forth
> So great an object.'

Words have to happen here, words that mean places and people and all the things that people see and act and think and say. A love of words has to happen, at least a respect for words, an understanding of what words can do."

Shakespeare became almost a prayer:

> " 'Into a thousand parts divide one man [*or woman,* she amended],
> And make imaginary puissance;
> Think, when we talk of horses, that you see them
> Printing their proud hoofs in the receiving earth.
> For 'tis your thoughts that now must deck our kings,
> Carry them here and there, jumping o'er times,
> *Turning the accomplishment of many years*
> *Into an hour-glass.'* "

REDUCING CONFUSION OF AIMS

The Basic Issues Conferences

Miss Johnson apparently knew what her aims were in teaching English. Not all teachers, departments, and schools are so fortunate. In 1958 a series of conferences was held, with financial support from the Ford Foundation, to determine the basic issues in the teaching of English. The conferees were some of the national leaders, including elementary, secondary, and college teachers, in the American Studies Association, the College English Association, the Modern Language Association, and the National Council of Teachers of English. Their report listed and described thirty-five issues seriously needing study, research, and decision. Issue number 1 was stated in this way:

What is English? We agree generally that English composition, language, and literature are within our province, but we are uncertain whether our boundaries should include world literature in translation, public speaking, journalism, listening, remedial reading, and general academic orientation. Some of these activities admittedly promote the social development of the individual. But does excessive emphasis on them result in the neglect of that great body of literature which can point the individual's development in more significant directions? Has the fundamental liberal discipline of English been replaced, at some levels of schooling, by *ad hoc* training in how to write a letter, how to give a radio speech, manners, dating, telephoning, vocational guidance?

Two Thousand Aims?

More than a quarter of a century ago a researcher listed all the aims for English teaching that he could find in print. The result: 1,581 aims, ranging from a vaguely phrased "Teach appreciation" down to "Teach proper attitudes toward care of the teeth." If his count were brought up to date, the number might exceed 2,000. But in most schools there are only 180 school days per year. To attain 2,000 aims is impossible. Needed is a reachable goal or a group of closely interrelated reachable goals.

Yet school and community pressures are hostile to such simplicity. The home and the church have abrogated some of the responsibilities once assumed to be theirs. Increasingly, instruction in etiquette, in courtesy, and in moral values has been relinquished to the schools. Each time when a new task for the schools is suggested, somebody observes that the task involves reading and writing and speaking; he then suggests that, because of this involvement, the English class is the logical place to insert the new material. If teen-age telephone habits are bad, for example, a unit on using the telephone is recommended for the English classes, because telephoning means using the language. If an article in a national scientific magazine proposes (as at least one did) that much or most of the reading in secondary English classes should be about science, hosts of scientists and laymen applaud, urging that the reform be instituted at once. School administrators are assailed again and again with pleas of "Do this!" "Include this!" "Give this high priority!" Servants of the community, the administrators oblige as well as they can. They turn to their English teachers, saying, "There's a chance here for students to read and write and speak about something that the community wants to have read and written and spoken about. Will you try to incorporate it in your program, please." And the English teachers look through the course of study to see what can best be sacrificed so that they can include instruction in

> The health that is dental and the health that is mental
> (Good-bye, good-bye to the transcendental);

The importance of space and the Martian race
(And Browning goes, frowning, from his place);
The pageant we need for the Bicentennial
(And so we lose a Hardy perennial).

Increasingly, though, English teachers are resisting the intrusion of what is not germane to their work. They are learning to say no—politely, but still *no*. Their hands will be strengthened when they reach closer agreement about what is truly germane.

Competing Theories Concerning Aims

Four somewhat competitive theories exist among English teachers as to what really belongs in an English program. The most catholic of these, and the least defensible, is the *carpe diem* theory. In brief, this says that any topic involving the use of language is apropos and may be introduced at any time that seems suitable. Bicentennial celebrations and this week's football game, being of current interest, are therefore appropriate and easily motivated subjects for reading, writing, and speaking. An outgrowth of a partially mistaken reading of John Dewey, the *carpe diem* theory is built upon the partially correct idea that what children are taught should be closely related to whatever happens to be exciting at the moment.

The second theory holds that the English teacher's task is to improve *communication*. Communication is divided into two parts:

COMMUNICATION

Sending	Receiving

Each of these is in turn subdivided:

COMMUNICATION

Sending		Receiving	
Speaking	Writing	Listening	Reading

This four-part division does not necessarily mean, though, that each section will be equally emphasized in the classroom. Reading is broadly enough defined to include the reading and study of literature, to which the proponents of the communication theory would devote perhaps as much as a half of the time. Writing and speaking both involve study of the language (as do listening and reading to some extent), but, since writing skills seem to take longer to develop than do speaking skills, there is a tendency to devote more attention to the language of writing.

The *tripod* theory says that instruction should encompass language, composition, and literature as equal partners in the English curriculum. Language includes study of the history, grammar, and current use of the English tongue. Composition refers especially but not exclusively to written work. Literature means literary materials, not today's newspaper or an article in *Popular Mechanics*. The twenty institutes for teachers sponsored in 1962 by the Commission on English of the College Entrance Examination Board focused on the tripod and first called national attention to this method of limiting the English program.

In mathematics, *unified field theory* refers to a concept of Albert Einstein involving electromagnetism and gravitation. We may borrow the term for English to designate the belief that English is and should be a unified field. However, some professional leaders argue that language or rhetoric is the unifying force and that the English curriculum should be language-centered, while others assert that literature should be the center. Those favoring the emphasis on language or rhetoric advocate intensive study of the English language, much writing on linguistic topics, and much literary study concerned with analysis of the authors' use of language and rhetoric. Those who favor a literary center contend that writing should be mainly on literary topics, and that students may improve their use of language by wide and deep reading. A possibly friendly battle is developing between holders of these views. It should be friendly, because both believe in the unified field theory; the linguists would not omit literature, and the belletrists would not exclude study of the language and of rhetoric.

The Point of View of This Book

It is not intended here to arbitrate among these four theories, except to question the validity of the *carpe diem* philosophy. That philosophy has two major weaknesses, even though it may be successful in the classroom of an expert teacher. The first weakness is that it pays too much attention to the barely relevant: to current magazines or radio speaking or science fiction or community surveys, for example. These are not to be completely condemned; a student may "learn English" from any of them. But, if they are given major emphasis, the transitory conquers the permanent: *LIFE, si;* life, no. The second weakness is that coherent plans spanning several years are difficult or impossible, because no one can forecast what the demands of the minute (noun or adjective) may be. The English curriculum is in many schools almost chaotic because of lack of sequential planning; the *carpe diem* theory certainly promises no reduction of chaos. True, study of what is relevant in the immediate environment is important, and many suggestions later in this book pertain to use of the immediate environment. The point is that the purely happenstantial provides insufficient basis for methodical instruction.

The other three theories are similar enough that any one of them may be selected as the basis for a coherent program of English instruction. They differ in emphasis rather than in essentials. The communication theory stresses the interrelatedness of the sending and receiving of oral and written "messages," including literature; the tripod theory pays relatively little attention to speaking and listening, much to literature and composition and language as subjects for intensive study; the unified field theory says that speaking, listening, writing, and reading may all best be studied through their common denominator, language or rhetoric, or through their common greatest exemplification, literature.

This book does not favor any one of these theories above the other two. It is eclectic in that it is based upon the following beliefs:

1. A planned, sequential program in secondary English is essential, with adaptations for differences among communities and among individuals.
2. The functioning of the English language should be studied daily, sometimes as a thing in itself, more often as a key to the clarity and effectiveness of composition and literature.
3. Students should be steadily exposed to the best literature they are capable of understanding reasonably well.
4. Students should have regular practice in using the language through a planned sequence of written and oral compositions.
5. The proportionate amount of time devoted to speaking and listening will be less in English classes in a school requiring separate speech courses of all students, greater in a school with no such requirement.

THE TASK OF TEACHING LANGUAGE

The rest of this chapter will delineate the major tasks of the English teacher, to provide an overview of his responsibilities. (One of the glaring lacks of the English language is a common gender, third person singular pronoun. The author, being a man, will use *he* and *his* to refer to a teacher. This decision may be considered either as a bow to convention or as masculine arrogance.) Suggestions for accomplishing the tasks fill the other chapters.

Determining the Purposes of Linguistic Instruction

When, in past centuries, Latin was the center of the curriculum, a Latin teacher assumed that his responsibility was rather clear-cut: he was to teach all his students to conjugate verbs and decline nouns, translate from Latin into English, and compose in Latin. Hour after hour was given to reciting *hic, haec, hoc,* and the like.

For many years English instruction was strongly influenced by the Latin procedures. Despite the fact that English differs from Latin in being largely uninflected, students laboriously conjugated verbs, declined nouns, and parsed sentences—parsing consisting mainly of detecting everything detectable about each word, as well as a few things that had to be accepted on faith. The process was largely useless and purposeless, but teachers *assumed* that such kinds of drill taught students what they needed to know about the language.

The conjugators and the parsers have almost disappeared, but a few of their replacements are little less sinful. These are the teachers who believe, or act as if they believe, that definition and identification are the chief purposes of language study. Their students learn to parrot the textbook definitions: "A sentence is a group of words expressing a complete thought. The subject of a sentence tells what the sentence is about." The students identify, identify, identify, pinning labels on every word:

> Theirs not to reason why.
> Theirs but to do—or try.

More enlightened teachers, steadily increasing in number, recognize two basic reasons for teaching the English language, one cultural and one utilitarian. The cultural reason is that language is a uniquely human possession. Through its use man has attempted to express his emotions, his strongest beliefs, his highest ideals. With it he has learned to inform and to deceive. It can be as descriptive and interpretive as a painting, as beautiful and moving as music, as sky-reaching as architecture. Knowledge of the qualities of language is essential to cultural roundness and solidity; the person who does not know them has a gap in his education that knowledge of no other type can fill.

The utilitarian reason for teaching the English language is that the nation's work, the world's work, is dependent upon language. No type of industry or occupation listed in the yellow pages of the telephone book could long survive without language. The coming of automation, the reduction of the number of blue-collar workers, and the even greater increase of white-collar employees have made clear and accurate use of the language even more essential than before. The promotion of a man or a woman is more often dependent upon how well he or she communicates than it is upon his brawn or her baby-blue eyes.

Every English teacher has the task of spelling out for himself the details of these purposes and of examining the content and procedures of the work in language to make sure that they are all relevant to the goals he seeks.

Teaching How Language Works

Definition and identification reveal relatively little about the language, although obviously a knowledge of basic terms makes it easier to discuss sentence elements. Especially needed is manipulation of words, phrases, and clauses. Such manipulation, involving the re-arrangement of the sentence parts and the substitution of different words and constructions, can do more than anything else to show students the changes in meaning and emphasis that are possible.

Part of the manipulation consists of work in semantics. Sentences are shifted from reportorial language to affective (emotional), and vice versa. Denotations and connotations are studied. The omnipresent role of metaphor is discussed.

In addition, a study of the history of the language helps to reveal pertinent characteristics of today's English. For example, knowledge of the medieval shift away from numerous inflections tends to clarify why word order is now so important. The growth of complex sentences, replacing many simple and compound structures, has led to the possibility of more precise expression today. The addition of progressive verb forms has lent further enrichment. Most dramatic of all, at least from students' point of view, is the steady growth of vocabulary through the centuries, with borrowings from every continent and almost every nation.

Choosing a Grammar

Three systems of grammar and a number of variations of each are available to today's teacher. Traditional grammar, with its eight parts of speech and Latin-derived concepts and terminology, is still the most familiar variety and, therefore, the one with which most teachers are at home. Structural linguistics stresses the language of speech as primary, with the written language a derivative; instead of parts of speech it describes four form classes and about a score of kinds of function words. Generative, or transformational, grammar is based upon the assumption that most English sentences are transformations of a few basic or "kernel" sentences.

The three types of grammar exist in several versions but are beginning to be combined. Some recent texts, though traditionally oriented, include definitions modified and made more accurate by modern research. Some structuralists are paying increased attention to the application of linguistic theory to classroom practice; some writers of structuralist textbooks use as much familiar terminology as they can, and some are increasing their attention to the written form of the language. Although some transformationalists are chiefly interested in perfecting their system for purposes of machine translation and machine composition, others are linking transformational grammar with the classroom.

It is probable that the English grammar of the future will represent a blending of grammars (though some scholars deny the possibility). The theories of sentence patterns of the transformationalists, the work of the structuralists on phonemics and intonation, and a large proportion of traditional terminology may well compose the blend.

This is a time of transition in the teaching of grammar. Teachers in each department have the task of choosing a grammar that they know, in which they can believe, and with which they think they can lead students to significant understanding. They have the added responsibility of keeping their minds open, so that, when additional research and experimentation clear up some of the presently muddy waters, they can shift toward the grammatical content that is proving most true and most helpful to students.

Teaching Usage

Usage is defined thus in Webster's *Third International:* "the way in which words are actually used (as in a particular form or sense) generally or among a community or group of persons." Grammar, in contrast, is the description of word forms, sentence parts, and sentence patterns; it is based upon usage. Grammarians observe, for example, that *are* and *were* rather than *is* and *was* represent the general "educated" usage after *you,* even when *you* means only one person; they formulate a "rule" (really a description) that says that verb forms normally regarded as plural follow the second person pronoun in the singular as well as the plural. Many persons then oversimplify, saying that *you are* or *you were* is "correct" and *you is* or *you was* is "incorrect." Actually, correctness is not involved, but only linguistic conformity or etiquette. The grammatical "rule" would be quite different if usage had established *you is* and *you was* as the forms normally used by "educated" persons.

Teachers have the task of clarifying such matters for their students. They themselves need to know about fluctuations in usage, for instance, that the double negative was once in favor or that the logical *you was* battled valiantly against *you were* before succumbing. They need to know that individual usages vary in different parts of the United States and other English-speaking countries. They should know also that, although it is possible to describe levels of usage (e.g., formal, colloquial, slang, substandard), the levels of demarcation are far from precise, and words or constructions tend to slip across the boundaries. (For this reason, Webster's *Third International* abandoned the designation of words as "colloquial.") They should attempt to show students that for social and economic reasons, not because of "rightness" and "wrongness," it is wise for them to make infrequent use or no use of substandard expressions.

The teaching of spelling is the teaching of one kind of usage. A quick comparison of Chaucerian and modern spellings will reveal to anyone that orthography is not a permanently fixed thing. Today's teacher gives instruction in those spelling usages that happen to be widely accepted today. The spelling *musick* is dead; *music* is today's version; tomorrow's may be *miuzik* or even a group of symbols in a now unknown alphabet.

Improving students' usage is an important job, but not the central one that some teachers have made it. Few students have over a hundred or so frequently employed substandard usages (aside from unconventional spellings) that need to be eradicated. A systematic, reasoned procedure for accomplishing the uprooting should occupy only a small fraction of class time.

Providing for Individual Differences

In a heterogeneous sophomore class in Emville, the thirty students reveal wide differences in linguistic sophistication. There are five or six for whom *he done it* represents a normal mode of expression, a dozen who say *if I was you,* and twenty-seven who are often unsure about *her* or *him.* Five in the class retain enough of their earlier instruction to be able to classify most words grammatically and to designate their functions within a sentence as *subject, predicate, object,* or *modifier,* but knowledge of this sort has slipped from the minds of the other twenty-five, leaving them virtually unmarked. None of the students know much about the history of the language; most have never even conceived the idea that language has a history: it is only something that is here and presumably always has been here, unchanged since the Tower of Babel.

Some of the students can learn much more rapidly than others, for the IQ range is from 81 to 144. Tests of verbal intelligence reveal as great a disparity.

The teacher's task is simple to state, difficult to achieve: to bring each student up to the highest degree of linguistic sophistication and skill possible for him.

THE TASK OF TEACHING COMPOSITION

"Composition" is defined here to include both oral and written attempts to convey information, opinions, or emotions. It covers both factual and imaginative presentations. It includes the mechanics of paragraphing, punctuating, and capitalizing, and it considers morphology, syntax, and semantics to the extent that they affect communication.

Helping Students To Find Something To Say

Good teachers of English have always been concerned at least as much with substance as with mechanics, but in the past few years the insistence upon solid content has steadily increased. No longer is a student's paper given a top grade simply because it has no misspellings, poor sentences, or solecisms; top grades are reserved for papers that say something, that say something significant, that say it neatly and accurately.

Students who complain that they have nothing to talk or write about are usually those who have never learned to marshal their resources for attack upon a topic. They stare out the window and finally turn in a blank or nearly blank paper. A skilled teacher makes certain that all students *can* talk or write on at least one of the topics; he motivates the students to want to express themselves; and he helps them to learn to uncover in their own minds, or in other sources, whatever bits of information are relevant.

Teaching Principles of Organization

The taillight of an automobile doesn't belong in front; a spark plug isn't inserted in the exhaust pipe. The parts of a composition can be put together as methodically as the parts of an automobile. The effectiveness of the whole, even its clarity, depends in large measure upon the arrangement of the parts—the organization.

Organization is important in both small and large units of discourse. At the University of Nebraska Curriculum Study Center, two useful terms have been invented: *micro-rhetoric* and *macro-rhetoric*. *Micro-rhetoric* refers to the principles of organizing and expressing a sentence or perhaps a paragraph; *macro-rhetoric* describes the organization of a larger unit, whether a composition, a textbook, or a novel. Although the Elizabethans employed well over a hundred rhetorical terms, a few principles are basic and permanent. It is these few principles of organization and expression that the English teacher needs to teach thoroughly. They blend imperceptibly with the next part of the task, the teaching of structure and style.

Teaching Structure and Style

Within the framework of the good composition, the sentences march or trip toward an inevitable conclusion. In the poor composition, they plod or stumble or wander or reverse themselves.

The teacher teaches micro-rhetoric so that each sentence can make its contribution to an entire paragraph, and each paragraph its contribution to a larger unit. Each clause, phrase, or word, each figure of speech, serves a purpose. Correctness of spelling, punctuation, verb forms, and the like is taught because incorrectness distracts from the receiving of the message; the message is of major importance, and nothing must be allowed to prevent its reception. Sentence structure is taught because not all possible forms of sentences are equally good for all purposes. Style is taught because some structures and some words are appropriate for certain purposes but not for all. Transitions are taught because they are signposts that remind the reader of where he has been and show him where he is going next.

Providing for Individual Differences

In the Emville sophomore class, five of the thirty students like to write and have a fairly clear understanding of a writer's obligation to a reader. The other twenty-five are good-natured and agreeable; they go through the motions of composing just as they do calisthenics in physical education class, with no idea of why they are doing what they are doing. One of the teacher's jobs is to motivate composition, to make it, if not exciting, at least purposeful.

The same five sophomores can organize compositions in a variety of ways, can vary sentence structure, and reveal at least the beginnings of individualized styles. Twenty of the others can organize chronologically but are lost when a topic requires some other order. Five blurt out whatever comes to their tongues or pens, regardless of order. Of these five, two seem incapable of assembling sentences into a coherent paragraph, let alone a longer piece of writing; in fact, they can barely assemble words into a written sentence.

The teacher must do as much as he can for all of these students, realizing that the slowest five will never catch the best five, that the gap between will constantly widen, but realizing also that some improvement in composition is possible for everyone who is at all educable. Yet, in composition as in other parts of English and in other school subjects, some teachers and some schools are highly successful with students of one level of ability, much less successful with others. A New York State publication, for example, shows that, of three selected schools, one did exceptionally well with students of high ability, poorly with average and low-ability students; a second school ranked near the top in success with average students, near the bottom with those of high and low ability; the third did excellent work with low-ability students but ranked in the bottom quartile with the others. The ideal, difficult to attain, is to effect the greatest improvement possible in all students.

THE TASK OF TEACHING READING AND LITERATURE

Providing for Individual Differences

Individual differences in reading ability are easier to demonstrate statistically than are differences in linguistic knowledge or composi-

tion skill. In the Emville class that we are using as an example, eleven
of the thirty sophomores read below the tenth grade level, with one
at fourth grade, two at sixth, two at seventh, two at eighth, and four
at ninth. Twelve read at the tenth grade level, and seven above it,
including three at eleventh, two at twelfth, one at thirteenth, and one
at fifteenth. How can a program be developed that will satisfy equally
well the needs of one student who reads like a fourth grader and another who reads as well as a college junior?

Other pertinent individual differences exist in this not atypical
class. The range of IQ's is from 81 to 144. Sixteen of the students
are boys; fourteen are girls. Most of the students were fifteen years
old in September, but one was thirteen, five were fourteen, and two
were sixteen. A poll of the class has revealed an interest in twenty-
three different vocations. What literature can appeal to boys and to
girls, to the mentally slow and the mentally quick, to the thirteen-year-
old and the sixteen-year-old, and to the future plumber, the future
housewife, and the future college professor?

How can such diverse students be motivated? For many students
the club that we call a report card is a sufficient incentive to work.
But the wise teacher of literature knows that students who read only
to earn a grade often do not learn to love reading. It is easy to
motivate a few students even without grades, because the most
capable or most ambitious students are usually self-starting and virtually self-propelled. But the self-starters are all too rare. With the
other students more than one type of motivation is needed.

Selecting and Apportioning

In the early 1960's, American publishers were bringing out over
18,000 books a year. Excluding Saturdays and Sundays, that amounts
to about 70 new books published each day—70 books that may or may
not be grist for the English teacher's mill. Seventy books—perhaps
20,000 pages every day. And already there existed many thousands
of books. Wherever the teacher or his students turn, reading material
is abundant. On the newsstands vie the occasionally quiet but generally flamboyant covers of hundreds of magazines, including dozens
of uncomic comic books, each trying to outshout the others. In the
newspapers, stories of crime or politics or war or scandal are picturesquely summarized in tall headlines. The libraries, the classrooms, and a small percentage of homes offer more quiet choices.
From this vast body of printed material, growing so fast that any

person can read only a tiny fraction of the daily output, the teacher must help his students find what they can most profitably use.

An old argument, still far from settled, concerns the proportionate amounts of time that should be devoted in English classes to contemporary literature and to literature that has lasted the hundred years often considered requisite to becoming a classic. The increasing tendency is to stress the classic without ruling out the contemporary that is well written and that has special appropriateness for a given class. But does this solution apply equally well to students of all levels of ability?

In the search for proportion, teachers need to decide also whether all the material read must be Literature (capitalized), or whether the inclusion of some transitory, well-written, but not particularly artistic prose may be justified. And they need to decide how much of each course should be devoted to each of the major literary types: fiction, non-fiction, poetry, and drama.

Approaching

Chapter 2 will consider the principles involved in planning the order of literary selections. But, after that decision is reached, presumably by an entire department or a larger group, the individual teacher still needs to decide what approaches to each selection will be likely to bring best results with a particular class. The choice of approaches depends upon the instructional aims and upon the characteristics of the class. The six basic approaches, which will be discussed and illustrated in later chapters, are these:

1. The *historical*, in which the emphasis is upon the author and the background of the selection.
2. The *sociopsychological*, which emphasizes the social and psychological aspects of the literature.
3. The *emotive*, which stresses the beauty or the pleasure implicit in the selection.
4. The *didactic*, which involves a study of the author's purpose and perhaps the moral implications of the selection.
5. The *paraphrastic*, which involves a summary of what the author has said.
6. The *analytical*, which attempts a study of the selection on the basis of its literary characteristics.

Guiding Individual Reading

Every English teacher requires, or at least encourages, individual students to read material in addition to that read by the class as a whole. In recent years emphasis on such reading has been increasing; it is regarded as one way to provide for individual differences. More and more, "outside reading" is being brought "inside": Students are urged to relate their individual reading to the class discussions of reading done in common. To some students, the opportunity to do outside reading is welcome; others consider it onerous, an undesirable chore. Nearly all students detest a traditional book-report day on which each is expected to discuss his book in accordance with some creaking formula.

The teacher's task here, then, is to lead students to want to read extensively and at progressively higher levels, and to find ways by which students may share the enlightenment their individual reading has brought them.

THE TASK OF TEACHING LISTENING

In 1928 Paul T. Rankin made a study of the relative amounts of time devoted by adults to listening, speaking, reading, and writing. He found that almost a half of the time involved in some sort of communication was used in listening. Yet instruction in listening was almost absent from the school curriculum.

Little was done about this situation until the middle 1940's. It was generally taken for granted that everyone knows how to listen. During the forties, though, and through much of the fifties, more and more articles on listening appeared, and English teachers' interest in this aspect of their work increased. A few teachers jumped to the conclusion that since about half of communication time is spent in listening, about half of English instruction should be devoted to listening. Now, in the 1960's, teachers realize that such a conclusion is unrealistic. They are striving for a modest but effective expenditure of time that will enable students to learn better such skills as following oral instructions, distinguishing between main and supporting points in a lecture, and analyzing the kinds of appeals made, for example, in a radio or television commercial or a political plea.

Relationships between listening and reading have gradually become apparent. Reading is the act of receiving, by means of the eye and the nervous system, a communication in written or printed symbols that have been infused with meaning. Listening is the act of receiving, by means of the ear and the nervous system, a communication in audible symbols that have been infused with meaning. Since both reading and listening involve receiving a communication, one may rightly expect some similarity between the two acts. W. W. Hatfield, in the *English Journal,* years ago pointed out these similarities:

1. Purposeful listening, like purposeful reading, is more successful than that which is without purpose.
2. Listening, like reading, is of various types, each of which must be mastered through practice.
3. Careful listening, like careful reading, involves attending (giving one's mind) to what is being communicated.
4. Semantic dangers (problems in word meaning) are even greater in listening than in teaching.

THE TASKS THAT ARE SHARED

Some responsibilities are common to all teachers in secondary schools. Such responsibilities are usually listed as the general aims of the school, and statements of such aims are almost as numerous as schools themselves.

Most widely known of the statements is the set of seven "Cardinal Principles" promulgated a half-century ago by what was then the United States Bureau of Education. According to these principles, the secondary teacher needs to guide its students toward the following goals: (1) health, (2) command of fundamental processes, (3) worthy home membership, (4) vocation, (5) citizenship, (6) worthy use of leisure, and (7) ethical character. All secondary teachers share in working toward these goals. The English teacher has partial responsibility for each goal. The study of literature may contribute to mental health. Reading and writing are two of the fundamental processes. What a student reads, as well as his interactions with his teachers and fellow students, may affect his family relationships. His reading will probably affect his vocational choice, and his success in English may determine in large measure his success in his vocation. Discussions of ethics and of morals, and the understanding of human beings that he gains from literature, may influence a student as a citizen. In an age of increasing leisure, what a student learns from his reading may affect the way he spends the hours away from his job. The standards of rightness revealed in literature, the fact that in English class a student can discover dramatically that both ideas and actions have consequences, may help to develop his ethical character. Teachers of other subjects contribute in their own ways to the realization of the seven "Cardinal Principles," but the English teacher's contribution is certainly no less than theirs.

A somewhat more specific list of general objectives is this one, prepared as a guide for the Champaign, Illinois, public schools:

1. To master the basic skills of reading, writing, mathematics, and speech.
2. To develop the ability to think clearly, critically, and creatively.
3. To acquire a desire for knowledge that will lead to continued growth and to the best development of one's potentialities for the common good.
4. To develop a respect for high moral values and to incorporate them into a personal code of living.
5. To understand the rights and duties of members of a democratic society in order to become responsible citizens.
6. To gain a knowledge of our history and an appreciation of our culture.
7. To acquire an understanding of the people and culture of other countries.
8. To develop respect for other persons and to be able to live and work cooperatively with them.
9. To develop habits of safe and healthful living, including the wholesome use of leisure time.
10. To develop skills, understanding, and attitudes that will help one to make a constructive contribution to society.
11. To learn about the natural resources of the world and to develop a feeling of social responsibility toward their use and conservation.
12. To understand the significance of the family for the individual and society, and to strive to become a worthy family member.

The central purpose of the educational program defined by these objectives is that boys and girls be helped to develop their intellectual skills to a degree which is consistent with their present and potential capacities— that they be taught to think logically, critically, and creatively. Our students must be able to solve problems of the present and problems of the future.

Our teachers and administrators accept the responsibility for translating these objectives and high purposes into day to day educational practice. They deal with knowledge, meanings, generalizations, and useful concepts. Knowledge is organized and presented as subject matter. This subject matter receives regular and constant scrutiny to insure that what is taught is what is most worth knowing. A process of continuing evaluation, selection, expansion, and elimination is always underway.

The staff is concerned not only with what is taught but how it is taught. Today's student must learn better, more rapidly, and with more efficiency than ever before. More and more, our students are being led to inquire into problems and discover answers, shades of meanings, and relationships for themselves.

This concern with better selection of subject matter and with improved methodology of teaching begins with individual teachers in the classroom.

The English teacher's share in attaining each of these twelve objectives is obvious. But it must be remembered that his is not the sole responsibility. These objectives he shares, but beyond these he has his own task, which is unique and which no other teacher can perform, though other teachers can supplement it: the task of helping students to understand the nature of language, to use it as a tool for the sending and receiving of messages, and to employ it in comprehending the best that has been written so far by the best minds of men.

The slogan "Every teacher a teacher of English" is high in motive but unattainable in general practice. The simple fact is that few teachers of other subjects know enough about language and literature to teach them. They have necessarily specialized in other subjects and have had insufficient time, even if they had the will, to master English in addition to their specialty. In two ways, however, the teachers of other subjects may and should reinforce the work of the English teacher, just as he is constantly reinforcing or supplementing their work. One of the ways is for these other teachers to let students know that they regard good English as important. They can insist on good organization, correct spelling, accurate punctuation and capitalization, and usages in accord with those most generally approved today. Second, the teachers of other subjects have the responsibility of teaching the vocabulary, spelling, and special reading skills required by their subjects. They are responsible, for instance, for definition, pronunciation, and spelling of such words as *theorem, enzyme, appellate,* and *pizzicato.* The mathematics teacher is responsible for instruction in reading an algebra problem—a very different thing from reading a short story. The social studies teacher is responsible for instruction in reading graphs—a very different thing from reading poetry. To such an extent every teacher may be a teacher of English.

ENGLISH IN THE SPACE AGE

Time is defeating space. A man can circle the globe in a couple of hours, and men are reaching toward the moon and the planets and are looking wistfully toward the distant stars. A human voice or a picture can be heard or seen thousands of miles away in a fraction of a second.

This age, we are told, is the Age of Technology, the Age of Science, the Atomic Age, the Space Age. This, the optimists say, is the Age of Endless Frontiers. This, the pessimists says, is the Age of Annihilation, the Age of the Last Man.

Human beings have felt themselves shrinking as they have learned more about the tininess of their earth in relation to the measureless stretches of a void only thinly sprinkled with suns. Once man could believe that he inhabited the center of the universe, and that he himself was the principal preoccupation of God. Now it is easier to believe that he is an almost invisible dot on a pebble.

When man thinks of his relations with his fellows, it is easy for him to despair. He says, "I want to live long, and I want my children to live forever." But his actions contradict his words. A mad, apparently irrepressible death urge is upon him. If lemmings could talk, perhaps they would discuss summer sunshine as they rush to drown themselves in frigid waters.

Paradoxically, science has given man a choice between destroying himself and enjoying for the first time in his history ample food, clothing, and shelter, as well as ample hours to play, to meditate, and to explore beyond undreamed horizons. Science has given man the opportunity to choose. Man must make the choice. Science cannot.

Perhaps no lemming can stop the lemmings, and perhaps no man can stop man. Churches are trying, but some nations and many persons are godless. A few leaders are trying, but their cries are engulfed in the shouts for more destructive weapons.

Perhaps, if this turns out not to be the Age of the Last Man, the teachers of the humanities will be given some of the credit. Not just North American teachers of the humanities—such conceit ill becomes us—but also European, Asian, African, Australian, and Central and South American ones.

For the humanist has a vision—or should have. He does not know exactly how to attain his vision. He is trying to define a purpose in life, and if he is wise he will never attempt to impose his purpose on someone else. But he keeps groping toward his vision, and as a teacher he encourages others to grope toward theirs.

The teacher of English is a humanist, and should wear the badge proudly. He should have his vision, his ideals, his hopes. His mind must extend beyond the covers of a textbook, beyond the four walls of a room. He has a job to do—a job that has been described in prosy factual terms in this chapter. But he needs vision to do that job well, a vision that shows him clearly the distinction between semicolons and sonnets, between a unit and unity, between means and ends. In an age when the life of man is the stake, success on the part of one teacher in distinguishing between the trivial and the vital may affect the decision.

THE IDEA BOX

The Idea Box, which you will find at the end of each chapter, has three purposes: (1) to suggest teaching devices of proved worth, besides those discussed in the chapter itself; (2) to mention other aids or materials or sources of materials; and (3) to list articles and books that provide additional information. Many of the titles listed refer to articles in the *English Journal*, both because those articles are readily available and because they contain suggestions made by specialists in high school English.

As Louis Zahner has said, ". . . no classroom practice is sound unless it stems from sound theory and can be traced back to it." The practices described in the Idea Box appear to be based on sound theory, though it cannot be claimed that all are of equal merit. Certainly the Idea Boxes contain many more tactics and techniques than any one teacher can or should try. However, from the richness each teacher may select the ideas that best fit his temperament and the needs of the classes he instructs. What will work well for one teacher in one situation may work less well in other circumstances, but every idea presented here has been used successfully in somebody's classroom.

The items in the Idea Boxes following the first three chapters are less specific than those in the rest of the book because of the broad topics of those chapters.

NEEDED RESEARCH

Needed Research in the Teaching of English (Government Printing Office, 1963), a report of a conference involving about fifty national leaders, refers to many topics about which we know too little. The book is useful for a graduate student searching for a topic for a dissertation, but it also has value as a corrective for persons who believe they already know most answers.

ENGLISH IN A CHANGING WORLD

Lou LaBrant considers the implications for English teaching of several developments of the past half-century, such as the decline of the immigrant population, our world orientation, the abundance of printed material, the mass media, and increased knowledge of the English language. The article "As of Now" is basic for perspective. *English Journal,* XLVIII (Sept., 1959), 295.

In the same issue is another important article, "The Professional Status of the Teacher of English," by Robert C. Pooley (p. 309). Dr. Pooley writes frankly of the not too esteemed status and describes what it should be.

CHECK LIST FOR THE BEGINNING TEACHER

Under the headings "organization," "pitfalls," and "self-evaluation," Elizabeth S. White presents a valuable check list of "Tips for the Beginning Teacher." *English Journal,* XLVII (Sept., 1958), 349.

For prospective teachers interested in democratically run classes and much emphasis on small-group work, a companion article (Oct., 1959, p. 414), Grace Daly Maertins' "Organizing the Class To Care for English Needs," is valuable.

"CONFLICTING ASSUMPTIONS IN THE TEACHING OF ENGLISH"

G. R. Carlsen analyzes seventeen conflicting "traditional" and "modern" assumptions and defends the modern. Though Carlsen is sometimes unfair to the traditionalists, his article is basic for understanding some genuine conflicts. *English Journal,* XLIX (Sept., 1960), 377. Mrs. Marice C. Brown, in a reply, argues that a preferable middle ground exists: "A Reexamination of the Middle Ground," *English Journal,* L (March, 1961), 188.

THE BROAD VIEW

". . . the teaching of literature will not be improved much if English teachers just keep looking at their own courses; they must try to understand what the particular role of literature is in the total curriculum pattern." George Henry, *English Journal,* XLIV (Oct., 1955), 383.

SUPERIOR AND LOW-ABILITY STUDENTS

John W. Myres, "Identifying Students of Superior and Low Ability," *English Journal,* XLIX (Oct., 1960), 485, discusses contrasting characteristics of the two groups:

Superior	*Low Ability*
1. Possesses a long attention span	1. Possesses a short attention span
2. Enjoys mental independence	2. Has limited creative ability
3. Understands complex directions	3. Tends to learn by simple mental processes
4. Is interested in many subjects	4. Is interested in few subjects
5. Analyzes and discriminates	5. Lacks discriminatory ability
6. Learns through own mistakes	6. Has limited ability to be self-critical
7. Relates thoughts, illustrations, and problems to real life situations	7. Is interested in present concerns and problems
8. Is energetic, self-directive, resourceful	8. May enjoy group activity
9. Is capable of abstract thinking	9. Is limited in ability to do abstract thinking

LIMITATIONS OF STANDARDIZED TESTS

"It is risky to group pupils for instruction or to predict future academic success on the basis of test scores alone." "Only when a pupil scores consistently high can we be sure that he is an exceptional student, and only

when several test scores are low should we classify him as retarded."
"[Tests] do not identify the student who possesses such valuable attributes
as originality, creativity, imagination, initiative, and perseverance." These
are among shortcomings defined by Eleanor F. McKey, "Do Standardized
Tests Do What They Claim To Do?" *English Journal*, L (Dec., 1961), 607.

TEACHING SLOW LEARNERS

1. Class atmosphere should be relaxed and friendly.
2. Slow students need much chance to practice skills, less emphasis on
theory and abstractions.
3. They must be enabled to succeed as often as possible.
4. They profit from concrete examples; hence, the inductive approach is
especially useful.
5. Many audio-visual aids should be used.
6. Activities should change often, with much student participation.
7. Instructions and assignments must be clear and definite, and may need
repetition.
8. Often homework should be started in class.

THE SLIGHTLY EDUCABLE

It has been estimated that as many as 20 per cent of students (excluding mental defectives) can never master material of above fifth or sixth
grade difficulty. To require such students to undertake reading or other
assignments permanently beyond their capacity is folly. Yet they may be
taught reading and language skills that will help them to develop into useful citizens.

STIMULATING THE ACADEMICALLY TALENTED

Phyllis Peacock (*North Carolina English Teacher*, Oct., 1959) lists these
ways of stimulating superior students: "(1) not *more* but *more challenging*
activities; (2) new ideas, new ways of treating traditional materials; (3)
emphasis on 'power-to-do,' not accumulation of facts; (4) challenge to do
extensive reading; (5) challenge to do *intensive* reading; (6) a great variety
of written work to gain power in analyzing, organizing, and thinking creatively; (7) extensive vocabulary growth."

THE GIFTED BECOME EXPERTS

C. P. Rossier finds it useful in teaching gifted students to enable each
to attain a degree of mastery in a certain literary or linguistic area. "It
contributes to pride in his own accomplishment and to status in the eyes
of his fellow students." (It should help in teaching individual study, too.)
Each student, along with his classwork, takes on an individual project for
the semester or year, makes progress reports, and prepares a final paper.
Clearing House, XXXIII (March, 1959), 415.

ADVANCED PLACEMENT PROGRAMS

Increasingly, many of the most able of high school upperclassmen are
enrolling in advanced-placement, college-level courses, which can earn them

either college credit or admission to advanced college courses. For details, write College Entrance Examination Board, Princeton, New Jersey. An informative article is Edwin Sauer's "Programs for the Academically Talented in English: What Are the Gains?" *English Journal,* XLIX (Jan., 1960), 10.

"FROM HIGH SCHOOL INTO COLLEGE"

Research by G. R. Carlsen revealed that failures in college result not from lack of knowledge of grammar, but from fear of asking questions, confusions in the library, inability to take notes, inability to state ideas for oneself, bafflement in using textbooks, and lack of fluency. *English Journal,* XLV (Oct., 1956), 400.

TEACHING AIDS IN THE ENGLISH LANGUAGE ARTS

This publication, revised every few years, offers annotated descriptions, sources, and prices of bulletin-board materials, films and filmstrips, recordings, tape recordings, tests, magazines, reprints and free helps, and guides to books and reading. It may be purchased from its publisher, the Illinois Association of Teachers of English, Urbana, Illinois, or from the NCTE.

2

THE IDEAL ENGLISH PROGRAM

THE FLOWING TIDE

In order to understand the present status of, and the future possible developments in, the teaching of secondary English, one needs an overview of the past. It is the purpose of this section to offer a glimpse of historical background.

Early American Schools

In the seventeenth and eighteenth centuries, and a large part of the nineteenth, children learned their letters and the fundamentals of reading at home, or in a reading school or a "dame school," the latter taught, very often, by a physically and monetarily enfeebled widow who herself had to spell out the hard words. Or sometimes the children were taught the fundamentals and a little more by men who had a smattering of knowledge in a dozen or maybe three dozen different fields.

The Latin grammar school was for a long time the nearest equivalent to our high school. In that name, the word "Latin" is of special importance. The Latin grammar school was intended primarily to prepare students to enrol in college, and colleges required Latin for admission. Harvard, in the mid-seventeenth century, had stipulated that its entering students should be able to "read any classical author into English and readily make and speak true Latin, and write it in verse as well as prose; and perfectly decline the paradigms of nouns and verbs in the Greek tongue." Not until 1817 was English grammar required for college entrance. The Latin grammar schools, of course, taught what the colleges said was necessary.

Even in the eighteenth century, though, there were some signs of revolt against domination by colleges and against a confining emphasis upon the classics. For example, the Philadelphia Academy, founded in 1753, had three "schools," or departments: Latin, English, and mathematics. Its emphasis upon English language and literature was much greater than that of the Latin grammar schools.

In these early schools, the stress in all subjects was upon individual instruction. Classes like those of today were not common until the middle of the nineteenth century. In the Latin grammar schools, and usually in the academies, each student progressed at his own rate and recited individually. The recitation was generally just that—a re-citation in which the student repeated more or less verbatim what he had read in his book. The emphasis in these schools was steadily upon memory, not upon interpretation and only seldom upon creation.

Narrowness of curriculum finally killed the Latin grammar schools. They were gradually supplanted by academies, which—in Massachusetts and some other states—the law required every large town to establish. The courses offered by academies were diverse. Subjects that today might be labeled English included biography, composition, declamation, extemporaneous speaking, grammar, moral philosophy, intellectual philosophy, penmanship, pronunciation, and rhetoric. All these were usually taught as separate courses, with little concern for orderly development or avoidance of overlapping.

It was the influence of the defunct Latin grammar school, plus changing college entrance requirements, that caused classics of English literature to be widely studied in the academies. The Latin grammar school had fostered the tradition of teaching certain selections from Latin and Greek authors; the academy, with its emphasis upon the vernacular, substituted English (not American) classics for the ancients. Johnnies-come-lately like Burns, Scott, Wordsworth, and Irving were ignored in most schools, although the students sometimes smuggled in and read surreptitiously some little volume by a man named Byron. Through their entrance requirements, the colleges gradually reinforced the tendency of secondary schools to teach selections from a limited list of accepted writers. The usual reason advanced was that all literate persons deserve to share the most noble literary productions—generally meaning Chaucer, Shakespeare, Spenser, Milton, Addison, Pope, Johnson, and a few others chosen for their religious and moral tone.

In writing and speech, the academies specialized in grammar, rhetoric, and declamation. The grammar taught in the academies presented a perversion of the English language, for which grammarians and textbook makers were chiefly to blame. Representative of these men was Lindley Murray, whose influential grammar was published in 1795. Murray and his like assumed that English is similar in nearly all respects to Latin, and therefore referred to such things as dative case, ablative case, gerundives, etc., disregarding the fact that the English language simply does not possess some of the forms that they tried to find. The result of teachers' following these pseudo-learned grammarians was numberless hours spent by students in parroting nonsense. The students "knew grammar" when they finished, but what they knew—and happily forgot—were definitions that were often inaccurate, paradigms that were valueless, and mistaken linguistic conceptions that would have been foolish if not impossible to apply.

The teaching of rhetoric was often better conceived than that of grammar. Some teachers, of course, were satisfied with mere verbalism and praised the student who could echo the definitions of synecdoche, litotes, amphibology, and anaphora. Others demanded slavish imitations of the "polished periods" of Addison. Some over-emphasized the four forms of discourse—exposition, narration, description, and argumentation—which are seldom found entirely separated. But many taught methods of organization, suggested ways of improving sentence structure, and offered constructive help to the student searching for the exact word. Some of America's most vital political documents and most vivid pieces of literature came from the quill pens of men who had learned rhetoric in academies.

Declamation was the father of elocution, both now in equal disrepute. At its worst, declamation consisted of mouthing turgid memorized speeches and accompanying the vocalization with measured arm movements. At its best, it offered students the chance to think about issues of local or national concern, to prepare a talk concerning those issues, and to deliver it before an audience. If declamation is to be blamed for much Fourth-of-July bombast, it is also to be praised for men like Daniel Webster and Henry Clay who were big enough to adopt the virtues of declamation and to sublimate its vices.

The methods used in the academies were dictated to some extent by the aims, which were summarized thus by the New York Regents in 1839: "The great purpose of education [is] to store the mind with useful knowledge." Note the verb "store." Schools were not to teach students to observe, to interpret, to reason, or to apply; they were only to pour facts, grain by grain, into students' minds. Dickens tells of schoolman Thomas Gradgrind who mentally refers to "the little pitchers before him, who were to be filled so full of facts"; changing the metaphor, Dickens calls Gradgrind "a kind of cannon loaded to the muzzle with facts, and prepared to blow [the pupils] clean out of the regions of childhood at one discharge."

Drill and more drill, memory work and more memory work, quotation and re-citation, examination and re-examination—these were the methods widely employed. Each school followed certain variations of the procedure, of course, and within the school each instructor often had his own favorite assignments and pet drills.

Nineteenth-Century Reforms

The mid-nineteenth century was a time of unrest and exploration in American education. Academies had become increasingly subservient to the colleges, shaping their curriculums in accordance with what the colleges demanded for entrance. The feeling grew that some other kind of school, a "practical" school intended primarily for students who did not expect to attend college, should be created. A few persons felt also that state-supported public secondary schools should be made available for all who wanted to enrol. Dissatisfaction with the methods and results of the academies was not uncommon among those who as students had labored there.

Boston, cultural pioneer of American cities, led the revolt when in 1821 it established an "English classical school," later to be named the "English High School." English literature, mathematics, science, history, and logic superseded Latin and Greek in this school, as in most of the few other high schools opened elsewhere before the Civil War. These schools, unlike the majority of the academies, were supported and controlled by the public. They did not become numerous until after the Civil War, but by 1896–97 there were 5,109 public high schools in the United States, in addition to more than 2,000 private high schools.

The nineteenth century also brought a demand for increased school equipment (including libraries), and an interest in improving the training of teachers and their methods of teaching. But it was not sufficiently generous in investing dollars in education; it did not eliminate the subservience of secondary schools to colleges; it did not establish adequate prerequisites for entering the teaching profession; and it did not get far enough away from the old idea of education as a storing away of information. Lincoln Steffens says in his *Autobiography,*

No one tried to interest me in [my school subjects]; they were put before me as things I had to have to get into college. The teachers of them did not appeal to my curious, active mind. The result was that I did not really work at them and so got only what stuck by dint of repetition: the barest rudiments of a school education. . . . The elect were, for the most part, boys who had been brought up to do their duty. They memorized whatever their teachers told them to learn. Whether they wanted to know it, whether they understood it or no, they could remember and recite it. Their own driving motives were, so far as I could make out, not curiosity; they rarely talked about our studies, and if I spoke of the implications of something we had read or heard, they looked dazed or indifferent.

In the latter nineteenth century and the early twentieth, the colleges maintained more rigid entrance requirements than now. In effect, college authorities said to high school administrators and teachers, "For entrance, we require . . . . We have no control over your curriculum, *but* your graduates cannot pass our entrance examinations unless they have studied . . . ." The high school teacher of English had at least three choices. He might ignore the colleges and teach whatever he believed his students would find most profitable, regardless of whether the colleges prescribed it; he might teach superficially those things that the entrance examinations stressed and, since this shallow treatment would leave a little time, teach with equal superficiality whatever else he wished; or he might devote all his time to teaching aimed at having students pass the entrance examinations. Since most honor came from getting one's students into college, and since the college prospects were usually the children of influential citizens, the teacher most often took the third course.

Let us pause for a moment to glance at a typical teacher of English in the 1890's. He stands beside his desk in a fairly well lighted classroom. Before him, in desk seats securely screwed to the floor, sit thirty students. (Most people still call them "scholars" in the 1890's.) The only books visible in the room are one in the teacher's hand, several on his desk, a large dictionary on a table, and a closed book on the desk of each student. A stereoscope and some stereoscopic views—the teacher's own property—are near the dictionary. (The teacher has daringly but vainly asked for a magic lantern which he might use to project pictures.) The teacher himself is a graduate of a university but in his college days did not plan to become a teacher; when a year in business proved unsatisfactory, he found that any college degree was sufficient passport to teaching. His interest in helping students learn, however, compensates to some extent for his lack of professional training.

The class has been studying Burke's "Conciliation"—required by many colleges. The teacher's questioning, by modern standards, is inept in that he usually probes for facts only, calls upon students in a fixed order, and lacks direction and logical progression in his questions. "What quality of Americans does Burke name first, Charles?" "Mary, what does *mediately* mean?" "No. Next." "No. Next!" "What quality does Burke name second?" "In the sentence 'Religion in this new people is no way worn out,' what two figures of speech does Burke employ, Wilbur?"

And so on and on. Not all teachers of English were like this example; some were less adequate, others were infinitely more resourceful and probably more successful, but the example approximates the type.

Twentieth-Century Developments

Not until after 1911 was there a concerted effort to raise the standards of English teaching. Comparatively few professional organizations existed in the nineteenth and early twentieth centuries. In English, the only national group was the National Conference on Uniform Entrance Requirements in English, whose narrow aim was indicated by its title.

Some of the most enlightened English teachers, however, realized that their efforts to teach young people were being hampered by over-specific entrance requirements and perhaps even by their own deficiencies as teachers. A group of them, at a meeting in Chicago in 1911, tried to work toward desirable changes in college entrance requirements. Had they stopped with that aim, their accomplishments would have been negligible. But they did not stop; instead they formed a permanent national organization for the improvement of English teaching. This fledgling organization, the National Council of Teachers of English, has since become one of the most potent educational groups in America. Major advancements in English teaching since 1911 are linked inseparably with the history of the NCTE.

The first issue of the *English Journal,* sponsored by the NCTE but financed during its first years by one of the NCTE's founders, James Hosic, appeared in January, 1912. Since that time the Council's list of periodicals has grown to five: *Elementary English* for elementary teachers, the *English Journal* for secondary teachers, *College English* and *College Composition and Communication* for college teachers, and *Abstracts of English Studies* for those interested in concise summaries of scholarly work. The *English Journal* is the most widely read professional publication for high school English teachers. Teaching English without the *Journal* is like keeping house without a cookbook: it can be done, but menus are likely to lack balance, variety, and flavor.

In addition to professional journals, the Council makes available surveys and research by fifty or sixty committees and commissions, and serves as a distribution center for literary maps, recordings, filmstrips, and other teaching aids. Perhaps even more important, it has gradually assumed more and more professional leadership, working both by itself and in cooperation with other national organizations and the federal government for higher standards in teacher education and for improvement of the curriculum.

During the twentieth century the high school population has increased tremendously. Previously, those who attended high school were usually only those fortunate enough to possess high intelligence, considerable family wealth, or both. The secondary school was looked upon as primarily a steppingstone to college. Today, neither wealth nor unusually high intelligence is characteristic of the majority of secondary school students. The high school is for everybody, and the majority of those in the high school age group now attend from one to four years beyond the eighth grade. For approximately half of these students, high school is not a preliminary to college but is terminal education. However, since the middle 1950's, half or more of high school graduates have been knocking on college doors. Since colleges gradually found it impossible to accommodate all who clamored for admission, they adopted more and more rigorous screening policies, saying in effect to high schools, "We can accept only those of your graduates who seems to us to be promising college material. We do not insist, as colleges formerly did, that your graduates must have taken specific courses and studied specific things, but we do require evidence that they can read a page with understanding, that they can write and speak with reasonable fluency and with attention to accepted modern usage, and that they can think and can organize their thoughts."

In twentieth-century English classes has occurred an interesting change in emphasis. At the beginning of the century, as in preceding centuries, teachers taught the subject. That is, they took the point of view that the grammatical concept or the literary selection was the important thing. They drilled and pounded until the concept or the facts about the selection had penetrated almost every skull. Then, under the influence of John Dewey and his "progressive" followers, teachers began to teach the child. In an extreme form of their view, only the child matters—the child's immediate needs, the child's interests today. Now, at last, we have moved to an understanding of the fact that the verb *teach* takes two objects: We teach *somebody something*. Neither the subject nor the child can be disregarded. We must pick from the immensity of our subject those things—facts, skills, understandings, perhaps attitudes—that the child needs and will need; we must prepare his mind to receive this knowledge, helping him to see its present and future significance to him; we must assist him to make it an irrefragable part of his being—not for the sake of the subject but for his sake and that of the society in which he lives and will live.

Another change that has occurred in the very recent past is an intensification of interest in secondary English teaching on the part of persons and groups that previously had remained aloof. College professors of English for several generations had assiduously cultivated their own gardens, teaching their students, conducting their research; they complained about the quality of incoming students but did little or nothing to improve that quality. In the mid-1950's, however, they began to realize that the preparation of secondary English teachers was at least as much their responsibility as it was that of professors of education. A few of them visited high school classes. More of them met with high school teachers to examine their common problems or to advise on curricular matters. Many colleges and universities re-examined their programs for preparing teachers. Some prominent professors took an interest in improving standards for certification, which in many states were pitiably low. The result of this interest by academic professors has been greater insistence upon a solid body of content in secondary English classes, along with increased study of ways to present that content sequentially instead of haphazardly. Teachers are being better prepared. Often working side by side with professors of education, professors of English are now making substantial contributions to improved secondary programs. Many high school graduates, as a result, are better educated in English than ever before.

Foundations and the federal government have also become interested in the improvement of instruction in English. Research in educational television and the other mass media has been conducted with foundation and government grants. Inaugurated by the federal government in 1961, Project English has underwritten much of the cost of extensive curricular experimentation, a large number of research studies, numerous significant conferences, and programs for enhancing or updating the preparation of teachers. These facts signify that business and government are becoming more aware than ever before that the study of English is not only central in the curriculum but also vital to the continued well-being of the nation.

But utopia has not been reached. The secondary English curriculum in many schools is still chaotic, still unnecessarily repetitive of some content and neglectful of other content, still largely unstructured. The constant burgeoning of new knowledge complicates the problems of choosing what should be taught. The study of the teaching and learning processes moves far ahead of classroom practice. New tools for teaching appear every week, varying in value but deserving of more time for consideration than a busy teacher, supervisor, or administrator can give. Many teachers are inadequately educated in subject matter, educational principles, or both. A changing world makes changing demands upon every teacher; today's rocket world has needs in communication different from those of a horse-and-buggy world. English teachers need to seek out, distil, and instil what is of permanent value in their subject, give primacy to that, and teach it as effectively as they can; then they need to superimpose those facets of their subject that are secondary in importance but are needed because of the demands of the present decade or century. The permanent remains at the heart of what we should teach, remains constant. The elements that should change, and that reveal why no curriculum can be forever fixed, are those that refer specifically to this moment in history.

FROM THIS ABUNDANCE

The Block Concept of Curriculum

Any planned curriculum must be based upon two facts.

The first is that children grow and develop but do so at different speeds; they differ in abilities. Two six-year-olds, both enrolled in the first grade, may be four years apart in mental age; six years later, in junior high school, they may be eight years apart in mental age; in senior high school, ten years may separate their minds.

The second fact is that each academic subject has its own inherent structure, its own anatomy, its own gradient of difficulty. This is perhaps best illustrated in mathematics or physics, in which some of the best minds have recently been engaged in analysis, determining which items logically should come first, which next, what is dependent upon what. Language, composition, and literature have their structures, too, though we cannot yet define them with finality.

A curriculum must be related to children's varying growth patterns, and it must present subject matter arranged in a sequential order. Curriculum committees entrusted with decisions about scope and sequence have for years been aware of these interlocking needs and have struggled to meet them. Typically they have decided rather arbitrarily that certain parts of the program are suitable for the seventh grade, others for the eighth, and so on. In schools with homogeneous grouping they have prescribed certain content for low, average, and high levels in each grade. What they have attempted is represented diagrammatically in Figs. 1 and 2.

Heterogeneous Classes

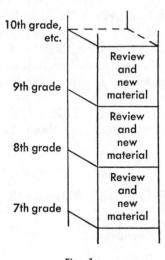

Fig. 1.

In effect, knowledge is conceived of as assignable to blocks, which are piled one upon another as a child moves through school. In schools without homogeneous grouping, all seventh grade children, for example, study the same block, which therefore must be thought of in terms of capabilities of an average child (though within the class some adaptation is possible). In homogeneously grouped classes, as Fig. 2 shows, the blocks for the average level correspond to those for the heterogeneous groups, but low-level ninth graders may be tak-

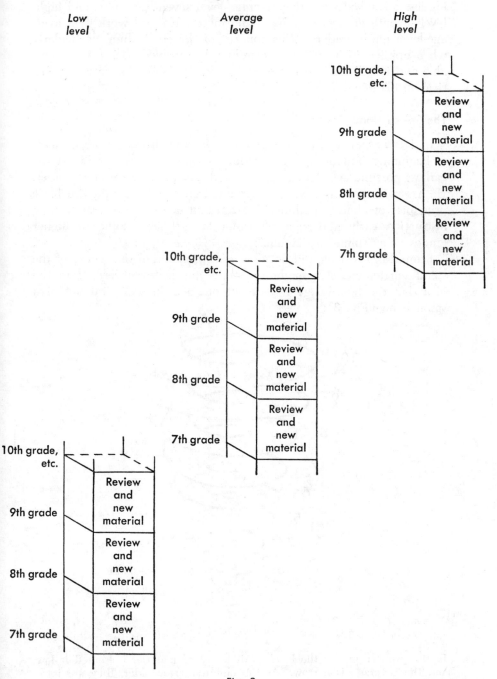

Homogeneous Classes

Fig. 2.

ing less advanced work than average-level seventh graders, and high-level seventh graders may be taking more advanced work than average-level ninth graders. This concept of the curriculum, particularly when applied in homogeneous groups, has proved useful and workable and is still the concept most frequently used as a basis for curriculum planning.

The Spiral Cone Concept

In *The Process of Education* (1960) Jerome Bruner wrote in favor of beginning fundamental instruction in each significant topic at the earliest possible age, returning to it and developing it in later grades. He asserted that even very young children can be taught the basic principles of almost anything. He referred to the process of starting instruction early and then returning to the same topic in higher grades as a "spiral curriculum."

Bruner, in his book, did not develop in any detail the theory of the spiral curriculum. He might or might not have subscribed to the idea that the best image is that not of an ordinary spiral but of a spiral cone (Fig. 3).

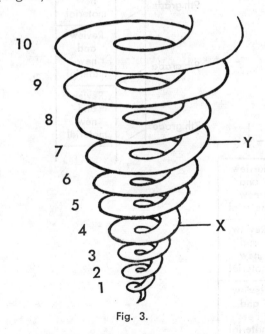

Fig. 3.

In the primary grades the level of difficulty of material presented is low, and the coverage is narrow. As the children grow older, they are introduced to more difficult material, they do more with it, and they cover more of it. Hence curriculum coverage rises and broadens simultaneously.

Different children of the same chronological age will be at different places on the cone. If the differences are not great, they may be accommodated by simple adjustments in the quantity of material presented. (In the illustration, for instance, less able children who are on the sixth ring of the spiral may be visualized as being on the inside of the cone, covering a limited amount of material of sixth-ring difficulty; their more able classmates will be on the outer edge, covering more material.) But when differences between children of the same age are considerable, when two children are at widely separated points on the spiral, they cannot be expected to master identical work. Of two ten-year-old children, for instance, one may be at point X on the spiral, the other at point Y. Through varied assignments, grouping, or a rather drastic revision of our usual concepts of grade level, it is possible to provide for each child what he needs at the particular point he has reached on the spiral.

. . . If all children were of equal ability and could progress at the same rate, it would be a relatively simple matter to decide upon a subject-matter sequence that would be logical. But since children (happily) are not identical, they are not all ready for the same learnings at the same time. The spiral cone concept provides for sequential progress in subject matter without ignoring variations in children.[1]

If the spiral cone concept were ever fully realized, it would have far-reaching effects upon education. It would involve an upward extension of the ungraded primary system, in which children in their first three years are taught what they need to be taught, without regard to whether the materials or skills are traditionally first, second, or third grade. A child who reads early, for example, is moved quickly into third grade materials or even above; a child who is slow in learning to read stays with the simplest work until he has mastered it. For several years some schools such as those in Melbourne, Florida, have experimented with ungraded classes in either the elementary or the secondary schools, with notably excellent results. If the plan is carried to its logical culmination, some children of fifteen or sixteen may reach the top rung of the secondary spiral in all subjects, pass college entrance examinations, and go to college at an age considerably below average. Other students, for whom high school represents terminal education, may have reached only a relatively low rung because of lack in ability or in motivation; after twelve years of elementary and secondary education, they would receive their high school diplomas but would not proceed to college, because their test results would be too low. On the other hand, a student who

---

[1] J. N. Hook, "The Emerging English Curriculum," *The American Behavioral Scientist*, Nov., 1962, p. 36.

after twelve years had almost reached a college-level rung could, if he wished, attend secondary school for an additional year without being sneered at for falling behind the rest of his class; in an ungraded system such designations as "sophomore" or "senior" are scarcely needed.

Among the specific implications of the spiral cone for English departments, perhaps the most important is also the most obvious: the need to plan the sequence of content. A second implication is flexibility of scheduling, so that whatever a given group of students (often of different age levels) needs, could be offered to it.

TOILERS IN THE DEEP

No curriculum, regardless of how well it is planned, will be successful unless the teachers know their subject matter, know children, know how to teach, and possess suitable personal qualities. Hence, in a chapter on "The Ideal English Program," it is imperative to describe in some detail the characteristics of a good teacher of English.

Human Qualities

Mark Hopkins was a great teacher because of *what he was;* likewise, *every successful teacher today is successful because of what he is*—not simply because of what he knows or what special skills and abilities he possesses. Knowledge and skills are naturally of great importance. Many teachers get into difficulties because they lack one or the other. But the success of a teacher depends in large part upon his personal qualities.

The capable English teacher of today is first of all a human being, not an automaton like the man who supervised a Lancasterian schoolroom, not a drillmaster like the teacher of the nineteenth-century "infant school." The word "human" refers to the possession of qualities held in common with other persons; it is the antithesis of "artificial." Some teachers of English have felt that their calling entitled them to don a special cloak of superciliousness; their knowledge of the "finer things of life" in their opinion justified an attitude of ill-concealed contempt for those whose cultural attainments were less than their own. By artificial standards they thus set themselves apart from the rest of humanity; in their exclusive clique, most non-members were considered barbarians who had traveled little in Keats's realms of gold and who sometimes said "hadn't hardly." Members of this limited clique thought of "we and other people," not of "we, the people."

Fortunately, English teachers with such artificial, highbrow attitudes have always been rare and are seemingly becoming more so. The English teacher realizes that he is a member of society and that, like almost everyone else, he has something to contribute to the betterment of society. He does not consider himself superior to his students except in his knowledge of a specialized subject matter. He knows that he merely happens, through an accident of chronology, to be older and more experienced and better trained in one phase of knowledge. With William Lyon Phelps, he knows also that every student in his classroom is better informed concerning some subjects than he is. For these reasons the teacher does not pose as the final authority on life and life's problems; he does not assume a false air of superiority.

Respect for One's Work

Although he is always ready to grant that the work of others can be as significant as his own, the successful English teacher nevertheless has a deep sense of the worthwhileness of his own work. He does not teach commas simply because the course of study says that he should, or teach Shakespeare because Shakespeare is always taught in English, or teach oral English because he does not have to prepare lessons for the days when students make speeches. He teaches these things and everything else because of what they can do for his students. He teaches his students to organize their thoughts, to express themselves clearly in an age when clarity of thought and statement may save humanity from extermination, and to understand the thoughts and feelings of other persons in the classroom, in a distant state, on the other side of the world, or in another century. Teaching those things is important. A word is only a group of inky curlicues, a punctuation mark is only an ink spot, and a sentence is only a conglomeration of curlicues and spots—until the teacher makes of them something meaningful, a representation of man's ability to think thoughts bigger than himself. From ink in students' fountain pens and from ink that was once wet on a printing press, the teacher creates constructive thoughts, orderliness, understanding, and tolerance. His is a job that challenges by its bigness.

Tolerance

The teacher himself possesses the tolerance that he tries to instil in his students—not in the narrow sense of "tolerating = enduring," not that he "tolerates" Protestants, Catholics, Jews, Negroes, Mexicans, Japanese, obstreperous boys, and girls who can converse only on movies, clothes, and dates. Mere tolerating is not being tolerant. One may tolerate (endure) a mouse simply because one cannot get rid of the mouse. But one is not truly tolerant of mice unless one likes and respects them and tries to see the mice's point of view. That is difficult as far as mice are concerned; when one thinks of mice, one thinks in terms of *I* and *they*. Probably most English teachers think about mice in the same way, but the effective teacher does not put any students into the same category with mice. He does not merely endure students. He likes them, respects them, tries to see their point of view, and thinks of them in terms of *we,* not *I* and *they*.

Take Johnny, for example. Johnny is often a troublemaker.

Johnny: High school freshman. Age fifteen. I.Q. 80. Two years in first grade. Mechanical ability. Little ambition. A school problem for nine years. Juvenile court record. Parents divorced.

Some of his teachers merely endure Johnny because he has to stay in school, against his will and theirs, until he is sixteen. Over their coffee a couple of these teachers call him a bad one and say that the reform school is the place for him. But, since they cannot get rid of Johnny, who to them is a "mouse," they tolerate him. The more human teacher, though, whether his subject happens to be English or something else, is tolerant of him. He asks Johnny to ride around a few blocks with him in his automobile to try to find the source of a noise. "It ain't—uh, isn't—nothin' but loose tappets," says Johnny. Maybe the teacher already knew that, but he thanks Johnny for helping him. He makes Johnny feel proud of himself. He talks with Johnny, finds out what makes him tick. He tries unobtrusively to help him. Johnny won't ever be president, or mayor, or alderman. But he'll be a good auto mechanic, unless the reform school gets him first. A little more tolerance and a little less tolerating will make Johnny a useful citizen.

Adaptability

The successful English teacher is adaptable. Perhaps he grew up in New York City and is teaching in Littleville. Maybe he was born on a Nebraska farm and is teaching in Los Angeles. Possibly the school has had three different superintendents in the last three years. Maybe at nine o'clock the teacher has a class of super-par college-preparatory seniors, and at ten o'clock a class of subnormal ninth graders who can read a simple poem by John Masefield and get only the idea that the author is saying something about ships. Regardless of the contrasts he faces, the teacher must be flexible enough to do the right thing at the right time. He can lead his college preps through a stimulating discussion of why Hamlet was Hamlet, and spend the next hour in helping the freshmen comprehend Masefield the Incomprehensible. The day before the big game, he can relate some of the items in the lesson to the only topic that at the moment interests nine-tenths of the class, and yet help the students to learn as much as usual. When the class mood is a rollicking one, the teacher can be frolicsome, too, and, when war or other shadows emerge from the nebulous world that is generally around the students but not of them, he can be as serious as an owl in hearing their opinions.

Alertness

The successful English teacher is physically and mentally alert. Alertness makes him eager, imaginative. He is not a dead fish. He teaches because he likes to teach, and he wants to make his teaching as effective as possible because it is more fun that way. So he experiments—tries first this, then that. Scientific accuracy? Possibly. Control groups? Could be. But whether or not his experimentation is scientific, he works imaginatively to improve his teaching. He never teaches a course twice in exactly the same way. Beneath his calmness he is restless, pioneering; goaded by his desire to serve better than ever before, westering he explores.

The teacher's imaginativeness reveals itself frequently in creative writing—not necessarily for publication, but for writing's effect upon him. He likes to write; he must write. And he knows that he can better interpret literature if he himself has suffered a few of the pangs of literary parturition. More important, he knows that through writing he can better understand the difficulties of the thirty-three juniors who have to turn in a finished composition on Friday. So the teacher fills a desk drawer with his poems, his essays, his stories, his first draft of The Great American Novel, and then he starts on another drawer.

Sense of Humor

The teacher, being truly human, has a sense of humor. He agrees with the thesis of Leon Ormond's book *Laugh and Learn,* that people learn most readily when the conditions of learning are made pleasant. Learning is apparently somewhat like digestion. A person can eat more and digest more readily if mealtime is enjoyable. But if one is tense at his meals, he does not swallow much, and what he does swallow gives him indigestion. A classroom is similar to a dining room; the teacher is the host.

So the successful teacher says in effect, "In my classroom, smiles will not be unholy or laughter blasphemous. I'll try to be as good fun in class as I think I am at a party. It's a happy coincidence of the English language that 'human' and 'humor' are so much alike. What lifts human beings above the other animals? A musician may say that it's his musical ability, a scientist that it's his possession of a useful thumb, a linguist that it's his flexible use of language, a minister that it's his religion, and a historian that it's knowing the events of the past. But 40 million American kids and I know that man became man the first time he ever laughed at anything more subtle than another's misfortune. It's human to have a sense of humor. A class should never become riotous, but a few laughs per day do any class good. And the teacher, too. As somebody once said, 'He who laughs—lasts.' "

Professional Attitude

The capable teacher is also professional in his outlook. That means that he wants to improve the profession, help others who are in it, bring other capable persons into it. It implies that, although he tries to improve the working conditions of his profession, he will not whine about them or boast about how much more money he could make in industry. Being professional means that he subscribes to professional magazines, attends worthwhile professional meetings (without spending much time shopping), and backs worthy professional activities. It includes his own carefully formulated code of professional ethics. And it means that he regards his work—the enrichment of the minds of youth—as the finest way he has of defending his own right to existence, of justifying the ways of a man to God.

Academic Qualifications

It has been said that what a teacher is, is as important as what he knows or what skills he possesses. In other words, in the opinions of many qualified observers the teacher's personal qualifications are as significant as his academic or professional ones. But no one can deny the need of a well-stocked mind and for familiarity with educational principles and procedures. Professor Ralph Boas, writing in the *English Leaflet,* based the following statement on long years of observation: "There is something fatal about the human mind which particularly affects teachers, so that all too often one finds enthusiasm and vitality without any sound basis in scholarship, or else pedantic scholarship without any real imagination or human sympathy."

Like Professor Boas, you no doubt have observed many instances of the dichotomy of which he speaks. But you have probably not been so unfortunate that you have failed to meet teachers who combined praiseworthy personal qualities with exact and extensive knowledge and with ability to impart that knowledge. Such teachers, in your private state fair, you mentally award blue ribbons.

It is difficult to say specifically what academic knowledge the capable teacher of English possesses. Faculties in teacher-training institutions often discuss that question heatedly when they consider what academic competences they should attempt to instil in their prospective teachers. Considerable agreement exists, however, concerning several of these competences.

A committee of the NCTE named, in 1961, in *The National Interest and the Teaching of English,* the following academic competences:

I. The teacher of English should have a certain fundamental and specialized knowledge of the English language and its literature, together with certain abilities and skills which enable him to perform expertly in his discipline.

A. In language, he should have:

1. A fundamental knowledge of the historical development and present character of the English language: phonology (phonetics and phonemics), morphology, syntax, vocabulary (etymology and semantics), the relations of language and society.
2. A specialized knowledge of the English language which is appropriate to the teacher's particular field of interest and responsibility.
3. An informed command of the arts of language—rhetoric and logic; ability to speak and write language which is not only unified, coherent, and correct but also responsible, appropriate to the situation, and stylistically effective.

B. In literature, he should have:

1. A reading background of major literary works which emphasize the essential dignity of the individual man. This background:
   a. Implies a knowledge of major works, writers, forms, themes, and movements of the literature of the English-speaking people.
   b. Reflects intensive study of many literary pieces.
   c. Includes familiarity with some of the outstanding literary works in English translation, or in the original language, of the Greek, Roman, Norse, Italian, French, Spanish, German, Slavic, and Oriental peoples.
2. A specialized knowledge of whatever writers and literary works, forms, themes, media, and movements are appropriate to the teacher's particular field of interest and responsibility.

3. An ability to analyze and evaluate independently the various forms of imaginative literature as well as the utilitarian forms of verbal expression, and the insight to use suitable critical approaches in order to discover their literary and human values.

Some of the implications of the points just listed may need discussion.

First, the capable teacher is able to read well, both silently and aloud. His silent-reading speed is reasonably great—perhaps 400 words a minute for easy material; but he is aware of the fact that some material must be read very slowly. His level of comprehension is high. That means that he has a large vocabulary, some knowledge of semantic principles, an understanding of sentence and paragraph structure, and an ability to see the relationship of each part to the whole. His ability to read critically is sufficiently developed that he can distinguish assertion from evidence and can avoid being misled by card stacking, bandwagon arguments, and other devices used by the propagandist. His oral reading is clear and expressive. Several persons have said that there is an element of the "ham actor" in every good English teacher.

Second, the capable teacher can speak and write clearly and agreeably. He adjusts his speaking and writing to the group he is addressing. He applies the principles of grammar and rhetoric but carefully avoids a stilted, pseudosuperior style of presentation.

Third, the competent English teacher has read very widely. Several courses in English literature and a couple in American have not left him with the impression that he "knows literature." He is aware that no one person can know literature. But he fills in some of the gaps in his knowledge by reading from Sophocles, Virgil, Dante, Racine, Goethe, Lagerlöf, and a host of other major writers from non-English lands. Since literature did not come to an abrupt halt in 1900, he reads modern authors as well as those of yesteryear, but, in all his reading, he tries to discriminate so that he spends but little time upon the trashy or highly transitory. And since he is a teacher of the young, he at least skims a large number of books that are especially suitable for young people; then, when Susie, future housewife, or Raymond, future scientist, wonders what to read next, the teacher can offer appropriate suggestions.

Related to a knowledge of literature, but never to be substituted for it, is the fourth competence, a knowledge of literary history. The two should not be confused. Knowing the dates and details of Shakespeare's career is not the same as knowing Shakespeare's plays and sonnets. It is desirable, however, for the teacher to have a pattern of historical reference, an understanding of the social and intellectual background of past centuries, by means of which he can see each author clearly in perspective.

Fifth—and this is an academic competence closely related to professional ones—the capable teacher knows how to show the present social implications of literary selections. To use a trite but nevertheless excellent example, the teacher understands the parallel between the career of Macbeth and those of twentieth-century dictators. Or, for another example, the teacher sees in Benét's *Western Star* a portrayal of good and bad human characteristics still strong in Americans. One reason why literature lasts is that its characters are always around us.

Sixth, the capable English teacher has some idea of the relationships between English and other areas of learning. English is the most far-reaching subject in the curriculum. It extends into history, economics, science, music, art—in fact into all divisions of human knowledge. No person can imagine all its ramifications. But the capable teacher knows, for instance, that Shakespeare's Julius Caesar, the Caesar studied in Latin, and the Julius Caesar of ancient history are all the same man; he knows that English history and Milton's life are inextricably tangled; he realizes that many modern poets cannot be read with much comprehension by one who is ignorant of science.

Seventh, the able English teacher is more than dimly aware of the existence of movies, stage plays, newspapers, and radio and TV programs. He has standards for judging each of them, and he sees the relationship of each to English.

Finally, it is highly desirable for the teacher of English to have a substantial knowledge of at least one foreign language. Other languages shed light upon English, make possible the reading of some literary masterpieces in the original tongue, and reduce provincialism. However, a superficial knowledge of another language does comparatively little good. Assuming that there is not enough time to learn two languages well, it is better to study the same language for several years rather than two or three languages for a year or two each.

Professional Qualifications

So much for the personal qualities and the academic knowledge of today's successful teacher of English. Now we turn to a list of abilities and skills needed in the classroom.

1. Ability in planning a course of study in English. The high school English course is crowded at best. To plan the inclusion of those things that students may most profitably learn, to

eliminate the harmful or the non-essential, and to apportion time wisely require knowledge and forethought.

2. Skill in providing for individual differences. Not all students need or are able to learn the same things. Not all will respond equally to the same stimulus.

3. Competence in improving students' reading. Some high school students cannot read on the high school level and therefore require remedial work. Those who are already able to read rather effectively need help in the further development of their reading skills.

4. Competence in arousing interest in literature and appreciation of it. The potential interest of literature is high. Helping students to discover this interest is often a problem.

5. Skill in improving students' oral and written English. The negative approach—the mere elimination of errors—is inadequate. Students need to be helped to learn to use language effectively as a tool for the expression of organized thoughts.

6. Ability to teach satisfactory listening habits. Everyone except a few ceaseless tongue waggers spends more of his time in listening than he does in talking or writing. The skills involved in competent listening are little less complicated than the skills of reading.

7. Skill in guiding cocurricular activities. To the English teacher usually fall one or several cocurricular activities. Properly guided, these may contribute generously to the development of better citizens and better-informed citizens.

8. Ability to lead classes through semester after semester filled with stimulating, broadening, and pleasant hours. At the end of a year's work, the capable teacher is never completely satisfied with what he has accomplished, but, as he considers the progress made by individuals and by groups, he feels a gratifying inner warmth. At such moments, life *is* worth living.

The beginning teacher who has read the foregoing pages may feel that impossible ideals have been set up. Rest assured, they are not impossible. The author has sat in the classrooms of many teachers who have possessed in considerable measure the personal, academic, and professional qualifications that are here summarized. Being in those classrooms was an agreeable experience. The students were alert and friendly. There was no feeling of tension. Learning was cooperative; it was enjoyable. Students were learning constantly, and what they were learning would be of lifelong value to them.

RIDING THE WAVES

The usual organization for the teaching process still involves the traditional trio of students, books, and teacher. It has long demonstrated its effectiveness, and most of this book is devoted to discussion of the ways in which the role of the teacher may be played most successfully. However, recent experimentation and technological developments have shown that traditional patterns are not inviolable. It is the purpose of this section to give an overview of some of the innovations, a few of which will be discussed in greater detail later on.

A Fivefold Procedure

Five main kinds of activities now engage the attention of students in some experimental schools. These are meetings in large groups, meetings in small groups, individual work in a language laboratory or a center with teaching machines, independent reading, and teacher-student conferences.

Such an arrangement is made possible in part by team teaching. Although specific plans differ, team teaching in general involves an attempt to make effective use of the special skills and knowledge of each teacher.

To make the mechanics clear, let us envision a senior high school with 1,000 students of English, to be taught by eight teachers who share the services of two or three teachers' aides. Mr. Bell, let us assume, is especially strong in literature; Mrs. Wright, in writing; and Miss Lang, in language.

Let us assume further that team teaching and a three-track system of grouping are used throughout the school. A room that will seat up to 300 students is available for the use of not only English teachers but also teachers of other subjects. (Alternatively, closed-circuit television would be employed.) It is reserved for the English department for nine class hours a week. The enrolment in the various tracks is as follows (A represents high ability):

10A	70	11A	60	12A	50
10B	260	11B	200	12B	180
10C	70	11C	60	12C	50

Each student spends one period a week in a large group meeting. When there is reason to focus on literature, Mr. Bell is in charge of the large group. He may, for example, introduce or summarize a unit or clarify concepts or terminology that the entire group will need. Sometimes he lectures; at other times he may show an appropriate film or present a guest speaker. If one of the other seven teachers is particularly well versed in the kind of literature being studied at the time, Mr. Bell will assign the responsibility for a large-group meeting to that teacher. The teachers responsible for the small-group meetings will attend the large group, because they are expected to relate the work of their discussion sections to the large-group presentation. Thus, since Mr. Bell and three other teachers share responsibility for the eight sections of 10B, all four of them will be present at the large-group 10B meeting on Monday. The four confer regularly on the content and the emphasis of the 10B work; so do the two teachers responsible for 10A; and so on.

When the emphasis is on writing, Mrs. Wright is responsible for the large group. When it is on language, Miss Lang is in charge. Mr. Bell, Mrs. Wright, and Miss Lang will each meet, on the average, three large groups each week, although sometimes the arrangement of the work will give one or another of them more or fewer large-group meetings in a particular week.

This school has, in all, thirty-two discussion groups, as follows:

10A	2	11A	2	12A	2
10B	8	11B	6	12B	6
10C	2	11C	2	12C	2

Because of the time required in preparing for the large-group presentations, Mr. Bell, Mrs. Wright, and Miss Lang each have charge of only two discussion groups, though they frequently sit in with other groups in order to keep informed about the specific kinds of problems that need clarification. The remaining twenty-six discussion groups are divided among the other five teachers. Each discussion group meets two periods a week. Thus Mr. Bell, Mrs. Wright, and Miss Lang each have an average of seven class hours a week, plus observations in a number of other classes. Each of the other teachers has about ten class hours a week, plus attendance at two or three large-group meetings.

The remaining time of all the teachers is given to individual work with students, to lesson preparation, and to paper grading. The individual work consists of conferences with students, guidance in selection of programs for individual students' use with the teaching machines or the language laboratory, and guidance of students' independent reading; ten hours per teacher per week are explicitly designated for these kinds of work with individuals.

Mr. Bell's program for a given week, then, may look like this:

Period	Mon.	Tues.	Wed.	Thurs.	Fri.
1	LG [2]	dg	ic	dg	ic
2	obs [3]	LG	obs	ic	ic
3	dg [4]	ic	LG	dg	obs
4	ic [5]	obs	ic	obs	ic
5	ic	prep	prep	prep	prep
6	prep [6]	prep	prep	prep	prep

Mrs. Wright's and Miss Lang's weekly programs would be comparable. The programs of the other five teachers would differ in that those teachers would seldom have responsibility for large groups, except to attend; the number of hours of observation in other classes would be smaller; and the number of discussion groups would be larger.

The English program of a student in a given week would look something like this:

Period	Mon.	Tues.	Wed.	Thurs.	Fri.
1	LG	dg	tm or ll [7]	dg	ir [8]

In the large group the student would listen and take notes. In the discussion group he would, of course, participate in consideration of the material being treated in the unit. In the work with teaching

[2] Large group.
[3] Observation of other teachers' classes, sometimes including large groups.
[4] Discussion group.
[5] Individual conferences and other work with individuals.
[6] Preparation, evaluation, etc.
[7] Teaching machine or language laboratory.
[8] Independent reading.

machines or in the language laboratory he would concentrate on phases of English with which he himself needed special help; this work might be, but need not be, directly related to the content of the unit. For example, if the class were studying literature, his teaching-machine hour might conceivably be devoted to punctuation or sentence structure because his deficiencies were greatest in those areas. If schedules permitted, he might also have access to the machine or the laboratory during certain other hours of the week. Part of his composition writing could also be accomplished in the laboratory period, with assistance available from the teacher in charge. The independent-reading period would allow him to browse, to read, and to check out books, usually in the classroom library but sometimes in the main library of the school. Conferences with the teacher would occur in either the laboratory period or the independent-reading period.

The teachers' aides would be assigned for specific parts of the day to assist each teacher. They would be responsible for such routine matters as checking attendance, filling out various forms, marking objective tests and spelling papers and the like, duplicating materials for use in the class, and—if their qualifications were sufficient—helping in the laboratory and in supervision of independent reading.

If, instead of using a block curriculum concept, the school followed the philosophy of the spiral cone, only minor adaptations of the plan just described would be required. There would be no such designations as 10A, 10B, and 10C. Instead, a variety of units would be available throughout the day, units so planned that, at any given time, work needed by various groups of students would be available. Thus some students whose greatest need was the improvement of reading would find it possible to concentrate on that for a length of time; meanwhile other groups would be working on language, on composition, on simple literary materials and concepts, on the higher reaches of literature, or on units that combined language, composition, and literature. The composite of large groups, discussion groups, laboratory work, and independent reading would still be employed.

In a very small high school the fivefold procedure cannot be followed, because of the limited numbers of both students and teachers. However, a language laboratory, perhaps shared with teachers of foreign language, is not out of the question, nor is a program of independent reading. In other words, provision for individual differences is quite possible.

In both small and large high schools, effective teaching is now going on that does not employ any of the elaborate organization described in this section. Preliminary experimentation suggests, though, that teachers are less heavily burdened and students learn more in a program that involves large and small groups, laboratory work, independent reading, and individual conferences.

The Physical Environment

Most school buildings are composed of a number of rectangular boxes. In each box designated as an English classroom are placed a desk, a number of chairs, and perhaps a filing cabinet or two. Along the walls are chalkboards, some bulletin boards, and usually a few shelves for books. More elaborately equipped rooms may have a tape recorder, a record player, a stand for an unabridged dictionary, a clock, possibly a television set, a projector, and a few other items.

Inside such a box, excellent instruction may and does occur. Nevertheless, rooms specifically planned by English teachers for English teaching may bring still better results.

Especially needed is a materials center for the English department, a center in which may be kept books, supplies, tape recorders, records and record players, portable television sets, projectors, maps, picture files, and other materials and equipment for the use of the department.

One design now employed in some schools places all the English classrooms in a hexagon or an octagon, with a materials center in the middle, as is shown in Fig. 4. One corner of each room may be

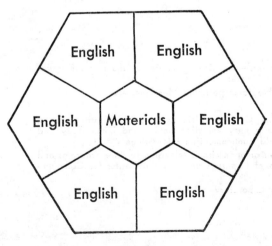

Fig. 4.

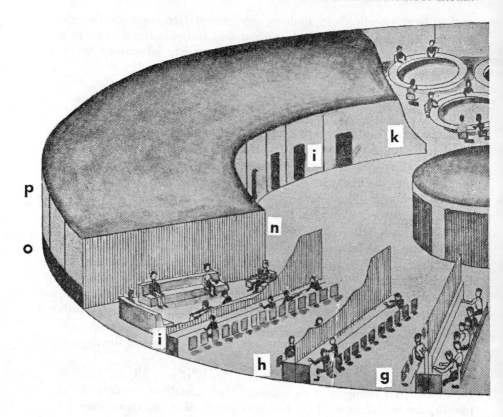

KEY

a. Department Headquarters—coordination center of the research, guidance, programing, teaching and testing staffs

b. Student File—accessible to Department Headquarters

c. Faculty Lounge

d. Departmental Material Center—distribution center of discs, tapes, films for classroom use; communication center and home study unit interchange; and world communication interchange

e. Television Unit—closed or open circuit television to show programs and lessons or to supplement Departmental Material Center for Communication Center viewing

f. Speech and Listening Laboratory

Fig. 5.

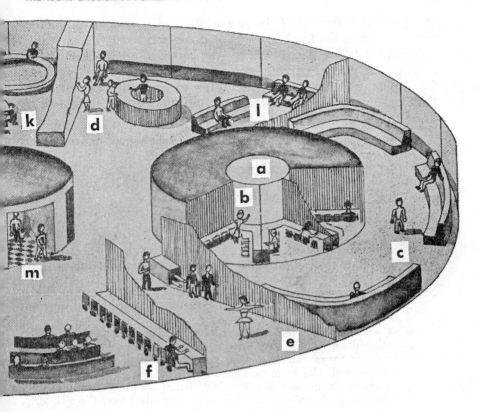

KEY

g. Reading Laboratory
h. Writing Laboratory
i. Conference Rooms—small teacher group discussion rooms
k. Multipurpose Rooms—test taking area and large classroom and audi-
    ence activity
l. Student Lounge
m. Elevator and Stairway Banks
n. Folding Walls
o. Solar Panels—providing uniform heating, cooling, and lighting
p. Sun Control Windows

separated from the rest of the room with a glass divider; this corner may be used as the teacher's office and conference room.

A more elaborate plan is that of "the language arts suite, including a number of general purpose rooms and a variety of rooms designed for variant functions." Suggestions for such a suite are made by Dr. Stanley B. Kegler of the University of Minnesota High School:

a) departmental offices (where teachers might retreat to be students for a while);
b) the instructional materials center;
c) a television unit for both closed and open-circuit television;
d) speaking and listening laboratories;
e) language laboratories;
f) special rooms for remedial instruction (which often takes place with relatively small classes);
g) writing booths or rooms;
h) conference rooms for student and teacher-student discussions (glass paneling allows for adequate supervision);
i) a relatively secluded area to which students might retreat to do the independent reading so important to literary growth and development;
j) at least one room into which a large number of students might be gathered for lectures associated with team-teaching;
k) provision for movable panels or partitions to provide an opportunity for the small classroom approach associated with team-teaching;
l) provision for expansion and adaptation when more nearly perfect teaching machines and programmed materials become available.[9]

Something approaching the Kegler suite is the "center for teaching communication in the school of tomorrow," depicted by Ruth Stickle and Jean Paul Budinger in their simplified sketch in the golden-anniversary-convention program of the NCTE, reproduced here as Fig. 5.

Perhaps such departmental arrangements will become realities in the future. The concepts they represent are important today because they reflect what some teachers, though by no means all, believe may lead to improved teaching and learning. Conservative—and often excellent—teachers say that book, child, and teacher are enough. Liberal—and often excellent—teachers admit that book, child, and teacher are basic, but they contend that the interactions among the three may be bettered if other ingredients are added.

[9] "Planning the Language Arts Classroom," *American School Board Journal,* Aug., 1962, pp. 28–29.

THE IDEA BOX

WHO IS THE GOOD TEACHER?

"The difference between a good and a mediocre teacher lies mainly in the emphasis the former puts on the exploring part of the mind, the aspects of learning that reveal meanings and lead to further understanding. . . . Mediocre teachers . . . stress memory at the expense of intelligence." (Northrop Frye, *Design for Learning*, 12–13.)

STRANDS

G. R. Carlsen, in the *High School Journal* for February, 1962, urges curriculum planners to think in terms of strands that will be woven sequentially through the English program. For example, in language, the seventh grade study might emphasize how we communicate; the eighth, history of language; the ninth, sociology of language; the tenth, semantics; the eleventh, the structure of English.

A PRINCIPLE FOR A CURRICULUM

"The best preparation for a period of rapid change consists of a firm grounding in those things *least* likely to change or that will change most slowly. Many of the subjects that seem at the moment to be most 'practical' are the very ones that will soon be outmoded by the swift march of events." Paul Woodring, *General Electric Forum*, IV, No. 3 (Oct.–Nov., 1961).

SEQUENCE IN THE CURRICULUM

Nine points to be considered in planning a sequential curriculum are discussed in J. N. Hook's "If a Curriculum Is To Be Sequential," *English Journal*, LI (Feb., 1962), 79. They include definition of *English*, average levels of expectation, grade placement of demonstrably useful items, a consistent writing program, grade placement of instruction in reading skills, a common literature program, opportunity for review, enrichment and dilution, and the analogy of the spiral cone.

"ORGANIZATION OF AN ENGLISH DEPARTMENT"

Specifically designated responsibilities for the department head, coordinators for each grade, a reading coordinator, an audio-visual chairman, a speech chairman, and each teacher—these make "machine-like" efficiency for a department, say Lorena A. Anderson and Eunice P. Benson, *English Journal*, XLVIII (March, 1959), 145.

UNION HIGH SCHOOL REVAMPS ENGLISH PROGRAM

Union High School, Mount Vernon, Washington, with the help of a sympathetic administration and public, reduced class size, developed a curriculum, formulated an in-service program, and planned to hire teachers who know English well. Pat Hayden describes the procedures, which resulted in substantial improvement without being revolutionary, in the *English Journal*, LII (Jan., 1963), 49.

"ESSENTIAL CONDITIONS FOR TEACHING WRITTEN COMPOSITION"

Lois Grose presents a reasoned description of proper working conditions including modest teaching load, writing laboratory, teachers trained in composition, departmental meetings, efficient grading of themes, team teaching, and the use of opaque projectors and teaching machines. *English Journal*, L (April, 1961), 246.

COMMUNICATION

In "A Course in Communication for High School Seniors," *English Journal*, XLIX (Feb., 1960), 108, Robert Lewin describes a comprehensive course stressing literary and linguistic symbols, with attention to mass media and modern theories of communication.

ENGLISH ADJUSTED TO NEED

Among numerous experiments, Evanston, Illinois, Township High School has tried a program in which students spend most of their time in their "own" class but part of the time in a large group and about three weeks of each semester in a section addressing itself to students' greatest needs. Thus, those most in need of improved mechanics were placed with a teacher specializing in that topic, those needing help with reading went to a reading section, etc.

PROS AND CONS OF TEAM TEACHING

Favorable: fewer preparations per teacher; more thorough preparations; cross-fertilization of teachers; playing from each teacher's strongest suits; provision for individual differences in small groups; greater variety in presentations; economical use of films, etc.; more student responsibility for his own learning; useful practice in listening to lectures, note taking, etc.; fairer evaluation of students; ease in administering tests.

Unfavorable: intensive preparation required for large-group presentations; difficulty of recognizing student lack of understanding in large groups; need for reaching many kinds of students with a single presentation; tendency to make teaching too subject-centered; revisions and reorientation required each time team personnel changes; occasional incompatibility of team members; loss of close teacher-student relationship; disciplinary problems in large groups; danger that lectures will constitute basis for all testing; in some schools, lack of suitable rooms and equipment.

FIVE TYPES OF TEAM TEACHING

1. Part- or full-time helpers (lay readers, secretaries, audio-visual helpers, etc.)
2. Trading (informal exchanges of class hours to capitalize on teachers' individual strengths)

3. Cross-departmental (use of specialists in other departments such as history and music, for certain purposes)
4. Coordinate teaching (with team members as equal partners in planning and in assuming responsibilities according to their specialties)
5. Hierarchy (one teacher, the "team leader," responsible for major presentations and supervision of the whole team)

TEAM TEACHING: AMERICAN HISTORY AND ENGLISH

In English 11 at Miami's Palmetto High School, correlation of history, social sciences, music, art, writing, speaking, and reading is stressed, with teachers of English taking the lead in an "American Studies" program. Among the features: units on "The Dream of Freedom," "The Dream of the Land," "The Hope of the City," "The Individual and Society"; weekly themes, with instruction in grammar and usage based on needs revealed in students' writing; extensive reading including American classics; much use of audio-visual material; lectures by specialists in art, music, etc.; for some students, a month of special help from the school's reading expert.

A DESCRIPTION OF TEAM TEACHING

Dorothy Kell, in the 1961–62 issue of the *Baltimore English Bulletin*, describes several team-teaching experiments. For example, in study of *The Red Badge of Courage*, two large- and three small-group meetings occupied each week. In the large meetings, slides, maps, and lecture predominated, with one hour for a program of Civil War music supplied by the music department. The small groups read, discussed, and were tested. Other team-teaching units included Shakespeare plays, humor, literature of foreign lands, and composition.

MORE ARTICLES ON TEAM TEACHING

Anderson, Robert H., "Team Teaching in Action," *Nation's Schools*, May, 1960.
————, "Team Teaching," *NEA Journal*, March, 1961.
Drummond, H. D., "Team Teaching: An Assessment," *Educational Leadership*, Dec., 1961.
Ford, P. M., "Different Day for the English Teacher," *English Journal*, May, 1961.
Searlin, Thomas, "A Critical Look at Team Teaching," *The Instructor*, Oct., 1961.
"Team Teaching," *Illinois Education*, Nov., 1961.
Weiss, Thomas M., and Mary S. Morris, "Critique of the Team Approach," *Educational Forum*, Jan., 1960.

ABOUT THE UNGRADED SCHOOL, MORE OR LESS

Although *Individualizing Instruction* (Part I, 61st Yearbook, National Society for the Study of Education, 1962) warns that "Ungraded structure is . . . no panacea for problems of curriculum and instruction," neither is any other system. John W. Gardner, in *Excellence* (New York: Harper

& Row, 1961, p. 112), says, "The academic lock step which developed in
many of our schools in the 1930's and 1940's, in which all youngsters are
advanced a grade per year regardless of IQ and performance, was among
other things a device for preventing invidious comparisons between individuals." And *The Pursuit of Excellence* (Rockefeller Bros. Fund, Inc.,
New York: Doubleday & Co., Inc., 1958, p. 30) asserts, "Adequate attention to individual differences means rejecting a rigid policy of promotion
by age."

AN UNGRADED SYSTEM

For a description of an ungraded English program, see M. F. Noall and
M. Nuttall, "Hurricane, Utah, High School Ungraded English Project,"
Bulletin of the National Association of Secondary-School Principals (Jan.,
1962), p. 185. Sophomores, juniors, and seniors are grouped according
to ability and skill and assigned to sections accordingly. The five teachers
each specialize in literature, grammar and usage, composition and creative
writing, speech, or reading; a student spends seven or eight weeks each
year with each teacher. The article says that hearty praise for the plan
has come from teachers, students, and parents.

AN UNGRADED PROGRAM FOR SUPERIOR STUDENTS

High-ability tenth, eleventh, and twelfth year students are admitted to
a special ungraded program at Schenley High School, Pittsburgh, described
as follows: "Since the basic structure of the course is a three-year sequence
of thematic units, a student may enter the class at the beginning of any
sequence. The student's progress toward intellectual maturity in English
is marked, not by changing grade level designations or by speed, but by
his reading of the more difficult selections for group and independent
reading, his understanding of the subtler points of both content and style
in the literature read, and his demonstration of increasing mastery of
speaking and writing skills." (From an unpublished report.) Three units
are based on language, three on literary types, one on literature and the
fine arts, and thirteen on universal themes in literature; writing and speaking are incorporated in all units.

JUNIOR-SENIOR ELECTIVES

University High School, Iowa City, Iowa, lets juniors and seniors elect
their English from this group of semester-long courses: Readings in English
Literature, Moments in American Literature, Landmarks of Literature, Individualized Reading, Writing Problems, Writing Laboratory, Creative
Writing. Speech electives are also available. Teacher-pupil planning,
small-group discussions, individual projects, and some use of college professors as lecturers are other features of the program, which G. R. Carlsen
described in the April, 1962, *English Journal*.

"AN ENGLISH LABORATORY IN ACTION"

Barringer High School, Newark, New Jersey, uses a special room to
assist small numbers of students with specific problems in language skills.

Grayce F. Salerno describes the laboratory in the *English Journal*, LII (Jan., 1963), 37.

A SCHEDULING PLAN

In Peekskill, New York, High School, all sophomore English classes meet at the same times; all junior classes, at other times; all senior classes, at still other times. This makes team teaching easier to arrange. One hour a day is set aside for a teachers' planning period.

ENRICHMENT FOR THE ABLE

Mildred Rock, in the *NEA Journal* for October, 1958, recommends these materials and techniques for enriching the curriculum for able students: use of college texts and selected paperbound books with upperclassmen, detailed analysis of literature, weekly creative or expository writing, semantics, essay tests, and research papers. (Note, though, that some college teachers object to high school use of college text material.)

PROGRAMS FOR THE ACADEMICALLY TALENTED

An NEA conference in 1958, chaired by Dr. James B. Conant, made these recommendations for able students in English: (1) selection on composite basis of reasoning power, creative ability, academic aptitude, achievement, work habits; (2) flexible class schedule; (3) ability grouping in large high schools, enrichment in small; (4) small seminar classes; (5) more advanced goals for these students, not just more work of the same kind the others do; (6) advanced reading skills taught through literature; (7) mandatory four years of English; (8) teachers with social sensitivity, broad interests, detailed knowledge of English, effective instructional methods, willingness to use mass media; (9) rich library resources; (10) diagnostic tests to make possible skipping of what students already know; (11) articulation with elementary and junior high schools; (12) reading lists for summer; (13) continuation of program from elementary school into college.

TWO VIEWS OF THE DIEDERICH PLAN

A plan formulated at a teachers institute at Rutgers in 1959, under the leadership of Paul B. Diederich, involves lay readers, conference time, two days of free reading, one day of "self-correcting homework," and only two days of class meetings a week. Diederich provides details in "The Rutgers Plan for Cutting Class Size in Two," *English Journal*, XLIX (April, 1960), 229. In the October, 1960, issue, Laurence Niblett develops the argument supported by his title, "The Rutgers Plan: Not Enough of the Right Kind of Help."

THE OVERHEAD PROJECTOR

For an article by a man who has successfully made extensive use of the projector in teaching language and composition, see Edwin L. Peterson's "A Magic Lantern for English," *NEA Journal*, LVIII (Oct., 1962), 18. See also Robert W. Wheeler's "Some Uses of the Opaque Projector," *English Journal*, L (Sept., 1961), 417.

BREAKS WITH TRADITION

1. Arcadia High School, Phoenix, Arizona, is experimenting with a program based upon the idea that we learn best by imitation. Students imitate pronunciation, use of vocabulary words in context, model sentences, model paragraphs, model essays. Joseph P. Collignon, "Teaching Them To Write," *Clearing House,* XXXVII (Nov., 1962), 142.

2. In Evanston, Illinois, Township High School, "final" examinations have been given in April. Advantages: better motivation, and opportunity to reteach important things that students have not learned. For details, see the article by Barbara Pannwitt, *Clearing House,* XXXIII (Nov., 1958), 139.

THE PROFESSIONAL THEATER IN THE SCHOOL

Other large cities might well emulate New York and Pittsburgh, which use small professional casts to perform suitable plays on a regular schedule during school hours in secondary schools. Thus, *Romeo and Juliet* was presented in 154 New York schools in one year; a program offering a condensed history of the theater attracted over 100,000 students in a year.

HELP FROM OTHER DEPARTMENTS

The Virginia State Board of Education recommends (1) that teachers in all subject areas encourage pupils to apply principles of effective writing in all writing assignments; (2) that, in preparing examinations, teachers in all subjects consider the appropriateness of one or more essay-type questions; (3) that spelling and composition be given due consideration in grading pupils in all subject fields.

ALL-SCHOOL ENGLISH

Through such devices as having geography papers written in English classes, or mathematics papers on "How To Find a Batting Average" scrutinized by the English teacher, a small Texas school involved all its teachers in improving English. Carrie Stegall, "Now They Are Real Buddies," *English Journal,* XLIX (Feb., 1959), 78.

TEACHER LIBRARIAN

The interdependence of teachers and librarians is becoming more clearly recognized. According to Joseph Mersand, past president of NCTE, this may mean "that the status of the librarian may have to be changed from that of a cataloger to teacher librarian or counselor. She will have to become acquainted with our courses of study, will have to learn something about teaching library skills, and do everything possible to make the library a beehive of wholesome and worthwhile activity." *SRA Insight,* Winter, 1963, 6.

HIGH SCHOOL—COLLEGE ARTICULATION

A series of articles by an NCTE committee on high school—college articulation is available in the *English Journal* for September, 1961, and February and March, 1962.

CHECK LIST

"A Check List for Evaluating the English Program in the Junior and Senior High School," *English Journal*, XLIX (April, 1962), 273, provides 55 basic questions and 108 subquestions.

BASIC PLANNING

AVOIDANCE OF SNIPPETS

Although it is essential, for purposes of clarity and specificity, to discuss one by one the various facets of the teaching of English, the beginning teacher must remember that as a rule English instruction is not chopped up into snippets. That is, reading, listening, writing, and speaking (or, if you prefer, language, composition, and literature) constitute a whole, with the elements woven together to form a smooth fabric. Therefore, in the teaching of English, it is usually wise to combine various types of activities. Instead of teaching the semi-colon today, "Miniver Cheevy" tomorrow, the complex sentence Wednesday, a short story Thursday, and public speaking Friday, it is better to plan one's work in units that will incorporate, to some extent, all the aspects of communication. The unified field theory described in Chapter 1 has the advantage that it recalls constantly to the teacher's mind the essential unity of English.

There has been too much atomization in the teaching of English. Granted that one must occasionally take time out to teach the use of the hyphen, the meaning of "ambidextrous," the spelling of "balloon," the usefulness of the appositive. Granted that one must work to improve reading skills, to increase the understanding of Edgar Lee Masters' poetry or the prose of Thoreau. Granted that one must help Lloyd to organize his oral presentations and help Jacqueline to distinguish between main ideas and details when she listens to a speech. Granted that individual students need special help with commas or with clear placement of modifiers or with specific problems in diction. The point still remains that, if each of these things is taught as an entity, as something existing in a vacuum and unrelated to anything else, much of the meaningfulness is lost. Yet, too often, capitalization has been taught only for the sake of capitalization, and Addison's essays have been taught without reference to any other essays, without reference to the students' own writing, and without opportunity for discussion of their social and literary implications. The English course thus became a hodgepodge of apparently dissimilar elements.

If, however, the teacher of English takes the broad view of his subject, if he conceives of his task not as the teaching of unrelated fragments but as the teaching of the whole art of sending and receiving communications in English, if he has an overview of the whole English curriculum and understands the relation of his part of it to the rest, and if his goal is to help each student progress as far as he can in all phases of communication, English is meaningful to all students. They then learn to use semicolons when there is a reason for this learning, they improve their reading because a reason exists for trying to make the improvement, they talk before the class because they have something to say; they learn English, that is, because English is worth learning and is interesting to learn.

PLANNING THE TOTAL PROGRAM

In taking the broad view the teacher must, as has just been said, consider the total English program and the way that his work fits into that program. In most good school systems the general plan for the three, four, five, or six years of secondary English has been carefully thought out so that the new teacher need only learn what the plan is and then fit his own materials, ideas, and techniques into it. Many of our best city systems now possess cooperatively developed K-12 or K-14 plans. Few or no states now have rigid curriculums that the teacher is expected to follow minutely, but a number of states now have flexible curriculums or curriculum guides that allow considerable departmental variations and teacher initiative; some of the state associations of teachers of English have been instrumental in building these guides. Many states still do not have such guides, though, with the result that each school system plans its program to fit its own peculiar situation.

Useful in curricular planning are the publications of the Curriculum Commission of the National Council of Teachers of English, although they have been criticized as too socially oriented and too little subject-matter-centered. Whether the charge is true or not, teachers should be familiar with *The English Language Arts,* which gives an overview of curriculum planning on all levels; *Language Arts for Today's Children,* which offers detailed suggestions for elementary school work; and *The English Language Arts in the Secondary School,* which provides for secondary English teachers rich and concrete suggestions based on the actual needs of junior and senior high school students.

The beginning teacher may be employed in a fairly large system; if so, he will have little voice in working out the curriculum until he gains considerable experience. But he is more likely to be employed in a small school in which there may be only from one to six English teachers. In such a situation, unless a curriculum is already firmly established and in no obvious need of revision, he will have a large share in the development. Even if there is a curriculum, sooner or later he will participate in revamping it. The "good" English curriculum of 1920 is not good today, because social, political, economic, literary, and educational developments have outmoded it, and today's "good" curriculum will need revision in a few years. The law of life, ceaseless change, is never repealed. At the center of any satisfactory curriculum remain a number of lasting verities, which must be taught to each successive generation of students. But, around the center, the other parts of the curriculum eddy restlessly.

It is desirable for the beginning teacher to "make haste slowly" in curriculum construction, because experience as well as theory is needed in the building of an inclusive, coherent, sequential program. If the beginner is in a large school, he should place considerable reliance on his more experienced colleagues. But, if he is the only English teacher in the school, he may have to formulate his curriculum as well as he can, test it, and in later years make whatever changes are required.

The planning of the work for several grades and varying levels of student ability may seem an insuperable task. Fortunately, in addition to the publications of the NCTE, there are many other aids. It is well worthwhile to spend some time examining the printed or mimeographed curriculums of a number of representative schools; copies of these are available in any adequate college library. The objectives for each year deserve the most attention, because these statements of objectives represent experienced teachers' reasoned opinions of what it is best to emphasize at each grade level. Some of the statements of objectives, it must be admitted, are so general as to be meaningless. But it is possible to examine a number of such curriculums and arrive at an approximate consensus of what may be expected of students in the different grades. One may note particularly the grade placement of various kinds of written work, patterns for organizing compositions, types of sentences, varieties of literature and literary concepts, and kinds of oral activity.

As the reports and recommendations of the curriculum-study centers sponsored by the United States Office of Education appear, they should be given especially careful attention. Beginning in 1962 a number of such centers were established, each with a somewhat different emphasis, but all charged with the responsibility of developing and testing an English curriculum sequence for designated grade levels. With federal funds amounting to about a quarter-million dollars each, as well as local support, these centers represent the first large-scale, systematic, well-financed attempt at curricular development in English. Their directors include some of the leading English teachers in the country.

Up-to-date high school textbooks also offer assistance. Although such books, of necessity, are aimed at large groups and may contain some materials unsuitable for a particular school, or omit other highly desirable materials, the beginning teacher can lean rather heavily upon them, confident that what they include is at least approximately right for the designated grade level. The dangers, though, are that the teacher may come to rely almost exclusively upon a particular set of textbooks and that what his students receive will therefore be relatively impoverished. No set of textbooks can contain everything that should go into an English curriculum for a given school.

Statements of minimum essentials have now largely gone out of existence. At one time such statements appeared in numerous curriculums, reflecting the belief that, in order to merit a passing grade, a student must reach a specified level of performance. Minimum essentials were attacked on several scores—some educators saying that minima tend to become maxima, others declaring that it is absurd to give a student a failing grade simply because he misspells a couple of required words or leaves out a vital comma, and still others expressing the belief that no hard-working student should fail only because he lacks the intelligence to master the minima. Some conservatives still contend, however, that the only way to establish and maintain standards in the schools is to formulate and observe statements of minima; a child who does not come up to the standards for the end of the first grade should repeat that grade and repeat it until he does reach the minima, even if he is twelve years old before he reaches grade two. A middle ground between those who oppose and those who favor minimum essentials is that of the educators who say that we need information about average levels of expectation for each grade; this information will affect teachers' evaluation and will help to show whether each school is doing as much for its students as is possible. Until such information is obtained through research, however, statements of minimum essentials will serve to indicate what levels of attainment may be expected of most students in each grade.

In planning the long-term program, the teacher has as the first step the setting up of objectives, both general and specific, for each year. Then, with the objectives before him, the teacher asks himself, "What types of work and what materials will best lead to the attainment of these objectives?" That leads to unit planning.

PLANNING OF UNITS

Answers to the question "What is a unit?" may vary widely. Here are two extremes: One teacher said, "I'm teaching a unit on Frost's 'Death of the Hired Man' today." To her a unit meant simply having students read and discuss a single poem and perhaps bring in some related material. But in a Minnesota rural elementary school all eight grades worked for a whole year on a "unit" called "Improving Our School," with all the elementary subjects incorporated in the unit. More typically, though, the term *unit* refers to an organized study, lasting from one week to eight weeks and centered upon a given theme, to which everything in the unit is in some way related.

Some units are devoted entirely to composition, others entirely to literature, still others to a combination of the two. As has already been suggested, a good unit often combines work in reading, writing, listening, and speaking. The number of possible subjects for units is limitless. Very often a concept is central, such as "Caution vs. cowardice," "What makes a plot?," "How authors delineate characters," or "The essence of tragedy." A linguistic item may be the focus: "English in Chaucer's time," "Emotive and reportorial language," "The versatile verb," etc. Skills may sometimes be stressed, as in "Reading for greater comprehension" or "Learning to write good letters." A large number of unit topics are suggested in The Idea Box, pages 78–81.

It was once the practice of some teachers to plan the organization of a unit to the last detail. Their lesson plans for the unit indicated that five minutes would be devoted to this, ten minutes to that, and so on. The teacher gathered every scrap of material in advance. The class moved in rigid conformity to schedule, regardless of whether or not the desired learnings had been attained.

Then, under the leadership of a few "progressive" educators, some teachers went to the other extreme, that of planlessness. In effect, they appeared before their classes, asked "What shall we do during the next four weeks?" and did whatever the majority of the students wished, whether or not it conformed closely to the objectives of the course. If the students wanted to read and discuss comic books, they did so; if they wanted to spend their time in planning for the junior-senior banquet, they did that.

Of course there was learning in both the carefully planned and the completely unplanned units. Students often learn in spite of themselves and their teachers. But the present tendency is toward planning by teachers that is flexible enough to permit some alteration in accord with legitimate student requests or unexpected developments.

"Teacher-student planning," strongly advocated by many educators and classroom teachers not many years ago, seems much less popular today, perhaps because it was often unsuccessful, or perhaps because of the analogical argument that a doctor's patient does not assist in choosing the medication. However, sometimes teachers do encourage class participation in unit planning, at least to this extent: After the teacher considers the objectives for the school year, chooses in their light a promising and appropriate theme for the unit, and ascertains whether the most essential materials are available in suitable quantities, he draws up a general (not a detailed) plan for the unit and submits it to the class. He explains the chief purpose of the unit and attempts to arouse students' enthusiasm or at least interest. Then the students discuss what the outcomes of the unit may be, what materials they will be able to supply, and how the work may be divided so that each gets to do something that he is particularly interested in or that he especially needs.

Variations of this procedure are endless. Some teachers prefer to begin by submitting to the students several choices, any of which would lead to realization of some of the year's objectives. After the selection has been made, teacher and class together set up specific objectives, choose materials, plan activities, and divide the labor. A number of teachers like to employ student committees, each of which is responsible for part of the work of the unit.

In a well-planned unit, not all students are doing exactly the same things. Some of the reading and exercises are performed in common, but individual and group work, tailored to special needs, is also included.

More than books should be used in most units. Movies and film-strips often fit in. Sometimes, through coincidence, radio or television programs are appropriate. Magazines, newspapers, and radio scripts may often be used. Occasionally a field trip is desirable. Outside speakers, or teachers in other departments, may be invited to talk to the class. The students' own activities may be varied. The good unit does possess much variety, life, interest. It is as a rule infinitely preferable to the old day-to-day assignment routine: "Tomorrow study pages fifty-eight to sixty-seven."

Details of unit planning vary, but the following description is reasonably typical.

1. *Scope:* a general statement of what will be covered and what apparently related material will be excluded.

2. *Objectives:* a list of desired outcomes. Objectives are often subdivided into general and specific. The general should not be huge and amorphous, such as "Learn to be a better citizen." Instead they should be general only in that they exclude concrete detail; e.g., "Learn to be tolerant of those whose home backgrounds differ from ours." The objectives are normally stated in terms of the outcomes for students; i.e., not *teach* but *learn.*

3. *Activities:* the specific reading, writing, problems, laboratory experiments, field trips, and other experiences that will be included. These activities form the basis of separate, more detailed lesson plans which develop each activity or group of activities fully enough for a day's classwork. Often the first activity is an "initiating" or "introductory" or "motivational" one intended to arouse students' interest and support and provide essential background. The last activity is called "culminating" in current jargon and is intended to summarize or in some other way bring to a head all the other activities. It may be combined with 5, Evaluation. Activities may be varied to provide for individual differences; if so, the unit should show how this is to be accomplished.

4. *Resources:* the books and other text or library materials, *realia,* audio-visual aids, laboratory equipment, field trips, and anything else needed for successful completion of the unit. Often the resources are divided into those for student use and those for the teacher.

5. *Evaluation:* the ways in which the success of the students and the success of the teacher may be judged.[1]

---

[1] J. N. Hook, *Hook's Guide to Good Writing: Grammar, Style, Usage* (New York: The Ronald Press Company, 1962), p. 482.

DIAGNOSIS, LESSON PLANS, AND EVALUATION

Diagnosis

Faced with his four or five classes—perhaps 100 or 175 students—the beginning teacher may feel a temporary bafflement. How can he get to know these young people? How can he discover what they are and what they need to learn?

The principal's files will probably yield some information concerning the age, background, physical handicaps, academic records, test scores, etc., of most of the students. It is usually inadvisable, though, to spend much time in studying these records until one gets to know the students fairly well in class. The mere reading of a hundred or so sets of data will leave in one's mind no clear impression about individuals unless one is already somewhat familiar with each student. Therefore, except for a brief preliminary examination of the records, the principal's files may be ignored for a few weeks. Then, if the teacher wishes specific information about individuals, he may ask the principal's permission to consult the files again. What he finds there should be taken with some salt, however, and should not be regarded as final.

For example, the file may show that freshman Herbert had difficulties in passing some of his subjects in the seventh and eighth grades, that his IQ is 97, and that disciplinary action was once taken when Herbert stole a fountain pen. To the teacher, Herbert has seemed a pleasant, well-behaved boy who is capable of doing at least average work. In this instance, the teacher's judgment *may* be more reliable than the statistical data, for the simple reasons that Herbert is an adolescent and that adolescents change rapidly. Perhaps Herbert, in a moment of adolescent irresponsibility, did steal a fountain pen; he should not, however, be regarded as a confirmed thief whose every movement must be watched. Perhaps his IQ is slightly below normal, but psychologists today are aware that the IQ test scores are not entirely reliable and that the IQ may change somewhat over a period of years. The process of growing up may have caused Herbert's troubles in eighth grade English; perhaps now he is mature enough that those troubles are lessened. In other words, data of the sort usually in the principal's office need to be supplemented by personal observation; these data may be of considerable value at times, but they should never cause a teacher to decide that one student is hopeless, that another is a genius, or that a third is doomed to mediocrity.

Within his classroom the teacher has a number of ways of learning about individuals. He should learn students' names quickly, for obvious reasons. The easiest way to do so is to make a temporary seating chart at the first class meeting. Fifteen or twenty minutes' homework studying each chart, plus a quick review before class, should enable him to call each student by name on the second day. The students will be pleased that they have so quickly lost their anonymity; they will be happy that they are not addressed as "the boy in the green shirt" or "the last girl in the row" or "yes, you"; and they will immediately gain respect for the teacher. If the teacher wishes to change or discard the seating arrangement after he has learned to attach the right name to the right face, he may, of course, do so.

After learning students' names, the teacher may begin making mental notes of individuals' characteristics. The notes are for the sake not of classifying but of understanding. Thus the teacher may note that George seems sullen in class and rather hostile toward the other students; the teacher will then be on the alert to discover the reasons for George's attitude and eventually to plan a little campaign to make George more cooperative. Or Helen may appear to be unusually intelligent and well informed; the teacher may search for ways of making use of Helen's intelligence for the benefit of both Helen and the rest of the class.

How a student talks, how he reads aloud, how he listens, how willing he is to contribute to class discussion, what information he brings in from his own background, how he reacts to a literary selection—all these are straws in the wind, bits of evidence that will help the teacher to understand him. Particularly valuable, though, is noting what and how he writes. In a page or two of a student's writing, one can find much more than the fact that the student does not know how to punctuate or to spell "there." One may discover his ambition, hopes, fears; much of his background; glimmerings of his developing philosophy of life.

Besides learning about students from administrators' data and from observation in class, the teacher may—and should, if there is time— talk with the students individually. The subject of conversation is relatively unimportant; it may be schoolwork, but it may almost as well be football or clothes or a movie or anything else. From such conversation the teacher may draw valid conclusions about what a student is and what he needs.

There are also numerous standardized tests available for diagnostic purposes. Such tests are of value as indications of what points need to be stressed in whatever units are planned.

Lesson Plans

A lesson plan is a fairly detailed outline of the work proposed by the teacher for a single class period. Some department heads, supervisors, or principals require that lesson plans be turned in for a week or two weeks in advance, so that in case of the teacher's illness a substitute will know what is to be covered. In other schools no such requirement exists.

Ordinarily it is desirable for beginning teachers to make more detailed lesson plans than experienced teachers need. For the experienced teacher a statement that covers the purpose, the materials, and the main points to be included is enough. Many old-timers, in fact, carry their lesson plans in their heads. But the beginner will feel more comfortable and probably do a better job if he has outlined each lesson rather carefully.

No specific kind of outline will cover all lesson plans. Most often, though, the following three points will be covered:

Objective or Objectives. These should be limited enough to be attained in the period. Usually they will represent a small segment of the objectives of the total unit.

Activities. These generally include (1) an introduction that relates the day's topic to previous work, or presents the beginnings of new material and (2) a chronological ordering of the things to be done during the hour, together with key questions to be asked if discussion is involved. If the class works in groups, the tasks for each group are specified.

Materials Needed. This is simply a list of any books, pictures, recordings, or other materials the teacher should be sure to have in class.

Evaluation

Every teacher needs to give considerable thought to evaluation, even before entering the classroom. How will he be able to determine whether his classes are making satisfactory progress? Upon what bases shall he grade the work of individuals?

The first of these questions is somewhat easier to answer than the second. The teacher may ascertain class progress in a number of ways. For one thing, he may, at the end of a semester or year, roughly estimate the progress of the class toward the attainment of the objectives that have been set up. That is, he will re-examine the objectives and draw conclusions concerning how fully they have been reached.

But the estimate will be more than a guess if he compares the known performance of his class with lists of minimum essentials, with reading-ability norms, with composition scales, and with norms of literature-appreciation tests. A comparison of paragraphs or longer pieces of writing prepared by the students at the beginning and the end of each term is often enlightening. Likewise, a consideration of improvement in students' ability to make well-organized and reasonably well-delivered oral presentations is possible, particularly if a few recordings are made at the beginning and again at the end of the term. Certain less tangible but no less important aspects of improvement can hardly be measured but should be thought about: such things as class spirit, cooperativeness, willingness to assume responsibility, initiative, judgment, tolerance, and understanding and employment of democratic principles. Some especially helpful suggestions concerning evaluation are detailed in Chapter 18 of *The English Language Arts*.[2]

The basis for evaluating the work of individuals is often determined by the administration. In some schools no student who attends class with fair regularity is permitted to fail. In others a grading curve must be followed by all teachers: perhaps 15 per cent A's, 20 per cent B's, 30 per cent C's, 20 per cent D's, and 15 per cent F's. In such a system the top 15 per cent must be given A's, even though some do not deserve this mark of distinction, or even though more than 15 per cent have displayed consistent excellence; likewise, 15 per cent must fail, even though they may have been fairly successful in reaching the objectives of the course. In a large number of schools, written comments are superseding grades; at the end of the course the student either is or is not given credit. Much could be said in favor of this plan, although some teachers complain that it destroys the initiative of potentially superior students to whom grades are an incentive. In still other systems the administrators have other rules of thumb concerning grading, rules which of course the teacher must follow whether or not he agrees with the principles involved.

But suppose that you—not "the teacher" but *you*—suppose that you may decide for yourself how you will separate the sheep from the goats. How will you determine who passes, who fails, who is "average," who deserves the coveted top marks?

You will doubtless find that making individual evaluations, "passing out grades," is the most painful part of teaching. Here is Edwin, slow, inaccurate, retarded in reading, but cooperative, likable, and hardworking; he ranks near the bottom of the class in almost everything

[2] New York: Appleton-Century-Crofts, Inc., 1952, pp. 417–40.

he tries. Must Edwin be given an F? Here is Joan, who almost never exerts herself but does work of consistently high quality. Should Joan be given an A, or should the top grades go usually to students like William, who is less able but more conscientious and who through strenuous effort does first-quality work? If Clara ranked very low at the beginning of the term, but now does work as good as that of the majority of the class, should she be given a B because of her marked improvement, a C because she is now doing C work, or a D because the average of all her grades is D? Several students are exactly on the borderline between two grades; either grade could be justified. Should you give them the higher or the lower grade?

Unfortunately there are no pat answers to questions like these. The plan of writing comments instead of grades on report cards eliminates many such problems; at the end of the term, only the decision to pass or to fail must be made, and, since relatively few students are generally near failure, only a small number of decisions must be reached. But if your school does not employ the pass-fail system of grading, you have to decide about Edwin, Joan, William, Clara, and the others.

Most helpful will be a definite interpretation of what each grade means. You may not agree with the definitions that follow, but they may serve as a guide to your further thinking.[3]

The grade of A is distinctly a mark of superiority. It represents much more than mere competence in meeting assignments. There is a "plus factor" involved: The A student not only does what is expected of him but goes beyond it. He dares to be himself; he dares to use his initiative; he does not require prodding. Even his occasional failures are magnificent failures; like the late Babe Ruth, he strikes out with a mighty swing. He works well with the group and often assumes leadership in group undertakings.

The grade of B indicates a high level of accomplishment, with the "plus factor" diminished. It represents less originality, less artistry, less depth of analysis than the A; yet all three qualities are sometimes present. A student may receive a B because he is in ability an A student who has not lived up to his potentialities, or because he is in ability a C student who has worked hard enough to pull himself up by his own bootstraps, or because he is an able student who does most things well but does not possess a sufficient amount of ability, initiative, or aggressiveness to merit an A. The B student usually cooperates well with the group and sometimes assumes leadership.

[3] If your school uses a numerical rather than an alphabetical system, substitute 92–100 for A, 84–91 for B, 76–83 for C, 68–75 for D, below 68 for F.

The grade of C represents mediocrity of accomplishment (in the old sense of *"mediocris,"* meaning "in a middle state"). The student who is given a C has done what he was asked to do, but probably little more, possibly a little less. The quality of his accomplishment is neither high nor low. Sometimes a C is given a student poorer than average in ability who has worked hard enough to deserve it; sometimes it is given to a capable student who does not try to live up to his ability. Usually, though, the C goes to the student who is not very high or very low in native ability, energy, and productiveness. The C student cooperates fairly well with the group but rarely volunteers to lead.

The grade of D covers a multitude of sins such as carelessness, indifference, sluggishness, or laziness. Or it may come as the result of virtually insurmountable handicaps such as low native ability, slowness in learning, or physical defects, over which neither teacher nor student has much control. Or the D may result from lack of reading skill, lack of ability to speak and write well, or inability to concentrate —all of which may be subject to correction. The D student is often pathetically eager to learn and hence may cooperate well; sometimes, though, he may be surly and resentful until the teacher gets his confidence. Only in the few areas where he believes himself skilful is he willing to accept leadership.

The grade of F indicates indifference and failure to try. It is not given to the student who plugs away, doing his pitiful best. In high school English (not necessarily in mathematics and kindred subjects) everyone who tries conscientiously to reach the objectives of the course deserves to pass. But the one who regularly loafs, who apparently does not care, who procrastinates, who fails to cooperate, who does not do the work that others do, deserves an F.

Now for a few additional comments. It is wise to talk about standards of grading with your classes. Perhaps you and they can draw up a list of criteria, maybe a modification of the one you have just read; the students will then understand that a grade is not the result of the teacher's whim. Ask your classes what they believe you should do in borderline cases. Their answer may be that such decisions must be based upon little things that otherwise might not be considered: such things as the score on a spelling test, a voluntary report in literature, extra care in revision of written work, etc. Or the class may decide that the student's cooperativeness and willingness to accept responsibility should determine whether he ought to receive the higher or the lower grade.

Beginning teachers tend to give too many high grades, especially at the start of the year. They are often surprised that so many students are bright and cooperative, and as a result they give mostly A's and B's. Then, as the year moves on and their understanding of the students increases, the grades begin falling, to the detriment of class morale. It is much better to grade conservatively at the start, giving few A's and B's and many C's and D's (always accompanied by constructive suggestions for improvement). Then, when the students who are really doing superior work have clearly emerged from the pack, they may be given suitable rewards. And, of course, when a student who normally does C or D work makes a spurt, he too should be rewarded.

A large number of F's, however, is usually a greater criticism of the teacher than of the class. If many students fail to try, the teacher is not supplying adequate motivation. In such cases, strenuous introspection is in order and a change of tactics is usually indicated.

As a rule, the quality of work that a student does in the last few weeks of a term should have greater bearing upon the final grade than should the work of the first few weeks. Thus, in the case of Clara, who was mentioned on page 75, the final grade should probably be a C, since she has been doing C work during the last few weeks.[4]

If a school has adopted the spiral cone concept explained on pages 38–40, there are special implications for grading. The only A's would be given to students who have considerably surpassed the norms of accomplishment for their age. B's and C's, however, could go to any students who are working conscientiously, even though their level of accomplishment is below average for their age. The grade of D would represent general sloppiness and indifference. An F would be given rarely, and only to a student who hardly tried at all and who was frequently absent without excuse. Such a grading system would provide strong motivation for the less able student, since he would know he could make B's by hard work. Restricting A's to students of high accomplishment would motivate able students. Since, with wide adoption of the spiral cone concept, colleges would rely mainly on entrance examinations for admitting students, the fact that many students of average or even below-average ability might have B grades would not matter; they could enter the college of their choice only if they passed required tests. Colleges have already learned that they can rely but little upon students' high school grades in predicting collegiate success.

[4] Further discussion of the grading of written work is included in Chapter 8.

THE IDEA BOX

REVISING A CURRICULUM

Helen F. Olson, of Seattle, writing in *Educational Leadership*, XIX (Feb., 1962), 302, develops several steps for curriculum revision. Included are forming a steering committee, which examines research and courses of study and initiates discussion and planning; planning sequences in reading, observing and listening, organizing thought, speaking, writing, and specific language skills; forming committees for each grade level, to develop course outlines for specific grades; trying out, revising, and then "publishing" the curriculum.

"A DISCUSSION VIEW OF CLASSROOM DISCUSSION"

In an article packed with useful suggestions for conducting discussion, Gladys Veidemanis urges emphasis on "Why?" and "What are the implications?" Among other tips: Students are asked to agree or disagree with a statement, finding support in the literary selection; teacher lists adjectives, and students discuss to whom each best applies; students hypothesize how the author's tone and handling would have to change if the story were told from someone else's point of view. *English Journal*, LI (Jan., 1962), 21.

ARTICLES ON SUCCESSFUL UNITS

Alm, Richard S., "What Is a Good Unit in English?" *English Journal*, XLIX (Sept., 1960), 395.

Alwin, Virginia, "Developing a Unit," *English Journal*, XLVIII (Sept., 1959), 315.

———— "Planning a Year of Units," *English Journal*, XLV (Sept. 1956), 334.

Bennett, Robert A., "Unit Ideas for the New School Year," *English Journal*, XLIX (Sept., 1960), 400.

Carriar, Shirley M., "Christmas Story Project: A Junior High Unit," *English Journal*, XLIV (Nov., 1955), 469.

Carruthers, Robert B., "The Unit Test," *English Journal*, XLVII (Sept., 1958), 339. Examples of good and poor questions.

Kegler, Stanley B., and John S. Simmons, "Images of the Hero: Two Teaching Units," *English Journal*, XLIX (Sept., 1960), 409.

McKean, Robert, "Students Like Thematic Units," *English Journal*, XLV (Feb., 1956), 82.

Ojala, William T., "Thematic Categories as an Approach to Sequence," *English Journal*, LII (March, 1963), 178.

Scheurs, Esther J., "Senior English Cook Book," *English Journal*, XLV (Jan., 1956), 13. Bringing the mechanics of English into a unit.

Willey, Wilbur, "A Thematic Approach to the Teaching of English," *English Journal*, LI (Dec., 1962), 643.

SUGGESTED TOPICS FOR UNITS

The grade levels designated for these units are not necessarily the only ones to which each might be adapted. It must be emphasized that this is intended to be not a comprehensive list but only a suggestive one. And it must also be stressed that these are *not* plans for a year's work in English, since there is no interrelation of units, and since more units are suggested than could profitably be taught.

Seventh Grade

1. When the West was young
2. A wet sheet and a flowing sea
3. Young heroes and heroines
4. The roar of traffic
5. "This is the forest primeval"
6. Nature rambles
7. Houses and homes
8. It's fun to laugh
9. Holidays in foreign lands
10. Pets, birds, and animals
11. The secret of everyday things
12. Far from here
13. What the past gave us
14. People you'll like
15. The wind and the rain
16. Rhythm for moderns
17. Family and friendship
18. "This is my country"
19. Fantasy
20. On the telephone
21. Questions and answers
22. Talking together
23. For reading aloud

Eighth Grade

1. Great moments in science
2. Happy hobbies
3. With the explorers
4. Wild animal trails
5. Ceiling unlimited
6. Courageous companions
7. A poetical calendar
8. Food for thought
9. "America the beautiful"
10. "O pioneers!"
11. Humor is where you find it
12. When the world was very young
13. Sportsmanship
14. Tall tales
15. Myths
16. Travel in an armchair
17. Inventors and inventions
18. "The play's the thing"
19. Sights, sounds, and smells
20. We want to climb
21. Subways and elevateds
22. Fun on the farm
23. The art of conversation
24. Getting along with people
25. Who are our friends?
26. We read together
27. Giving directions
28. Power with words

Ninth Grade

1. They sought gold
2. Adventure ho!
3. You make your own luck
4. Wampum
5. Famous young Americans
6. Fine arts
7. The time is now
8. My personal opinion
9. Heroes of civilization
10. Great moments in freedom
11. For laughing out loud
12. "By the sweat of thy brow"
13. Iron horses and others
14. The world we want
15. "My dear Watson"
16. Now that spring is here
17. Who has seen the wind?
18. Daily, including Sunday
19. Our neighbors in foreign lands
20. You are tuned to channel—
21. Magicians of science
22. Team play
23. Ballads
24. A great American
25. Know your school
26. Manners of today
27. How to study
28. What's worth seeing here?

29. This state of ours
30. Planning a vacation
31. Telling stories

32. Panels for information
33. Making announcements
34. Hard to explain

Tenth Grade

1. They had to be brave
2. People in the sky
3. "And the soil was fertile"
4. The city awakes
5. What is this thing called life?
6. They knew what they wanted
7. He has a sense of humor
8. Smokestacks
9. The inscrutable Orient
10. Man with a test tube
11. Social rights and wrongs
12. "Sermons in stones"
13. Sports and hobbies
14. Traveling light
15. Science: friend or foe?
16. Industry then and now
17. Our expanding frontiers

18. People are interesting
19. Man dreams
20. Curtain!
21. Pictures in poems
22. Epic poetry
23. Neighbors to the south
24. Neighbors to the north
25. Pictures in words
26. Our Who's Who
27. "What's in a name?"
28. Men across the seas
29. Bravery in our land
30. Social graces
31. Today's paper
32. "As others see us"
33. Two ears and something between

Eleventh Grade

1. Slowly the wheels turn
2. America was younger then
3. Thinking about college
4. Making a better America
5. The American short story
6. America sings
7. Behind the footlights
8. Great Americans
9. Look who's laughing
10. The future and your share in it
11. Movies: art form
12. Mystery and suspense
13. The right job
14. These minds of ours

15. Understanding Europe
16. It's an art!
17. Science for everybody
18. Mankind—how and why?
19. Why are people human?
20. First person singular
21. The power of suggestion
22. "My love is like a red, red rose"
23. For men are brothers
24. Poems of feeling
25. The American city
26. Our community's place in history
27. Letters in our lives
28. The modern magazine
29. First aid for thinking

Twelfth Grade

1. Historical fiction
2. They paved the way
3. England sings
4. England's theatrical heyday
5. The story of books
6. Preparing for college
7. America dreams
8. Living twenty-four hours a day
9. What is greatness?

10. What is success?
11. How people live and how they should live
12. A touch of whimsy
13. Living and earning a living
14. Voyage to the mind
15. On getting along with people
16. Love and marriage
17. Latin American literature
18. A man's religion

19. The universe and I
20. Living with the arts
21. Does human nature change?
22. Citizen of the world
23. Intelligent man

24. "Varied carols I hear"
25. Occupations in our community
26. Interviews
27. Letters that mean business

MISSIONARY WORK

In Oakland, California, schools, "outstanding teachers, with particular specialties, are released from regular teaching for several weeks to work with teachers in other schools." In the February, 1957, *English Journal*, Myrtle Gustafson and four other Oakland teachers show how the plan works.

TERMINAL STUDENTS

1. Most of the December, 1954, *English Journal* is devoted to specific suggestions for course offerings for students who do not expect to go to college.

2. In the September, 1955, *English Journal*, Helen Thornton describes the English program in a large city technical school.

3. The New England Association of Teachers of English, in working on plans for "general" students, decided to try to instil in them a desire (1) to speak clearly, distinctly, and to the point; (2) to listen intelligently; (3) to spell common words and to learn to find others in a dictionary; (4) to read with understanding newspapers, magazines, and books within their range; (5) to write straightforward sentences; and (6) to be mature and responsible citizens. Dorothy Potter gives some details in "Operation Utopia," *English Journal*, XLII (Dec., 1953), 501.

ENLIVENING EXAMINATIONS

1. Joyce Steward in Madison, Wisconsin, prepares interesting tests combining objective and essay questions, for example, "lead paragraphs" about selections read, "feature stories" on themes in literature, "Truth or Consequences," "featured players." "New Dress for Tests," *English Journal*, XLIV (Jan., 1955), 34.

2. For an especially thoughtful analysis of tests and testing, see Paul B. Diederich, "Making and Using Tests," *English Journal*, XLIV (March, 1955), 135.

3. Helps for your upperclassmen are available in J. N. Hook, *How To Take Examinations in College*, "College Outline Series" (New York: Barnes & Noble, Inc., 1958). College entrance examinations are also discussed.

TESTS

A useful annotated list of tests is available in *Teaching Aids in the English Language Arts*, a publication of the Illinois Association of Teachers of English, obtainable from the NCTE. Types of tests include written language skills; reading and literature; listening, vocabulary, and study skills; and achievement.

4

THE IMPROVEMENT
OF READING

BASIC PRINCIPLES

First Principle: Reading Is Complex

If reading consisted merely of pronouncing printed words, reading problems would almost cease to exist. Even with a relatively unphonetic language like English, daily short periods of instruction would in a few months or years enable a person to "read."

But pronouncing words is not reading. Reading involves apprehending as much as possible of the meaning and emotion and purpose of the writer. It involves thinking about the meaning, emotion, and purpose, relating them to what one already knows. It often involves enjoyment. With today's knowledge of electronics it is at least theoretically possible to construct a machine that can scan a printed page and reproduce vocally every word on the page. But that machine could not really read, for the mental reaction that is the most important part of reading would be missing.

Some children in our schools are like this hypothetical machine. They know most or all the words on the page, but they cannot tell except in very general terms what they have read.

Goethe, when he was already elderly and famous, said, "The dear people do not know how long it takes to learn to read. I have been at it all my life, and I cannot yet say that I have reached the goal." And Goethe is believed to have been one of the most intelligent men of all time! Yes, reading is complex.

Take the apparently simple items of speed and comprehension, for example. Hundreds, even thousands, of articles have been written about speed and comprehension in reading, and some exorbitant claims have been made. Some persons, it is said, have learned to read up to 10,000 words a minute. (That would mean, according to some calculations by Professor V. E. Leichty of Michigan State, that a book about the size of the one you have in your hands could be read in seventeen minutes.) The theoretical maximum—with a machine to turn pages—is 40,000 words a minute. But somewhere comprehension fails to keep pace with speed. For most persons, reading easy material, that somewhere is in the 250 to 500 WPM (words per minute) range. Speed is not the sole criterion of excellence in reading; neither is comprehension. Rather, quickness of comprehension marks the able reader. In contrast, the poor reader grasps the meaning slowly if at all.

The problem of teaching reading is complicated because no two persons will or can react in exactly the same way to the same set of black stimuli on the white page. Tom and Jerry, next-door neighbors of the same age, may look alike, but note a small part of the tremendous array of possible differences that may make Tom a poor reader, Jerry a good one:

Tom	*Jerry*
has somewhat defective vision	has excellent vision
has an IQ of 105	has an IQ of 115
has traveled little	has traveled extensively
lives in an almost bookless house	lives in a house with a good library
is mainly interested in autos and sports	has wide interests
wants to become an automobile mechanic	wants to become a lawyer
likes practical jokes	likes puns and limericks
thinks school a waste of time	likes school moderately well
moves his lips when he reads	does not move his lips in reading
reads everything at same speed	varies speed of reading
read two books last year	read twenty-five books last year

Second Principle: Everyone Can Read Better

Perhaps Tom will never becomes as good a reader as Jerry, because Tom's characteristics and environment are unlikely to change enough to enable him to catch up. But, helped by good teachers, Tom can learn to stop moving his lips, to vary his reading speed, to become interested in books about autos and sports and some other subjects, and to carry some books and magazines into his bookless home.

Jerry, however, although he is already an able reader, can become still more able. In fact, the chances are that the gap between him and Tom will steadily increase, even though Tom's improvement is considerable. Jerry can increase his vocabulary, his speed of comprehension, his retention of details, his ability to find main ideas, his ability to skim, his ability to draw conclusions, his understanding of people in literature, his ability to find material, his expressiveness in reading aloud, and undoubtedly some of his other partially developed skills.

Everyone—even you, presumably an excellent reader—can read better. So many skills are involved in reading that no one can have reached his potential in all of them.

Because of the increased realization of this fact, most high schools now stress what is called *developmental reading*. Instead of assuming as formerly that students have mastered reading in the elementary schools, high school teachers attempt to develop for each student the skills in which he is least proficient.

Third Principle: To Read Well, One Must Want To Read Well

Unless Tom can be led to realize that reading can bring him something that he wants or needs, he will probably never learn to read well. And if Jerry complacently believes that he knows all about reading, his improvement is not likely to be great. Motivation, then, becomes a key.

The principles for motivating better reading may be summarized in the form of six axioms:

Axiom 1. *Each student should understand what reading can do for him.* People read either for pleasure or for information or both. A student may be led to increase his reading skill if he can be shown that reading, both now and later, can contribute to his pleasure and to the knowledge that he himself requires or will require.

Example A. Louis. Age fourteen. IQ 85. Eighth grade. Fifth grade reading level. Failed third grade. Would probably leave school at sixteen and become an unskilled laborer. Working slowly and with easy materials pertaining to sports and model airplanes, in which Louis was especially interested, the teacher was able to help the boy convince himself that newspapers, magazines, and even a few books could give him pleasure. Special help in technique made reading less burdensome for him.

Through a unit on democracy at work, Louis (and the rest of the class) became aware that good citizens need to keep informed about political, social, and economic issues. During the year, Louis' reading ability increased to seventh grade level, and his attitude toward reading was improved.

Example B. Mabel. Age fifteen. IQ 101. Tenth grade. Tenth grade reading level. Not a college prospect. Mabel had no strong reading interests, although she voluntarily read local news, motion picture magazines, and love stories. The teacher led Mabel to see that news did not have to be local to be interesting, showed that some love stories are more realistic and worthwhile than those Mabel had been reading, and interested the girl in fiction and non-fiction pertaining to home life and home problems. Mabel's reading ability improved only one year in two semesters, but she was choosing *Good Housekeeping* and *Seventeen* instead of *Romantic Mirror.*

Example C. Charles. Age sixteen. IQ 135. Eleventh grade. College reading level. A prospective lawyer. The teacher's task with Charles was to show him the value of certain reading skills in which he was least strong: skimming for central ideas or for specific points, determining word meanings from context, and varying his speed according to the material. The teacher also helped him to see that wide reading of adult books would assist him in preparing for his legal career.

Axiom 2. *Each student should know how well he reads.* This implies that students' reading should be tested at regular intervals. Although most educators consider it generally wise to withhold from students their IQ scores, they do not say the same thing about scores on reading tests. It seems inadvisable to post the scores of students, but each should be told privately what the tests show about his own reading. If his score is low, he should be given encouragement and advice designed to help him improve. If it is high, he should be shown that further improvement is possible and desirable. Every student should be in competition, not with other students but with himself.

Axiom 3. *Each student should know that his reading can be improved.*[1] The experienced teacher will be able to tell the child about similar former students whose reading ability was bettered. The inexperienced teacher can find brief case histories in some of the items listed in The Idea Box, pages 108 ff. If a student's reading ability is very low, the teacher can encourage him by referring to whole classes of poor readers whose reading improved much more rapidly than would have been expected. If the student is already rather proficient,

---

[1] Sometimes improvement is contingent upon the elimination or reduction of physical handicaps. The teacher needs to watch particularly for defects in vision or hearing and recommend appropriate medical care.

the test results will certainly show that some of the skills may be further developed.

Axiom 4. *Each student should be kept aware of his progress.* Simple, teacher-made tests should be administered frequently, and standardized tests given at regular intervals—two or three times each year. Although there is usually insufficient time for a conference after each test, the teacher should encourage the students by giving evidence of individual progress, and may occasionally be able to pay a sincere compliment to the whole class on its improvement.

Axiom 5. *Reading materials should be appropriate.* Intrinsic worth, interest, and degree of difficulty should all be considered. Quality must not be sacrificed. "Where a need for intensive remedial work exists, it is of unusual importance to secure the highest possible levels of quality in form and content of the materials." [2] This does not mean that the practice materials should be "literature," but they should be worthwhile.

Many studies have been made of the reading interests of young persons. John J. De Boer summarizes many of the findings:

Boys like vigorous action—exploration, pursuit, conflict, triumph, surprise. They like the David-and-Goliath type of story, the real life or fictional hero in either the Edison or Daniel Boone category. Often they enjoy stories of sports and science. Many come to love Stevenson, Dickens, Dumas, Mark Twain. Girls, on the other hand, read stories of home and school life, romantic love, careers for women, mystery stories, and sentimental fiction. Girls are more likely to read boys' books than boys are to read girls' books.

Curiously, the factors of intelligence and socioeconomic status do not markedly affect young people's interests.[3]

Jo M. Stanchfield studied the reading preferences of eighth grade boys, listing in rank order fifty types of subjects. The top ten were explorations and expeditions, outdoor life, tales of fantasy, everyday-life adventures of boys, historical fiction (with some characters of their own age), sea adventure, sports and games, war, humor, and science fiction. At the bottom were teen-age romance, fairy tales, music, family and home life, plays, art, and poetry.[4]

[2] Arthur I. Gates, *The Improvement of Reading* (3d ed.) (New York: The Macmillan Co., copyright 1947 by Arthur I. Gates), p. 122. By permission of The Macmillan Co., publishers.
[3] "What Does Research Reveal About Reading and the High School Student?" *English Journal*, XLVII (May, 1958), 277–78.
[4] "The Reading Interests of Eighth-Grade Boys," *Journal of Developmental Reading*, V (Summer, 1962), 256–65.

An Iowa study that covered grades seven through twelve was based on the responses of 510 students to the question "If you could have an author write a story-to-order for you, what would you have him put in it?" The following table summarizes the most frequent replies:

Junior high boys:		Senior high boys:	
Mystery	16%	Adventure	46%
Sports	15%	Mystery	25%
Science fiction	15%	Sea stories	25%
Adventure	15%	Comedy	24%
Animal stories	13%	Historical	23%
Sea stories	10%	Science fiction	21%
Junior high girls:		Senior high girls:	
Romance	65%	Romance	66%
Mystery	20%	Career	36%
Career	12%	Mystery	32%
Comedy	11%	Adventure	30%
		Comedy	28% [5]

Most high school students prefer a simple style, brevity, and straightforwardness; they dislike difficulty, wordiness, slow movement, monotony, sentimentality, and lack of worthwhileness.

An experienced teacher can estimate fairly well the difficulty of a selection. He knows that students find a selection difficult if the vocabulary is beyond them, if the word order is unusual, if sentences are long and complex, if statements are highly compressed, if the language is strongly metaphorical, and if abstractions are numerous. Should you be dubious about your own ability to judge difficulty, you might apply some such scale as the Lorge formula, which involves counting the number of words in a sample passage, and the number of sentences, prepositional phrases, and "hard words" in that passage.

One caution is imperative, though: A teacher is responsible for helping his students to grow. If *all* reading materials are based only on their current interests, growth is slowed unnecessarily. Always the good teacher is introducing his students to materials that, in both difficulty and significance of content, are just a little above the students' present levels.

Axiom 6. *The classroom atmosphere should be pleasant.* Learning is most efficient when the environment is friendly and free from tension. Even in a rather gloomy, unattractive building, the attitude of the teacher can make a class cheerful and cooperative.

---

[5] Mary L. Smith and Isabel V. Eno, "What Do They Really Want To Read?" *English Journal,* L (May, 1961), 343–45.

Fourth Principle: Many Teachers Share in the Responsibility for Improving Reading

If there is any one feature of the total reading program about which the experts are in agreement, it is that all the high school teachers have a share in the responsibility, even though the major part of the burden falls upon the teacher of English. In summarizing the experts' idea of an ideal all-school developmental program (which no school yet claims to have achieved) Margaret J. Early lists these ten points. Note that teachers of subjects other than English have responsibility in numbers 1, 3, 4, 5, and 7, and possibly in one or two more:

1. Continuous instruction in reading skills from kindergarten to grade twelve for *all* pupils
2. Integration of reading skills with other communication skills: writing, speaking, and listening
3. Specific instruction by subject-matter teachers in *how to read and study* in their special fields, using the basic reading materials of their courses
4. Cooperative planning by all teachers so that skills will not be overlooked or overstressed
5. Adjusted reading materials in all subjects for slow, average, and superior students
6. Guidance in free reading
7. Emphasis on the uses of reading as a source of information, as an aid to personal and social development, and as a means of recreation
8. Corrective or remedial instruction for seriously retarded readers
9. Measurement of growth in skills by means of standardized and informal tests; study of students' application of techniques in all reading tasks
10. Evaluation of the uses of reading through study of the amount and quality of voluntary reading; study of effect on achievement in all school subjects; effect on percentage of drop-outs [6]

Examples may make this point more specific. Social studies teachers should give suggestions on how to read and study social studies material, and should teach students how to interpret maps, graphs, and charts. Music teachers, in addition to teaching the reading of music, should be sure that students can read and understand such terms as *pianissimo* and *glissando;* teachers of health and physical education should teach necessary technical vocabulary. Science and mathematics teachers, in addition to giving specific vocabulary instruc-

[6] "About Successful Reading Programs," *English Journal,* XLVI (Oct., 1957), 395.

tion, need to teach the peculiar skills involved in reading problems and formulas. All teachers who require reports should help students learn to locate and use appropriate materials.

Fifth Principle: There Is No Single Right Way To Teach Reading

Perhaps this principle is a corollary of the first, that reading is complex. Research has shown repeatedly that students may improve their reading abilities when taught by various methods or combinations of methods. Unfortunately some researchers or experimenters, loving their own brainchildren best, have tended to make exaggerated claims for the methods they have used successfully. Thus machine users, for instance, being able to demonstrate that students improve speed and perhaps comprehension through mechanical aids, have urged that reading accelerators be lined along the walls like slot machines in Las Vegas. Some persons who favor phonetics would apparently ignore everything else. Some who think that small vocabularies are poor readers' biggest handicaps would spend day after day on vocabulary-building devices. Some have found that extensive reading, unaccompanied by any formal instruction, may result in considerable gains, and hence have argued that all that is needed is to turn children loose in a library. And so on, ad infinitum.

The significant point is that there is a degree of truth in most of the claims. However, each of the dozens of recommended methods is likely to lead to a special—and rather limited—sort of improvement. The best program, then, it would seem, would be a balanced one that borrows some parts from each of the proved methods.

That is the kind of program outlined in the rest of this chapter. It is based on the five principles of which you have just read. It presupposes an interested school administration, and cooperation from other teachers as recommended in the fourth principle. It describes special help for special cases, then attempts to suggest some of the many ways in which reading instruction can be brought into the English classroom, and finally considers how the student can be helped to help himself through extensive out-of-school reading.

READING IN SPECIAL CLASSES

Various Types of Special Classes

In a free society, with local control of schools, it is to be expected that organizational patterns will differ widely, because of peculiar

local conditions and also because of the varying beliefs and understandings of administrators and leading teachers. The weakness of
such diversity is that inevitably some patterns will be inferior to others;
the strength is that opportunities to experiment are constantly present
almost everywhere, and out of countless experiments may evolve a
system that many communities can accept and find effective.

In a study of 107 special reading-improvement programs in Illinois
high schools, Loren V. Grissom found three patterns in operation. In
Group One were schools that provided special, ability-grouped English
classes in which much emphasis was placed on reading. Schools in
Group Two offered one- to two-semester reading classes in addition
to the regular English classes, and tried to place in them those students
whose reading levels were below the levels that intelligence tests and
other measures showed to be possible for them. The schools (usually
large) in Group Three made varied provisions, typically including
remedial English-reading classes for low-ability classes, special reading classes for students reading below their ability levels, and voluntary, non-credit clinic periods for students deficient in certain skills
and for college-preparatory students who wanted to become better
readers.[7]

Classes for Needlessly Retarded Readers.   These are usually the readers
whose reading levels are one or more years below their apparent
ability, as measured by intelligence tests and other means. For
instance, if a ninth grader with an IQ of 100 is reading at sixth or
seventh grade level and if he seems to have no serious visual or other
handicaps, he would be a candidate for such a class. Such readers are
very numerous.

Ordinarily, the special classes for such students are treated as temporary substitutes for regular English work. For instance, twenty
ninth graders are put into the special class for a semester or at most
a year, and they receive English credit for the reading course. Perhaps ideally they should take both English and reading, but most
school programs are too crowded to permit such doubling up. At the
end of a semester or a year, if the teaching has been successful, most of
the students will have made sufficiently substantial gains that they will
have approached their potential as of that time. For instance, ninth
grader Carol, IQ 90, may have started the term with sixth grade reading ability and finished it with eighth. That, for Carol, would
represent her present potential. If her IQ were 100 or 110, though,

[7] "Characteristics of Successful Reading Programs," *English Journal*, L (Oct.,
1961), 461–64.

it would be hoped that she would reach the ninth grade reading level or above as a result of the corrective instruction.

In this type of special class, the teacher attempts to find, through diagnostic tests, the major reading weaknesses of the individuals and of the whole class. Geared to the entire class is instruction in those reading skills in which most of the students are deficient. This instruction is supplemented by some individual assignments and activities, intended to help students overcome weaknesses not shared by the majority.

Organization of such classes varies considerably. Here are a few examples of patterns followed in some schools:

1. Non-credit reading laboratory—selected students sent there two or three hours a week, during study periods; individualized instruction, geared to specific needs of each student

2. Workshop—taken for credit either in addition to or in place of English; enrolment limited to fifteen or twenty per period; both group and individual instruction

3. Reading period—one period a week taken from regular English class, for intensive work on reading improvement

4. Concentrated work on reading—typically a three- or four-week period, sometimes in summer, when other work is laid aside for group and individual work on reading problems

5. Daily reading session in English—fifteen or twenty minutes a day devoted to instruction and practice in reading

6. Elective reading course—student initiative, both for electing the course and planning work for self-improvement

Classes for Mentally Retarded or Otherwise Handicapped Readers. Among the eighth grade students in one school are Clayton and Dolores, with IQ's of 76 and 78; Joachim, who has just arrived in the United States and knows no English; Blanche, with a serious speech defect; Glenn, with a serious visual defect; Bill, with a drunken father and an irresponsible mother, no interest in school, and a record with the juvenile courts; and Louise, who has never been more than two miles from home, and who is responsible for most of the care of several younger brothers and sisters. All feel lost in regular classes, yet their needs are obviously not the same. No single formula will help all of them, but the school cannot afford the individual tutelage that might make each of them a better reader, a better student, a more productive adult citizen.

Some schools would put Clayton and Dolores and other mentally handicapped children into special classes called "General English" or something else; in those classes the work would be sufficiently simple that the slow learners could succeed with it reasonably well. Clayton and Dolores can hardly be expected ever to read up to their grade level; their potential, as eighth graders, is probably about fourth grade level. Their other language skills are likely to be comparable.

But suppose that Clayton and Dolores stay in "General English" all through high school. And suppose further that they or their parents think they should go on to college. (After all, they have a high school diploma, haven't they?) This kind of situation exists fairly frequently. In fairness to colleges, to other students, and to Clayton and Dolores, the school administration should state clearly, with reasons, that Clayton and Dolores are not suited for college work. A good guidance program in the school should steer them toward technical training rather than toward college.

Some schools would keep Clayton and Dolores in regular classes, and in small high schools there may be no other solution. In that case the teacher must realize that much of the work will pass over their heads, but that many special assignments within their reach are possible. Dolores and Clayton may profit especially from well-conceived group work.

If the school has enough students like Joachim, the new arrival, they may be put together into a class for foreign students. Much work is now being done to improve the teaching of English as a second language. New York City, in particular, has worked out detailed plans for teaching the large number of Puerto Ricans and others to whom English is almost an unknown tongue. Los Angeles and other places in the West and Southwest are also working steadily on methods of teaching their Spanish-speaking students in particular. The techniques are specialized ones and cannot be described here.

Blanche and Glenn, with their severe defects in speech and vision, probably need first some specialized doctors' care that few schools can provide. The school can, however, help in making arrangements with appropriate local, county, or state authorities. Then Blanche and Glenn may be placed in a class small enough for considerable individual help.

Bill has an emotional problem caused by family troubles. A psychologist who works with the school may be helpful. So may a teacher, if the teacher can find one small opening in Bill's armor, one interest that can be capitalized upon, one subject that Bill is willing to read a little about. If Bill's intelligence is about normal, he may well be placed for a while in a reading class for the needlessly retarded.

Otherwise he may be provided for in a "General English" class or even in a regular one.

Louise, the girl with limited experience, obviously needs reading materials that will give her some hints about the rest of the world. She will probably find herself in the same class with Bill. Both of them may profit from and find interesting some stories about other young people with problems similar to theirs.

Perhaps the severely handicapped children like the seven we have just observed pose the biggest problem that teachers encounter. Many, perhaps most, of such children, though, can be sufficiently helped that they can contribute wholesomely to society. The teaching and other assistance that they need are expensive, but it is better to spend four or five hundred dollars annually on Bill now than to spend a thousand dollars or more a year to keep him in prison later. It is more economical to spend generously for the others now than it is to maintain them the rest of their lives as public wards.

Classes for the Gifted. In Gouverneur, New York, the rather small high school has "efficiency classes" for sophomores, juniors, and seniors who are in the top fifth in intelligence. These classes are intended to help the most able students reach their potential. From such students the majority of tomorrow's leaders will come, yet in most schools they have insufficient opportunity to grow as much as they are able. Gouverneur's efficiency classes stress efficient reading and study skills. Each student selects five fields of specialization, and, under guidance, reads extensively in these fields and concurrently is given special instructions in developing the reading skills in which he is least advanced.

Other schools are conducting different experiments in an attempt to find ways of taking down the bars that surround the most able students in many places. These experiments are among the very significant ones in twentieth-century America.

Devices Used in Special Classes

Only a book devoted solely to reading can explain in detail the various methods and devices employed. Here we can look at just a few of them, in summary form, under three headings.

Learning Methods of Word Attack. Phonics teaches a child to "sound out" many words. Research has shown that the phonics approach works best with words that are already in the child's speaking vocabulary.[8] In addition to learning the usual sounds of letters, the student needs to learn the sounds of such consonant combinations as *bl, st, str, ng,* and *gr,* and such diphthongs as *aw* and *ou.*

Obviously, though, we do not want the child to have to sound out the same word again and again. Perhaps he uses his knowledge of phonics and learns the word "belong," let us say. He should, later, through the use of flashcards and similar elementary techniques, be helped to recognize "belong" at a glance. Still later he may be helped to read at a glance a group of words, like "belong to me," in which the word appears.

A number of reading workbooks contain picture aids and other devices for increasing each student's ability to recognize words.

Increasing Speed. The slow, word-by-word reader often fails to grasp the meaning because the phrases and clauses never take shape in his mind. He may understand "John—and—Paul—came—to—the—bridge," but, if the sentence contains a few more phrases and clauses, he loses the entire thought. Speed in itself is not a very important goal, but as a tool of comprehension it is.

Students should be told how one reads. As you know, the eye does not glide smoothly along from left to right but moves in a series of little jumps. The more jumps, or pauses, the less speed. Students may be given simple, teacher-made or class-made exercises such as flashcard exercises or groups of phrases arranged vertically on the page; the purpose is to learn to take in the whole phrase at a glance. Working in pairs, students may observe each other's eye movements, as the reader tries consciously to read each line with the fewest possible fixations.

Reading in which the student forces himself to read at his top speed is often productive. For this purpose the material selected should be very easy, preferably two grades or more below the student's reading level. It should be on a subject interesting to the student. With such material the student can be encouraged to compete against himself, keeping time charts and figuring out his own reading speed.

The usefulness of tachistoscopes, pacers, and other machines has been hotly debated. Undeniably, boys especially are fascinated by them, so motivation is made easier. Undeniably also, their use can result in greatly increased reading speed. However, doubters say that the increased speed is not uniformly transferred to reading done without the machine, that just as great gains may be made by reading easy

---

[8] Paul A. Witty and Robert A. Sizemore, "Phonics in the Reading Programs," *Elementary English,* XXXII (Oct., 1955), 355–70.

material at top speed, that the acquired high speed is not necessarily retained, and that after a couple of years the gains in comprehension, which accompanied the machine-made increase of speed, may disappear. The upshot of the discussion appears to be that machines are useful, especially for motivation, but not indispensable.

Improving Comprehension.   Frederick B. Davis has listed the following types of comprehension: defining words as used in the context, understanding the pattern of organization, identifying the main thought, finding answers to questions discussed in the passage, drawing inferences, recognizing literary devices, identifying the tone or mood, and determining the writer's purpose or viewpoint.[9]

Direct questioning, on whichever of these types a class is ready for, is often the best and simplest approach, for example, "What is the main thing the author says about seashells?" "What is the meaning of 'sound' as the author uses it?" "Can you figure out the meaning of 'bivalve' from the way the author describes it?" "What does he say causes the roaring that we hear when we hold a large shell to our ear?" "How many kinds of shells does he name?" "What are the two main classes of these shells?" "What shows you that the author loves the sea?"

Many variations are possible, including the writing of a title for the passage, writing a "headline" about it, thinking of other words the author could have used to express the same idea, thinking of another possible pattern of organization, adding to what the author says, choosing the best summary sentence, reducing each of the author's sentences to a word or a phrase, and discussing how the passage would have been different if the author's purpose or viewpoint had been different.

READING IN REGULAR ENGLISH CLASSES

On the high school level much of the teaching of reading takes place in regular English classes, most often in connection with the study of literature. Chapters 5, 6, and 7 of this book treat in some detail the teaching of literature; if the recommendations in those chapters are followed, improvement in reading ability will almost inevitably result. There are, though, some specific techniques that a teacher may consciously employ with the improvement of reading as his major goal. It is the purpose of this section to discuss those techniques. However, much more experimentation is necessary before we shall

[9] "Comprehension in Reading," *Baltimore Bulletin of Education,* XXVIII (Jan.–Feb., 1951), 16–24.

know the very best ways of incorporating reading instruction in the regular English program while still teaching adequately everything else that must be included. Perhaps as much as 95 per cent of the research so far reported has dealt with special classes or individual problems rather than with reading in the regular English class.

The well-balanced English program includes some reading done in common by the whole class or by sizable groups within the class, and also reading done by individuals or by small groups. In this section we shall concern ourselves especially with reading in common.

Before the Students Read

A reading program is likely to be most effective if the teacher knows how well each student already reads, if students' interest is aroused, and if students' probable difficulties with assigned selections are anticipated.

Testing. Some schools as a matter of general practice give all entering students a reading test. Some give such tests annually, to measure each student's growth. Some give them at the beginning and end of each year.

If your school tests reading regularly, you should study the test results for your students. Do not look only at the total scores, but also at the scores on various parts of the test. These parts vary according to the test given but are likely to have such classifications as speed, word comprehension, sentence comprehension, paragraph comprehension, finding answers to questions, selecting main ideas, drawing inferences, and observing organization. If you find that most of your students are especially weak in certain of the items tested, you may slant your instruction somewhat toward those items.

If your school does not have an established and consistent testing program in reading, perhaps you can arrange one for your classes. It is probably best to plan to give different forms of the same test at the beginning and the end of the same year. The comparison may please you or humble you, and may affect your teaching in subsequent years.

Do not be reluctant to talk with your classes about the kinds of things that reading tests measure—and why. Analysis of the parts may help your students to understand more clearly the components of reading skill.

Skills To Be Emphasized. In Pennsylvania, instruction in reading skills is legally required in grades seven and eight. A number of junior high schools have chosen to emphasize these skills:

1. Word Recognition Techniques
   a. Meaning aids
   b. Visual and structural aids
   c. Auditory and phonetic aids
2. Comprehension Abilities: reading to
   a. Retain information
   b. Organize
   c. Evaluate
   d. Interpret
   e. Appreciate
3. Basic Study Skills
   a. Locating information
   b. Use of general references
   c. Use of visual materials
   d. Organizing
4. Basic Meaning Development
   a. Paragraph meaning and organization
   b. Word meaning [10]

In later grades, these skills may be developed further, and more advanced skills such as skimming and "reading between the lines," may be added.

Building an Interest in a Selection.   You yourself read with the liveliest mind and the greatest understanding that which interests you. Your students are no different. They will start an assignment—and complete it—with most success if they have a glimpse in advance of what it may mean to them.

Often a simple factual question is enough, or a question that relates the selection to the students' lives, or one that poses a problem. Here are a few examples, related to familiar pieces of American literature:

(Irving's "Rip Van Winkle") If you had gone to sleep twenty years ago and woke up today, what changes would you soon be aware of?

(Henry's "Speech in the Virginia Convention") All of you have heard "Give me liberty or give me death!" What caused Patrick Henry to give the famous speech ending with that sentence?

(Hawthorne's "The Minister's Black Veil") How would you react if your minister or one of your teachers started wearing a black mask to church or school?

(Poe's "The Purloined Letter") If you wanted to hide a letter in your room so that very thorough searchers could not find it, where would you put it?

(Peattie's "What Life Means—An Answer in Nature") Ruling out such things as bombs, what is man's greatest weapon?

Sometimes a little background information—a kind of quick stage setting—can provide the impetus for careful and intelligent reading. For example, for the Donald C. Peattie selection, you might tell the class that Mr. Peattie spent three years studying intensively the animals and plants in a single square mile of land near Chicago. From his

[10] U. Berkley Ellis, "Developmental Reading in Junior High School," *Journal of Developmental Reading*, VI (Autumn, 1962). 41–49.

observation of insects and small animals he not only learned much about them but also about human beings. "Can any of you think of anything that we might learn about ourselves by watching ants or bees or chipmunks?"

Sharing of students' experiences may also whet a desire to read a selection. One teacher knew, for instance, that one of the boys in her class had done a little amateur panning for gold during the past summer. Before her class read Jack London's "All Gold Canyon," she asked this student to relate his experiences to the class and explain just how panning is done.

Anticipating Difficulties. It is not possible to anticipate all the difficulties that individual students may conceivably encounter in their reading. However, a teacher can reduce some of the problems. The amount of such anticipatory assistance should be greater for young students and slow-learning groups than for older students and quick learners.

Suppose that reading tests or the teacher's observations have revealed that a class has difficulty in understanding organization and grasping main ideas. A brief outline, mimeographed or placed on the board, may be of considerable help. For a variation, especially useful with exposition, the numbers of main and supporting points may be supplied, with the students to fill them in: I. . . . A. . . . B. . . . II. . . . , etc. Or a list of key questions, each pointing toward the main idea of a section, may be prepared.

Questions about the meaning of important paragraphs or sentences may also be presented to the class in advance to help them improve comprehension still more. It is especially desirable to ask questions about paragraphs and sentences that *must* be understood if the student is to comprehend the selection.

There are differences of opinion about trying to anticipate difficulties with vocabulary. Some teachers like to pick out a few of the important "hard" words and define them in advance. Others argue that new words are best learned in context. You may want to experiment to see which method you prefer. Any general work that the class does in vocabulary building (see Chapter 12) is valuable for reading as well as for writing, speaking, and listening.

If you use an anthology for the central reading material of the course, do not overlook one source of help that can save you hours and hours of preparation. That is the teachers' handbook, which is available as a companion to several of the best anthologies. One such handbook contains 504 pages, crammed with aids and suggestions. For every selection or group of selections, the authors of the handbook have prepared background information, an explanation of possible procedure, and a suggested assignment that guides the student's reading, as well as ideas for class discussion and follow-up. You will not find useful in your classes every suggestion in a handbook, but judicious choice can save time and enrich teaching.

Thinking and Talking About What Was Read

In the discussion and other activities that follow the reading of a selection, the students concentrate their attention upon the selection and related items. But the teacher has an eye on the future reading of the students, and uses the present selection as a base for future operations. That is, he uses it to develop skills that the students will find useful in later reading in the course and in reading they may do throughout their lives.

The points and methods of attack will differ according to the needs of the class. With some groups the steady emphasis will have to be upon simple comprehension and relation of each selection to the students' lives. With other students the stress may be upon some of the more advanced skills—"depth reading," as one teacher has called it.[11] Here is a brief discussion of a few of the reading-improvement techniques that have been proved workable.

Understanding Details. The study of details may best be related to finding answers to fairly general questions. For instance, if a class has read excerpts from *Robinson Crusoe,* a before-reading question may have been, "If a person is shipwrecked on an island, what problems will he face, and how can he solve those problems?" After reading, the question is "What problems did Robinson Crusoe face, and how did he solve them?" The questions become more and more specific: "How did Crusoe 'plow' his land?" "How and why did he build a fence?" "What troubles did he encounter in making utensils?" "How did he keep track of time?" "How would you have coped with these same problems?" "Are there any problems that Defoe seems to have overlooked?" The advantages of this method are first, that it does not stress details for the details' sake; second, that it gives purpose and therefore adds interest to the search; and third, that it makes the details easier to remember, because they are placed in a framework.

Paraphrasing. When a selection seems rather difficult for students, a small amount of paraphrasing may be necessary. (Paraphrasing is discussed at greater length in Chapters 5, 6, and 7.) Suppose, for

[11] See the series of three articles by Naomi Gill in the September, 1953, September, 1954, and December, 1955, *English Journal.*

instance, that the class has read Wilfrid Gibson's poem "The Ice-Cart."
Although this is not a difficult piece, some slow students may not understand it. A brief summary by one of the students, perhaps like the
following, may help. "The narrator, working in a hot office, sees a
man delivering ice and imagines that he himself is suddenly trans-
ported to a polar region, where he sees white bears, swims with seals,
and then lies on an ice floe while gentle snow falls upon him, covering
him deeper and deeper as he sleeps peacefully. Suddenly the iceman
cracks his whip, and the narrator awakes in the grimy heat." More
detailed paraphrase may be used to clarify particular lines or groups
of lines. For instance,

> . . . I was swimming, too,
> Among the seal-pack, young and hale,
> And thrusting on with threshing tail,
> With twist and twirl and sudden leap
> Through crackling ice and salty deep—
> Diving and doubling with my kind. . . .

may require paraphrase to make clear the point that the narrator
dreams that he himself actually *is* a seal.

Mastering New Words. The words chosen for class discussion will
vary with the class. The principle behind the choice is this: Which
of the probably unfamiliar words in this selection will be of particular
use to the students in this group? For instance, in the long first
paragraph of Lamb's rather well-liked "Dissertation upon Roast Pig,"
these words may be unknown to many students: "obscurely," "Mundane
Mutations," "designates," "mast" (i.e., nuts and acorns), "lubberly,"
"Younkers," "conflagration," "antediluvian," "new-farrowed," "utmost,"
"consternation," "negligence," "premonitory," "nether," "retributory,"
"cudgel," "callous," and "ensued." Instead of spending most of the
class hour in defining all these words, it may be more profitable to
pick out three or four (perhaps "obscurely," "utmost," "negligence,"
and "ensued"), discuss their meanings, and have students construct
original sentences with them. Some of the words ("Mundane Mutations," "mast," "lubberly," and "Younkers") your students may never
encounter again and never need.

As often as possible, meanings should be figured out by the students,
using contextual clues. "The following dialogue ensued" easily reveals
the meaning of "ensued." "His nether lip" is obviously either his
upper or his lower lip, and, since moisture overflowed it, it must be
the lower. Students are more likely to remember words whose mean-

ings they have deciphered for themselves than they are those that have been defined for them by teacher or dictionary.

Students should be encouraged to ask questions about word meanings, word relationships, word peculiarities. "Are there any words in the paragraph that you do not understand?" is a good opening. And perhaps it need not be mentioned that the teacher should not discourage questions by making every question the occasion for student labor: "Look it up in the dictionary, George." Dictionary use is of course important, but too often teachers have unintentionally employed the dictionary as an apparent punishment for curiosity. And curiosity is the most vital ingredient in motivation.

Understanding Allusions and Figures of Speech. Naomi Gill [12] refers to the difficulties that teen-agers have with allusions and figurative language. To many of them, she says, such expressions as "Herculean effort," "crossed his Rubicon," "built a better mousetrap," "old school-tie," and "the shot heard round the world" are meaningless. Daniel Webster's "brow like a mountain" doesn't denote intelligence to them; "As soon as she left, she was the life of the party" doesn't seem funny; "clippership clouds" are commercial planes; "mahogany-faced sea captains" are only red-faced; and "His nose was a topographical error" has not even one meaning, let alone two or three.

The teaching of figurative language may be somewhat more difficult than it once was, because, although the basic rhetorical figures remain the same, their possible content has been infinitely enlarged. Many of our students tend to be extremely literal-minded, perhaps because much in their environment encourages literalness: constant emphasis upon the tangibles of science, matter-of-fact newspaper accounts, prosaic television dramas, and endless analysis of sentences in English classes. It seems important, though, to teach what the basic figures are and to talk about them when some of their more interesting examples appear. (See also Chapters 7 and 12.)

The teaching of allusions becomes much more difficult every year, and no systematic approach appears feasible. Even a hundred years ago human knowledge was much less than it is now, and the possible content of allusions was consequently much less. It has been estimated that the sum total of human knowledge is now doubling every ten years! Think, then, of how many more things a modern author may allude to. Only an omniscient person could unfailingly grasp allusions.

[12] " 'Depth' Reading II: The Figures," *English Journal*, XLIII (Sept., 1954), 297.

If we define allusions more narrowly—perhaps restricting them to classical and Biblical—we can study myths in school and the Bible in church school, and thus familiarize students with Orpheus and Lazarus. Otherwise we must content ourselves with examining the content of each allusion as it appears.

Finding Main Ideas. Authors and editors are usually rather generous in supplying aids to understanding. Titles, chapter titles, headings, subheadings; paragraphing, transitions, "arrow words" (such as "especially significant"); use of additional space for important points; heightened style; mechanical devices (such as italic or boldface type) —these are some of the helps offered to the reader. But many high school students, and adults too, remain largely unaware of such bounty.

Particularly when dealing with expository material, the teacher may seize the opportunity to point out some of these aids. Simple questions are useful: "What do you suppose the author will discuss under this heading?" "Why does he use three paragraphs to discuss this topic?" "Why is this sentence italicized?"

Also of value in helping students to find main ideas is calling for one-sentence summaries of paragraphs, then one-sentence summaries of groups of related paragraphs, and then one-sentence summaries of entire expository selections. Class discussion of why one summary is better than another is useful.

Drawing Conclusions. Nobody can write everything about anything. If it were possible, it wouldn't be artistic. Something has to be left to the reader, who works with the writer to draw from words their threads of thought. An artistic writer does not insult his reader by telling too much. He seldom says, "The moral of all this, dear reader, is that . . ." He makes clear and explicit what he must, and leaves implicit what the reader presumably already knows or can deduce for himself.

Unaided, few children are adept at between-the-lines reading. They see what the author sets before them, and no more, just as they see cornflakes on the breakfast table without awareness of farmers, tractors, marching rows of corn, dinosaur-necked corn pickers, trucks, elevators, trains, dietitians, ovens, packaging machines. To help them see more than words on a page requires patience, skilful questioning, tolerance of differing opinions—and a teacher who himself can read beneath the surface.

What, for instance, is Thurber driving at in "The Secret Life of Walter Mitty"? A student said, "Mitty's wife henpecked him so much that she drove him crazy, that's all." "Is he crazy?" the teacher asked.

"No," said some students, "he's just a dreamer." "Do you ever dream of being a great athlete, a great doctor, a great actor, or anything else?" "Yes, of course, maybe we all dream a little," the students admit. "Does Thurber seem to like Walter Mitty?" "Yes, but he seems a little contemptuous of him, too." "Does Thurber think it's bad to day-dream?" "No, only if it's overdone." And out of such inductive discussion, such Socratic questioning, the students conclude that Thurber is saying that it is human nature to dream great dreams, to imagine that we are someone else, and that dreaming is not bad unless it is carried to such an extreme that it becomes madness—that it is less bad to dream you are a dozen great men than it is to be sure you are Napoleon.

Often, especially in non-fiction, it is desirable to have students draw conclusions about the attitude and the purpose of the author, or even about his probable honesty. This is often called critical reading. For instance, in an article on a political question, the students may find as much as possible about the author, try to discover whether he would have any reason to weight his arguments unfairly, and examine the arguments carefully to see whether any important considerations have been omitted.

Understanding Human Beings. An important segment of drawing conclusions is drawing conclusions about human beings. One of the virtues of wide and intelligent reading is that it can introduce us to a much greater variety of persons than we are ever likely to know in real life. But authors do not tell us about all these actual and fictitious beings. Instead they show them to us, and from the persons' actions and their words we must try to understand them; from such understanding may come truths that we can apply to our own lives, our own relationships with others.

In *Giants in the Earth*, Rölvaag shows Per Hansa, Norwegian pioneer in the Dakota territory, and Beret, his wife. He shows Per Hansa performing brave acts, but he does not tell us that Per Hansa is brave. He lets us observe Per Hansa talking to the land and the land talking to him, but Rölvaag does not say, "This man is a poet." He lets us know that Per Hansa is disgusted because Hans Olsa does not get up and work despite his frozen legs, but Rölvaag does not say that Per Hansa is not really cruel—that it is just difficult for him to realize that many are less strong than he. Beret weeps and worries and makes dire predictions and indulges in mystic fancies; Rölvaag does not tell us that she is basically kind and delicate and loving but obsessed with terrible fears of an unfamiliar world. The reader must live with Per

Hansa and Beret in the book and learn about them as he would in real life, draw conclusions about them as he would if he shared their roof. He may or may not come to admire and love them, but if he lives with them he will attain much understanding of them, of others like them who drove their oxen toward the sunset, of his own ancestors, of himself, of his friends who have strengths and failings like those of Per Hansa and Beret.

Understanding Literary Devices.   In addition to reading for meaning, all classes to some extent—and able classes in particular—may be led to an understanding of certain literary forms and formalities.   In poetry, for instance, they may note that a sentence does not necessarily end with the line, but they may see also the musical effects of rhyme and alliteration and assonance, the purpose of repetition, the reasons for and the effects of the great condensation characteristic of much poetry. In short stories they may observe the author's technique in plotting, the way he flashes bits of the setting on our mental screen, the things he does *not* say.

Special Problems in Reading

At convenient and appropriate times in the regular English classroom, the teacher and class may work on special ways of improving reading.   Three of these ways are varying speed according to difficulty, locating information quickly, and scanning and skimming.

All three of these may be taught as matters of efficiency.   It is not efficient to spend five minutes reading a page of easy material, although it may be efficient to spend twenty minutes reading a onepage poem or a complicated problem in mathematics.   A reader who races through everything at 500 WPM may be no better than one who always slogs along at 100.

The library catalog and the table of contents and the index of a book represent wasted space to many students.   Yet their efficiency as readers may be considerably improved if they learn to use these tools. Sometimes even college students thumb through a whole book to see whether it says anything about toadstools, when in thirty seconds they could find the answer in the index.   Housewives may spend fifteen minutes in hunting percolators in the mail-order catalog.

To locate information, students need to know the alphabet, know it thoroughly.   In addition, they need to know what kinds of information the cards in the library catalog contain, and what the difference is between a table of contents and an index.   Then they need much practice, including some plain drill exercises, in using these three valuable tools.

For the teaching of scanning (i.e., searching quickly for a specific bit of information), the following procedure is generally effective: The teacher asks the students to bring to English class a textbook used in their history or science class. In one chapter the teacher finds the answer to a certain question, and he asks that question: "How close is Mercury to the sun? Find the answer in Chapter 4." The students who locate the information most quickly are asked how they did it. They will usually refer to the headings and subheadings, which show them where to read more carefully. They may also mention that the first sentence of each paragraph generally contains valuable clues.

In skimming, the technique is somewhat different. Skimming enables a student to discover quickly what a whole article or book is about. For instance, a student may wonder whether he wants to read a certain novel. He may skim by glancing through the first few pages to discover vocabulary difficulty and approximate setting, skip a number of pages and read quickly a paragraph or two, and repeat this process until he has made up his mind.

READING OUTSIDE THE CLASSROOM

Guided Free Reading

According to John C. Dana, the twelve rules for improving reading are the following: "1. Read. 2. Read. 3. Read some more. 4. Read anything. 5. Read about everything. 6. Read enjoyable things. 7. Read things you yourself enjoy. 8. Read, and talk about it. 9. Read very carefully, some things. 10. Read on the run, most things. 11. Don't think about reading, but 12. Just read." [13]

As teachers, we are less interested in turning out graduates who have read than we are in turning out graduates who read. But, as Dr. Ruth Strang points out, "Reading will not be persisted in unless it brings satisfaction." [14] That means that during the school years we must cultivate in our students the habit of reading by giving them the opportunity to read widely in materials they can enjoy.

In some schools, extensive reading is completely free; that is, students may read anything and in any amount they desire. In others, it

[13] Quoted in Ruth Strang, *Problems in the Improvement of Reading in High School and College* (Lancaster, Pa.: The Science Press, 1940), p. 273.
[14] *Ibid.*, p. 54.

is almost completely guided, with the teacher making the selections. The happy medium is apparently "guided free reading," in which students choose from a long but carefully selected list representing various types and levels of difficulty. The teacher and librarian may both offer specific suggestions to individual students. They steadily recommend books just a little above the level of those the student is now reading, and encourage him to avoid restricting himself to one kind of subject matter.

Methods of conducting guided free reading vary. The most nearly typical procedure seems to be to set aside part of each class hour, or part of a week or other period of time, in which the students read whatever they select from the books and magazines that have been made available. In some classes there is no follow-up; in others there is class or group discussion regarding any topics of interest. For such a reading program to be successful the students must be surrounded by appropriate books and magazines, they must be led to read because reading is fun, and they must be taught by a person who is himself well read, quick to offer suggestions, but willing to slip unobtrusively into the background as the young people explore the variegated joys of reading.

Also frequently employed is the procedure of relating both in-class and out-of-class reading to the unit being studied. In some ways this is preferable, especially because the reading is likely to be purposeful and because subsequent class discussions will have unity and afford opportunities for all to participate. The unit on "Back-Country America" in Chapter 4 of *The English Language Arts in the Secondary School* (NCTE, 1956) describes in detail such a procedure.

Providing Materials for Extensive Reading

In a decreasing number of schools, the English teacher simply tells his students, "Go to the library and pick out a book for your next book report." Modern schools leave less to chance. They encourage reading in class but also set aside an occasional class period for reading in the library. During library periods, many different procedures may be followed: permitting browsing, having students spend only five minutes with a single book, spending periods with different types of books, giving library instruction, suggesting books, conferring with some students while others browse, etc.

Classroom libraries are assuming increased importance. The books, perhaps 50 to 100 in number, are changed at rather frequent intervals and may be "advertised" in various ways such as those suggested in

The Idea Box, page 115. These books may be borrowed by the teacher from the school library or, if sufficient funds are available, may be purchased for classroom use and circulated from room to room. The paperbacks, if wisely chosen, are a boon to schools with little money; some publishers of these books are now making an effort to print more titles that teachers want and students enjoy. Some schools collect a fee of fifty cents or so per year from each student and buy classroom books and magazines with the money; the wisdom of this practice is at best debatable. Interest in the classroom collections may be built up by having students suggest many of the titles.

Checking on Outside Reading

"Book-report days" are still among the most detested in those schools where students make written or oral reports according to old, creaking formulas. But, since some teachers want records to help in guidance and to pass on to the teacher who will have the class next year, they feel a compulsion to continue the system of reports.

It is not necessary, however, to follow any dull routine pattern for reports. Here are a few tested devices (others are listed in The Idea Box, pages 115–117):

1. A small group of students reads the same book. The chairman and teacher prepare a list of thought questions to be answered independently before the class. Differences of opinion may lead to discussion, and create class interest in the book.

2. ". . . a bright-eyed bookworm with wide reading experiences might be asked for a careful statement of theme, a high-level analysis of some character's motivation, a discussion of some structural aspect of the author's craftsmanship, or a comparison with another piece of literature. Most important, reporting must not be a case of either this or that for an entire class." [15]

3. Students who have read books on similar topics (occupations, animals, history, etc.) exchange information about their books before the class.

4. A student tries to "sell" a book to another student, who believes that he would not like it.

5. "Conversation circles" with student chairmen discuss books on similar topics.

6. The class prepares a "newspaper" with stories based upon books read.

7. On a spindle, each student places the name of a book he has read. By the next day, the teacher has added a pertinent specific question concerning the book. In class, the student answers the question.

[15] Stephen Dunning, "Everybody's Doing It—But Why?" *English Journal* XLVIII (Jan., 1958), 33. Mr. Dunning stresses the need to have book reports reflect "common purposes that both teacher and student can hold as honest, valuable, and realistic."

8. Students may work out dialogs, monologs, pantomimes, short plays, or television dramatizations, pertaining to the book read.[16]

9. Students prepare appropriate book jackets including "blurbs." Advanced students write reviews, criticisms, and evaluations.

10. "Tell the story again from the viewpoint of another character in the story." "Show how color or key words or ideas run through the story. Discuss their purpose and effectiveness." "Place yourself in the protagonist's position and relate how plot would have been affected with you as the hero." "Imagine the character in the book in a different setting. . . . Change mood, time, or setting and show how it affects characters and plot." "Imagine an eighteenth century schoolboy, accustomed to reading Shakespeare, Milton, Addison, etc., reading your book. What would be his reactions?" "Write a letter in the style, with the feeling, in the character of the subject of the biography, e.g., Thoreau writes to President Johnson." "What characteristics of the main character are present in all successful men and women? What are his or her unique characteristics?" [17]

11. One of the simplest and best methods of providing a motivated check on reading is to have the students record whatever reading they do, together with a brief comment. The Cumulative Reading Record (NCTE) is ideal for this purpose. The teacher encourages the students to bring into class discussions references to their reading, just as adults do. Since the teacher notes carefully what each student has been reading, he may frequently address to a student a question upon which his recent reading should throw some light. The class soon learns to expect and welcome such casual questions, and reads more carefully because of them. At the same time, students are learning that their outside reading may be related to many topics of discussion. They thus gradually acquire a more adult view of reading than they may gain from some other devices.

THE IDEA BOX

TWO TYPES OF READING

Ruth G. Viox (*The English Record*, Fall, 1957) says that junior high students need two types of reading instruction: for information and for appreciation and enjoyment. Separate lessons should be planned for each purpose, for example, skimming, speed practice, and instruction in study skills for the first, and understanding characterization and plot development for the second. Some skills may be taught in both types of instruction, for example, vocabulary building, noting details, making inferences, and evaluating ideas.

MOTIVATION OF READING

1. "To build interest, occasionally start a story orally, and then finish it with silent reading." (Iowa City Junior High School.)

---

[16] For details on scripts, see Donald Noble, "Television Script Book Reports," XLIX (April, 1960), 259–61.

[17] These and other suggestions are taken from Howard S. Rowland, "Alternatives for the Book Report, *English Journal*, LI (Feb., 1962), 106-13.

2. "I have found that if a senior sees a new book on a teacher's desk or sees her reading it, he often becomes interested in it." (Mary Hart Finley, Madisonville, Ky.)

3. G. R. Carlsen believes that books which students like satisfy one or more of these desires: "First, the desire to find self-importance, self-confidence; second, the desire to see one's self as a part of the onflowing human race, to see one's feelings and emotions as a part of the pattern of all human life; and, third, to assess one's self in terms of the position that one can assume in society and adult life." "Behind Reading Interests," *English Journal*, XLIII (Jan., 1954), 7.

4. Thomas Battista reports in the March, 1962, *Bulletin* of the NASSP that retarded junior high readers were motivated when the teacher brought to class samples of the reading materials they would need to cope with in their chosen occupations such as truck driving, auto repairing, police work, cosmetology, and the like. The state driver's manual was especially helpful.

VIVE LA DIFFERENCE

Boys, says G. R. Carlsen, like an expansive book, with lots of elbowroom; girls like a confined book. Boys like emphasis on incident; girls like to read about interrelationships of people.

READING EIGHTH GRADERS LIKE

A study of eighth grade boys' reading likes and dislikes, reported by Jo M. Stanchfield in the Summer, 1962, *Journal of Developmental Reading*, revealed that superior, average, and poor readers all liked approximately the same kinds of subject matter. All groups placed outdoor life, explorations, tales of fantasy, and everyday life adventures of boys at the top of the list; at the bottom were art, poetry, plays, music, family life and homelife, and fairy tales.

PREFERENCES OF JUNIOR HIGH BOYS AND GIRLS

Lorene Novotny, in the February, 1960, *Kansas Studies in Education*, summarizes likes and dislikes of 128 seventh gratlers: "In fiction, the boys preferred stories of frontier heroes, wars of our country, the jungle, western adventure and Indians. Girls preferred stories of teenage romance, adventures of girls, funny stories, and pioneer life. Least attractive to boys were modern sea stories, modern travel stories, teenage romance, and adventures of girls. Least attractive to girls were sea stories of the past, football stories, and stories of jet planes."

DEVELOPMENTAL VS. REMEDIAL READING

Developmental reading assumes continuous and steady progress toward reading goals, while remedial reading implies serious interference with such growth. Continuous instruction is the keynote of developmental reading: special attention to specific reading difficulties is characteristic of remedial reading. So says Robert Karlin, *Reading Forum*, Spring, 1962.

DEVELOPMENTAL READING PROGRAM IN ACTION

"Though we are organizing our program as a 'developmental program' for all our pupils from the tenth grade Z group to the twelfth grade Honor group, it is understood that 'developmental' includes 'remedial' work where necessary *at any level* (meaning an attempt to correct errors in the procedures of all pupils). No course in literature is to be discontinued, because those courses are already developmental in a reading program. The greatest change consists of introduction of greater emphasis on the techniques of reading." (Barbara Phillips, Albuquerque, N. M.)

HANDBOOK FOR DEVELOPMENTAL READING

A *Handbook for Instructors in Developmental Reading*, prepared by teachers in Indiana, offers many suggestions as well as a thirty-six-lesson instructional program; it is published by Psychotechnics, Inc., 105 W. Adams, Chicago 3.

NEWSPAPER HEADLINES

"From newspapers select short, interesting items with better than ordinary headlines. Number the headlines and corresponding articles for purposes of identification, cut off the headlines, and distribute the articles, giving easiest reading matter to poorest students. Headlines are kept at the teacher's desk. Each student reads his article and writes an original headline for it. As the teacher calls numbers, each student reads his article and the headline he has written. Then the teacher reads the one which was in the newspaper. The class compares them and makes comments. Students seem to enjoy a lesson of this type and do good work with it." (Mary Halloran, Braintree, Mass.)

ADDITIONAL TECHNIQUES IN TEACHING READING SKILLS

1. If any of your students move lips or tongue while reading, help them to understand that doing so retards their reading. Tell them of the student who had difficulty in breaking himself of moving his lips and tongue. He finally put a piece of tape across his lips and rigidly held his tongue against the roof of his mouth. After a few days he was able to dispense with the tape; his reading speed was nearly doubled.

2. Usually tests of reading speed should be accompanied by tests of comprehension, since speed without adequate understanding has no merit. However, at monthly or bimonthly intervals, students may time themselves in reading selections of comparable difficulty (selections chosen by the teacher). They may thus discover whether their reading is becoming more rapid. The teacher may, if he wishes, have the class answer questions to test comprehension.

3. Delwyn G. Schubert, in the December, 1954, *Clearing House*, suggests several ways to change word readers into phrase readers. Among them: Encourage rapid reading of easy, interesting material; read aloud to the student, overemphasizing word groups, and have him imitate; use flashcards with phrases; have pupils draw diagonal lines between word groups; have students match phrases in opposite columns, with a time limit.

4. Alan Robinson suggests emphasis on three comprehensional skills: finding key words in a sentence, finding key sentence in a paragraph, and finding the main thought in a paragraph that contains no topic sentence. "A Cluster of Skills: Especially for Junior High Schools," *Reading Teacher,* 15 (Sept., 1961), 25.

5. Asking questions as one reads is probably the best way to remember, suggests Delwyn G. Schubert (*High School Journal,* Nov., 1957). A quick survey of a chapter before reading may help one to perceive relationships that otherwise would be missed. Giving oneself a quiz after reading is also helpful.

6. A student's ability to read humor understandingly is a good guide to his level of comprehension and general maturity.

7. Students are given paragraphs of simple instructions for doing something that may be performed in the classroom. Each does exactly what his instructions tell him.

8. Students read an untitled paragraph. Each suggests an appropriate title.

9. To assist visualization, students may draw or describe suitable pictures to accompany certain scenes in fiction.

10. Direct experience helps to clarify meaning. Thus, one class visited a newspaper plant and then read articles on how newspapers, magazines, and books are printed. The material was comprehensible because the students had something tangible to which to relate the words on the page.

11. To clarify sentence meaning, one student may read a sentence, and two others may restate its idea in two different ways.

12. To increase power to understand details, students may read a passage that contains many sensory images, and find words or phrases suggesting pictures, odors, sounds, tastes, or feelings.

13. For the same purpose, the teacher may supply a paragraph and three or four questions, one of which is not answered in the paragraph.

14. Students should frequently answer thought questions, not merely factual questions, based on paragraphs or articles.

15. Students may read two short articles about different inventions (or people, countries, etc.) and then decide how they are alike and how they differ.

16. The teacher prepares short paragraphs describing a person's actions. Students decide the person's purpose in acting thus. For instance, Ralph was invited to a dance. He washed his father's car, volunteered to help his mother, and remarked to his father that he wished he could take Jane to the dance. Why did Ralph do these things?

17. Students read a fable and then decide what familiar proverb it illustrates.

18. From a few clues in a paragraph, students decide what the setting is, or who the chief character is, or the approximate date of the incident.

19. In one column are several half-sentences; in a second column are the half-sentences needed to complete the first ones. Students are to find in the second column the words that logically complete each sentence.

20. Important tools in reading are the library catalog and *Reader's Guide to Periodical Literature.* Perhaps the best way to teach their use is to

employ teacher-made or student-made problems, such as "Where can you find information about skin diving?"

21. To improve skill in locating information, the teacher prepares specific questions answered in various reference books. Students use the indexes, tables of contents, etc., and find the answers as quickly as possible. If the teacher desires, the class may be divided into teams for an information-finding contest.

22. To improve skill in scanning and skimming, students are given a limited amount of time to find in a magazine a specified item of information, or to prepare for writing a brief summary that will give the central idea and chief supporting points. The length of time permitted may gradually be shortened.

23. Have students rapidly examine a chapter in any one of their texts, preferably a chapter with subheadings. Ask them to list six to ten questions that they believe the chapter would answer. At another time you may have them draw up a skeleton outline of a chapter, and perhaps fill in the outline with the most important details.

24. Using a chapter with subheadings, ask students to indicate what is probably the chief question answered under each subheading. Then have them find and write the answer to that question.

25. Students read a paragraph, write an already familiar fact or idea related to the paragraph, and then point out how the two are related.

26. Some schools are experimenting with the plan of three different textbooks in each subject. Students are not segregated by ability but are given easy, average, or difficult texts. The plan has been both praised and severely criticized.

27. Useful films and filmstrips on reading, using the library, and similar topics are available from Coronet, Encyclopaedia Britannica, Inc., and other sources.

28. One of the few controlled studies of teaching reading in regular classes is reported in Wallace Z. Ramsey's "An Experiment in Teaching Reading in High School English Classes." *English Journal*, XLVI (Nov., 1957), 495.

29. Improving reading of plays and poetry is the topic of Rosemary S. Donahue's "A Problem in Developmental Reading." *English Journal*, XLII (March, 1953), 142.

30. To improve students' ability to read critically, try constructing some relevance tests. Write a statement about any topic, and below it write three to five other statements. Students are to decide which of these statements are relevant to the first one. Similarly, to improve use of the card catalog, *Reader's Guide*, and indexes, you may write a statement and then ask under which of several suggested topics the students would look to find further information.

31. Critical reading may also be improved by asking questions concerning plausibility: "Does —— seem to be a real person such as you might meet?" "Could this event have happened?" "Would it be probable?"

RANK ORDER OF READING DIFFICULTIES

When 827 college students and adults were asked to rank their reading difficulties in order of importance, this was the result: 1. Word-by-word reading, 2. vocalizing, 3. backtracking, 4. daydreaming, 5. monotonous plodding (not changing speed), 6. rereading, 7. word blocking (unfamiliar words), 8. clue-blindness (ignoring headings, key phrases, etc.), 9. finger following, 10. word analysis (giving a word more meaning than context necessitates), 11. head swinging, 12. number attraction (being stopped by a number). John W. Purcell, "Poor Reading Habits: Their Rank Order," *The Reading Teacher*, XVI (March, 1963), 353.

INFORMAL READING DIAGNOSIS

Nila B. Smith's *Graded Selections for Informal Reading Diagnosis* (New York University Press, 1959), offers selections of varying difficulty. When a student reaches a selection on which he scores below 80 per cent, the level at which his further instruction should be based has been revealed.

LINGUISTICS AND READING

1. In recent years the possible application of linguistic principles to reading has attracted much attention. The key book (though it is mainly concerned with elementary reading) is C. C. Fries' *Linguistics and Reading* (Holt, Rinehart & Winston, Inc., 1963). Fries recognizes three stages of reading: "transfer," when the child learns to recognize the relationships between spoken language and that in print; "productive," involving response "to the meanings that are signalled without the use of the signals themselves"; and "vivid imaginative realization," which permits vicarious experience. Most students, but not all, in junior high school have passed the transfer stage; the emphasis in instruction, however, must be related to the stage in which each student is.

2. Among the few articles on this topic are two in *The Reading Teacher*: Dolores Durkin, "Linguistics and the Teaching of Reading," XVI (March, 1963), 341; and Rosemary G. Wilson and Helen C. Lindsay, "Applying Linguistics to Remedial Reading," XVI (May, 1963), 452.

ON RAPID READING

Arthur Heilman, Director of the Reading Laboratory at the University of Oklahoma, discusses objectively the emphasis on extremely rapid reading, whose protagonists often seem to imply that almost everything should be read at a speed of 1,000 or more WPM. His conclusion: "If it turns out that rapid reading is accepted only as . . . a tool to be used where appropriate, the results may be primarily good. If for a great number of people rapid reading becomes a goal in itself, modern man will simply have become *more* obsolete." *Journal of Developmental Reading*, V (Spring, 1962), 163.

A DEVICE FOR TEACHING CRITICAL READING

Ellen L. Thomas, in the February, 1960, *Reading Teacher*, describes packets of materials collected from newspapers, magazines, pamphlets, advertising, etc. A caption is on each packet: "Has the Writer Proved His Point?" "Is There a Hidden Motive?" "Who Would Want You To Believe This?" etc. Students choose a clipping, read the material, and attempt to answer the captioned question.

WHAT'S NEW IN THE LIBRARY?

Students in Norwalk, California, High School prepare a little quarterly magazine called "A Look at Your Library," listing and annotating new acquisitions and giving brief biographies of authors.

READING WITH A TAPE RECORDER

One study in South Bend, Indiana, reported in the *Indiana Teacher* for September, 1962, suggests that playing a tape recording while eighth grade students follow the copy in their books is helpful in improving reading skills. The experiment should be replicated a number of times with different groups before being considered valid.

READING LISTS

Available from the Division of Extended Services, Indiana State College, Terre Haute, is "Literature of Recognized Excellence for High School Students," an inexpensive list of several hundred classic or near-classic titles, arranged by types.

The Wisconsin Council of Teachers of English (WCTE) has prepared a popular leaflet, "Reading List for College-bound High School Students," available in quantities at low cost from the NCTE or WCTE.

DESIGN FOR READING

A device for encouraging students to read books of different kinds is "My Reading Design," which has separate forms for junior high and for senior high. For a sample, write Reading Circle, Inc., North Manchester, Indiana.

GUIDANCE FOR INDIVIDUAL READING

Books, Young People, and Guidance, by Geneva R. Hanna and Mariana K. McAlister, Harper & Row, 1960, relates principles of book selection to characteristics of adolescents. It suggests ways to stimulate reading and offers suggestions for book reports.

MACHINES FOR AIDING READING

For a favorable view of tachistoscopes, etc., and discussion of their selection and use, see Murray L. Miller, "Devices and Instruments for Use in High School Reading Instruction," *High School Journal,* XXX (Jan., 1956), 227.

CLASSROOM LIBRARY

"We have such animal stories as *Big Red* or *Wilderness Champion* for those juniors who are slow readers and whose reading vocabulary is rather limited. We have *Oliver Wiswell, Anthony Adverse, Oil for the Lamps of China,* and *The Yearling* for those students who have graduated from the Zane Grey type of novel. Then there are more difficult books for the most able readers." (Eleanor Vossler, Osawatomie, Kan.)

MOTIVATING OUTSIDE READING

1. "At the beginning of the semester, a junior boy says, 'Do you have any stories about sports? That's all I'm interested in.' I recommend *All-Conference Tackle, Career Coach,* or *Goal to Go*—not classics, I admit, but at least these books serve their purpose because upon finishing them this boy will say, 'Do you have any more like those?' I now have the motivation I have been striving for—an aroused interest in reading. I must be especially careful not to violate his trust by suggesting a book that, according to literary standards, is a classic, but according to his standards is difficult and boring. He is not ready for such a selection, and insistence on specific books to be read for credit is no procedure to follow if we are attempting to teach the student to like to read. Gradually, though, his reading horizon can be broadened to include far-away places, various professions, means of communication, etc." (Eleanor Vossler, Osawatomie, Kan.)

2. Raise the question, "What are the adventure zones in our world?" Get answers referring to things other than places. Then encourage reading in these zones.

3. "A touch of comedy may go further than a casual suggestion from a teacher. Post a large 'Bugs Bunny' poster which reads 'How about a Good Book, Doc?' Cards describing good books can be inserted in a window in the poster. Or one might have the cartooned figure of a diver (Gay Nineties suit); above it, 'Thinking of Taking the Plunge? Try Poetry.' Post below it some titles of quickly read poems." (Elaine Charles, Central High School, Grand Rapids, Mich.)

4. On the bulletin board put book reviews, pictures, and newspaper clippings referring to books. Better, let students do so.

5. "I post on the bulletin board 'best sellers' (not necessarily current books) that I recommend for the particular age group." (Marguerite Chamberlain, Franklin, N. H.)

6. The teacher's reading of brief, carefully selected excerpts from a book may make young readers eager to read it for themselves.

7. A meaningful and satisfying book for a student meets these two criteria, claims Dwight L. Burton: "first, the book must be within the intellectual power of the student; and, second, the student must be able to identify himself in some satisfying manner with the characters of the story." "There's Always a Book for You," *English Journal,* XXXVIII (Sept., 1949), 371.

8. After reading books about various countries, Ruth Raymond's students in Keene, New Hampshire, hold discussions on such topics as Interesting People We Meet in Books, Problems Solved, Description of a Scene, Maxims and Aphorisms, Humorous and Witty Lines, Customs of the Countries.

MORE SUGGESTIONS FOR BOOK REPORTS

1. Let students consult *Book Review Digest* to discover what can be told about a book besides its story.

2. Often the form of a book report may be predetermined by the reason for reading the book. If, for example, a student reads a book about electronics in order to learn about electronics, shouldn't his report tell of some of the important things he had not known before?

3. In lieu of a report, allow a student to make a poster to advertise a book he has liked.

4. Have students prepare an advertisement for a book, such as a book club might use. (Esther Urie, Hartford, Vt.)

5. A week in advance of the date when reading reports are due, ask for titles of books being read. On the due date, select four or five somewhat related books for reports. The other students simply record their reading, but all must read, since they do not know who will be called upon. (Marguerite Chamberlain, Franklin, N. H.)

6. For a short oral or written report on fiction, have each student state the main character's big problem and its outcome. (Anna Haig, Bronxville, N. Y.)

7. Let students give oral or written reports, not summarizing the story but presenting their ideas concerning the author's motives and methods. (Paul Hassett and Harold R. Hansen, Menomonie, Wis.)

8. In Kennebunk (Maine) High School, most reports are written. The questions to be answered are changed for each report to prevent monotony. (Thomas Maynard.)

9. "Let students print titles of books read beside their names on wall charts; indicate the subject, e.g., aviation or careers or history, so that pupils will be encouraged to build a varied reading experience." (Iowa City Junior High School.)

10. Have a "Talk-About-Books Day" once a month. (Iowa City Junior High School.)

11. Margaret Boutelle lists sixteen questions, any one or two of which may be used as the center of a book report. Among them. "What handicaps did the main character have, and how did he overcome them?" "What interesting facts about geography or history did you learn?" "What social customs were described as typical of the period or place?" "Did the book change your way of thinking in any manner?" *English Journal*, XL (Dec., 1951), 574.

12. In El Cerrito, California, junior high school students hold "Book-of-the-Week-Club" panels. Five students review books they have read, and the class chooses the one most adequately presented as its book of the week.

13. Gregory Coffin, of Marblehead, Massachusetts, duplicates especially good student-written book reviews for his class, and in the margin points out whatever is particularly commendable. *English Journal*, XLII (Dec., 1953), 510.

14. Donald Noble, of Alvin, Texas, has his students write parts of the script of a television play as a book report. For detailed instructions, see *English Journal*, XLIX (April, 1960), 259.

15. Many variations of a point-credit system are in use. Instead of stipulating that a student read a certain number of books, this plan requires earning a certain number of points. Long, difficult books carry more points than short, easy ones. Defects of this plan, however, are numerous, as in any plan that makes a quantitative prescription for all students.

16. Have each student keep a diary of his reading, with titles and comments. Collect the diaries a few at a time, and read excerpts to the class.

17. Encourage summer reading by allowing students to check out books

before the end of the school term. Get parents' signatures to ensure that the books will be returned.

18. "Select from the book a scene which will show some special power of the author, such as power to build a dramatic, a humorous, or a pathetic scene, or to express his observation of life and his philosophy about it, or create characters and pictures. Prepare it for presentation to the class as a radio script or as a reading." (Ada M. Bing, *English Journal*, XLII (March, 1953), 156.

19. Be sure to keep a permanent record of each student's outside reading.

20. Students may write a paragraph on each of two topics, choosing from six presented: (1) the character I'd like as a friend; (2) with specific reference to incidents, characters, or theme of this book, why I'd like to read another book by this author; (3) what makes the ending of the story satisfactory; (4) referring to at least two ideas in the book, why other students would find it helpful and not just entertaining; (5) comparison of the setting with my own environment; (6) permanent impression left upon me by the author's insights into human nature. Christine Yoder, *High Points*, Nov., 1961, p. 16.

21. The day before a book review is to be written, Elizabeth S. Sloat, Nazareth, Pennsylvania, puts on the board three or four general, thought-provoking questions, which are changed for each review. She thus leads students to search in their books for more than the superficial.

22. Charles E. Lapp suggests these ideas for junior high reports: (1) Student reads a quotation from the book and then writes a story of a moment in his own life that is related to the quotation. (2) Student thinks of himself as the main character and writes about something he would have done differently. (3) Student tells why the book would make a good movie, commenting on needed deletions, probable cast, etc. (4) Student conducts an imaginary interview with the author. *Clearing House*, XXXV (Feb., 1961), 337.

SIMPLIFIED CLASSICS

A simplified classic is obviously not the same as the classic itself. Usually little remains except the story. If you feel you should teach such books to slow readers, anyhow, or suggest them for outside reading, Donald J. Assuma gives the reading difficulty of about eighty of them in the February, 1953, *English Journal*. A shorter list is in the April, 1951, *English Journal*.

TO KEEP YOUR CLASSROOM LIBRARY BOOKS ATTRACTIVE

Remove the jacket when the book is checked out, and replace it when the book goes back to the shelf.

BOOK CAFETERIAS

More and more schools are installing small bookstores especially for sale of paperbound books. The stores may be staffed by students under faculty supervision and should be open regularly at stated hours. Profits may be used for classroom libraries or other commendable purposes. Only books should be sold—not candy, etc. Titles should be faculty-approved but may be student-suggested. Prices should be publishers' list prices. Titles displayed should be changed frequently.

PAPERBOUND BOOKS IN PRINT

This quarterly catalog, published by the R. R. Bowker Company, lists most paperbound books (of American publishers) currently in print. It is essential for any school library and useful in making selections for classroom libraries. Other books from the same company include *Textbooks in Print* (annual) and *The Literary Marketplace* (concise information about publishers, annual).

YOUR OWN READING RECORD

After reading a book, article, or story that they may wish sometime to call to the attention of a student or students, some efficient teachers spend five minutes in writing pertinent bibliographical information on a 4" by 6" card, along with a brief summary or interpretive comment. A collection of such cards can be invaluable.

5

ALLOWING LITERATURE TO LIVE

WHY DO WE TEACH WHAT WE TEACH?

The Misguided Misguiders

If one visits a number of secondary school classes in which literature is being taught, one is likely to see some excellent, obviously
purposeful teaching and also some that, though it may have a purpose, is misguided and, hence, misguides students in the quest for
what literature has to offer. Let us pay imaginary visits to a few
classrooms (described in exaggerated or even burlesque terms to
make a point) and evaluate the instruction we see in each.

Miss Plodd teaches English in a junior high school. The room is
plain and unadorned. So is Miss Plodd's teaching. She and her class
plod methodically through their anthology. The second day of the
term they began with page 1, and on all the "literature days" since
then they have followed the same procedure.

"Class, open your books to page 226," says Miss Plodd. "Charles,
you may read the first stanza."

Laboriously, Charles begins reading Lowell's "The Vision of Sir
Launfal." When he finishes, Miss Plodd corrects his mispronuncia-
tions. Then she asks Charles to tell her what the stanza is about.
He doesn't know. Miss Plodd asks for volunteers. Melissa, who
always knows the answers, summarizes the stanza to Miss Plodd's
satisfaction. The class is, therefore, ready for the next stanza. "Lor-
raine," says Miss Plodd, "you may read the next stanza."

When we pause to think about what Miss Plodd does, we wonder why she does it. First, why is she a slave to an anthology? Anthologists carefully prepare books with which most students in a particular grade can cope; they arrange selections according to some sort of order; and they provide study aids that are often well conceived, useful, stimulating, and insightful. But probably no anthologist would recommend that his book be used in the way that Miss Plodd employs it. Different classes need different materials. "The Vision of Sir Launfal" may be entirely suitable for some students or some classes, entirely unsuitable for others. In addition, the anthologist would certainly recognize that, though his arrangement of materials would be ideal for some schools, it would be desirable for others to alter the arrangement to suit their special needs. And he would urge that many assignments be from outside his anthology—that, for instance, the vast resources of paperbound literature be partially explored.

We wonder, secondly, why Miss Plodd follows so persistently the read-paraphrase technique. As an occasional device, it is certainly useful. But, employed too much, it has weaknesses besides the fact that it engenders boredom. For one thing, by focusing attention on separate stanzas or paragraphs without any synthesis, it gives students no conception of the whole work. It is the entire work and the contributions that each part makes to the whole work that are important. For another, the read-paraphrase technique pays no attention to nuances of style. Also, though Miss Plodd's procedure involves oral reading, direct instruction in oral reading would probably bring greater improvement in that skill than does mechanical plowing through of a number of stanzas or paragraphs.

Let us now look briefly into the classroom of Mr. Tinkertoy. While Miss Plodd's classroom is unadorned, Mr. Tinkertoy's is adorned so much that it is cluttered. Mr. Tinkertoy is perhaps a born teacher of industrial arts who somehow missed his calling. In one corner of the room, boys are sawing and hammering. In another, students are carving soap. In another, girls are dressing dolls. Along one wall, boys and girls are busily painting a mural. On desks and tables and walls and on the floor and suspended from the ceiling are guillotines (*Tale of Two Cities*, you know), Globe Theatres, Roman Forums, rafts (*Huckleberry Finn*), drawings of frogs that can't jump, and pictures of emaciated Rip Van Winkles. If you would see Mr. Tinkertoy's monument, look around him.

An occasional Globe Theatre may be all right—say one per decade. Even an occasional guillotine is endurable, though it probably reveals little about Sidney Carton. Handicraft may make a few students slightly less reluctant to come to English class. But what does Mr. Tinkertoy think he is teaching? Does he really believe he is teaching literature? Can anyone understand better the interactions of Julius Caesar, Brutus, Mark Antony, and Octavius because he has hammered together or carved out a Roman Forum? If the time in Mr. Tinkertoy's class is given mainly to such activities, he should give back half his salary.

Mr. Mechano is a cousin of Mr. Tinkertoy. "This is the Age of Science," says Mr. Mechano. "This is the Age of Electronics." So Mr. Mechano persuades the principal to persuade the superintendent to persuade the school board to permit him to buy every schoolroom gadget that American ingenuity and business enterprise can produce. Mr. Mechano's classroom looks like a disorganized electrical repair shop. There's a TV set, of course, as well as a radio, a tape recorder, and a hi-fi with wires running here and there, threatening to trip or decapitate the unwary. There are a phonograph, a slide projector, a filmstrip projector, a silent-movie projector, and 8- and 16-mm. sound projectors. There are an overhead projector, a dismantled tachisto-scope, a dozen reading pacers, and four brands of teaching machines. Mr. Mechano is presently much interested in teaching machines and is trying out all available programs that will fit his machines and bemoaning the fact that eleven other programs would require six other types of machines that the school board refuses to buy him. He spends his evenings repairing the gadgets in his classroom, aided by a half-dozen boys who ought to be at home doing their mathematics or reading Thomas Hardy or Julian Huxley.

This is indeed the Age of Electronics, and every English teacher should know what audio-visual aids are available to help him do his job. But Mr. Mechano goes to the extreme of substituting the machine for the book. His students have the opportunity to see visual inter-pretations of literature and to hear oral interpretations of literature; what they do not have is the opportunity to read literature.

Here is Miss Toynbee's room. Miss Toynbee is a literary historian. Her students read about American and English literature. On an examination her juniors can give the birth and death dates of any Mather of Lowell you care to name, can arrange ten titles in chrono-logical order, and can name the chief characteristics of the Colonial Period, the Revolutionary Period, and all the other Periods. Her seniors do equally well with the Age of Chaucer, though the only Chaucer they have read is the first twenty lines of the Prologue; they can contrast the Age of Classicism and the Romantic Period, but they have read only a few couplets by Pope and something by Wordsworth that they persist in calling "daffy dills." Miss Toynbee teaches as she does because she mistakenly believes that colleges insist upon literary history. She should ponder a statement by Paul Farmer, past president of the NCTE, reporting on the kinds of abilities and knowledge that students need to cope with College Board examinations: "First, emphasis should be shifted from facts about literature to the reading and understanding of literature itself."

Here is Miss Boas' classroom. Miss Boas is a cultural anthropologist or a sociologist. Her classes sometimes read literature and sometimes discuss literature. They sometimes get excited about literature. They also read sociology, psychology, anthropology. They talk about inter-relationships of people and about the effects of the Industrial Revolution upon American life, and right now they are exploring the mores of the upper classes through the medium of Cleveland Amory's *Who Killed Society?* Last week they discussed *Huckleberry Finn* as a treatise on Negro-white relationships. If you ask them the differences between a novel and a work of non-fiction, they look at you blankly.

Finally, we sit in Mrs. Tiny's classroom. Mrs. Tiny specializes in detailed analysis. Somewhere she read the statement (and a true statement it is) that classroom concentration on a relatively few pieces of literature is better than dips into great numbers. So she concentrates. Her class spends three weeks on "The Rime of the Ancient Mariner." They analyze every stanza, every line, almost every word. They anatomize every simile, every metaphor. Mrs. Tiny expects her class to know not only iambics and anapaests but also amphibrachs, pyrrhics, and choriambs. Woe to the student who fails to recognize metonymy!

If we had time, we could also visit the classes of Miss Gush ("Isn't this *lovely!*"), Mr. Homer ("Only the classics are worth reading."), Miss Free ("What shall we do today, Class?"), and a few others. These and the six into whose rooms we have ventured have one thing in common: unawareness of why literature should be taught. All of them are constantly on the periphery of literature. They keep their students on the periphery with them.

Perhaps all of them teach as they do for one central reason: They themselves do not know how to read literature or why to read literature. More specifically, they do not know how to read a page and relate that page to other pages. Their colleges have failed them. Some college teachers of literature are historians like Miss Toynbee, sociologists like Miss Boas, or analyzers like Mrs. Tiny. These three high school teachers are teaching in the way that somebody else taught them. Miss Plodd probably teaches as she does because it is an easy way to get through the class hour and requires no elaborate planning. Mr. Tinkertoy and Mr. Mechano are following their own bents; maybe literature as literature is unknown to them, so they substitute something superficially related to literature.

Yet, one affirmative statement should be made about these teachers. Something good can be said about every one of their procedures. Miss Plodd emphasizes getting the basic meaning, and, without such understanding, it is impossible to reach the higher goals. Mr. Tinkertoy helps his students to visualize, and visualization is important to literary grasp. Mr. Mechano is alert to modern aids. Miss Toynbee realizes the importance of relating one part of learning to another. Miss Boas is right in stressing that literature is about people. Mrs. Tiny is right in requiring intensive reading and in teaching a certain amount of terminology. Miss Gush's enthusiasm for literature, Mr. Homer's desire to teach worthwhile material, and Miss Free's willingness to listen to students' opinions are all commendable. Yes, there is something good in what every one of these teachers does. The something bad is that they go to such extremes that their teaching lacks balance. Each has a gimmick that he or she overemphasizes.

Three Reasons for Reading Literature

Why do we teach what we teach? That question might be phrased differently as "Why should we teach what we should teach?" or "How can we determine what we should teach?" It is related, obviously, to the even more basic question, "Why read literature?"

Let us consider that question, "Why read literature?" and then see how our conclusions may guide us in selecting literature for high school teaching and also in determining what we do with that literature.

We read literature for three interrelated and overlapping reasons: for pleasure, for information of a kind not available in an encyclopedia, and for a means of sharing in our cultural heritage. We cannot separate these three with definite partitions, but, nevertheless, we can try to look at each in turn.

Pleasure. We get our pleasures from different things, and the most truly educated persons are probably those who are most versatile in their joys. Such persons may turn in succession to a book, an art museum, a science exhibit, a kitchen stove or a jigsaw, a fishing rod or a set of golf clubs, a baseball game, a lecture, and the late late show on television.

He who knows how to read well enough can obtain a variety of pleasures vicariously. Though a baseball story by Ring Lardner should not be substituted for an afternoon in Yankee Stadium, the Lardner story may make the next baseball game a more vivid experience. The players on the field emerge as human beings; the Lardner reader is a better baseball fan because he realizes that baseball uniforms cover players who in background and temperament are themselves far from uniform.

Vicariously one could travel under the sea with Jules Verne decades before the first submarine was built. Vicariously one can visit lands that one may never see even with today's jet travel. Vicariously one can go back into the past and live as one's ancestors lived. Much of the pleasure of literature comes from such vicarious experiences. They help to create a versatility of pleasure.

Part of the pleasure for one who knows how to read well comes from a conscious recognition of artistry. We applaud what is done well, whether the act is one of juggling, painting a picture, playing the piano, or arranging words. The literary artist, though perhaps depicting "what oft was thought," chooses his words so that we may add "but ne'er so well express'd." We derive pleasure from the artful simplicity of Housman or Frost or Hemingway, from the resonant voice of Milton, from the dilettante extravagances and metrical experimentation of Swinburne, from the barbed satirical mastery of Swift or the gentleness of the remonstrances of Addison. The musics of Poe and Lanier have their beauty, and so has Millay's cry of exultation, "Oh, world, I cannot hold thee close enough!" and so has Robinson Jeffers' bitter anguish.

Some years ago an advertiser ran a series of ads using the slogan "It's fun to be fooled, but it's more fun to know." It is fun to read literature even though one does not recognize the writer's techniques, but it is more fun when we do know what the writer has done to move us. If we can note how he has assembled the parts of a plot, how in a poem he has blended together rhythm and diction to suit his purpose, how in a play he has characterized in only a few sentences, our appreciation is heightened. This does not mean that we have to count all the similes or scan all the lines, but it does mean that we analyze enough to identify the key aspects of the writer's craft.

Other parts of the pleasure can be identified. There is, for example, the pleasure of the puzzle, comparable to that of solving the Chinese box or ring puzzle; we attain this pleasure when we outguess the detective in a mystery story, or we attain it when we extract the essential kernel from a difficult lyric poem. There is also the pleasure of satisfying our curiosity about people, of comparing them with ourselves, of identifying ourselves with some of them, and of observing how they will react when they are thrust into changed surroundings or faced with unaccustomed obstacles. This is related, no doubt, to the pleasure obtained from discovering how things turn out—the age-old love of a story, which has its incipience in curiosity. Then there is the pleasure of intellectual stimulation—the stimulation that comes from new ideas and insights, thinking about these insights, and formulation of one's own conclusions.

Information. The pleasure of intellectual stimulation is related to the second reason for reading literature: It gives information of a kind not available in encyclopedias. If we want facts, we go to reference books. But, if we want insights different from those afforded by facts, we go to literature.

Dr. Sterling M. McMurrin, former United States Commissioner of Education, speaking on "Education for Freedom in a Free Society," said,

> One of the major deficiencies in our national effort to meet the challenges before us is the almost complete failure of the American people to recognize that the strength of a nation lies in its art and music and literature, and in its philosophical sophistication and the quality of its social sciences, just as much as in its physics and chemistry or its electrical engineering. When we raise the question of the survival of our Nation it is a question in proximate range of statesmanship and machinery. But when we speak of the decline or rise of our culture and the strength of the Nation for the long haul ahead, it is a question of the full cultivation of our spiritual, artistic, moral, and intellectual resources. Those who suppose that great music or great poetry or a knowledge of classical literature is not essential to not only the quality but even the survival of a nation and its culture are quite unaware of the lessons of the past.

The insights that are deeper than mere facts are so numerous and varied that they can only be illustrated. In Crane's *Red Badge of Courage* is a portrayal of fear and self-finding more revealing than any of the studies made by psychologists. In Jonathan Swift's satire is a revelation of human weakness; it is a warning; it is a sermon. We recognize that we are the Lilliputians who will go to war over which end of an egg should be cracked first; we recognize that we are sometimes the Yahoos, with their repulsive habits; we recognize some twentieth-century scientists in the eighteenth-century scientists ridiculed by Swift. (Maybe the greatest need of this century is a reincarnation of Jonathan Swift.)

From the poetry of Robert Frost we learn once more the value of elemental things. The greatest accomplishment of the hired man in

Frost's poem was his ability to load a hay rick tall and secure, every forkful in its place. The hired man reminds us of the bootmaker in John Galsworthy's short story "Quality," who made such good shoes that it took years to wear them out. We contrast the work of the hired man and the bootmaker with the shoddy workmanship, the built-in obsolescence, of so many items we buy today, and we wonder why we have lost what we have lost, and what the consequences may be, and what we may do to regain integrity and the pride that was once ours in a job well done.

From books like Mark Twain's *Life on the Mississippi* or O. E. Rölvaag's *Giants in the Earth* we can learn more than the history books tell us about the lives our ancestors lived. These are not glamorized, sleek presentations. Mark Twain's Mississippi is not just a broad, beautiful river with picturesque scenery along both banks; it has sand bars and mud, rough and sometimes violent men, sweat and confusion. Rölvaag's pioneers are both brave and fearful; in Beret, the pioneer wife who lacked the strength and the balance needed in a new land, we have one of the most sensitive portraits in all literature.

The humorous writers give us insights, too. Ogden Nash's famous four-line parody of "Trees," in which he laments that unless the billboards fall he'll never be able to see a tree, is more eloquent than most hour-long speakers on the conservation of natural resources. A drive along U.S. 1 in the East reveals the truth of Nash's lines.

Cultural Heritage. History classes bring parts of our cultural heritage to students; so do classes in science, mathematics, art, music, and so on. Can we in English identify as basic to our common heritage a number of literary selections that every American should know? Once the colleges, through their entrance examinations, in effect determined such a canon, including works like "The Bunker Hill Oration," Burke's "Speech on Conciliation," "Evangeline," "Idylls of the King," *Hamlet,* and *Macbeth.* After the turn of the century such dictation was rightly opposed. But the net result has been that we Americans have so little reading in common—on any academic level—that Professor William R. Parker, of Indiana University, has asserted that even among his graduate students in English he cannot count upon all of them to know any given work of literature.

It seems unfortunate that television rather than literature provides a common bond among most Americans. The man on the street or the woman at the bridge party can refer to any of a dozen currently popular television programs with fair assurance that the others present will understand the reference. Next week new programs, new allusions; next year many or most of this year's programs will be off the air, supplanted by something else. Without hostility to television one can justify the statement that it is ephemeral, it lacks roots, and it provides but a transitory bond. Literature could provide a permanent bond for us.

The NCTE's *National Interest and the Teaching of English* makes the case for literature in our cultural heritage in this way:

> The young who study our language and literature come into the best contact possible with the dreams, hopes, and aspirations, as well as with the roots of our culture. The rich texture of myth and folklore of lumbering, pioneering, and railroading stimulates the imagination and is a vehicle for the perpetual transmission of the American heritage. Only through the imagination do the complex natures of our various regions—Down East, the Old South, the prairie, the corn belt, and the mining town—become ingrained in our rising generations. Many of the books our youth read suggest the richness which we define as our heritage—*Our Town, Huckleberry Finn,* "The Devil and Daniel Webster," "The Death of the Hired Man," *Abe Lincoln in Illinois, The Scarlet Letter, Moby Dick.* These stories are founded upon an older and wider tradition, but one still ours—*David Copperfield,* "The Ancient Mariner," "The Deserted Village," "Elegy Written in a Country Churchyard," *Robinson Crusoe, Macbeth.* And this literature depends upon and blends with an even older tradition—the temptations of Faust, the mystic Bluebird, the penetrating humor of Don Quixote, the wanderings of Ulysses, the heroic figures of Greek and Roman myth, the just and overseeing God of the Bible. The base of the heritage is as broad as the humanistic tradition.[1]

SELECTING

On the basis of valid reasons for reading and teaching literature, it is possible to answer some of the questions often asked about choosing the literature to be taught.

Should Only Classics Be Assigned?

College entrance examinations decades ago demanded familiarity with prescribed classics; even if they had not, the typical English teacher of 1910 would have cringed at the suggestion that that vulgar upstart Jack London be taught. William Lyon Phelps early in the century was regarded as dangerously radical when he encouraged his Yale students to read Stevenson.

But the old order changeth. London and Stevenson have attained respectability and have made the going easier for such of their de-

[1] P. 16.

scendants as Ernest Hemingway and C. S. Forester. Out the window have gone Burke's "Conciliation," Halleck's "Marco Bozzaris," and Landor's "Iphigenia and Agamemnon." Less attention is paid to Alexander Pope, and the name of Carlyle is never uttered in some classrooms. Most teachers today try to select for study only those pieces that have something clearly worth saying to today's young people and that say it well; these teachers realize that some of the old and some of the new meet this requirement.

Extremists exist on both sides, of course, though they are relatively few. Battling for an almost exclusive diet of classics are some teachers who argue that little contemporary literature is as good as what has stood the test of time; that the classics, because they are so well presented, can have even more appeal for adolescents than do materials whose chief virtue is contemporaneity; and that, if students are not exposed to the world's finest writing in high school, many of them will never read a line of it. On the other side are some teachers who assert that most classics are too difficult for teen-agers, difficult not just in language but also in conception and scope; only mature minds, these teachers say, can grasp what Shakespeare is really talking about or what Milton is saying about the ways of God.

A middle ground seems to be best. We must face the fact that most of the reading our students do after graduation will be taken from contemporary materials—newspapers, magazines, books-of-the-month, etc. As teachers we need to make this reading more discriminating than it would have been if we had never existed. We can teach discrimination only by introducing to our classes many varieties of reading and by helping students to understand the similarities and differences among those varieties. We need to present Homer, Chaucer, Hawthorne, and others, with sufficient skill that our students will not only see what has made these writers live but will also be able to use them as touchstones for the evaluation of other literature. The classics should be taught as samples of the best thinking and writing that man has yet achieved, and as expressions of the sensitivity of unusually perceptive human beings. Those children who are intellectually able to realize the mental and emotional penetration of great writers will have as a permanent possession the desire to find in other literature that which is no less evocative.

When a teacher is considering a selection, he should give it a high mark if it is readable by his class and if it will introduce students to some of the personalities who ought to be known to almost everyone. Somewhere in their high school careers students should become ac-

quainted with Apollo, Minerva, and other mythological characters; *[mythi.*
with such semilegendary figures as Horatius, King Arthur, Marco *Jr. High]*
Polo, and William Tell; and with such literary immortals as Oedipus,
Sinbad, Chaucer's Knight, Cervantes' Don Quixote, Swift's Gulliver,
Addison's Sir Roger, and Irving's Rip Van Winkle. It is doubtful that
a modern American can be called truly "cultured" or even "educated"
if such names are meaningless to him. Students in junior high school
are usually ready for the myths of Greece, Rome, and Scandinavia, and
for simple versions of the Round Table stories and other legends. But
greater maturity—the near maturity of high school upperclassmen—is
essential for an understanding of the Knight and other Chaucerian *[Sr. High]*
characters, Sir Roger, and Oedipus or Antigone.

The contemporary has its virtues, too, if it is carefully chosen.
Some of today's contemporary literature will be tomorrow's classics.
The first teacher to introduce O'Neill, Wilder, Hemingway, Steinbeck,
Faulkner, or Frost to his students was departing from the classical
canon, but today we realize that he chose well. The important point
to remember is that, while modern writers of first rank are worth
including, little class time should be spent on the tenth raters—or even
the third.

How Difficult Should the Literature Be?

It is impossible to assess literary difficulty with exactitude. Formulas
have been devised in the attempt, but, since they involve counting
polysyllables and measuring sentence length yet cannot provide a
yardstick to the difficulty of conceptions, they are hardly satisfactory.
Readability formulas show, for example, that *Tom Sawyer* and *Huckleberry Finn* are equally difficult books, but anyone who has read and
understood both stories realizes that Huckleberry Finn is infinitely
more complex, multilayered, hard to grasp. Edgar Dale illustrates
clearly how simplicity of words may conceal depth of meaning:

In Dostoevsky's novel *The Brothers Karamazov*, Father Zossima asks:
"What is hell?" and answers, ". . . it is the suffering of being unable to
love." A fifth grader can pronounce these words, recognize them percep-
tually, but can he *read* them? He can't get the meaning because he is
conceptually immature.[2]

But how can a student's conceptions mature if he is constantly exposed to immature conceptions? There is a way out of the apparent

[2] *Newsletter,* October, 1962, p. 2.

dilemma. The principle of pleasure that we have discussed implies that what we teach should be capable of bringing pleasure to our students at the intellectual or maturational level they have attained at that time. In other words, a selection should not be so far beyond the understanding of students that there is no possibility of pleasure. Yet it should be slightly beyond their full comprehension. Robert Browning provides the justification:

> Ah, but a man's reach should exceed his grasp
> Or what's a heaven for?

A well-chosen literary selection should stretch the student slightly; it should make him extend himself. If it does not stretch him, it provides no new challenges; he might as well spend his time before the TV set. But, if it is so far out of his reach that even utmost stretching will not bring him close, he will give up in despair.

Fortunately, many pieces of literature are comprehensible in part to most students, more fully comprehensible to others. Consider the analogy of an apple tree, laden with fruit. By stretching, every student in the class can reach the apples on the lowest boughs. Other students, by stretching, can reach apples on higher branches. Perhaps the ladders supplied by college and maturity will be necessary before any of the students can reach the apples at the top of the tree. But the other apples, some of them reachable by all students, are worth the picking.

Must Only Literature with a Capital L Be Assigned?

Perhaps no one can define exactly the line a writer must cross in order to be an author of literature. It may be helpful, though, to recall Van Dyke's definition of "literature": "Literature consists of those writings which interpret the meanings of nature and life, in words of clearness and power, touched with the personality of the author, in artistic forms of permanent interest." A sale bill seldom possesses any of these characteristics, nor, usually, does a news story about yesterday's murder or last night's basketball game. The purpose of the sale bill or the news story is utilitarian—to give information. But a non-utilitarian selection such as a story in a pulp magazine is not necessarily literature.

For practical purposes, as a rough guide only, the line between "mere reading" and "literature" might be drawn thus:

"Mere Reading"	"Literature"
1. May be utilitarian or affective (emotional)	1. Is always affective [3]
2. If utilitarian, has primary purpose of informing	2. Gives an author's personalized interpretation of life
3. If affective, lacks one or more of the last three qualities listed under "Literature"	3. Is clearly, strikingly written
	4. Is in an artistic form of lasting interest

Briefly, the question to consider is this: Should any material that is not literature be admitted to the high school English course?

The answer appears to be a qualified "yes." In their lives after graduation, many students will have more occasion to do utilitarian reading than affective. They will, for example, read recipes to find out how to bake a cake, timetables to discover when they will arrive in Denver, and newspaper and magazine articles to get information and form opinions. The English department has not done its duty if its students are graduated without knowing a great deal about how to read various kinds of utilitarian materials.

But, although the inclusion of some utilitarian reading is highly desirable in each year of the junior and senior high school, there is seldom a strong reason for including any affective material that lacks one or more of the qualities of literature. Outside the school's jurisdiction, students will sometimes read "Superman" and Spillane. In class, however, they may read with profit selections that are of no less interest but are of satisfactory quality. Eventually, through the teacher's guidance, most (but not all) will search in their reading for qualities the comics and the pulps do not possess.

The "yes" may be qualified further by adding that most of the abilities requisite for reading utilitarian material should be developed in the elementary grades and junior high school. Many seventh, eighth, and ninth grade textbooks offer material of the sort needed to help the student in his work reading, and the resources available in newspapers and magazines are nearly limitless. In the senior high school, the English teacher needs to help each student develop further his skill in reading utilitarian materials. A considerably larger proportion of the time, however, should be devoted to literature than to "mere reading." [4]

[3] It must be noted, though, that some utilitarian selections are on the borderline between "mere reading" and "literature." For example, some of Ruskin's prose dealing with art or with the dignity of labor is utilitarian in that it strives to inform, but it also possesses the characteristics listed here under "Literature."

[4] A unit in the reading of newspapers and another in the reading of magazines are desirable, probably in the sophomore and junior years.

You will recall that one of the reasons for reading is to obtain information that transcends the factual. It is, therefore, wise to ask about almost every selection, "Will it provide insights valuable to today's students?" Ruled out, then, will be an article about fighting forest fires, if it provides nothing more than information about how to fight them. Ruled in will be an article or story on the same topic, if it sheds light on human nature and on the age-old conflict between man and nature. Novels by George R. Stewart, for example, might do this— *Fire* deals with forest fires and the men who combat them; *Storm* concerns the human effects of a fierce storm that sweeps from the Pacific across the western part of our country. Ruled out will be stories of conflict for conflict's sake—the bang-bang stories with little motivation, little probing of character: stories that hardly rise above children's backyard play-fights against the "bad guys." Ruled in will be stories of conflict that show why men fight, that show conflicts that may be more internal than external. *No* to Zane Grey; maybe *yes* to Walter Van Tilburg Clark, Conrad Richter, A. B. Guthrie, Jack Schaefer, Oliver La Farge.

Should the Whole Class Read the Same Literature?

The diagram shown as Fig. 6 represents a desirable reading plan for a class.

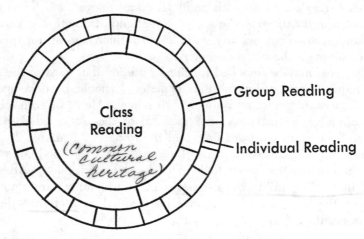

Fig. 6.

The material read by the whole class helps to provide for the common cultural heritage discussed on pages 126–127. In addition it makes possible some instruction in close reading, analysis of style, discussion of what to look for in literature, explanations of how each part contributes to the whole, and examination of the author's purpose. It assists students in relating literature to life, in distinguishing one type of literature from another, in learning the special techniques to apply to each type, and sometimes in seeing how literature grows not only from the author's experiences but also from the age in which he lives. Class reading may be regarded as an ideal form of the kind of reading it is hoped each student will do later on his own, alone with a book he has chosen, a book that he has no obligation to discuss with a teacher or anyone else.

Group reading, used especially in thematic units but possible also in other arrangements, involves reading of the same or very similar material by several students in a class. They discuss within the group, perhaps with the aid of questions or in a framework prepared by the teacher, and they usually find some way to share their reactions with the class, maybe through panel discussions, reports, or dramatizations. The material read by a group is teacher-approved, although students may assist in the choices and sometimes select their group on the basis of what is to be read in it. Groups of good readers may read more material and more advanced material than groups of poorer readers. Hence the groups provide for differentiation on two grounds: the nature of the material and the abilities of the students.

In individual reading, perhaps no two students in the class are reading the same book. Some of the choices should be perfectly free; some may be free within prescribed limits such as those of a literary type or a list of books on the same or varied subjects; some should be chosen in conference between teacher and student. The amount of individual reading should be larger than the amount of class or group reading. In many schools, supervised individual reading has become the heart of the reading program. It should never replace class and group reading, however, because those have values not otherwise attainable.

ARRANGING AND APPROACHING

Arranging the Course in Literature

Four principles of arrangement are widely used in planning the reading for a course:

1. In chronological order
2. According to types of literature

3. In units based on central themes
4. Around students' experience (sometimes overlaps no. 3)

In addition, teachers occasionally employ various combinations of the above arrangements, or modifications of them. For instance, a variation of the chronological approach is the "culture-epoch" plan, in which each unit is centered upon the literature and other cultural elements of the Colonial Period, the Revolutionary War Period, etc. Less frequent is the organization of a course with a few authors or a few classics as centers of interest or points of departure. The "guided free reading" mentioned earlier might also be called a method of arrangement. Correlation with history or some other subject is a plan followed in some schools. A few teachers, it seems, follow no plan of arrangement but merely teach whatever they want to whenever they want to.

Each method of arrangement has its good qualities and its drawbacks. The major pros and cons are as follows:

ARRANGEMENT BY CHRONOLOGY

Pros	Cons
1. Chronology, since it follows the inexorable calendar, affords the most orderly plan of procedure.	1. Learning to enjoy literature is much more important than learning who wrote what when.
2. Students learn the pattern of development of literature.	2. The literature that students usually find least interesting is presented first.
3. Students learn some of the relationships between literature and history.	3. When time runs short, modern literature is likely to be neglected.
4. Students do not stay with one type long enough to become bored with it.	4. Sometimes the chronological course in literature degenerates into a course in literary history.

ARRANGEMENT BY TYPES

Pros	Cons
1. Students learn to distinguish literary forms.	1. It does students little real good to be able to identify a type of literature.
2. Comparison of work of different authors who used the same medium is facilitated.	2. Too much stress is put upon distinctions that are not always clear-cut (e.g., between short story and essay, or novelette and novel).
3. Students learn how writing of each type has changed.	

4. Students who like one type may be stimulated to further reading in that type.
5. It is easy to combine this arrangement with some other.

3. Students acquire no idea of the whole pattern of development of literature.
4. If much time is devoted to a type that some students dislike, that part of the course is a desert for them.
5. The selections often have no continuity or similarity other than being of the same type.

Arrangement by Units and Themes

✓ *Pros*

1. The reading is related to general topics (adventure, science, etc.) in which students are usually interested.
2. Selections from different countries and different centuries may be introduced in the same unit.
3. Students do not stay with one type long enough to become bored with it.
4. Students may readily be stimulated to do additional reading on a topic that they enjoy.
5. Differences in authors' points of view may be studied.

Cons

1. Sometimes selections are chosen not because of their quality but because they pertain to the theme.
2. Students acquire no idea of the whole pattern of development of literature.
3. Some students may not be interested in the general topic of the entire unit.
4. Regular use of this arrangement becomes tiresome.
5. There is danger that sociology and history may be stressed too much, literature too little.

Arrangement Around Student Experiences

✓ *Pros*

1. This arrangement emphasizes not the literature but the experiences that students can obtain with and through literature.
2. Students' problems may be the focus; thus, students get help in regulating their own lives.
3. Students are urged to do more independent reading than in other arrangements.
4. Individual differences create less of a problem in this arrangement than in others.

Cons

1. The material read may sometimes be of inferior quality.
2. Only unusually competent teachers generally succeed with this arrangement.
3. Independent work is difficult to grade.
4. Students' laziness often makes independent work slipshod.
5. Students acquire no idea of the whole pattern of development of literature.

The fact that no one method of arrangement emerges as superior to all the others should cause no particular surprise or alarm. It has previously been remarked that there are no panaceas in teaching. If someone could find a plan of arrangement that has no weaknesses . . . but that is only utopian dreaming. It is necessary to take what is available, improve it if possible, but use it effectively.

Arrangements by themes and around student experiences have been found most satisfactory in the seventh, eighth, ninth, and tenth grades. Fine distinctions among types usually make little impression on students in those grades. Likewise, their sense of chronology is as a rule insufficiently developed to make a chronological organization meaningful; the year 1880 to most fourteen-year-olds sounds no nearer in time than 1680, and not much nearer than 1492. But the seventh-to-tenth graders can profitably study a number of selections about pets, holidays, pioneers, the sea, the mountains, Latin America, etc. Or they can read, with enjoyment and benefit, poems that emphasize rhythm, varied selections that add to their experience of city or country life, stories that give them vicarious experiences, etc.

Arrangement by types or chronology is better suited to the eleventh and twelfth grades, although even in these years long-continued exposure to lyrics or essays should probably be avoided. (Lyric poetry is so intense that few persons read much of it at one sitting. Lyrics are on the spice shelf of literature; none of us would make a meal of cloves.) The average sixteen-year-old, according to some psychologists, has reached or passed the average mental age of the whole population. If he will ever be able to learn about the types and the chronology of literature, and if these things are worth teaching, then the ages of sixteen and seventeen would seem to be the logical time to present them.

There are various ways of attaining a little variety in arrangement. Among possible variations of the above procedures are these:

1. Use the chronological order, but begin with modern literature. After a while, raise the question, "How did our literature get to be this way?" Then go back to early literature and work forward, keeping the question uppermost and drawing many comparisons between past and present writings.

2. Within the chronological order, have several units based on types or experiences, for instance, war in Elizabethan literature, the eighteenth-century essay in England, love of home in modern literature.

3. Teach a classic and then a similar modern work, or vice versa, for example, *Treasure Island* and *Mutiny on the Bounty*.

4. In the type organization, use several illustrations of one type to develop the same theme.

The Six Basic Approaches

The basic approaches to a literary selection have been mentioned in Chapter 1: (1) historical, (2) sociopsychological, (3) emotive, (4) didactic, (5) paraphrastic, (6) analytical. Each has its strengths and its weaknesses.

The Historical Approach. The historical approach emphasizes the biography of the writer and the literary and historical events of the age in which he lived. Overemphasis upon this method often makes literature appear secondary to the history and biography, but its skilful use helps the student to see literature as a changing, developing art. Perhaps more important, it helps him to place *himself* in the calendar of man's development.

The Sociopsychological Approach. The purpose of the sociopsychological approach is threefold. The teacher attempts to help students increase their knowledge of people, add to their understanding of the age in which the literature was written, and apply this knowledge and understanding to current living. The sociopsychological approach of necessity overlaps the historical but differs in that flesh is restored to the bones exhumed by the archeologist (although a capable history teacher, it must be added, never presents a parade of skeletons); it differs also in that an attempt is made to compare the flesh and nerves of the there and then with the flesh and nerves of the here and now. The chief weakness of the sociopsychological approach is that it may lead to neglect of some of the qualities we call "literary." Its compensating virtue is that it demonstrates that people were people even in the fourteenth century, and that people are still people; it helps to define people.

The Emotive Approach. The emotive approach has two subdivisions, perhaps not equally praiseworthy. The teacher may say in effect about each literary work, "Isn't this pretty? . . . See how many pretty things the author has named, and how attractively he has pictured them. . . . Isn't that a beautiful simile? . . . How many beautiful similes can you find?" Or he may say in effect, "Literature is fun. It is written to be enjoyed. Let's have some fun with this play." The weakness of the isn't-it-pretty variety of teaching is that it may degenerate into mere gushing; the defect of the this-is-fun variety is that, if overused, it may neglect the mental growth that is essential in education. But the virtue of either emotive approach is that, skilfully employed, it can awaken doubters to a realization that beauty and pleasure may originate outside Hollywood.

The Didactic Approach. The didactic approach, if carried too far, involves a relentless hunt for "morals." "Tennyson's poem teaches us that we can learn great truths even from humble little things like flowers, doesn't it, Wilhelmina?" "No, John, I think that the moral of the 'Ancient Mariner' is much broader than that we should not kill albatrosses." But in favor of the didactic approach, if it is not carried to ridiculous extremes, is the fact that most students enjoy finding a significant idea, a memorable thought capsule, even though they dislike preachiness. The didactic approach actually involves studying the author's purpose and his observations upon life. These observations may or may not be ethical principles or "morals." The search for the author's purpose, together with subsequent discussion of it, leads to improved reading ability and to a thoughtful attitude toward what is read; noting the author's apparent beliefs may sometimes provide assistance in the student's formulation of his own philosophy of life.

The Paraphrastic Approach. In the paraphrastic approach, teacher and class repeat in their own words what the author has said, the intention being to uncover the exact meaning lurking behind each of the author's sentences, paragraphs, or stanzas. The usual objection to paraphrasing is that it involves stating only the approximate meaning, since "saying the same thing in different words" is very seldom saying actually the same thing. Paraphrasing is valuable, however, in the interpretation of abstruse literature; even though the connotations of some of the author's words will elude the paraphraser, he and his classmates may come near enough to the meaning to make the effort worthwhile.

The Analytical Approach. The last approach may be called the analytical, although this term is too restricted. The analytical approach involves examining the ideas, the imagery, the mechanics, and the tone of a piece of writing in order to discover what each contributes to the total impression. The constant aim is to help the student to see the selection as a whole, by assisting him to see the function of each part. Just as a shop teacher discusses a carburetor in terms of its function in making an automobile run, a literature teacher may use the analytical approach to show, for example, that the repeated references to sleep in *Macbeth* serve purposes of characterization and assist in the development of the theme. In other words, the goal of the analytical approach is synthesis through analysis. The weakness of the approach is that in distorted form it becomes what students call "picking to pieces." Its value is that, through its use, students can discover that true literature does not just happen but results from careful planning, selection and rejection of details, and painstaking workmanship. An even greater value is that, if the teacher uses the analytical approach competently, the students improve in their reading ability by learning to distinguish tree from grove in whatever they read.

These six approaches may not seem, on the surface, to be all-inclusive, but a little pondering will show either that other so-called approaches are subdivisions of these six or that they are not truly approaches at all. The use of audiovisual aids, for example, does not constitute an approach, for such aids are tools or vehicles that may be used in any of the six basic approaches. The same comment applies to games and other special devices used by many teachers; they are actually vehicles.

Choosing the Approaches

The constant use of any one of the six approaches is objectionable on at least two counts: loss of interest and failure to show the versatile attractiveness of literature. Obviously, day-after-day repetition may lead to boredom for both students and teacher. If students are given the impression that authors write only that their works may be analyzed, or if they are led to believe that knowing literature means merely knowing literary history, they are likely to say, "Literature! Nobody cares about that stuff except English teachers, and they wouldn't either if they didn't get paid for it!" Not one "pure" approach but, rather, a multiple approach is best in the teaching of literature.

Since literature is many-sided, any one approach will reveal only a few of its attractions. A poem, an essay, or a novel is a castle, located deep in a forest. One person, the historian, explores its surroundings and says, "Now I know all about this castle." The sociopsychologist collars a couple of the inhabitants of the castle, puts them behind glass, and says, "If we observe how these inhabitants act, we shall know not only about this castle called Literature but also about Living." The emoter stands at the edge of the clearing, looks at the castle, and says, "Isn't it just darling, and aren't we having fun!" The moralizer looks up at one of the spires and says, "Atop that shining spire is a gem of wisdom for all of us. Let us ascend and grasp it." The paraphraser walks slowly around the castle, pausing to examine the surface of each stone with a magnifying glass. Upon completing the circuit, he says, "After careful inspection, I conclude that the intention of the builder of this castle was so and so." The analyzer studies the architecture, noting what each wall, each buttress, each arch contributes to the building; then he says, "Now I know all about the castle that is worth knowing." But like Saxe's six blind men, each "prates about an Elephant not one of them has seen." Each has acquired part of the truth about the castle, but a merging of all of the observations would give a much better understanding of the whole edifice.

If, then, no single approach is to be used, what should the teacher do? Should every literary selection be historified, socialized, glorified, moralized, paraphrased, and analyzed? Obviously not. The hourglass would run dry; human patience would not endure; and possibly the selection would become thin and frazzled. But sometimes two or three different approaches may be used with the same work or within the same hour. And all six approaches may be used at different times with different selections. Within a unit, probably only two or three approaches would be used, but, with a new unit, the approaches might well be changed.

The choice of approach should be made in the light of the objectives of the study, the characteristics of the literature, and the knowledge, ability, and interests of the class.

For example, a junior class is to read some of Whitman's poems including "I Hear America Singing," "When I Heard the Learn'd Astronomer," and three or four of the war poems. The teacher's immediate objectives are to interest the students in poems with no rhyme and little rhythm, and to help the students to realize that Whitman's poetry is still alive and vigorous a century after it was written. Most of the members of the class are also enrolled in American history, in which they have been studying the Civil War. The class is slightly above average in ability.

Any one or any combination of the six approaches *could* be used in these circumstances, but some would seem more desirable than others. The poetry is not so difficult as to justify the paraphrastic approach, and only a confirmed emoter or moralizer would be likely to insist that either the emotive or the didactic approach is peculiarly valuable in the study of Whitman. The historical might be employed to a slight extent, in order to relate Whitman to American history, and also, through a brief biographical sketch, to show that Whitman knew what he was writing about. But the sociopsychological and analytical approaches would be best.

Using the sociopsychological approach to (for example) "I Hear America Singing," the teacher and the students could compare the occupations of Whitman's time with those of today, and could discuss the role that singing played—and still plays—in people's lives. Wars, unfortunately, are not yet ended; students can realize that "Come Up from the Fields, Father" is an extremely human and even timely poem. Cer-

tainly there is no better way to show that a poem is alive than to show
that it lives. The analytical approach will help the students to see
that poetry may be poetry even though it does not rhyme and does
not possess a da-dum da-dum da-dum rhythm. The slow-moving,
burdensome opening lines of the "Learn'd Astronomer" give way to
shorter, more direct lines as the narrator leaves the lecture room; the
long lines are appropriate for the Ciceronian periods of the lecturer,
and the short lines equally appropriate for the almost wordless thoughts
of the stargazer. Whitman's words such as "gliding" and "mystical
moist night air," may be shown to be exactly the ones essential to his
purpose. The contrast between the lecture "with much applause" and
the "perfect silence" in which the narrator looks at the stars ties the
poem together. The analytical approach, that is, synthesis through
analysis, will show the students the whole poem, will show them that
it *is* a poem.

A different set of circumstances warrants a different approach.
The teacher of an eighth grade class reading its first play probably
uses the emotive this-is-fun approach. Markham's "Man with the Hoe"
usually demands the sociopsychological approach. Bacon's essays are
clarified by paraphrasing. During the Christmas season, a class profitably and enjoyably expands the "moral" of O. Henry's "Gift of the
Magi." The careful construction of Galsworthy's "Quality" and of
dozens of other selections justifies frequent use of the analytical approach. In Latin American literature, if the teacher wishes to emphasize the basic similarities between Latin Americans and other
Americans, he uses and reuses the sociopsychological approach. Since
Wordsworth's life colored everything he wrote, the historical approach
to his poetry is a promising one. These are only examples and do not
take into consideration specific classes or specific objectives as the
teacher must do when deciding which approach or approaches to use
with a given piece of writing.

The Need for Variety in Teaching Literature

Recently a high school junior said, "I like English this year. Got a
good teacher. She makes it interesting, doesn't kill it off the way some
of 'em do."

"How does she make it interesting?" he was asked.

"Oh, I don't know. I never thought about how she does it. I
imagine it's variety, though. We do lots of different things in class
and read lots of different kinds of things. Other years we just repeated
the same kind of thing over and over—for instance, last year, when

we had to pick all the literature to pieces. It got awful dry, like—well, like just practicing shooting free throws in basketball would be. I like basketball, and I know that free throws are important, but, if there wasn't anything to basketball except standing in the same spot and doing the same thing over and over, I'd quit."

THE IDEA BOX

"LITERACY AND LITERATURE"

James R. Squire finds evidence that Americans' reading habits and tastes are superior to what the voices of doom assert. Good statistical ammunition here. *English Journal*, XLIX (March, 1960), 154.

LITERATURE ISN'T SCIENCE

We must never forget that literature belongs to the humanities and that "humanities" by definition refers to that which is *human*. If the study of literature is permitted to degenerate into analysis and classification, or even into mere explication of pattern and imagery, it becomes less human, more scientific, more mechanical.

WHAT WOULD YOU HAVE DONE?

"Discussions of literature should frequently center around human motivations—why characters acted as they did and in what ways the students would have reacted differently." Dwight L. Burton, "Teaching Literature to Our Youth Today," *English Journal*, XLIV (May, 1955), 274.

"STAGES OF GROWTH IN LITERARY APPRECIATION"

Margaret Early discusses the stages of (1) unconscious enjoyment, when the reader "knows what he likes but doesn't know why"; (2) self-conscious enjoyment, when he "gradually moves away from a simple interest in what happened" and toward interest in character, emotions, and literary interpretation; and (3) conscious delight, when the reader "responds with delight, knows why, chooses discriminately, and relies on his own judgment." "Among the readers who achieve this final stage we do not expect to find many high school students or even many university students." *English Journal*, XLIX (March, 1960), 161.

"PLANNING A LITERATURE PROGRAM FOR THE JUNIOR HIGH SCHOOL"

The Houston supervisor of secondary English, Ruth E. Reeves, details a program intended to bring a junior high student to a point where he can say "what an author meant, and . . . prove that the author meant that, although he did not say exactly that in words and although the student may not agree with him." *English Journal*, XLVIII (Oct., 1959), 374.

"TWO BASIC CONVICTIONS ABOUT TEACHING LITERATURE"

Anthony Tovatt supports these convictions: ". . . with the teacher rests the final responsibility for making choices that are governed by his best assessment of what a particular class needs"; ". . . literature must always be meaningful for the student in the *present* if it is to be meaningful for him in the *future.*" *English Journal*, XLIX (Nov., 1960), 528.

POETS VS. ESSAYISTS VS. NOVELISTS

Malcolm Cowley, in "The Story Teller's Story" (*New Republic*, Dec. 9, 1957, p. 20), asserts that lyric poets are primarily concerned with moods, essayists with social and psychological principles, and novelists with changes that occur in people. Though Cowley's statements are no doubt oversimplifications, they are certainly worth considering with a class.

RAISING STANDARDS

"*To improve, not simply the quality of books studied, but rather the quality of literary experience undergone:* this should be the emphasis when speaking of raising standards. . . . Literary sensitivity and literary maturity cannot be divorced from the individual's rhythm of growth and breadth of experience." Louise M. Rosenblatt, "Literature: The Reader's Role," *English Journal*, XLIX (May, 1960), 304. (Be sure to read the whole of this excellent article.)

UNDERSTANDING A CHARACTER

Select several short speeches of a character, and ask the class to suppose that all they know of the character is found in those speeches. What conclusions about him can they draw? For example, Middleton in Cooper's *The Prairie:* "God in Heaven protect us! There is no time to lose, old man; each instant is a day; let us fly." "Let us mount and ride; is life not worth a struggle?" "We will ride into the centre of the whole tribe, and put their manhood to the test." "This resignation is maddening! But we are men, and we will make a struggle for our lives."

WHAT IS THE STORY ABOUT?

Professor Randall Stewart, of Vanderbilt, recommends asking the apparently simple question "What is the story about?" But the student who starts to recount the events should be stopped. "No, that's the story, but what is it *about?*" With enough prodding, students name the main topic: idealism, justice, etc.

VERIFYING A GENERALIZATION

As a step toward more connected writing about literature, each student is asked to write a general statement about an author, a work, a character, the plot, the setting, the style, or a concept. Then he finds and copies a short passage proving or at least illustrating the generalization, or he draws from the work some other kind of relevant evidence.

"ENGLISH LITERATURE FOR THE NON-COLLEGE-BOUND"

Dorothy Bratton describes techniques that interested her terminal seniors in a somewhat chronological study of English literature. *English Journal,* XLV (Feb., 1956), 84. ✓

JUNIOR GREAT BOOKS

Initiated in Louisville, Kentucky, and spread to schools scattered throughout the country is a Junior Great Books Program in which children from the fifth through the twelfth grades are exposed systematically to the ideas, attitudes, and values of great books. The technique of Socratic dialog is usually stressed. A *Leader's Guide* has been prepared by Dr. John Ford, of Bellarmine College.

A GREAT BOOKS CLUB

1. In Merrill, Michigan, Edgar Madden organized a voluntary Great Books Club, whose student members bought, read, and discussed such books as Anne Frank's *Diary of a Young Girl,* Heyerdahl's *Aku-Aku,* and Hilton's *Lost Horizon.* The account is in "Popularizing Reading in the Small High School," *English Journal,* LII (Jan., 1963), 46.

2. It's a sought-after honor to be invited to join the Great Books Club in Denby High School, Detroit. Only able juniors and seniors who read ten or more books from a selective list may join and take part in the after-school discussions of Homer, Dickens, Emerson, Thoreau, Shaw, etc.

BUILDING AN INTEREST IN BOOKS

✓ 1. Encourage students to start their personal libraries now. In a PTA talk, you might suggest that parents buy books as presents, and give specific criteria for selecting them. Let parents know that you are willing to give advice concerning books suitable for Johnny or Susie.

2. If you are a teacher-librarian, let students help to select new books for the library. They can write for publishers' catalogs, read advertisements and reviews, and discuss the most suitable books to be bought with limited funds.

FOR VARIETY IN TEACHING FICTION

1. If a story is told in the first person, discuss how it would have differed if another character had been telling it.

2. Try a "Mr. Anthony" program, in which two students representing fictional characters who are in conflict in a book present their stories to an arbiter.

NATIONAL BOOK WEEK

Use National Book Week (instituted in 1919) as an occasion for furthering interest in books. A book fair, art, exhibits on a particular theme, talks, contests, and community participation may be included. Cooperate with your librarian and principal on the project.

ON THE ADVANTAGES OF *why* AND *how* QUESTIONS

Who, what, when, and *where* questions about literature are usually superficial. Try stressing *why* and *how* questions to encourage greater understanding and thought. Not "Who is Polonius?" or "What does Polonius tell Laertes?" but "Why is Polonius often considered a foolish person?" or "How does Shakespeare reveal what kind of person Polonius is?"

"AN EXERCISE IN COMPARISON"

Detailed comparisons of two literary treatments of the same topic are often helpful. Richard Stonesifer, for example, has his students compare Sandburg's familiar "Grass" with several paragraphs about grass in Jesse Stuart's *The Year of My Rebirth*. "An Exercise in Comparison," *Exercise Exchange*, IV, No. 3 (Feb., 1957), 8. Socrates A. Lagios does something similar with Hemingway's 1932 one-paragraph version of *The Old Man and the Sea* and the expanded 1952 version. "The Old Man and the Sea, 1932 and 1952," *ibid.*, X, No. 2 (March, 1963), 12.

WHY STUDY THE CLASSICS?

1. "Through the classics we can emphasize the best of nations, and unite pupils with the past to show them that man—no matter of what era or nationality—has always been basically the same, has always sought for himself answers to the great questions that men even today seek—What is life? What is love? What should a man do? What is good? What is bad? Why am I here? Where am I going? How should I live? What is worth living for? What is worth dying for? and the greatest, superseding all others, Who am I?" Clarence Hach, "The Universal in the Classics," *Illinois English Bulletin*, Oct., 1958.

2. The *English Journal*, in 1956–57, ran several lead articles on the appropriateness of certain classics in the modern high school, as follows: Chaucer, October, 1956; Tennyson's "The Idylls of the King," November, 1956; Poe's prose and poetry, December, 1956; George Eliot's *Silas Marner*, January, 1957; Scott's *Ivanhoe* and *Lady of the Lake*, April, 1957. Read these articles for careful, informed discussions. In *Clearing House*, January, 1952, J. E. Logan argues that we should teach poor students "the SPIRIT of the great books instead of spending so much time on analyzing obscure passages."

THE HISTORICAL APPROACH: A DEFENSE

An eloquent plea for the historical approach is Robert E. Spiller's "Is Literary History Obsolete?" (*College English*, XXIV, Feb., 1963). Professor Spiller argues that teachers should "start with the work of art as the analytical critics demand, but move outward to the context. . . . Remember that American literature is the expression of the civilization of the United States, English literature is the voice of the British people, and Greek literature speaks for Athens; but also remember that a good tragedy is a fine drama and a bad one is melodrama whenever or wherever or by whomsoever it was written. The two ways of considering literature are supplementary, not mutually exclusive."

ANECDOTES FOR MOTIVATION

Sometimes an anecdote may provide insight and, hence, motivation. For example, Robert Stevens, of Arizona State College, recommends this anecdote for students who think that any piece of literature not filled with action is dull: A man journeyed to Arizona to see Niagara Falls, but all he found was the Grand Canyon. He was disappointed at first, but, the longer he looked at the canyon, the greater his pleasure. He realized that he was seeing something no less beautiful or exciting than Niagara would have been.

LITERARY "TRIP"

"We begin our English literature course by taking a 'trip' to England. This involves writing letters to travel bureaus, keeping a diary, reading background materials, compiling a bibliography, using reference tools, listening to records such as 'White Cliffs of Dover,' making a scrapbook of pictures and articles from periodicals, and finally presenting a travel talk." (Hortense Finch, Davenport, Iowa.)

CASEBOOKS

Now flooding the market are dozens of "casebooks," usually consisting of collections of essays on a central topic, often literary. Although intended primarily as source material for college composition, many of them are useful on the high school level as guides for teacher and student in literary interpretation. For example, a D. C. Heath and Company series includes Blake, Dickens, George Eliot, *Hamlet*, Pope, *Huckleberry Finn*, Swift, and others. To locate more, refer to *Paperbound Books in Print* or to advertising in *College English*.

TEACHING WORLD LITERATURE

1. Mark Van Doren says that teaching literature of another land is similar to teaching our own, in that what really matters is the work itself—what light does it throw upon the human predicament? He has this specific warning: "It is easier to lecture about the time and place of the book, the culture that produced it, its reputation in its own country or religion, its difference from any Western book—in other words, its unintelligibility." "Great Books—East and West," in *Approaches to Oriental Classics*, William T. DeBary, ed. (New York: Columbia University Press, 1959), p. 7.

2. A rich source of information and ideas is "Teaching World Literature in High School," *Illinois English Bulletin*, Dec., 1961, produced by a committee chaired by Mrs. Enid Olson. Among its many specific suggestions are these if a thematic arrangement is used: For a theme like "Search for a Better World," use parts of Plato's *Republic*, Bacon's *New Atlantis*, More's *Utopia*, Swift's *Gulliver's Travels*, and Hilton's *Lost Horizon*. For satire, try *Til Eulenspiegel*, *Reynard the Fox*, selections from Rabelais and from Voltaire's *Candide*, and Orwell's *Animal Farm*. For "Understanding Others," *Stories of Russian Life* by Chekhov, *Out of Africa* by Isak Dinesen, *My Country and My People* by Lin Yutang.

3. In teaching the literature of foreign countries, stress the similarities of people's basic needs, hopes, and characteristics; the differences are relatively minor and serve to add spice to life. How dull living would be if everyone were alike! Remember that the United Nations' publications avoid terms like "odd," "strange," "exotic," "inferior," and "superior" with respect to people and their customs.

"TEACHING LITERATURE OF THE ORIENT"

Elwood C. Karwand suggests useful titles and sources in literature of China, Japan, Korea, and India. *English Journal*, XLIX (April, 1960), 261.

BRINGING EARLY AMERICAN LITERATURE TO LIFE

1. Early American literature, consisting mainly as it does of political documents, often seems dull to students—and teachers. In Durham, North Carolina, Minnie P. Turner's students enlivened this study by preparing and producing dramatizations. "Living Through Early American Literature," *English Journal*, XLV (Feb., 1956), 92.

2. Gerhard Friedrich suggests content and approaches in "The Teaching of Early American Literature," *English Journal*, XLIX (Sept., 1960), 387.

"ANGLO-SAXONS FOR A NIGHT"

Messmer High School students, in Milwaukee, learned much about Old English literature and social customs in preparing for an "Anglo-Saxon Mead Hall Celebration," an invitational party. Sister Mary Madeleine Sophie, S.S.N.D., tells about it in the February, 1954, *English Journal*, p. 81.

FOR EXTENSIVE BOOK LISTS

Purchase from the NCTE the inexpensive pamphlets "Your Reading" and "Books for You." They contain annotated lists of hundreds of books suitable for junior and senior high schools. Also valuable: various booklists from the American Library Association, Chicago.

INTRODUCING A BOOK

A class that has studied a novel or a play may prepare a short program to introduce the book interestingly to next year's class.

LITERARY MAPS

1. Let students make their own. In American literature, a literary map of their own state or region is stimulating. Several state associations of English teachers have prepared printed maps, most of which may be purchased from the NCTE. A student in Dallas prepared such a good map for *Pilgrim's Progress* that the Dallas English Council printed it and it was distributed nationally by the NCTE.

2. If a literary map of your state exists, its chief value may be to dispel students' notion that famous authors have always lived far away. A literary map of the United States helps students to associate authors and their works with their locales. A literary map of the British Isles is perhaps most

valuable of all, since British place names mean little to American students, many of whom do not even know whether London is in the northern or the southern part of England. A collection of literary maps adds both color and informativeness to a classroom and may be referred to frequently for specific points.

HELPING THE GIFTED

Ruth Reeves, in the November, 1956, *English Journal,* describes in detail in "The Gifted Student in the Literature Class" the following special activities used in Houston schools for superior students of literature: solving problems (e.g., predicting endings), using the imagination (e.g., writing letters to or from characters in books), reading with full understanding, reading extensively, holding panel discussions, dramatizing, conferring on reading or special projects.

SOCIAL IMPLICATIONS OF LITERATURE

1. "I start from the premise that we all work for the betterment of our personal selves. Then I try to show students that their personal selves are bettered when other people are bettered. I utilize Tennyson's 'Flower in the Crannied Wall' to show that all things are interrelated. This is a new idea for most of them. It causes violent discussion and disagreement. When they finally realize clearly that their every action influences society in some way, some of them, at least, tend to adjust their conduct accordingly." (Robert L. Stevens, Flagstaff, Ariz.)

2. "The study of world literature developed a sense of 'one-worldness' in my students." (Mary Hart Finley, Madisonville, Ky.)

3. In *Literature and Social Sensitivity,* a pamphlet available from the NCTE, Walter Loban analyzes students' reactions to stories requiring an understanding of others, and offers suggestions for improving such understanding. In "Teaching Literature for Social Consciousness," *High School Journal,* XXXIX (April, 1956), 370, Beryl M. Parrish names and discusses many selections that help build social awareness.

GROUP WORK

In an increasing number of schools, students spend part of their time working in groups, sometimes on subjects assigned to the groups, sometimes on projects devised by themselves. For one account, see Mary Baloyan's "Enjoying Literature More Through Group Dynamics," *English Journal,* XLIII (Sept., 1954), 308. For another view, see James Squire's "Individualizing the Teaching of Literature," *English Journal,* XLV (Sept., 1956), 314.

LITERATURE IN MODERN LIFE

Spurred by a small bonus in grades, Carrie Stegall's eighth graders each day brought to class literary references they encountered in newspapers, magazines, television, movies, church, conversation, etc. "Who Cares about Literature?" *English Journal,* XLVII (Jan., 1958), 21.

ESTABLISHING A TIME SENSE

Time charts prepared by the class may help to clarify some time relationships. In a beginning study of American literature, for example, a stretch of chalkboard may be reserved. Ask the class to name a few great Americans, including authors, whom they remember. Arrange a chart with the names they suggest, putting each person in the period when he flourished:

1750–1800	1800–1850	1850–1900	1900–1950	Your birth	This year
Washington	Irving	Lincoln	London	Frost	
Franklin	Poe	Whitman	Cather	Steinbeck	
	Hawthorne	Twain	O'Neill	Hemingway	

Add other important names to the chart as study progresses. If space permits, a more elaborate chart may also list major historical events. In English literature a chart may go back to about A.D. 1000; in world literature, still earlier.

HUMANITIES COURSES

1. In Centralia, Illinois, an elective senior honors course, focusing on the tragic tradition in literature, considers the family of man, the Hellenistic contribution, Shakespeare, poetry, novels, and selected art forms. Sarah M. Bush, "A Humanities Course That Works," *English Journal*, XLVIII (April, 1959), 208.

2. In North Haven, Connecticut, the humanities course takes the form of "Cultural History." Seniors study the Hebrews (*Bible*), the Greeks (Plato), the Medieval Age (Dante), the Renaissance (*The Prince*), the Baroque (*Paradise Lost*), the Enlightenment (*Candide*), the Romantic Age (*Werther*), Impressionism (*Lust for Life*), the Modern Age (*The Stranger*). William A. Clark, "The Humanities Program in the High School," *English Journal*, LI (Oct., 1962), 474.

CENSORSHIP

1. All teachers should be familiar with the pamphlet "The Student's Right To Read" (NCTE, 1962), which explores the question of censorship of reading materials and recommends a specific procedure to follow ahead of time and in case censorship strikes.

2. Harry E. Hand recommends a "middle road" approach in selecting literature involving sex. See "Sex in the Modern Novel: A Teaching Problem," *English Journal*, XLVIII (Nov., 1959), 473.

SOURCES OF RECORDINGS

The NCTE sells numerous literary recordings, which members may buy at substantially reduced prices. Commercial catalogs include those of Schwann, available at most record shops, and Libraphone, Inc., Long Branch, New Jersey.

THE SUPERNATURAL IN LITERATURE

Sarah I. Roody uses the literature of the supernatural to expand students' understanding of the role of the imagination and of symbolism in literature. Poe, Dickens, Stevenson, Hawthorne, Burns, Coleridge, and Shakespeare are some of the authors she includes. See "From Bridey Murphy to the Magic Casements," *English Journal*, XLVI (Feb., 1957), 100. In Kirkwood, Missouri, Virginia Durham's seventh graders compare such supermen as Hercules and Atlas with Paul Bunyan and Pecos Bill. Louise Weller argues that mythology has value in vocabulary, reading, geography, art, music, literature. *Clearing House*, XXX (Oct., 1955), 71.

FOLKLORE

"Our American Folk Tradition: A Unit in American Literature," by Charles B. Willard, deals with American folk heroes. *English Journal*, XLII (Feb., 1953), 84.

THE ART OF QUESTIONING

Examples of poor and good questions based on Poe's "The Cask of Amontillado":

Poor: Montresor was a hypocrite, wasn't he?
Good: How do we know that Montresor was a hypocrite?

Poor: What happens at the end of the story?
Good: What word in the second paragraph foreshadows the end of the story?

Poor: Who is Luchresi?
Good: How does Montresor use the name of Luchresi to entice Fortunato into the vaults?

Poor: What were the motto and the coat of arms of the Montresors?
Good: How were the Montresors' motto and coat of arms appropriate?

DEVICES FOR REVIEWING

1. Try a "Stump the Experts" contest, with students asking questions of class "experts" who volunteer.

2. Let students make up questions involving recognition of stories they have read. For example, "In what story are combs, a watch chain, and a woman's beautiful hair significant?"

3. In junior high, try a variation of TV quiz contests, with play money.

4. Original plays may be used to review and clinch the subject matter of a unit.

5. Upperclassmen may learn a little about literary criticism through this method of review: Each student selects three or four of the important selections or authors studied, and in literary histories or critical works he finds two or three pertinent and specific sentences concerning each. He copies these and brings them to class, leaving out the names to be identified. The other students use the clues to name the work or the author.

6. Useful with either under- or upperclassmen is the game of five clues.

Each student prepares several sets of five clues for different works studied by the class. The first four clues are moderately difficult, though reasonable; the fifth is so easy that it almost gives away the answer. Classmates attempt to identify the work. For example, for "To Althea, from Prison": 1. "This building has known more of evil than of good." 2. "Yet sometimes good men and women have unwillingly spent time there." 3. "Once a poet dwelt for a time in this building, and was not especially unhappy there." 4. "In fact, he wrote, 'The birds that wanton in the air/ Know no such liberty.'" 5. "The poet was Richard Lovelace, who wrote a poem to Althea from this building."

7. Students may also construct *who, what, when, where, why,* and *how* questions for their classmates' review, with each student responsible for one or two questions in each category. Caution the class to ask important questions, not minor ones such as "When did Tennyson write 'Ulysses'?"

TESTS ON LITERATURE

1. Try asking some questions that probe for facts, some that require interpretation, some that necessitate relating a selection to other literature or to life.

2. For variety, give occasionally a short open-book test.

3. Help your students to learn to organize their answers.

4. On some occasions, let each student make out a set of final-examination questions that he thinks would be fair. Choose the questions from those submitted.

5. Before a short surprise test, allow two or three minutes for reviewing notes. This procedure encourages careful, methodical notetaking.

6. Dwight Burton suggests these methods of evaluation, in addition to objective and essay tests: observation by the teacher; records of voluntary reading; interest inventories, questionnaires, and attitude scales; performance in book reports or activities following reading; group discussion; small-group reports; and individual reports. *Literature Study in High Schools* (New York: Holt, Rinehart & Winston, Inc., 1960), Chap. 12.

6

TEACHING FICTION
AND DRAMA

THE APPEAL OF FICTION AND DRAMA

"Fiction carries a greater amount of truth in solution than the volume which purports to be all true," said William Makepeace Thackeray. In that sentence the key words are "in solution." A book of non-fiction says, "Here are facts, and facts, and facts." But in fiction the facts and the deeper truths that underlie facts are hidden, in solution. It is possible to read an entire novel, enjoy its story, and almost completely miss the "truth in solution."

The thoughtful reader of good fiction finds insights into human nature that may have eluded him in a score of books devoted to psychology, sociology, or anthropology. Fiction dramatizes; the psychology text merely explains. The dramatizing brings abstract principles to life and, in so doing, entertains through appealing to the universal love of a good story. "It is the first duty of the novelist to let himself be read—anything else that he gives you is a bonus, a trimming, a dessert," as George Saintsbury once wrote. It is to the combination, then, of readable story and underlying significance that the superior novel or short story owes its ability to hold the attention of a reader.

Fiction provides partial answers to age-old questions. "Who am I?" "Why was I born?" "Is life purposeless?" "Are people merely accidental excrescences on a planet that is but an atom in the universe?" Since no author is omniscient, the reader knows that he will never find complete answers to his metaphysical queries. But he knows also that from a clue here and there he can piece together a philosophy of life which will serve him, or that he can amend his existing philosophy.

It may seem contradictory to say that fiction also provides an escape from life, but so it does, and in that way it is closely akin to drama. "The world is too much with us"; it is often too humdrum, too tearful, or too frightening. The little boy escapes it by putting on a space helmet; the little girl bosses her family of dolls, anticipating the time when she can really give orders instead of obeying them; the adult, like Miniver Cheevy, may escape to the Medici or to the bottle, or to the book or to the theater.

The drama, of course, can also reveal truths about life, but it is especially successful (at least on the stage, where it belongs) in carrying us out of ourselves. Studying plays in school is an artificial activity, taking them from their medium, the stage, and exposing them to visual rather than auditory scrutiny. Yet there is still no feasible alternative. And, well taught, they can appeal almost as much to a reader as can a short story or a novel.

SOME OFTEN ASKED QUESTIONS

The answers to these frequent questions are no doubt too arbitrary, but let's risk them; they may provoke worthwhile discussion.

Q.: How should we select the novels we teach?

A.: That depends on your students, your purposes, and the over-all emphasis and plan for your course. In general, choose relatively short and "easy" novels for junior high, longer and "harder" ones for senior high. But ruthlessly reject any novel that you cannot respect for its literary quality. Your time and students' time shouldn't be wasted on trash.

Q.: Does this mean concentrating on *Silas Marner* and *Tale of Two Cities?*

A.: Who said there aren't other novels of high quality? With a junior high class, Annixter's *Swiftwater,* Forbes's *Johnny Tremaine,* Stevenson's *Treasure Island,* or any of a number of other books is fine. With a senior high class, the choice is much wider. Other novels by George Eliot or Charles Dickens may be better for some classes than the traditionally taught ones. See The Idea Box after this chapter for titles of a score of different novels and articles on teaching them. And look again at some of your own favorites to see how suitable they may be for your students.

Q.: Should all members of a class read the same novel?

A.: Not necessarily, though some reading in common is desirable. Sometimes try having three or four groups reading different novels, perhaps relating to the same theme. Use panel discussions, along with class discussions of questions all the novels can illuminate, to bring the class together. With able classes, sometimes each student may read a different book, and report to the class on what it seems to say about certain important questions.

Q.: How long should we spend on a novel?

A.: Seldom more than three or four weeks, often less. Frequently, potential enjoyment has been killed by prolonged study.

Q.: How much should be assigned at a time?

A.: If the novel is not too difficult and if the class is fairly able, it is good to have the whole novel read (with the help of a few guiding questions) before any discussion. But, with long or difficult novels, a series of perhaps ten or fifteen assignments may be necessary. It is important, though, to reserve some time for discussion of the whole novel, so as not to leave an impression that it is only a number of vaguely related episodes.

Q.: What kinds of questions should we ask?

A.: With young or slow students, stress *who* and *what* questions. With older or brighter students, ask *why* and *how* much more often. For example, "Why is Huck usually afraid to approach strangers?" "How does Clemens employ irony in the chapter where Huck dresses as a girl?" (The most overused question in the teaching of fiction and drama is "What happened next?")

Q.: What plays should we teach?

A.: Choose high-quality one-act plays for the junior high years. Move on, as your classes' abilities permit, to Maxwell Anderson, James M. Barrie, Rudolph Besier, John Galsworthy, Oliver Goldsmith, Kaufman and Hart, Sidney Howard, Lindsay and Crouse, Arthur Miller, Eugene O'Neill, Edmond Rostand, William Shakespeare, George Bernard Shaw, Robert E. Sherwood, and Thornton Wilder. With able students, Sophocles, Euripides, Aeschylus, Ibsen, and the like are possible.

Q.: Which plays by Shakespeare?

A.: You'll not confine yourself to Shakespeare, of course. Today

the most popular choice, by far, is _Macbeth._ Others frequently taught
are _Julius Caesar_ (especially with sophomores) and _Hamlet_ (generally seniors). _As You Like It_ and _Merchant of Venice_ seem to be
slipping. _Taming of the Shrew_ and _Twelfth Night_ appear to be gaining favor. A _Midsummer Night's Dream_ is a good opener. _Henry V_
and _Romeo and Juliet_ perhaps deserve more attention, as does _Henry
IV_, Part I.

Q.: How should we teach a play?

A.: Remember that it _is_ a play. Use much reading aloud, as well
as considerable prepared (but not memorized) and some impromptu
dramatization. Help students to visualize the action as stage action,
for example, to be aware of what other persons are doing while one
is speaking. Stress characters and characterization. Discuss theme
and underlying meanings, especially with advanced students. Three
weeks is usually enough time for a full-length play, though the range
may be from a few days to four or five weeks.

Q.: To what extent should composition and the study of language
be related to fiction and drama?

A.: Increasingly, good schools are asking students to write on litera-
ture-oriented topics, especially in the junior and senior years. It would
be unwise, however, to devote _all_ compositions to literature, because
students need to learn to write on other topics also, to be successful
in college and in various occupations. The study of language is often
profitable in connection with literature. Such topics as these may be
considered: How does Shakespeare's language differ from ours and
from Chaucer's? What peculiarities of sentence structure and diction
mark the stories of Hawthorne, Irving, Poe, Cooper, Hemingway, etc.?
How does stage conversation differ from actual conversation?

Q.: Which of the six basic approaches should be used with fiction
and drama?

A.: All, at different times. Often two, three, or more will be used
with a single work. The choice depends upon the needs of the class,
the purpose of the study, and the characteristics of the literature being
studied. Details about the use of each approach follow.

The Historical Approach

The historical approach has greater value for juniors and seniors
than for younger students, although driblets of literary history and
background may well be offered throughout the high school years.
The teacher's intentions in using this approach are to present authors

as human beings and to clarify time relationships—to show that people for many years have been much like us, and to give the students some understanding of the continuity of literature and the relationship between history and literature. Adults who lack such understanding are likely to carry distorted mental pictures like those of a character in Dos Passos' *Manhattan Transfer:* "I always think of history as lithographs in a schoolbook, generals making proclamations, little tiny figures running across fields with their arms spread out, facsimiles of signatures."

Traditionally, the historical approach has meant study of the history of American and English literature. At its worst, this study has degenerated into the memorization of names and dates: "In what year did Dickens die?" "Give the titles and dates of three novels by Thackeray." "What happened in 1881?" At its best, it has brought recognition that each writer is an outgrowth of his age, that his characteristics were shaped by the time in which he lived. The historical approach disagrees with the theme of such a book as *Shakespeare Apart,* whose author declared that Shakespeare was apart from, different from, and superior to, everything else in his age; the historical approach says that Shakespeare and every other author is not *apart* but *a part.*

In other words, the historical approach should relate writers and works to their backgrounds. A few suggestions to show how this may be accomplished are given in the following paragraphs.

Clues from the Literature Itself. Often a piece of writing affords many clues concerning the author and his time. Shakespeare, Goldsmith, Fielding, Austen, Dickens, and Twain come readily to mind as illustrations, but such writers as Chekhov, de Maupassant, Galsworthy, Irving, Poe, Harte, Jewett, and O. Henry also reveal much about themselves and their ages. Discussion that locates in literature the characteristics of an author and of his era is valuable.

Wide Reading Pertaining to the Period. One story or one book should often lead to more reading of similar material. How one book may enrich another is obvious: Bret Harte and Edward Eggleston throw light on Mark Twain and his America; Jane Austen, Charlotte Brontë, George Eliot, and even Thomas Hardy make Dickens' England even more real; the writings of Defoe's contemporaries bring eighteenth-century England alive. Fiction and non-fiction alike serve a useful purpose. The student just introduced to Latin American literature may read about ancient Peru in Victor Von Hagen's *Highway to the Sun* before reading about more recent Peruvians in Thornton Wilder's *Bridge of San Luis Rey.* Books such as Frederick L. Allen's *Only*

Yesterday and *Since Yesterday* and Mark Sullivan's *Our Times* interpret the years of the twentieth century when your students' parents were young and their grandparents not yet old.

Not all students will do the same supplementary reading, of course, but you should use every opportunity to let students share with the class the additional knowledge they have gained as individuals.

A teacher points out another value of studying the background of the age, with special reference to drama:

> The program of study . . . should emphasize . . . the causes for the emergence of particular dramatic forms and theaters during different historical periods. For example, students better perceive the intentions of tragedy once they realize that it has been the product not of disillusioned, depressed cultures, but of societies, like those during the times of Sophocles and Shakespeare, which have prized individual resourcefulness, personal freedom, and human happiness. . . . Similarly the comedy of manners or satirical drama should be seen in the context of the Restoration Period, broken loose from a decade of Puritan austerity, or of the eighteenth century, with its surface proprieties, material concerns, and inflexible class distinctions inviting the playwright's mocking or witty scrutiny.[1]

Biographies. You and your students should know the periodical called *Current Biography,* which ought to be available in your library. So ought the Kunitz and Haycraft books of biography: *American Authors 1600–1900, British Authors of the Nineteenth Century,* and *Twentieth Century Authors.* Referring to these sources should become an established practice for your students.

Some students like to read book-length biographies of favorite authors. Among those rather easy to read are

Meigs, Cornelia L., *Invincible Louisa* [Alcott].
Rumer, Godden, *Hans Christian Andersen.*
Waite, Helen E., *How Do I Love Thee* [E. B. Browning].
Winwar, Frances, *Immortal Lovers* [the Brownings].
Wector, Dixon, *Sam Clemens of Hannibal.*
Graham, Eleanor, *Story of Charles Dickens.*
Hawthorne, Hildegarde, *Youth's Captain* [Emerson].
Hawthorne, Hildegarde, *Romantic Rebel* [Hawthorne].
Peare, Catherine O., *Washington Irving.*
Peare, Catherine O., *Poet of Craigie House* [Longfellow].
Benét, Laura, *Young Edgar Allan Poe.*
Pearson, Hesketh, *Sir Walter Scott.*
White, Anne T., *Will Shakespeare and the Globe Theater.*

[1] Gladys Veidemanis, "Drama in the English Classroom," *English Journal,* LI (Nov., 1962), 544–45.

Visual Aids.   Maps, drawings, pictures, slides, filmstrips, and motion pictures have considerable value in the historical and other approaches. With such a work as *A Tale of Two Cities*, for example, one of the teacher's problems is to re-create for the students a world vastly different from their own. At least a partial solution is offered by the movie version, which familiarizes the students with the clothing, modes of transportation, etc., of the late eighteenth century.

Reports on the Period.   For years, a favorite device of teachers has been to ask students to give reports on the backgrounds of authors and selections.   Such reports are most worthwhile when the topics are carefully chosen and when there is opportunity for the class to ask questions and to provide supplementary details.   The reports need not be limited to history, geography, and famous names but may pertain to music, art, clothing, medicine, superstitions, schools, etc.   A student prepares carefully when he has a topic that interests him and when he knows that he may be subject afterward to questioning by the class.

Newspapers.   By preparing "newspapers" relating to a literary selection, students improve both their ability to write and their understanding of literature.   High school classics such as *Ivanhoe, A Tale of Two Cities*, and *Silas Marner* are especially suitable for journalistic enterprises.

A *Raveloe Gazette* or a *Roman Bugle* may contain news stories, sports stories, editorials, advertisements, etc., related to *Silas Marner* or *Julius Caesar*.   In such an activity, students find it necessary to carry themselves back mentally to an earlier day, which they try to re-create.

Radio and Television Programs.   Some radio and TV programs dramatize famous historical events.   Students should be encouraged to view such broadcasts and to talk about them in class, especially when the programs are related in some way to literature the class has read or is reading.   Some excellent kinescopes and tapes are also available, and have the advantage that they can be shown when they are most appropriate.

In addition, students enjoy preparing a simulated broadcast of their own.   An interesting method of presenting a historical incident with literary overtones is to produce a program called "——H.S. Was There" (using the initials of your high school).   Scenes like that of the tournament in *Ivanhoe* offer fascinating material for these pseudobroadcasts.

Some schools that are given radio time by a local station prepare programs of this kind for actual broadcasts.   Others present the programs before the assembly or before younger classes.

Time Charts. Textbooks often include time charts that show the chronological relationship between history and literature, or among the literatures of different countries. Unless students have these charts called to their attention, and unless they are asked occasional questions that can be answered only by reference to the charts, the students are likely to ignore them.

A few teachers, on the ground that people learn more by doing than by reading, have students prepare their own time charts. Some of these are elaborate, with pictures or drawings to illustrate the chief events.

Correlation and Integration. Most far-reaching of the attempts to relate writers and works to their backgrounds is a course in which literature and history are taught together. The theory is that history throws light on the literature, and vice versa. The strengths of this procedure are that it does demonstrate the fact that literature is inevitably an outgrowth of the social, economic, and political climate and that it does make history seem real—not merely "little tiny figures running across fields with their arms stretched out." One weakness is that it severely limits the literature to be included; since the histories of such countries as India or South Africa or Poland are unlikely to be covered, the literatures of those countries are usually completely ignored. A second weakness is that some important periods of history produced little literature of merit; in America, for instance, the periods of exploration, colonization, and the Revolutionary War are of great significance historically, but not much genuine literature, except for several masterpieces of political writing, appeared until the nineteenth century. A third possible weakness is that the integrated course demands a teacher about equally well prepared in both history and English, and about equally interested in each.

In recent years interest has grown in a "humanities" course, especially in one or more of the upper years of high school. Although definitions of *humanities* are as various as the definers, such a course sometimes includes literature, art, music, and simplified philosophy—all often related in some way to intellectual and social history. Rare is the teacher who is close enough to omniscience to teach such a course, but carefully coordinated team teaching may make it successful.

The Sociopsychological Approach

The historical approach to literature has been and is still widely employed, but on occasion it has been bitterly opposed. One of the more temperate opponents, Louise Rosenblatt, stated years ago in a still valuable book,

> Literary history has its values. . . . Yet those values should not be permitted to obscure the fact that all the student's knowledge about literary history, about authors and periods and literary types, will be so much useless baggage if the student has not been led primarily to seek from literature a vital personal experience.[2]

Miss Rosenblatt and many other teachers would largely dispense with literary history and would substitute for it an approach that would tend to develop the student as a thinking, feeling human being:

> He [the student] must be helped to develop the intellectual and emotional capacities for a happy and socially useful life. He must be given the knowledge, the habits, the flexibility, that will enable him to meet unprecedented and unpredictable problems. He needs to understand himself; he needs to work out harmonious relationships with other people. Above all, he must achieve some philosophy, some inner center from which to view in perspective the shifting society about him; he will influence for good or ill its future development.[3]

> .   .   .   .

> Thus as we attempt to develop the student's appreciation and enjoyment of literature, we must be concerned with furthering a parallel development of his emotional nature and his understanding of life.[4]

The way in which this growth is to be accomplished is suggested in this passage:

> Prolonged contact with literature may result in increased social sensitivity. Through poems and stories and plays, the child becomes aware of the complex personalities of other people. He develops a stronger tendency to notice the reactions of others to his own behavior. He learns imaginatively to "put himself into the place of the other fellow." He becomes better able to foresee the possible repercussions of his own actions in the life of the others. . . . Through literature the individual may develop the habit of sensing the subtle interactions of temperament upon temperament; he may come to understand the needs and aspirations of others; and he may thus make more successful adjustments in his daily relations with them.[5]

This approach is dubbed sociopsychological because, as was shown in Chapter 5, it involves making an attempt to learn about people both

---

[2] Louise M. Rosenblatt, *Literature as Exploration* (New York: Appleton-Century-Crofts, Inc., 1938), p. 72.

[3] *Ibid.*, p. 3.

[4] *Ibid.*, p. 64.

[5] *Ibid.*, pp. 217–18.

as individuals and as members of society. The value of the approach
is clearly indicated in the quotations from Miss Rosenblatt.

Methods of employing it are numerous. Even without any conscious
effort on the part of the teacher, students inevitably learn about human
characteristics when they read. Shakespeare's *Julius Caesar* illustrates
the strength of emotions and the constancy of human conflict; Goldsmith's *She Stoops To Conquer* shows that eighteenth-century ideas of
what is funny differed little from our own; Poe's "Gold Bug" demonstrates human ingenuity; Garland's "Under the Lion's Paw" exemplifies the misuse of power; Tarkington's *Seventeen* paints a kindly
humorous picture of young love; Wilder's *Our Town* shows how people
get along with one another in a small town; Connelly's *The Green
Pastures* portrays a highly humanized religion; and so on. Whether
the teacher wills it or not, students learn many social and psychological
truths from the mere act of reading.

But the teacher can and should expedite the learning of these truths.
He can do so through the kind of assignments he makes, through class
discussion and written work, and through examination questions.

Any assignment, of course, should be carefully planned and carefully made.[6] The assignment mentioned casually at any odd moment
during the hour or shouted at the backs of students leaving the classroom seldom brings good results. Likewise ineffective is the vague
assignment ("Read Act One of *The Merchant of Venice* for tomorrow").
The good assignment provides a reason for doing the work, specific
information concerning what the work is, and suggestions for accomplishing it efficiently. Mimeographed thought questions may
have considerable merit. In many schools, students are given mimeographed materials—including questions and suggested activities—for
an entire unit; the teacher may supplement these in any way that he
wishes. In some schools, students provide their own questions.

Class discussions should never be aimless. Although students may
often bring up points not thought of by the teacher (and should be
encouraged to do so), and although it is sometimes desirable to follow
a worthwhile tangent for some distance, a discussion should generally
center upon certain predetermined points. Often there are no definitely
right and wrong answers to discussion questions, but such questions
nevertheless have value in stimulating thought and in helping students
to see more than one side of controversial issues and to draw conclusions from the evidence.

Discussions involving the sociopsychological approach have as their

[6] This statement is as true when students and teachers plan the work together
as it is when the teacher makes each assignment.

focus the individual characters and the interaction among characters. Here is a list of questions typical of the kind that may profitably be considered at various times by a class. (In the schoolroom, of course, the wording would often need simplification, and examples might sometimes be required.)

Understanding a Character

1. What kind of person is _____? What is your evidence?
2. If _____ were living today, what kind of clothes would he choose? What books, magazines, movies, and music would he like?
3. What is there in _____'s character that makes him disliked (or liked, feared, laughed at, etc.)?
4. What would _____ do if he found himself in (a certain hypothetical situation)? How does this differ from what you would do?
5. Does _____ usually reason out what he should do, or does he merely react emotionally? Your evidence?
6. Is _____ actually true to life, or is he only a stereotype? (Teaching the recognition of stereotyped characters is one of the best services that a teacher can perform, since too many persons think in terms of the "typical" Negro, Jew, Mexican, Frenchman, Russian, etc.)
7. How and why does _____ change in the course of the story?

Understanding the Character's Relation to His Environment

1. Why do you suppose _____ is the kind of person he is? What clues concerning his background are included in the story? How has his background contributed to making him what he is?
2. If _____ had lived in a different century, would he have been the same kind of person?
3. If _____ had lived in such and such a country, how would his thoughts and actions have differed?
4. If _____ had been of the opposite sex, how would his (or her) decisions and actions have varied? Would he (or she) then have faced the same problems?
5. How does _____'s economic status affect his attitudes and his actions?
6. How has _____'s occupation affected his life?
7. Is _____ entirely responsible for what happens to him, or do outside circumstances beyond his control determine his fate?
8. Could this story have happened in the same way in a country with a different form of government?
9. If you were a native of another country and read this story, which customs would seem strange to you?

Understanding the Interaction of Characters

1. Which of these characters would you rather have as a close friend? A parent? A teacher? A brother or sister? An uncle or aunt? A companion on a desert island? A wife or husband? Which would you like least? Why?

able and informative discussion. Sometimes the teacher may be the
chairman; more often, one of the students should be. Usually the
whole class will be involved, but sometimes a student panel may assume responsibility. The teacher does not take the attitude that he
knows all the answers. The author Jesse Stuart, who also has been a
teacher, once wrote,

> [My students] will tell me that I am wrong about this or that. I never
> was able to tell my teacher that he was wrong; he was right, always right,
> definitely right. I listen to the student, often agreeing with him, for I
> know that I have him where I want him when I get him interested. Interest
> will bring about love for any subject. Lazy boys get interested in my classes.
> All of my students get interested. They do not take the textbook for every-
> thing. They go to the library of their own accord and look up material.
> Tho our library is small, it is one of the most widely used in this state.[7]

And some of the fun comes from activities related to the literature.
Generally there should be a choice of activities—not just a required
one.[8] Any activities genuinely in the spirit of the literature may be
adopted, provided that they have intrinsic worth for the students.
One teacher, whose class was reading *As You Like It,* asked each student to be responsible for a contribution that should grow out of the
play and in no way violate its spirit. As a result, two boys made
puppets and used them to act out scenes of the play; a girl with musical
talent composed melodies for the lyrics and sang them; some students
drew scenes on a long scroll, which they unrolled to present the story;
several built model stages; some drew cartoons; and some wrote
imaginary letters from Shakespeare, accounts of a visit to an Elizabethan theater, Elizabethan diaries, character sketches, or short plays of
the same type. Did they learn anything about Shakespeare or drama?
Probably, because they had enjoyed what they associated with Shakespeare and because they had to read carefully in order to make their
contributions.

Plays, as has been remarked, were written to be acted, not to be
studied. Since that is true, one of the best activities to employ when
a play has been assigned is to act it out. Students will take most of
the parts, but the teacher should not be simply a spectator. Before
doing any acting, the class must understand the events and the chief

---

[7] Jesse Stuart, "Teaching the Short Story," *NEA Journal,* XXXII (Jan., 1943),
p. 24.

[8] The author still recalls with chagrin his mistake in requiring all his tenth
graders to make soap carvings related to *Julius Caesar;* the waste of time must
have amounted to at least 200 man-hours, and the waste of soap, it was said,
caused a temporary shortage in the community.

characteristics of each role, just as professional actors must. In *Twelfth Night,* for instance, they must recognize that Orsino is lovesick; Maria, frisky; Andrew, cowardly; Toby, jolly and drunken; the singing fool, plaintive. Parts of the room, one teacher suggests, may be marked— Duke's throne, Olivia's palace, etc.; each of the players may be given a simple identifying token—Olivia, a veil; the clown, a dunce cap; Maria, an apron; Malvolio, a yellow cross-gartering made of crepe paper. Action must accompany reading of the parts—students bow or curtsy to the Duke, crouch behind imaginary trees, and laugh at Malvolio. Undignified? Perhaps, though not unduly. Shakespeare was a great dramatist partially because he knew when to unbend. His serious scenes owe much of their effectiveness to the contrast with the hilarious ones. May not we teachers follow the lead of this author whom we revere?

Another teacher who advocates much acting believes in releasing students' bodies as well as their thoughts—letting wiggling freshmen learn while wiggling, through wiggling. She makes much use of pantomime; in a study of myths, small groups of ninth graders volunteer to pantomime a myth of their choice, with the rest of the class to guess the story. An accelerated group writes plays of its own based upon class reading, and acts them out. Old Testament narratives are also acted: the discovery of baby Moses—a foot ruler in a dictionary; the plague of frogs—with everyone wanting to be a frog. Reviewing in June, someone giggles and says, "We ought to remember that. Don't you remember what we did . . . ?"

What has been said about the emotive approach deserves repeating: Literature can be fun.

The Didactic Approach

You have no doubt seen copies of old-fashioned elementary school readers in which a "moral" was obligingly supplied after each story. From the story the students were supposed to carry away a little lodestone of truth to guide their present or future behavior. Whether they kept the lodestones—who knows?

Even in our day some students expect to learn a moral from everything they find in a literature book. When the author began teaching, a student would sometimes politely remind him that he had neglected to tell the moral. In examinations a few of the students seemed to delight in writing, "From this story I learned that we should always. . . ."

The chief objection to the teacher's habitually stressing moral truths is that sermonizing results. Although educators are interested in graduating students who will be worthy members of a democratic society, and although they realize that knowledge of principles of conduct is essential to such worthy membership, they know that they cannot attain their ends by preaching in a schoolroom. Students do not behave themselves just because an author and a teacher form a coalition for that purpose; they do not become honorable men and women because they memorized morals in English 9A.

Anyhow, morals suggested by different authors may be confusing and contradictory. The moral of one story may be "Look before you leap" and of the next may be "Nothing ventured, nothing gained." Which is the student to believe? And a Saroyan story may not have a discernible moral.

Why, then, bother about the didactic approach at all? The answer is that it has value if it is not so narrowly conceived as it was by our colonial and nineteenth-century pedagogical ancestors. It does not mean merely moralizing; in fact, it often means something entirely different—the study of the purpose of an author. Since a writer is not usually a preacher, he does not as a rule try to instil any ethical principles; if such principles appear, they often do so accidentally or incidentally. But the writer does have a purpose in writing. Clayton Hamilton, in *The Art of Fiction*, defined it thus: "The purpose of fiction is to embody certain truths of human life in a series of imagined facts." These truths *may* be ethical principles, but often are not. According to Hamilton, the scientist collects and arranges facts, the philosopher uses these facts as the basis of a structure of belief, and then the artist takes over.

Accepting the correlated theoretic truths which the scientist and the philosopher have given him, he endows them with an imaginative embodiment perceptible to the senses. He translates them back into concrete terms; he clothes them in invented facts; he makes them imaginatively perceptible to a mind native and indued to actuality; and thus he gives expression to the truth.

The truths capable of illustration by an author are infinite. To suggest only a few, from short stories: Hamlin Garland's "Mrs. Ripley's Trip" shows the emptiness of Midwest rural life in the 1880's; William March's "Fourteen Men from Company K" demonstrates the painful futility of war; Pearl Buck's "The Enemy" declares that American principles become embedded in people who spend even a few years in the United States; Edgar Allan Poe's "Cask of Amontillado" shows to what lengths a warped mind will go for revenge; John Galsworthy's

"Quality" demonstrates that the honest independent workman suffers from the competition of modern mass production. These truths, or opinions, are not morals; they do not necessarily serve as guides to conduct. They are observations that enrich our understanding of life.

In using the didactic approach, the teacher asks three basic questions: "What does the author show about life?" "How does he show it?" "Why do you agree or disagree?" These questions may be supplemented by others, involving a discussion of incidents in the story and similar incidents familiar to the class. The students need not accept the opinion of the author if their own observation indicates that he is or may be wrong. For instance, the students may have known a craftsman who, unlike the high-principled bootmaker in "Quality," did not suffer because he dared to maintain top standards of workmanship in our competitive age. Galsworthy presented the truth as he saw it, but he may have been guilty of a misinterpretation, or he may have failed to allow for numerous exceptions. The teacher must not insist that the class accept every printed opinion as gospel.

The merits of the didactic approach are these: It teaches the student to read between the lines; it makes him think; and it contributes to the building of his personal philosophy of life. An author seldom makes a bald statement of his purpose; the student must put together clues to discover what the purpose is. That is, he must read thoughtfully, and then he must relate what he has read to other bits of his knowledge. From wide reading and much thinking, he eventually formulates a philosophy that may serve him in the manifold decisions of his present and later life.

The Paraphrastic Approach

Particularly useful in the study of difficult selections is the paraphrastic approach, which requires the translation of sentences, paragraphs, or longer passages into language readily comprehensible to the student. This approach has the disadvantage of leading to boredom if it is long continued, but sometimes it is indispensable if the student is to understand.

The employment of the paraphrastic approach may be illustrated by a passage from *The Merchant of Venice*, being taught, let us say, to a sophomore class getting its first taste of Shakespeare.

> SOLANIO. Believe me, sir, had I such venture forth,
> The better part of my affections would
> Be with my hopes abroad. I should be still

> Plucking the grass, to know where sits the wind;
> Peering in maps for ports, and piers, and roads;
> And every object that might make me fear
> Misfortune to my ventures, out of doubt,
> Would make me sad.

In this passage, students' difficulties arise chiefly from failure to understand the situation, the use of words in unfamiliar ways, peculiarities of sentence structure, and incomplete development of one or two thoughts. In other passages, the troubles might come from figures of speech or unknown words or allusions.

Let us examine the quoted passage carefully in order to find the specific sources of difficulty. In the first place, the student must have a picture of the scene. Antonio, Salarino, and Solanio are standing talking on a street in Venice (not floating in a gondola as one student thought). Antonio has complained of being sad—he does not know why—and Salarino and Solanio are suggesting that the reason is that he is worried about his ships at sea. Therefore the "sir" in the first line refers to Antonio; it suggests also the respect that Solanio has for the merchant.

When the student comes to "had I such venture forth," he may be temporarily baffled. For one thing, the clause is not constructed as we usually would construct it today. Recall to the class that we do sometimes say "had I known" or "had I been there" instead of using the "if" construction. "Venture forth" may be misinterpreted for two reasons: The words have meanings strange to us, and "venture" is here a noun and not a verb. Solanio therefore means "if I had such an investment at stake" or, in other words, "if I had so much merchandise at sea."

"The better part of my affections would/Be with my hopes abroad" causes little trouble except for the word "affections," which here refers to thoughts rather than love. Solanio is saying, "Most of my thoughts would be about the ships carrying my fortune." Some students may need to be shown that the sentence does not end with "would." Many students, in both silent and oral reading of poetry, stop completely at the end of each line.

"I should be still/Plucking the grass, to know where sits the wind" contains two difficult words and one undeveloped thought. "Still" has the old meaning of "constantly" or "always"; yet a student may think that "be still" means "be quiet." "Sits" refers to the direction from which the wind blows. But why does Solanio say that he would be plucking grass? Someone will probably realize that he means that he would toss blades of grass into the air in order to discover the direction of the wind.

"Peering in maps for ports, and piers, and roads" goes along with "I should be still." Solanio says that he would be constantly engaged in plucking grass and looking at maps. The word ("roads") does not mean highways, but anchorages.

"And every object that might make me fear/Misfortune to my ventures, out of doubt,/Would make me sad" needs a little elaboration and requires explanation of "out of doubt." Students may suggest objects that might appear to Solanio, who is on dry land, that could make him fear the loss of his ships. "Out of doubt" is misleading until it is translated as "beyond doubt" or "surely."

The entire passage, then, would be paraphrased in some such way as this: "Believe me, Antonio, if I had such a large investment at stake, most of my thoughts would be about the ships that carry my fortune. I should be constantly picking blades of grass and throwing them into the air in order to find the direction of the wind, or examining maps to locate ports, piers, and anchorages where my ships might be. Every sign I happened to observe that would make me fear the loss of my ships would surely make me sad."

This passage has been analyzed at some length because it exemplifies several of the difficulties that students often encounter. Students, because of limited experience, do make absurd misinterpretations. A near-classic example was given by the late C. H. Ward, who told of a boy's explanation of

> The stag at eve had drunk his fill
> Where danced the moon on Monan's rill . . .
> With one brave bound the copse he cleared.

To the boy, a stag is "when a fellow hasn't got any girl." This stag had been drinking one night at Monan's roadhouse (grill?) and, presumably when he was about to be arrested for intoxication, had jumped over the policemen (copse) and escaped.

Impossible? Ward assured us that it was true, and any experienced teacher can cite instances of misconceptions equally absurd but perhaps less funny. The late Reed Smith summarized a study showing that Masefield could not be identified by a single college freshman in a group of 44, that Malvolio was known to 4 of the 44, that Canterbury was known to 23, and the Koran to 14. Euripides was identified as "higher mathematics" or "a river in Asia Minor"; Falstaff was "a musical term"; the Koran was "the ruler of Japan." One of the author's

Introduce sentence constructions for back-ground "what with" construe. etc.

students confidently assumed that Macbeth's command "Be large in mirth" meant the same thing as "Laugh and grow fat."

Variations from normal wording or sentence structure often puzzle students. An intelligent girl once pointed out what she called a "misprint" in a British story: "The time was come"; to her, "was come" seemed an error. Hawthorne's "what with telling the news . . . Dominicus was delayed" baffles a youngster who has not previously encountered the "what with" construction. Some students may become lost in a sentence no more complicated than this from Bret Harte:

Of their married felicity but little is known, perhaps for the reason that Tennessee, then living with his partner, one day took occasion to say something to the bride on his own account, at which, it is said, she smiled not unkindly and chastely retreated—this time as far as Maryville, where Tennessee followed her.

Often an entire passage does not need paraphrasing, but only a word or two requires explanation. It is best if a student can supply the information; otherwise the teacher should try to do so. If the teacher cannot (and he may take comfort from the fact that there are numerous passages in Shakespeare and other authors concerning which scholars disagree), he, of course, should avoid bluffing, although he may hazard an intelligent guess. But his guesses need not be numerous, if he foresees students' probable difficulties and decides how to attack them.

The paraphrastic approach is not necessarily dull, although it is more susceptible to dullness than any other. If it is used only when needed, and if the presentation is enlivened with illustrations, this approach may be as interesting as its results are valuable.

The Analytical Approach

The analytical approach, often in combination with the sociopsychological, has in recent years become by far the most widely used, especially with above-average students in the upper secondary years. This tendency no doubt reflects the collegiate trend away from the historical approach and toward the kind of literary analysis advocated and demonstrated by the misnamed "new critics," who say that only the literary work itself is significant, not the circumstances of its composition.

The analytical approach is the most "literary" of all. It entails an analysis of literary characteristics, an examination of the ways in which an author achieves his effects. It involves investigation of the inter-

relationships among (1) setting, (2) style, (3) characterization, and
(4) plot. It also involves study of the effect of each of these upon
theme, and some consideration of other literary qualities such as irony,
paradox, and voice.

Setting. The setting of most modern fiction and drama usually is a
determining factor in theme, characterization, and plot. This was not
always true; in the "once upon a time" stories the setting is almost
anywhere and anytime. Today's authors realize, as Clayton Hamilton
reminds us, "that any given story can happen only in a given set of
circumstances, and that if the setting be changed, the action must be
altered and the characters be differently drawn." The stories in Kipling's *Plain Tales from the Hills,* for example, would be considerably
different if the setting were not India in Queen Victoria's time; tales
about China, or even tales about India as it was in Queen Anne's
time, would of necessity differ markedly from those that Kipling has
given us.

Setting is a matter not only of place but also of time and "moral
environment," to use a phrase of Burges Johnson. A story about
Chicago in 1950 differs from one about Chicago in 1920, and differs
still more from a story about Fort Dearborn in 1820. Moral environment similarly varies with both place and time. For example, in some
lands it is still immoral for a woman to leave her house without wearing a veil; in the United States our attitudes toward such matters as
divorce, dress, and woman suffrage are considerably different from
those of 100 or even 50 years ago.

Some questions that will make your students more aware of the
significance of environment have been listed on pages 162–163. Here
the special concern is with teaching the literary techniques employed
in presenting the setting.

Show Setting:
1. cataloging
2. suggesting

A writer of fiction may show the setting in either of two basic ways:
cataloging and suggesting. Sir Walter Scott and many of his contemporaries illustrate the catalog method, writing long paragraphs
of description, offering details and more details, describing almost
every tree in the grove. Modern writers sometimes use the catalog
technique, but tend more often to choose only a few representative
details that suggest the rest of the picture. They have adapted the
poet's technique of selecting and pruning. Thus, in Marjorie Kinnan
Rawlings' short story "A Crop of Beans," in which the setting has importance as a motivation of the action, a few phrases and sentences
like these set the stage: "live oaks and palmettos," "blinding blue of
the Florida afternoon," "swaying palms, precise and formal against a
turquoise sky," " 'Floridy don't make none o' her own troubles,' she

grumbled. 'They all comes in from some'eres else. Wind from the south an' cold from Texas,' " "a small melodeon . . . the sole ornament of the main room."

The dramatist's problem is different. Since plays are to be acted, not read, the spectators see the setting, or at least part of it, and do not need a description. Therefore, the dramatist merely gives some technical details concerning placement of exits and furnishings. Occasionally he may suggest or call special attention to a detail, or to something not visible on the stage, but primarily he presents only brief stage directions.

Teacher and class should now and then talk about points like those just discussed. Students may note the method that an author employs to portray the setting, and discuss the reason for including some details and excluding others. Often elements of the setting are tied closely to the action and the characters, as in the play *Emperor Jones* or in the novels *Return of the Native* or *Notre Dame*. Since this is true, questions that may be asked frequently are "What does [a certain part of the setting] show about [a certain character]?" and "What effect does [the setting, or part of it] have upon [a character]?"

When the class is occupied with a play, diagrams or pictures of the stage are often helpful. In a presentation before the class, a few lettered labels and some suggestions of furnishings are useful. Settings of Shakespearean plays, with their many changes of scene, require more visualization than do most others, although Shakespeare helped by letting his characters comment upon their surroundings. Thus King Duncan, before Macbeth's castle, remarks about the "pleasant seat" and the "sweet" and "nimble" air, while Banquo observes the "jutty, frieze, buttress [and] coign of vantage"; in *As You Like It,* much of Act II, Scene 1 serves to paint the Forest of Arden.

In summary, teacher and class will try to visualize the setting of each novel and play, and will try to decide why the author uses that setting, how he presents it, and what effect it has upon the characters or the action.

Style. Matters of style should be touched rather lightly in the high school years. Unlike setting, style is elusive and abstract. Even scholars and critics have failed to reach agreement on its definition. Such ingredients as choice and arrangement of words, sentence structure and sentence length, and tricks of expression are commonly recognized, but over and above all these is the mysterious element of personality that led Buffon to state, "*Le style est de l'homme même.*"

Some of the less subtle distinctions in authors' styles even an average class can discover. They can quickly become aware that Hemingway does not write like Poe, that Somerset Maugham's quietly dramatic sentences have no resemblance to Dorothy Parker's barbs, that O'Neill's characters do not talk like Goldsmith's, that Barrie's stage directions are distinguishable from Maxwell Anderson's. Further, they can learn to identify some of the causes of disparity, such things as Hemingway's terse tough-man-to-tough-man sentences, Poe's love of polysyllables and his use of mood-creating words, and Barrie's amiable chitchat.

An average class sometimes may profitably analyze the ways in which an author achieves a particular effect. They read, perhaps, Chekhov's "Grief," the account of the driver of a horsedrawn cab who find no one to listen to his lamentations over the death of his son. They read the concluding sentence: "Iona's feelings are too much for him, and he tells the little horse the whole story." They note the simplicity of that sentence, its shortness, its restraint; they see that a less competent author would have gone on and spoiled the effect. They wonder about the use of the present tense throughout the story, and comment upon how the use of that tense makes the action seem nearer and more real. Little things, they discover, make the difference between a good story and a great one—the selection of a word, the sound of a sentence, the emotional burden of a phrase, the color of a clause. A useful teaching device is to translate a "just right" sentence into a drab, feebly wandering one, or to substitute an abstract noun or a sickly verb for a vigorous word, and have the students note the loss; the power of the original is made apparent by the contrast.

Capable students may be led further. These are the students who like to write or who want to know the "how" of everything. Their curiosity is high. Use them as leaders of class discussions on matters of style. Ask them pointed questions about why an author chooses a particular word, why he uses short sentences in one place and long ones in another, how he builds up a feeling of tension or hatred or longing. These students will welcome such questions and dig deep for the answers.

Characterization.   Now let us turn to the matter of characterization. When one has finished reading a story or a play, how does one know that a character is noble, cranky, whimsical, fickle, or something else? One has learned from the author's use of one or more of the nine basic methods of revealing a character:

1. Telling what kind of person he is
2. Describing the person, his clothing, and his environment
3. Showing his actions

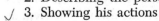

4. Letting him talk
5. Relating his thoughts
6. Showing how other people talk to him
7. Showing what other people say about him
8. Showing how other people react because of him
9. Showing how he reacts to others

Most elementary of these methods is the first. An unskilled writer says, "Fred was a grouchy old man," but an experienced author knows that showing is superior to telling and therefore uses one of the other devices.[9] Dickens frequently employs the second method, taking his reader down the streets and alleys of London to a black old gateway, or into a vast hall with massive but cobweb-covered furniture; there he meets someone whose person and accouterments Dickens sweeps before the reader's eyes by giving a single impression and then filling in details. Almost inevitably, authors employ the third and fourth methods to reveal character. For example, when Huck Finn disguises himself as a girl, Mrs. Judith Loftus readily penetrates his incognito but, thinking he is a runaway apprentice, aids rather than hinders his flight. These actions reveal both her quick intelligence and her kindliness. Further, almost every sentence that she speaks tells something about her. She says, "You do a girl tolerable poor, but you might fool men, maybe," and the reader knows from that one sentence that she is blunt, good-natured, not well educated, and slightly contemptuous of masculine acumen.

Since what a person thinks is often more significant than what he says, authors often take the reader inside characters' minds. A Shakespearean soliloquy does that, and so does O'Neill's device in *Strange Interlude*, where the characters not only talk to one another but also speak their true thoughts for the audience to hear. Novelists, of course, when they use the omniscient point of view, often recount what their characters are thinking. The last four methods of revealing character may be illustrated in almost any story or play.

In classroom consideration of characters, the analytical and the sociopsychological approaches are likely to overlap. The distinction, though, is that the sociopsychological approach emphasizes human beings and their interrelationships, whereas the analytical stresses the author's technique. Very desirable is a combination of the ap-

[9] For a detailed treatment of authors' methods of presenting characters and point of view, see Wayne Booth's *The Rhetoric of Fiction* (University of Chicago Press, 1961), one of the most scholarly treatments of the role of the author in the writing of fiction. Booth defends "telling" more vigorously than do most fiction theorists.

proaches, founded upon two basic questions: "What kind of person is____?" and "How do we know that he is?"

Plot. In a story or play, the characters are usually involved in a series of events called the "action" or "plot." (Some modern short stories, of course, are virtually plotless.) A plot is a more or less artificial tying together of incidents involving the same character or characters and leading to a solution of a conflict. The artificiality arises from the fact that the loose ends, common in real life, are concealed in the story, and only those persons and events essential to bringing the story to a conclusion are retained. In life, much conversation and many actions are aimless, but in a play or story the author generally reports only conversation and incidents that have a bearing upon the outcome; thus Shakespeare time after time plunges into the heart of a scene, ignoring the "Hello, nice weather we're having," etc. that would be typical of actuality. In life, dozens of big and little things happen every day, but, in a story, the author selects only those that move the narrative forward.

The easiest narrative structural unit to make clear to a class is the short story. Unaided, students will say only that the plot of a story tells what happens; prompted further, they will add that it involves moving forward in time. In your classes, you may try to show them that an author does more than move his characters forward, that he presents a series of closely linked episodes. Each episode is related to each other episode. Thus, in the familiar "boy meets girl" story, the very first episode generally suggests why he may love her, why he may lose her, why he may win her. The four episodes in such a story may be diagramed as in Fig. 7. Each part of the story is related to every

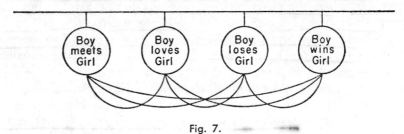

Fig. 7.

other part. Each incident grows naturally out of the preceding incidents. Each one, after the first, happens because of one or more of the others.

"We frequently speak of 'weaving' a plot," you remind the class. "By looking at the lower part of the diagram, you can begin to see what is meant by that expression; some of the lines cross one another, forming the beginning of a web. Naturally, the more episodes we have, the more interwoven the plot will be. That is, each episode introduces some complication and makes the plot more intricate, like this:" (and you show the diagram in Fig. 8).

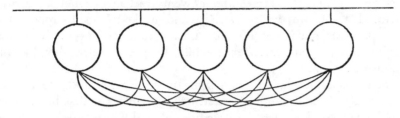

Fig. 8.

"The important thing to remember is that each part of the well-plotted story is related to every other part, is either the cause or the effect of one or more of the other parts. There are no unrelated segments. Each complication is present—at least potentially present—from the beginning, and each is solved at the end."

The diagrams of most stories are fairly easily evolved by a class (perhaps not by individuals) on the principles just explained. The value, of course, lies not in the diagraming but in the understanding of story technique and character relationships that results.

Nine short stories out of ten are constructed similarly. So are most novels and dramas, although in these the episodes, and hence the complications of the web, are more numerous, and digressions more frequent. Nevertheless, once the students have grasped the fundamental principles of plot, they have little difficulty in seeing how a novel or play, as well as a short story, is put together.

Understanding of principles of construction can add tremendously to anyone's enjoyment. Although the class should not be made to analyze painstakingly the plot of every story or play assigned, enough such analyses should be made to help the students see that stories do not "happen" but are built by an author who cleverly weaves together a number of essential and related episodes.

Setting, style, characterization, plot, and the relationship of each of these to the central idea—all of these are involved in the analytical approach. Like any of the other approaches, it is good if not overdone, if not allowed to degenerate into "picking to pieces." Just as a visit to an automotive assembly line gives one more complete knowledge of automobiles, and perhaps more interest in them, so an investigation of the assembly technique used by an author makes a story or a play more understandable and more enjoyable.

COMBINING THE APPROACHES [10]

A small boy had a bow and arrow—one arrow. He stood in the back yard, aimed at a target about twenty feet away, shot his arrow, retrieved it, smoothed the feathers, and walked back to repeat the process. Over and over he aimed, shot, and retrieved. It was a monotonous procedure. After a while, he got tired of shooting his one arrow.

Later, his father bought him some more arrows, and the two of them rigged up more targets, constructed just like the first but requiring the boy to shoot part of the time at a different angle. A little variety thus being added to his archery practice, his enjoyment was renewed. And, since he spent less time in retracing his steps and in refeathering his one arrow, his marksmanship improved more rapidly than before.

The scene was a classroom. "In what year was Robert Browning born, James?" "What do you know about his school days, Mildred?" "What was the title of his first important poem, Pauline? *You* should certainly know that." "Name three other long poems by Browning, Wilbur." "Where was he buried, Marcella?" "We shall now hear George's report on the years the Brownings spent in Italy."

The scene was another classroom. The class was studying *Julius Caesar.* The teacher said, "Ronald, read the first two speeches in this scene aloud and tell us what they mean." Then, "Lucille, read the next two speeches and tell us the meaning." So the hour crawled by. The following week the class was studying an essay. "Daniel, read the first two sentences and tell us what they mean."

One-arrow teachers they apparently were. They aimed, shot, retrieved, smoothed the feathers, and aimed again. Over and over their classes did the same thing, relieving their boredom only by horseplay or by raucous laughter at something not really funny.

The plea in this chapter has been that every teacher of English should have and use more than one arrow. The literature teacher is hunting big game for his class. Not tigers or elephants, but pleasure, and understanding of literature as a key to life, and understanding of literature as an influence upon life. No tiger was ever so large or so formidable or so much worth capturing as any one of these quarries.

---

[10] The following paragraphs are adapted from the author's article, "The Multiple Approach in Teaching Literature," in *They Will Read Literature,* NCTE, 1955.

Six arrows have been described. One should be used now, another tomorrow. Two or even three may be used almost concurrently. But no one arrow should be worn out. The teacher with six arrows is much more likely to hit the target than the teacher with only one.

THE IDEA BOX

SIDEWALK DRAMA

"Students can become conscious of sidewalk drama and even classroom drama in their own everyday lives, and make comparisons with that which they read." (Alma W. Roberts, Abbeville, Ala.)

SHAKESPEARE ISN'T DEAD

Teacher and class may gather from current magazines and newspapers allusions to Shakespeare or his characters.

RE-CREATING THE PAST THROUGH DRAMA

1. In the study of such a play as *Julius Caesar,* let the students imagine that they are twentieth-century people carried back to ancient Rome by a time machine; they write letters to their twentieth-century friends.

2. Prepare news stories or TV programs describing the events of the play.

WRITING STAGE DIRECTIONS

Students may add to their understanding of a Shakespearean play if they write some detailed—perhaps Barrie-like—stage directions for it.

THINKING ABOUT STAGING

Students may consider how a particular scene, or a whole play, could be most effectively staged. "This has good results in stimulating what otherwise may be dormant imaginations." (Harold R. Hansen, Menomonie, Wis.)

GROUP WORK WITH SHAKESPEARE

Gwen Buck divides her Illinois students into groups of four. Each group is responsible for detailed characterization of one person in the play, with passages to be cited as evidence. One member presents the findings to the class, for its reactions.

"SHAKESPEARE WITHOUT PAIN"

"When I am especially eager to have the class read a Shakespearean play, I speak skeptically about their doing so. I argue that the plots are exceedingly melodramatic, involving murder, insanity, suicide, and adultery. I point out that the stories are unoriginal and that Shakespeare's characters are often deplorably vulgar in speech," says E. M. Holmes, *English Journal,* XLII (May, 1953), 270.

BEFORE YOU TEACH *Macbeth*

Read these *English Journal* articles, preferably in this order: Elizabeth Arnold, "No More Hurly-Burly," LXI (Jan., 1952), 37; Herman O. Makey, "In the Literature Class," XXXIX (Sept., 1950), 360; Mary N. Gallman, "Macbeth Lives Again," XLI (Sept., 1952), 370.

GENERAL STUDENTS LIKE *Hamlet*

So says Priscilla Zink in "*Hamlet*—Caviar to the Generals," *English Journal*, XLIV (Jan., 1955), 37. The secret: Review constantly the plot of the play; emphasize action; never labor a point, but bring in frequent brief references to such important items as Hamlet's tendency to talk rather than to act; have written work on topics that each student can handle creditably. In the November, 1956, *English Journal*, William Fidone tells of the more sophisticated treatment of this play by above-average students, in his article "An Above-Average Class Studies *Hamlet*."

SHAKESPEARE AND MODERN EVENTS

In studying *Julius Caesar*, the students of Elizabeth Deur, in Kalamazoo, Michigan, cut out political cartoons from newspapers and find appropriate Shakespearean lines as captions.

INTRODUCING SHAKESPEARE

Some teachers employ recordings to introduce Shakespeare. Excellent is the Caedmon record "Shakespeare: Soul of an Age," with Sir Michael Redgrave and Sir Ralph Richardson. It includes biographical information and short selections from about a dozen plays.

WHO'S WHO IN SHAKESPEARE

"Who's who" questions may serve as the basis for either a game or a quick quiz, and may help students to recall essential facts. For example, ask who is referred to in "He doth bestride the narrow world like a Colossus" and "Yond _____ has a lean and hungry look;/He thinks too much; such men are dangerous," from Act I of *Julius Caesar*.

HOW WOULD A JOURNALIST TELL IT?

Occasionally a scene from Shakespeare (or some other author) may be rewritten by students in the style of a modern journalist. Examples would be the assassination of Caesar or Macbeth's victories (Act I). Comparing the original with the journalistic account, even though the news story is well done, may help students to understand and appreciate the original writer's artistry.

GETTING THE MEANING

Joseph C. Gainsburg, in "Play-reading with Dynamic Meaning," *English Journal*, XLI (Oct., 1952), 403, illustrates clearly how students can be helped to understand the between-the-lines meaning in such a play as *Elizabeth the Queen*.

Our Town

For an excellent critical analysis of this popular play, see Arthur H. Ballet's "In Our Living and in Our Dying," *English Journal*, XLV (May, 1956), 243.

A SEMESTER OF DRAMA

Washburn High School, Minneapolis, is among those schools offering a semester course in drama. Students study three modern plays and six by Shakespeare (*Macbeth, Hamlet, Romeo and Juliet, As You Like It, Twelfth Night,* and *Taming of the Shrew*). Recordings, films, a Shakespearean bulletin board, paraphrasing, memorizing, dramatizing, a matinee at a local university, and a term paper are included. For details, see Mary Alice Wells, "Appreciation Follows Understanding," *NEA Journal*, November, 1958.

"TEACHING SHORT STORIES"

It is good, for motivation, to have some before-reading discussion of a question related to the story. For instance, for "The Necklace": "What would you do if you had borrowed some expensive bit of jewelry to wear to a party and had lost it?" Other excellent suggestions are in Bernice Freeman's article, *English Journal*, XLIV (May, 1955), 284.

OPPOSING FORCES

In the study of a play or novel, analysis of the forces working for and against the protagonist—perhaps writing them in parallel columns—adds to the understanding. (Norman, Okla., High School.)

"TEACHING A NOVEL"

Marion Sheridan's article in *They Will Read Literature* (a portfolio available from the NCTE) gives almost a play-by-play account of teaching *Return of the Native.* "How To Read Fiction," by author Howard Pease, in the same portfolio, is addressed to students and develops clearly the idea of theme and symbolism in fiction—hunting for a "secret cargo," as Pease calls it.

ELIMINATING STEREOTYPES

Have students read a story with a stereotyped Negro, Swede, or Englishman, and then contrast this inferior presentation with a story containing a true-to-life person from the same racial or national group.

EXAMPLES OF FICTIONAL SCENES THAT MAY BE DRAMATIZED

1. Godfrey Cass and Silas Marner discuss the custody of Eppie.
2. Long John Silver is given the Black Spot.
3. Trial of Charles Darnay.

PUPPETS

English and art may sometimes be combined in junior high school classes.

Students make puppets and use them to present original plays or plays studied in class.

NOVELS FOR THE COLLEGE-BOUND

John W. Ragle offers his Vermont college-bound seniors an eight-week unit involving (1) two weeks of lectures on the history of novels, (2) four weeks of study of one or two influential novelists, (3) practice in taking and using lecture and reading notes, (4) writing a research paper, and (5) an oral report by each student. Good preparation for the rigors of college! *English Journal*, XLIII (Nov., 1954), 426.

BRANCHING OUT FROM THE NOVEL

One book, as has been said, should lead to another. After reading *Silas Marner*, one group of students read and reported on other novels in which a character undergoes a significant change. *Main Street* might lead to further reading about the small town. There are many other possibilities of this sort.

IF THE COMIC BOOKS BOTHER YOU

1. Don't give them the sweetness of forbidden fruit by banning or confiscating them. Some teachers have been able to use comics as stepping-stones to *Treasure Island, Sherlock Holmes, Paul Bunyan*, etc.

2. Beryl Sullivan's junior high school students read and reported on whatever they wished for a week. Many read comics. The comic stories were so similar that even their avid followers noticed their monotony.

3. In class, let students examine a number of comic books from the point of view of their truth to life.

LEEWAY IN READING

In "Fostering Interest in Reading," Lisbeth S. Jensen argues in favor of having students read widely in literature of their ancestral nations, in biography, in fiction, and in the fields of their special interests. *English Journal*, XLII (Oct., 1953), 367.

CHOOSING A NOVEL FOR CLASS READING

If enough copies are available, you may use the "loaded deck" method. Name several worthy novels, tell a little about each, and let the class choose the one they would like to read.

THE JUNIOR NOVEL

One of the phenomena of the past few decades has been the tremendous increase in fiction written especially for young people. Librarian Emma L. Patterson tells the story and analyzes the results in "The Junior Novels and How They Grew," *English Journal*, XLV (Oct., 1956), 381. Frank Jennings, though, thinks the average quality is too low. "Literature for Adolescents— Pap or Protein?," *English Journal*, XLV (Dec., 1956), 526. G. R. Carlsen, in "The Dimensions of Literature," *English Journal*, XLI (Apr., 1952), 179, suggests a yardstick for measurement of literary quality: literary merit, literary form, and content. Dorothy Petitt, in "A Search for Self-definition,"

English Journal, XLIX (Dec., 1960), 616, lists and describes twenty-five especially well-written books for adolescents.

IF YOU TEACH *Huckleberry Finn*

Despite the thousands of pages of commentary, the best statement made about *Huckleberry Finn* is still Mark Twain's own: "A book of mine in which a sound mind and a deformed conscience come into conflict and conscience loses." The novel may well be taught from that point of view, with emphasis upon Huck's "sound mind" and the way that his upbringing ("deformed conscience") has affected his thinking.

IF YOU WERE AN ARTIST

Sometimes ask students to imagine that they are artists employed by a magazine to illustrate stories or poems. Have them describe the picture they would draw or paint to illustrate an especially significant part of a literary work read by the class.

UNDERSTANDING FLASHBACKS

In dealing with a story using flashbacks, ask the students to rearrange the events, putting them into strict chronological order. Then discuss what was probably the author's reason for altering this sequence and what the story gained or lost as a result.

IF YOU TEACH *Silas Marner*

These ideas for enlivening are suggested in *English Journal* articles: (1) Have students prepare a map of Raveloe, using hints in the novel. (XLI, Jan., 1952, 41.) (2) Have them write the letters mentioned in Chapters 1, 3, and 10 of *Silas Marner.* (XLII, Nov., 1953, 463.) (3) Let students lead the discussion. (XL, June, 1951, 338). (4) Stage the trial for the custody of Eppie. (XXXIX, Oct., 1950, 452.)

AUDIO-VISUAL AIDS

To keep up with developments in audio-visual aids, send to the Bureau of Educational Research, The Ohio State University, Columbus, Ohio, and ask to have your name put on the mailing list for *The News Letter.* There will be a nominal charge.

WORTH ASKING YOURSELF WHEN YOU MAKE AN ASSIGNMENT

1. Will the work arouse wholesome curiosity?
2. Will it build rather than kill interest?
3. Will it help students to think?
4. Will it improve expression?
5. Will it teach cooperation and promote an interest in others?

MOTION PICTURES

1. Help students to set up criteria for judging movies. Authenticity, quality of acting, moral tone, propaganda values, informational values, plot, theme, setting, and characterization are among the points that might be included. (Lois Roquemore, Las Vegas, N.M.)

2. The teacher should help students to recognize movie stereotypes, propaganda, glittering generalities, and misrepresentation of social facts, for example, suggestions that winning the girl means lasting happiness or that the good life is the acquisitive life or that catching the criminal solves the crime problem.

3. The students establish standards for judging movies. Then, after having seen particular films, they indicate their quality by a traffic light display: red if the movie is poor, yellow if mediocre,,and green if good.

4. Try to preview each film shown in class. Also, do a little preteaching to point out certain things for which to look. A long movie may be presented in instalments. After showing, discuss such points as casting, acting, directing, theme, plot, significance, dialog, balance, music.

MORE ABOUT TEACHING SPECIFIC NOVELS,
SHORT STORIES, AND PLAYS

The following articles offer helpful teaching suggestions or literary analyses useful in the classroom. Except for those marked *CE* (*College English*), all are in the *English Journal*.

A Christmas Carol. Wrigg, William, "Dickens' Message of Christmas," XLVIII (Dec., 1959), 537.

The Crucible. Josephs, Lois, "One Approach to the Puritans," L (March, 1961), 183.

Cry, the Beloved Country. Marcus, Fred H., "*Cry, the Beloved Country* and *Strange Fruit:* Exploring Man's Inhumanity to Man," LI (Dec., 1962), 609.

Darkness at Noon. Fioravanti, Joseph A., "*Darkness at Noon* for Juniors," L (Sept., 1961), 416.

Ethan Frome. Bernard, Kenneth, "Imagery and Symbolism in *Ethan Frome*," CE, XXIII (Dec., 1961), 178.

A Farewell to Arms. Marcus, Fred H., "*A Farewell to Arms:* The Impact of Irony and the Irrational," LI (Nov., 1962), 527.

Gilbert and Sullivan. Fletcher, Paul H., "A Unit on Gilbert and Sullivan," LI (March, 1962), 203.

Great Expectations. Lindberg, John, "Conscience and Injustice in *Great Expectations*," CE, XXIII (Nov., 1961), 118.

Partlow, Robert B., Jr., "Point of View in *Great Expectations*," CE, XXIII (Nov., 1961), 122.

Stange, G. R., "Expectations Well Lost," CE, XVI (Oct., 1954), 9.

Huckleberry Finn. Cummings, Sherwood, "What's in *Huckleberry Finn?*" L (Jan., 1961), 1.

Gibb, Orson, "The Best Authorities," CE, XXII (Dec., 1960), 178.

Lane, Lauriat, Jr., "Why *Huckleberry Finn* Is a Great World Novel," CE, XVII (Oct., 1955), 1.

O'Connor, William Van, "Why *Huckleberry Finn* Is Not the Great American Novel," CE, XVII (Oct., 1955), 6.

Rubinstein, G. M., "The Moral Structure of *Huckleberry Finn*," CE, XVIII (Nov., 1956), 72.

Solomon, Eric, "*Huckleberry Finn* Once More," CE, XXII (Dec., 1960), 172.

Julius Caesar. Dean, Leonard F., "*Julius Caesar* and Modern Criticism," L (Oct., 1961), 451.

    Foster, Guy L., "Teaching *Julius Caesar* to Slow Learners," XLIX (Dec., 1960), 632.

    Harrison, G. B., "The Teaching of Shakespeare," LII (Sept., 1963), 411.

    Ryerson, Edward, "*Julius Caesar* Once Again," XLVII (Jan., 1958), 1.

"The Leader of the People." Grommon, Alfred, "Who *Is* 'The Leader of the People'?" XLVIII (Nov., 1958), 449.

Lord, Jim. Hunt, Kellogg, "*Lord Jim* and *The Return of the Native:* A Contrast," XLIX (Oct., 1960), 447.

Macbeth. Calitri, Charles, "*Macbeth* and the Reluctant Reader," XLVIII (May, 1959), 254.

    Dean, Leonard F., "*Macbeth* and Modern Criticism," XLVII (Feb., 1958), 90.

    Reynolds, W. J., "When Thou Doest *Macbeth,* Do It Quickly!" XLVII (Feb., 1958), 90.

1984. Thompson, Frank, "Orwell's Image of the Man of Good Will," *CE,* XXII (Jan., 1961), 235.

The Old Man and the Sea. Cotter, Janet M., "*The Old Man and the Sea:* An 'Open' Literary Experience," LI (Oct., 1962), 459.

The Pearl. Litsey, David M., "Comparative Study of Novels," XLVIII (March, 1959), 149.

The Red Badge of Courage. McColly, William, "Teaching *The Red Badge of Courage,*" L (Nov., 1961), 534.

The Return of the Native. See under *Lord Jim.*

The Rise of Silas Lapham. Van Nostrand, Albert D., "Fiction's Flagging Man of Commerce," XLVIII (Jan., 1959), 1. (Other business novels discussed in February, 1959, issue.)

Romeo and Juliet. Taylor, Gary J., "*Romeo and Juliet* and *West Side Story:* An Experimental Unit," LI (Oct., 1962), 484.

The Scarlet Letter. Cowley, Malcolm, "Five Acts of *The Scarlet Letter,*" *CE,* XIX (Oct., 1957), 11.

    Marcus, Fred H., "*The Scarlet Letter:* The Power of Ambiguity," LI (Oct., 1962), 449.

"The Secret Sharer." Burton, Dwight, "Teaching 'The Secret Sharer' to High School Students," XLVII (May, 1958), 263.

Shane. Dunning, A. Stephen, "Toward Maturity in Judging Fiction," XLIX (Jan., 1960), 22.

Silas Marner. Kanehl, Joy J., "*Silas Marner* on Trial," LI (Dec., 1962), 647.

    Thale, Jerome, "George Eliot's Fable for Her Time," *CE,* XIX (Jan., 1958), 141.

A Tale of Two Cities. Sister Mary Felice, "An Approach to Teaching *A Tale of Two Cities,*" XLVIII (Jan., 1959), 31.

"The Three Strangers." O'Connor, William Van, "Cosmic Irony in Hardy's 'The Three Strangers,'" XLVII (May, 1958), 248.

Tom Sawyer. Brumback, Doris A., *et al.,* "A Unit on *Tom Sawyer,*" LI (Jan., 1962), 51.

    Marks, Barry A., "Mark Twain's Hymn of Praise," XLVIII (Nov., 1959), 443.

Wuthering Heights. Goldstone, Herbert, "*Wuthering Heights* Revisited," XLVIII (April, 1959), 175.

7

TEACHING POETRY
AND NON-FICTION

POETRY

Why Read Poetry?

Dame Edith Sitwell prefaced *The Outcasts,* published on her seventy-fifth birthday, in 1962, with this comment: "It is as unseeing to ask what is the *use* of poetry as it would be to ask what is the use of religion. . . . Poetry is the deification of reality, and one of its purposes, amongst others, is to show that the dimensions of man are, as Sir Arthur Eddington said, 'half way between those of an atom and a star.'"

In *The Powers of Poetry* (Fair Lawn, N. J.: Oxford University Press, 1960) Gilbert Highet suggests more pedestrianly that poetry appeals for these reasons: It gives "the pleasure of following a pattern of sound," as music also does; because of its heightened language it is sometimes better than prose for telling a story; poetry is easier to remember than is prose (e.g., "Thirty days hath September,/April, June, and November" is easier to recall than "The months that have thirty days are April, June, September, and November"); poetry "can express general experience—can say what many men and women have thought and felt"; and, conversely, it can say what few of us have ever thought or felt, and thus broaden our experiences memorably.

These are good reasons, surely, and Highet skirts the pitfall of attempting to justify the reading of poetry by utilitarian reasons. Few persons make a living from poetry, and students should look dubious if a teacher suggests that knowing about Keats will ever put a dime into their pockets. The best reason for reading poetry is strictly non-utilitarian: It is the same as the reason for listening to music, watching ballet, or looking at a painting; that is, poetry can be enjoyable.

The more one knows about music, ballet, or painting, the greater may be one's pleasure. The more one knows about poetry, the more one may enjoy it. But many students are reluctant to do what is necessary to increase enjoyment. They claim (and rightly) that poetry is artificial, that people don't really talk like that. Some feel that, once they understand a poem, the result is not worth the effort. Some have become antagonistic because teachers have gushed too much about poetic beauties or have dismembered every line. Most of the objections, though, are to the difficulties of reading poetry. A poem is by its nature highly compressed; a single reading will seldom reveal many of its secrets.

The objections to poetry may best be met in terms of the main purpose for reading poetry: pleasure. Enjoying rhythm, treating the comprehension of compressed language as the solving of a puzzle, and discussing the broadly applicable human truths or the individual insights and emotions—these are representative of the kinds of pleasure we shall discuss in connection with the six fundamental approaches.

In discussing the principle that literature should be read for pleasure, Professor Fred H. Stocking objects to reading literature for moral awareness and improved ethics, "because I have known so many good people who read literature badly and as many bad people who read literature well." [1] He also objects to the use of literature to promote psychological health, because

I cannot fully respect the conception of literature as a kind of psychological medicine. In fact, I dislike all arguments which make literature a slave to something else. . . . We too often act as though pleasure were something shameful, at least in a school building constructed with taxpayers' money. . . . I like to think of literature as a great compendium of celebrations. All literary works say that life is full of wonder, that life deserves our admiring attention.

One of the complicating factors in teaching poetry is that not all students are ready for the same kind of pleasure at the same time. Wittick, in 1960, described five levels of appreciation: The first, which is evident in preschool children and may remain for a lifetime, is "conscious pleasure in strong rhythm and rhyme, even with nonsense syllables"; the second, which characterizes many upper elementary

[1] "The Two Jobs of English Teachers," *English Journal*, L (March, 1961), 165.

and junior high pupils, is a liking for limericks and other "fun poems"; third is the emotional and story appeal of narrative verse; fourth comes lyric verse in conventional patterns; and finally there is the "sometimes baffling pleasure of considering modern, experimental forms." [2] An implication of the Wittick classification is that there is some poetry that will appeal to any child, but not every child can be expected to like every poem, simply because he has not reached a sufficiently advanced stage of development. A second implication may be that the poetry selected for class discussion should ordinarily be on, or slightly above, the level presently attained by most members of the class, with a few "fun poems" or narratives interspersed for the slower students and a few relatively advanced poems for the advanced students.

The Historical Approach

Under the influence of the "new critics," who say that only the poem matters and not the circumstances of its composition, the historical approach has fallen into disfavor. It is certainly true that this approach may be abused—that it may, for example, become largely a matter of emphasizing unimportant biographical facts, dates, and the like. But the historical approach is justified in high school teaching when knowledge of the circumstances of writing will help to clarify the poem, when the poem sheds light upon the age in which it was written or which it describes, and when the poem relates to a historical subject.

No true poem, of course, has ever been written that did not grow from the author's current thinking and feeling. Some poems, however, illustrate his thoughts and emotions better than others. Here are three examples.

Bryant's "To a Waterfowl" developed from a personal experience. Twenty-one years old—not the gray-bearded, bald-headed old man pictured in the anthologies—Bryant was walking the seven miles from his home to Plainfield, Massachusetts. He was worried, uncertain. Because of lack of money he had not been able to complete his college work. He wanted to write and had written, but he knew that his writing could not yet support him. He had passed his bar examination, but had no law office, no chance to practice. On this day, a chilly one in December, 1815, he was going to explore the possibility of opening a law office in Plainfield. But the future was doubtful and dreary. The sun seemed to be setting on his bright youthful hopes just as it had already disappeared in the west. Then, also in the west,

[2] Summarized in "Developing Tastes in Literature in the Elementary Grades," *Elementary English*, XXXIX (Dec., 1962), 783.

Bryant saw a lone wild duck, flying rapidly southward. The young man noted the assurance of the bird, the straightness of its course. Certainly a higher Being was guiding it. And if that Being cared for this wild creature, need he, the poet, fear anything?

> He who, from zone to zone,
> Guides through the boundless sky thy certain flight,
> In the long way that I must tread alone,
> Will lead my steps aright.

Without an explanation like this, "To a Waterfowl" is just another poem. With the background, however, it achieves visible significance.

Poe's "Annabel Lee" has a less specific story attached to it than has "To a Waterfowl," but to appreciate it a class must be familiar with the story of Poe's tender love for his child-wife, Virginia, who had died three years before. They must know of her delicate loveliness, her singing ability, her lingering illness that often threatened death before it actually arrived. They should know that she had already inspired some of Poe's best work such as "Ulalume" and "The Raven." It is also helpful for them to realize that there is at least figurative truth in the line "She was a child and I was a child," because Poe never "grew up" to the conservatism and subdued emotionality that usually accompany adulthood. And the class should know, too, that "Annabel Lee" was probably the last poem that Poe wrote—that memory of his dead wife remained sharp within him up to the time he died.

Quite different is the background of Siegfried Sassoon's "Suicide in the Trenches" or any other of his bitter antiwar poems:

> In winter trenches, cowed and glum,
> With crumps and lice and lack of rum,
> He put a bullet through his brain.
> No one spoke of him again.

At twenty-eight, Sassoon himself had gone to war. He knew its filth, its heartlessness, its blood. Twice wounded, he was awarded the Military Cross for rescuing injured soldiers under fire, and he threw the decoration into the sea. Later he declined the D.S.O. because he had learned that war is completely futile. In his poems—indeed in his whole life after World War I—his chief aim was to fight war:

> You smug-faced crowds with kindling eye
> Who cheer when soldier lads march by,

> Sneak home and pray you'll never know
> The hell where youth and laughter go.

These illustrations should make it plain how knowledge of the poet may clarify some poems and make them vivid experiences, not dull words. Similarly, knowledge of the age in which a poet lived may often remove a poem from the realm of the abstract.

Chaucer's "Prologue" may serve as the example here. To us, who know medieval history and who are familiar with H. O. Taylor's *Medieval Mind*, R. L. Poole's *Medieval Thought and Learning*, and G. G. Coulton's *Medieval Panorama*, the knights, squires, yeomen, monks, friars, franklins, clerks, reeves, summoners, and manciples seem at least as distinct as next-door neighbors on a foggy day. But between our students and these characters is a brick wall in which we must make a few chinks if we cannot tear it down.

Consider, for instance, the Clerk:

> A Clerk ther was of Oxenford also,
> That unto logyk hadde longe ygo.
> As leene was his hors as is a rake,
> And he nas nat right fat, I undertake,
> But loked holwe, and therto soberly.
> Full thredbare was his overeste courtepy,
> For he hadde geten him yet no benefice,
> Ne was so worldly for to have office.
> For him was levere have at his beddes heed
> Twenty bokes, clad in blak or reed,
> Of Aristotle and his philosophye,
> Than robes riche, or fithele, or gay sautrye.

A combination of the paraphrastic and the historical approaches seems essential here: the paraphrastic to clarify word meanings and sentence structure, and the historical to add facts essential to understanding and appreciation. Unaided, some students will assume that the clerk sold groceries; Oxenford and Oxford they will suppose to be two different places; "nas nat" will be meaningless; and so on. The second line opens the way to a little discussion of medieval education. The line does not mean "Who'd turned to getting knowledge long ago" (as translated in one modern version) but means, rather, that the clerk had long since been familiarized with the "trivium" (grammar, rhetoric, and logic) and was probably studying the "quadrivium" (arithmetic, geometry, astronomy, and music); in other words, he was an advanced student. Line 6 offers opportunity to show some pictures of medieval costumes. Lines 7 and 8 point out that a more worldly scholar than the clerk might abandon his desire to become a priest in order to accept a position as secretary to some rich man or government official. Line 10 provides an opening for a discussion of what books were like before the invention of printing, and how costly twenty books would be. Line 11 might well be passed over quickly with only a mention of Aristotle's doctrine of the "golden mean" for the few students who might be interested. Pictures of medieval musical instruments would illustrate line 12, and a musically inclined student might find here a good subject for a report.

Not all the "Prologue," of course, is crammed with so many reflections of the fourteenth century as these lines are, but, nevertheless, this poem and many others have sufficient historical connections to make such study worthwhile and interesting. The poetry suggests the social history, and the social history enlightens the poetry.

Political history also has often been tied closely to poetry. Obvious examples are Emerson's "Concord Hymn" and Whitman's "O Captain! My Captain!" To teach these without reference to their historical background would be not only pointless but almost impossible. Somewhat less obvious examples are Longfellow's "Skeleton in Armor," which might be related to the puzzle of who really discovered the New World; ballads, both English and American, some of which have a historical foundation; "London, 1802," which demands an understanding of the England that Wordsworth described as "a fen of stagnant waters"; and Tennyson's "Locksley Hall," published in 1842 but foreseeing aviation, gigantic aerial wars, the steady advance of science, and a "Federation of the world" that has not yet been attained.

As a final and somewhat different example of the usefulness of the historical approach, consider Keats's "Ode on a Grecian Urn." Obviously, it is desirable in teaching this poem to comment upon Greek art and pagan religious rituals. But why does Keats say that the urn carries two quite different scenes, the one depicting love and pursuit and near frenzy, the other a sedate procession of pious persons on their way to perform an act of worship? The dichotomy is not characteristic of classical Greek art. As Gilbert Highet says, "The sculptor or painter who decorated a vase would not think of mingling half-naked bacchantes with decently dressed churchgoers, any more than we should put voodoo drums into a Bach choral prelude and fugue." But Keats knew that the Greeks were somewhat schizophrenic persons, in constant conflict within themselves. To quote Professor Highet again, "The conflict was a struggle between the life of reason, for which they were uniquely gifted, and the dark forces of the passions, to which they were terribly sensitive." Apollo, the god of reason, and Bacchus, lord of revelry, warred within them. Keats was sufficiently informed about the Greeks to recognize this conflict and to dramatize it in his poem.

When one of these close connections exists:

✓   poem   ←→   the poet's life
✓   poem   ←→   the poet's time
✓   poem   ←→   the time depicted in the poem

the historical approach is justified. It removes the poem from the pages of a book and places it in its proper context—in physical surroundings that may be made familiar, and among real people with fears, tears, joys, and aspirations not unlike our own.

The Sociopsychological Approach

Still more may the sociopsychological approach give vitality to a poem. In this approach, even more than in any of the others, lively discussion is desirable and essential. Many questions like those listed on pages 162–163 are as appropriate for poetry as for fiction and drama.

Most adolescents are keenly interested in people. They want to know how people act, why they act that way, what might cause them to act differently. Social relationships concern them deeply. Boy-girl and family relationships provide much of their conversational diet, but not infrequently they talk with utter seriousness about solutions of national and international social problems that most of us adults hardly dare to face squarely. Recently, for example, a fifteen-year-old boy was proposing answers to the problem of racial segregation—a boy with ordinary ability and the usual interests in athletics, airplanes, and automobiles. He was thinking seriously of an important matter, thinking with a fairness and an unselfishness that adults might envy. One could not help wishing that the fine idealism and the high seriousness that he shares with millions of other adolescents would not be worn away in a few short years. And one could not help wondering whether we might not come nearer to solving our biggest social problems if through education we could provide practical knowledge of humanity that might modify but not debilitate the idealism of youth. The idealist proposes solutions that often ignore reality; the realist—at least in one of his more extreme guises—scorns ideals and accepts the status quo as almost immutable. Somewhere between the two must lie a space where idealism and realism overlap. The Founding Fathers apparently located it. They knew people well; they were neither excessively idealistic nor excessively insistent upon maintaining the status quo. Our Constitution—indeed the whole basis of American democracy—lies in neither idealism nor jaded realism but in an awareness of rough reality and an equal awareness that a beautiful white Thule may lie beyond the horizon. Today's students are tomorrow's Founding Fathers. As teachers, we can say "Well done" to ourselves if we can help them to blend practical knowledge with ideals.

Poetry offers endless opportunity for adding to knowledge of human beings. It offers, too, tentative conclusions—guesses to be weighed and modified. The poet, even though he may be what Shelley called him, the legislator of mankind, does not know all the answers. But he does raise many questions and he does supply clues to help answer them.

In the following paragraphs we shall consider some familiar poems to illustrate the use of the sociopsychological approach. In the first group are poems about individuals; those in the second are about the relationships between two or more persons; those in the third refer to large groups.

Poems About Individuals. "Richard Cory." In considering Edwin Arlington Robinson's poem, the class would discuss the kind of man that Cory was—rich, handsome, courteous, and envied by all. But why did such a man commit suicide? What may have been lacking in his life? What really are the ingredients of a rich, full life? Other character sketches by Robinson, such as "Miniver Cheevy" and "Mr. Flood's Party," offer equally good material for consideration of the individual.

"Lucinda Matlock." Edgar Lee Masters has portrayed a woman who possessed the secret that Richard Cory apparently lacked: "It takes life to love Life." Cory was all superficiality; "he glittered when he walked." But Lucinda did not glitter; there was a depth in her that Cory could never have. She worked hard, gave birth to twelve children of whom eight died young, nursed the sick,

> . . . and for holiday
> Rambled over the fields where sang the larks,
> And by Spoon River gathering many a shell,
> And many a flower and medicinal weed—
> Shouting to the wooded hills, singing to the green valleys.
> At ninety-six I had lived enough, that is all—
> And passed to a sweet repose.

The teacher might ask the class why Lucinda was happy, whom they have known comparable to her, what are the ingredients of happiness. Masters' *Spoon River Anthology* and *New Spoon River* are filled with additional sketches, many of them suitable for class discussion.

"The Haunted Palace." Poe's poem is not about a palace but about "a mind haunted by phantoms—a disordered brain," as he himself explained. In dealing with this poem, the teacher would probably combine the paraphrastic and sociopsychological approaches, having the class explain first what the poem says about the palace and then translating it into what it implies about a human mind. The class would also supply its own illustrations. What, for instance, may have been the "evil things, in robes of sorrow, [that] assailed the monarch's high estate"?

"Ozymandias." What did Ozymandias look like? What did his appearance show about his character? What does the inscription on the pedestal show about him? Would you have liked to be one of his subjects? Can you think of two or three modern men who were like Ozymandias and shared his fate? If being a "king of kings" will not enable a person to be long remembered, what will? By asking such questions, the teacher will do more than clarify the character of the king in Shelley's poem; he will help the class to see that mere possessions and power do not insure immortality in the hearts of men.

"Excelsior." Like Poe's "Haunted Palace," Longfellow's poem has a double meaning. Ostensibly it is the story of a headstrong youth who perished while climbing a mountain. Actually it tells of an intelligent, fearless young man who was not satisfied with things as they are but ever strove to rise higher. Longfellow's summary should suggest appropriate questions for class discussion:

His motto is "Excelsior,"—"higher." He passes through the Alpine village—through the rough, cold paths of the world,—where the peasants cannot understand him, and where the watchword is "an unknown tongue." He disregards the happiness of domestic peace and sees the glaciers—his fate—before him. He disregards the warnings of the old man's wisdom and the fascinations of woman's love. He answers to all, "Higher yet!" The monks of St. Bernard are the representatives of religious forms and ceremonies, and with their oft-repeated prayer mingles the sound of his voice, telling them there is something higher than forms and ceremonies. Filled with these aspirations, he perishes, without having reached the perfection he longed for; and the voice heard in the air is the promise of immortality and progress ever upward.

A word of warning is in order here, however. Not every poem is like "Excelsior"; not every poem has a double meaning. Yet some teachers have spoiled a potential liking for poetry by insisting that students always read between the lines and locate things that simply are not there. Finding a double meaning in every couplet of Whittier's "Snow-Bound," for instance, is absurd. Older poets comparatively seldom introduced a multiplicity of meaning. (For a comment on modern poetry, see page 204.)

Poems About Two or More Persons. "The Cotter's Saturday Night." Poetry that clarifies family relationships has especial value in this age, when some persons fear that the family unit is disintegrating. A poem like this one by Burns affords a splendid opportunity to consider what family life was formerly like, how and why it has changed, whether the changes have resulted in improvement or loss, and what the future of the family unit seems to be. Involved in such a discussion would be a consideration of how much authority parents should exert; what assistance, advice, and cooperation a child has a right to expect from his parents; whether parents should interfere in their children's choice of friends; what parents have a right to expect of their children; whether grown children should contribute to meeting the household expenses; and so on.

"Forbearance." Emerson names only one quality for which he would value a friend, but suggests several others. As students enjoy talking about friendship, a teacher may use a poem like this as an entrance to a free discussion of the qualities that a genuine friend should possess.

"Maid of Athens," "The Indian Serenade," etc. To many high school students, especially juniors and seniors, love is real and love is earnest. They—at least the boys—may sneer at a Byronic or a Shelleyan effusion, but, nevertheless, some of them are themselves feeling, mayhap in a diluted form, the ecstasy and the pain described by a thousand thousand poets and poetasters. A certain amount of love poetry is therefore not inappropriate. The teacher probably should touch these poems lightly; he needs to make sure that meanings of phrases like "champak odours" are cleared up, but after that he may merely let the poems do their own work.

Sonnets from the Portuguese, "Maud Muller," "My Last Duchess," etc. We sometimes forget that our juniors and seniors are physiologically mature, or almost so; we forget that in other centuries or in other lands those who seem children to us would probably be husbands and wives and even parents; we ignore the steadily increasing number of teen-age marriages in the United States; we conveniently ignore the fact that tens of thousands of girls now in American classrooms will mother illegitimate children. What has this to do with literature? Only that young people need to know more about human relationships, and that literature helps to clarify such relationships. We cannot continue to dodge our responsibility; if people did not need to be educated, we should not need educators. And education is much more than dates and charts and the spelling of "psychology." It is a provision of the knowledge and a strengthening of the abilities requisite to satisfactory living in a complex world.

Selections like some of Mrs. Browning's *Sonnets from the Portuguese* portray the beauty of married love, and stress—without stating—that such love between a well-matched couple is worth waiting for. Whittier's "Maud Muller," read superficially, suggests that the Judge and the rustic Maud would have been happy if they had married; but pondering raises the question of whether this is true, whether they were suited for one another, what qualities a well-matched couple hold in common. (Bret Harte's pointed parody "Mrs. Judge Jenkins" mercilessly reveals Whittier's sentimentality.) Browning's "My Last Duchess" indicates how the pride and the jealousy of one of the partners may bring a marriage to a tragic end. Abundant are other poems, as well as short stories, novels, and plays, pertaining to different aspects of married life, although unfortunately most high school anthologies contain too few such selections.

Poems About Groups. "I Hear America Singing," "The Man with the Hoe," "The Cry of the Children." Much poetry enlightens the relationships not of a few people but of vast groups of people. Whitman's "I Hear America Singing" should lead to a discussion of means of earning a livelihood, of ways of enjoying one's work, and of methods of choosing a lifework; it might lead to a discussion of other selections pertaining to the building of skyscrapers, the life of a doctor or nurse, the work of a pilot, etc. Markham's "The Man with the Hoe" (read, of course, with a copy of Millet's painting before the class) may be introduced as the theme song of the early twentieth century, when laborers in America began to make spectacular gains. Mrs. Browning, in "The Cry of the Children," along with Dickens in his novel *Oliver Twist*, was partially responsible for the reduction of child-labor abuses in nineteenth-century England. Through selections like these, a class can learn that literature is indissolubly mixed with life—indeed, that literature may help to change and improve life.

"Come Up from the Fields, Father," "The Man He Killed." War and hunger, according to historian Carl Becker, are man's two greatest enemies, and at present it seems that war is more likely than hunger to extinguish the human race. It is usually not pleasant to read about war, but it is interesting to note that something—perhaps prolonged experience with war and prolonged reading about its horrors—has changed human attitudes toward it. Savage tribes and even the otherwise admirable Greeks apparently fought largely for the joy of fighting, killed for the pleasure of killing. Today most of us look upon war as something hateful, a childish way of settling disputes that man must outgrow if he is to survive. This modern attitude can be strengthened in our schools. Poems like Whitman's "Come Up from the Fields, Father," depicting a family which receives the news that its son and brother has been killed, and Hardy's "The Man He Killed," suggesting that the enemy is human also, are only examples of the many that accentuate man's greatest folly.

"Chicago," "Clean Curtains," "Mamie." In our increasingly urbanized life, writers frequently emphasize the problems inherent in dwelling within congested areas. Sandburg sees both the glory and the gloom of city life; he hears Chicago laugh "the stormy, husky, brawling laughter of youth," but he knows, too, that in Chicago is Mamie, from a little Indiana town, underpaid Mamie who has always dreamed and still dreams of "romance and big things off somewhere." In the city also are the new neighbors who put up clean curtains, but

> Dust and the thundering trucks won—the barrages
> of the street wheels and the lawless wind took their way—
> was it five weeks or six the little mother, the new neighbors,
> battled and then took down the white prayers in the windows?

Writers, it seems, tend to stress the undeniable squalor of the cities and to ignore the equally undeniable advantages of urban life. A good class discussion will consider both sides—what is good and what should and can be bettered.

Poems by and about members of minority groups. Probably poems by members of minority groups should not be singled out for special comment. That a Jew should write a poem is no more remarkable than that a Methodist or a Catholic should; that a Negro or Japanese or Mexican can write beautifully should excite no more surprise than the fact that an Englishman can. It is better to take each poem for whatever it happens to offer, regardless of who wrote it. Yet at the same time one must realize that we cannot bury our heads and thus conceal the presence of minority problems (or are they *majority* problems?). Therefore, when a class comes across a selection bearing directly upon such issues, the poem should be discussed as frankly as a poem about war or city life or country life or anything else. The students in today's classes are tomorrow's lawmakers, tomorrow's citizens who must live together. If the teacher can do anything to build in them a spirit of live-and-let-live, he should be more than pleased.

"The Building of the Ship," "Old Glory." Poems of patriotism many students like. The greatness of one's own land is a topic that most people never tire of extolling.

> Breathes there the man with soul so dead
> Who never to himself hath said
> "This is my own, my native land"?

The teaching of patriotism, however, is swinging slowly away from a narrow, chauvinistic variety to a broader type that interests itself in the possible contributions of a nation to world peace and world advancement. A poem like the conclusion of Longfellow's "Building of the Ship" and especially a more modern poem like Russell Davenport's "Old Glory" may illustrate what has been called "the higher patriotism":

> Old Glory! Guard the hopeful and the good,
> And lead us onward, unconfusedly,
> That in our freedom others may be free!

"The World Is Too Much with Us." Wordsworth's sonnet may serve as an illustration of many poems that help students to ponder some of the big and possibly abstract questions concerning human conduct and human relationships. Do we devote too much of our time to "getting and spending"? What else does life offer? Wordsworth advocates paying more attention to nature. Is he right? What could we gain from following his advice? What besides nature may make our lives truly rich?

For many more poems like those mentioned—poems that shed light upon individuals, upon the interrelationships among a few individuals, or upon the possibilities of rapport within large groups—the socio-psychological approach is invaluable if not indispensable.

The Emotive Approach

Robert Frost, teacher and poet, once said,

I don't want to analyze authors. I want to enjoy them. I want the boys in the class to enjoy their books because of what's in them. Here again, perhaps, I am old-fashioned. Youth, I believe, should not analyze its enjoyments. It should live. It doesn't matter what they think Hazlitt thought or tried to do in his works; what matters is the work, the story, the series of incidents. Criticism is the province of age, not youth. They'll get to that soon enough. Let them build up a friendship with the writing world first. One can't compare until one knows.[3]

And a state superintendent of schools who visited Frost's class said of him later, "He was neither raising his voice nor cutting up any pedagogical monkeyshines but rather talking to them as he might talk to a group of friends around his own fireside." [4]

If one had to follow a single principle in teaching poetry, that principle would be easy to choose: Poetry should be enjoyed. Enjoyment is intrinsic in the emotive approach, but it should never be divorced from the other approaches. That is, the teacher should never say, in effect, "Since I'm going to use the historical approach with this poem, we won't have any fun today." Both pleasure and worthwhileness should be a part of every approach.

The emotive approach stresses the pleasure more than the others do, however. This pleasure is inherent in the language, rhythm, story, emotional intensity, and pictorial qualities of poems. It may come also from the oral reading and other activities that may be associated with poetry.

The old but still useful *An Experience Curriculum in English* mentions a number of units in which enjoyment is to be the primary objective. Some of these, with titles of representative poems, are as follows:

1. To enjoy poems of delight in physical nature and in bodily activity. Carman's "Vagabond Song," Whittier's "Barefoot Boy," Emerson's "Snow Storm," Beeching's "Bicycling Song," Untermeyer's "Swimmers."

2. To enjoy poems of the merely ludicrous. Lear's "Owl and the Pussy Cat," Daly's "Mia Carlotta," Service's "Cremation of Sam McGee," limericks.

3. To enjoy poems in which rhythm or (and) onomatopoeia are prominent. Tennyson's "Brook," Lanier's "Song of the Chattahoochee," Shelley's "Cloud," Browning's "How They Brought the Good News from Ghent to Aix."

4. To share in expressions of friendship, tenderness for pets, friends, family. Bang's "My Dog," Tennyson's "Sweet and Low," Burns's "To a Mouse," Teasdale's "Grace Before Sleep."

5. To enjoy poems in which vivid sensory images are especially prominent. Wylie's "Velvet Shoes," Lanier's "Tampa Robins," Brooke's "The Great Lover," Southey's "How the Water Comes Down at Lodore."

[3] Quoted in Robert Newdick's "Robert Frost as Teacher of Literature and Composition," *English Journal*, XXV (Oct., 1936), 632.
[4] *Ibid.*

✓ 6. To enjoy poems in which suggestion is predominant. Guiterman's
     "Hills," Field's "Little Boy Blue," Sarett's "Four Little Foxes."
✓ 7. To enjoy poems of subtle humor or of humor mingled with other
     emotions or accompanied by didactic purpose. Robinson's "Mini-
     ver Cheevy," Holmes's "Last Leaf," parodies.
✓ 8. To share delight in intellectual experiences or poetic contempla-
     tion. Frost's "Stopping by Woods," Wordsworth's "My Heart Leaps
     Up," Milton's "Il Penseroso," Arnold's "Dover Beach."
✓ 9. To delight in poems with more intricate or more varied music,
     including free verse. Masefield's "Sea Fever," Poe's "Bells," Amy
     Lowell's "Patterns," Sandburg's "Fog."
✓ 10. To enjoy poems in which much of the charm is due to elaborate,
     exotic, or fanciful imagery. Frost's "Birches," Shelley's "To a Sky-
     lark," Teasdale's "Barter."
✓ 11. To enjoy poetic expressions of romantic love. Whittier's "School
     Days," Burns's "My Love Is Like a Red, Red Rose," Jonson's
     "Drink to Me Only with Thine Eyes," Byron's "She Walks in
     Beauty."
✓ 12. To enjoy poetic fantasies, in which beauty and imagination pre-
     dominate. Coleridge's "Kubla Khan," "Christabel," Yeats's "The
     Lake Isle of Innisfree," Tennyson's "Lady of Shalott." [5]

Poetry offers the sources of enjoyment suggested by these objectives,
and offers many more besides. We teachers know that, but how can
we get our students to know it?

The solution seems to lie in doing many things with poetry—not just
one thing again and again. One of the attractions of sports is that there
are many types of plays in each game, not the same play repeated ad
infinitum. Poetry can have the same appeal. Teacher and class can
(1) read aloud, (2) dramatize, (3) present choral readings of, (4)
sing, (5) discuss, (6) compare, (7) write about, (8) emulate or
imitate, (9) illustrate with words, (10) illustrate with pictures, (11)
listen to recordings of, (12) laugh about, (13) memorize (voluntarily),
(14) collect favorite poems or passages, and (15) with modern poetry,
serve as a cocreator. These methods of employing the emotive approach are discussed in the following paragraphs.

Oral Reading. That the teacher ought to read aloud with effectiveness goes without saying. Constant application of only one rule leads
to good oral reading: The voice should "do the thing shall breed the
thought." That implies, of course, that the reader must understand
what he is reading—its mood as well as its ideas. Then he makes his
voice convey the mood at the same time that he is presenting the
thought. When he is reading a serious passage, his voice suggests the

[5] Abridged from *An Experience Curriculum in English* (New York: Appleton-
Century-Crofts, Inc., 1935), pp. 53–62.

seriousness; for a light passage, his voice is lilting; in an exciting passage, his voice becomes tense, his breathing more rapid. This may sound difficult, but, if one really understands and *feels* a poem, the voice tends to adjust itself with little conscious effort by the reader. It is easy because it is natural; when one talks, he naturally adjusts his delivery to what he is saying. Good poetry is natural enough that one can read it without becoming pompous, oratorical, or even silky smooth or sickeningly sweet. Natural delivery has the advantages of placing pauses where they belong (not necessarily at the end of each line) and of avoiding excessive stress upon the accent, rhythm, or rhyme. Practice is essential, of course; but, if a college senior preparing to teach English devotes ten minutes a day through the school year to oral reading of various kinds of poetry, and keeps the above rule constantly in mind, his reading at the end of the year should be satisfactory. This is almost certain to be true if he has the opportunity to hear a few recordings of his reading, made periodically during the year.

Dramatization. Classes enjoy dramatization of poetry. A ballad such as "Get Up and Bar the Door" may be dramatized with little time-consuming preparation, as it falls readily into dramatic form. Two capable boys may work out a dramatization of "Sohrab and Rustum" that will help to clarify the action and the speeches. Some poems may be pantomimed effectively by one student while another reads. Reading of parts in such a poem as Poe's "Raven"—with a narrator, a speaker, and a hoarse raven—assists visualization and understanding.

Choral Reading. Choral reading has been made the subject of several books, and cannot be adequately discussed here. The proficient choral group attains majestic organ-like effects, but these are usually beyond the attainment of an English class, where choral reading is only one activity among many. Simpler effects, though, may be obtained rather easily. For example, in "Lord Randal" the girls may read the mother's questions, and the boys Lord Randal's replies. Other poems divide themselves naturally into three parts or four parts, or into parts suitable for a solo and a chorus. Junior high school youngsters, in particular, enjoy choral reading, although many senior high groups also like it.

Singing. Much poetry was written to be sung. Then why not sing it? If the teacher cannot lead the singing, there is usually a student who can. Ballads, perhaps one or two of the roisterous American folk ballads or cowboy songs like "The Old Chisholm Trail," make a good entering wedge. Later, lyrics by Shakespeare, Jonson, Burns, and others may be sung.

Discussing and Comparing. Discussions of poems should be lively and interesting. A good discussion inevitably involves more than one of the approaches. Comparisons between poems or between poets (e.g., Frost and Wordsworth, the rhythm of Chesterton's "Lepanto" and the rhythm of Lindsay's "The Congo") are invaluable.

Writing. Written work in connection with poetry seldom adds to the enjoyment. Sometimes, though, the members of a class, or a few students, become sufficiently excited over something they have found in a poem to want to put down their excitement on paper. This effect is unlikely to be reached often, but when it does it should certainly not be stifled. Also, a few students like to write verse of their own, verse possibly inspired by or modeled on something they have read. To get all students to engage in such an activity, some teachers use the group poem technique and find that classes that have written group poems tend to be more appreciative of the efforts of professional poets.[6] The author has taken a class for a walk around a city block or past part of a lake, asking them to be perfectly silent and to keep all their sensory organs alert. After returning, the students write on the board words and phrases indicating what they have seen, heard, smelled, and felt. (Young people tend to express themselves much more picturesquely than older ones; with a class of adults, the phrases obtained are generally trite ones like "rippling water," "swaying grass," etc.) Then they find some element that seems to tie most of the phrases together—usually a dominant impression. The last step is assembling the pertinent phrases in coherent order and applying a little polish to make the result reasonably like free verse. One such group poem, neither better nor worse than average, is this, written by a junior high school class before the end of World War II:

Gold Star

This morning's *Tribune* lying on the vine-clad porch,
And in the yard, a sleepy dog beside a sand-box waits;
Across the dewy lawn, the ice man strides,
While falls of sunlight through the graceful willows spray

---

[6] The poet Countee Cullen has his class write the first stanza of a Mother's Day poem; then individuals supply additional stanzas. He also encourages the writing of limericks and parodies, and gets good results from an exercise called "How Would a Poet Say This?" ("Snow is nature's salt." "Winds are violent songs in motion.") *High Points*, XXV, No. 7 (Sept., 1943), p. 26.

And radiant paint the quiet goldenglow.
They shine upon the porch, four empty chairs,
And on a golden star.

Illustrating. Since a poem is highly compressed, a class often profits from expansion of its meaning through illustration. The illustrations may be in words: examples of what the poet was saying, or experiences or scenes comparable to those the poet presented. Or they may be pictorial: photographs, drawings, or paintings supplied by both teacher and class to assist visualization.

Playing Recordings. Numerous recordings of favorite poems are available, some of them made by the poets themselves. A recording may be played before or after the class has read a poem, or both before and after. Perhaps the best source of such recordings is the National Council of Teachers of English, which will send a descriptive folder upon request.

Enjoying Humor. Shared laughter means shared enjoyment. A fairly large proportion of the poetry read should be light and amusing. Limericks, parodies, and some poems by Holmes, Field, Lear, Gilbert, Daly, and Nash are examples of appropriate light verse. Many collections of humorous poetry are available.

Memorizing. Memorization should be encouraged but not required. In too many instances, forced memorization has caused dislike,[7] and, in too many instances, the student, told that he must learn twenty-five or fifty lines, has chosen his lines solely on the basis of their brevity. Three suggestions on memorization: (1) If poetry is taught effectively enough, students will *want* to tuck away certain lines and brief passages. (2) Choral reading and dramatization tend to fix certain lines without the student's conscious effort. (3) If the teacher himself occasionally quotes a few lines pertinent to the topic being discussed, some students will be motivated to emulate him.

Collecting. Adolescents love to collect stamps, coins, matchbooks, records, and so on. Why not have them collect poems? As individuals or as a class they may make notebooks of favorite poems. In one small school, each senior class prepares a book of its favorites for presentation to the library; the books prepared by earlier classes are eagerly read and compared with what the present class is doing. In other schools, classes have collected poems on topics of particular interest to them: nature, city life, poetry to be sung, patriotism, heroism,

---

[7] It is probably now unnecessary to remind any teacher that memorizations of a poem should *never* be used as punishment.

etc. One all-boy class objected to reading poetry until the teacher commented that many other boys were similar to them in attitude and that this class might perform a real service by making a collection of poems that boys really like. The class prepared for the library a volume called *Poems for Regular Fellows,* which was composed of verse that the boys liked and that almost any teacher would approve.[8]

Creative Reading. Professor Marshall McLuhan, of the University of Toronto, has made an observation about modern poetry that may result in its having considerably greater appeal for your upperclassmen. According to McLuhan, most modern poets do not spell out a meaning as did their predecessors. Indeed, there is often no single meaning, but instead a large variety of possible meanings. Earlier poets expected their readers to be only consumers; modern poets tend to think of their readers as cocreators. A poem, then, presents a stimulus for creative thought on the part of the reader, and two readers of the same poem may emerge with widely different creative responses. For a high school class the significance of McLuhan's thesis appears to be that modern poetry provides an opportunity for a type of enjoyable intellectual activity that in the past has infrequently penetrated into classrooms. Freed from the requirement of saying that T. S. Eliot "means" so and so, students may find in his verse a rare richness of suggestion.

One caution is necessary, though, lest the McLuhan hypothesis be considered a sanction for "anything goes." Although more than a single interpretation of a poem may often be possible, complete freedom of interpreting is not. Lawrence Perrine says wisely that the best interpretation is

. . . that which most fully explains the details of the poem without itself being contradicted by any detail. If more than one interpretation satisfactorily accounts for all the details of the poem, the best is that which is most economical, i.e., which relies on the fewest assumptions not grounded in the poem itself.[9]

The authors of *The Dimensions of Poetry* say that a poem may be looked at as a physical object and as a process. The physical object is the lines, shape, scenes, and words of the poem; the process is

. . . the experience—what the reader *does,* and what happens to him when all the elements of the poem come alive in him. . . . The process is both

[8] Lieber Anker, "By Boys for Boys," *English Journal,* XXXIV (May, 1945), 276.

[9] "The Nature of Proof in the Interpretation of Poetry," *English Journal,* LI (Sept., 1962), 393. Be sure to read all of this extraordinarily helpful article.

exciting and demanding: The reader can set off an explosion from the chemicals the poet provides, making a carnival of stars out of a few plain words. But he must also approach the creation of a poem, through his own craft of imaginative reading, with the same close awareness, attention, and practiced skill that a pianist gives to music, or a skier to motion in sky and snow.[10]

The same authors quote from Walt Whitman:

The reader will always have his or her part to do, just as much as I have had mine. I seek less to state or display any theme or thought, and more to bring you, reader, into the atmosphere of the theme or thought—there to pursue your own flight.

It is not *only* the moderns, then, whose poems can be cocreated by the reader.

Some of these methods of employing the emotive approach will work better than others in your classes. You may wish to give each of them a brief trial and thereafter emphasize the six or seven that bring the best results in your school. The last one, creative reading, may well become one of your stand-bys.

The Didactic Approach

With the didactic approach, teacher and class find and discuss the author's viewpoint toward his subject. They may or may not accept that viewpoint. "Poetry does not demand our belief; it invites us to experience," as Miller and Slote say. The students examine the viewpoint from several sides, compare it with other viewpoints, and evaluate it in light of their own experience. Four poems will be discussed to exemplify this approach.

"Miracles." Whitman calls all commonplace things "miracles"—houses, bees, fish, rocks, food, companionship, the new moon. Is he right? A "miracle" is defined as a wonderful thing. What is wonderful about a honeybee? About a rock? How does Whitman's definition of "miracles" differ from yours? What are some things that you consider miracles?

"Mending Wall." Frost's poem has been taught as an argument between an internationalist and an isolationist, with the latter having the last word. Such an interpretation is not necessarily farfetched, because one of the pleasures of poetry is that it can be given wide application. There is danger, however, in saying that Frost *intended* to

[10] James E. Miller, Jr., and Bernice Slote, *The Dimensions of Poetry* (New York: Dodd, Mead & Co., Inc., 1962), p. 5.

convey any such idea, a danger of reading into a poem something that was not written into it. To apply the thought of a poem to something outside it is one thing, but to say that the "something outside" is really inside is perverting the poem. Frost merely says that two neighbors, of unlike temperaments, each spring mend the stone wall between their fields; one is opposed to the mending because he sees no need for walls, but the other, moving in the darkness of time-worn beliefs, insists that "Good fences make good neighbors." Without referring to international implications at all, a class can ponder the questions of why the two men were different, whether it is true that good fences make good neighbors, what kinds of fences we put up between ourselves besides physical ones, and whether people still tend to repeat the ideas learned in their childhood. Then, if someone sees that fences between neighbors are like fences between nations—good, but it should not be said that the fences-between-nations idea is in the poem itself.

"I Saw a Man." Stephen Crane's little poem is a good introduction to symbolism:

> I saw a man pursuing the horizon;
> Round and round they sped.
> I was disturbed at this;
> I accosted the man.
> "It is futile," I said,
> "You can never"—
> "You lie," he cried,
> And ran on.

A hint from the teacher will give the key that the horizon symbolizes ideals. The discussion then may center upon whether it is futile and senseless to pursue ideals that can never be reached. Who is right, the speaker or the pursuer of the horizon? What have men gained from seeking the ideal means of transportation, the ideal means of communication, the ideal form of government? Who is more likely to leave his "footprints on the sands of time"—the one who says "You can't" or the one who says "I can try"?

"Mother to Son." The mother in Langston Hughes's poem tells her son,

> Life for me ain't been no crystal stair.
> It's had tacks in it,
> And splinters,
> And boards torn up,

And places with no carpets on the floor—
Bare.
But all the time
I'se been a-climbin' on.

One young lad, catching the significance at once, remarked, "My dad was climbing up the ladder of success but came to a place where a couple of rungs were missing, and he fell through and had to start all over." Class discussion may profitably expand the metaphors. What are the tacks, splinters, boards torn up, and bare places in life's stairway? Does everybody find them? Is life for anyone a crystal stair? Wouldn't crystal stairs become tiresome after a while?

Use of the didactic approach, then, gives opportunity to explore authors' opinions, to elaborate upon them, and to agree or take issue with them. It is an approach useful in teaching students to think straight, and in developing their philosophies of life.

The Paraphrastic Approach

Several years ago a teacher pointed out some of the vocabulary difficulties that students encounter in Milton's minor poems. "Cloister" they confuse with "cluster," "furrow" with "furrier" or "burrow," "dame" with "Dane" or "dam," "hamlet" with "hammock," and "haycock" with "a bird that lives in the hay." Such students may read "The upland hamlets will invite" and get a mental picture of someone being lured by a slanting hammock; "the tanned haycock" is a sunburned bird; and "the studious cloister's pale" is a cluster of pale, overworked students. It is almost beyond the imagination to guess how students may interpret "sable stole of cypress lawn," "daisies pied," "country messes," and "Jonson's learned sock."

Then, besides the traps of vocabulary, there are the pits of allusion. In the first twenty lines of "L'Allegro" are at least ten allusions that will mean little or nothing to the average high school senior—words like "Cerberus," "Stygian," etc.

Morasses of sentence structure also abound. One example will suffice:

Straight mine eye hath caught new pleasures,
Whilst the landskip round it measures.

Even though a student knows that "straight" means "straightway" or "at once," "whilst" means "while," "landskip" means "landscape," and "measures" means "examines," the couplet is still unintelligible unless he also knows that "it" refers to "eye" and is the subject of the clause. If he does not realize this, he interprets the second line to mean that the landscape is examining something; but, if he does realize it, he can see that the couplet means, "Immediately my eye has seen new pleasures while it examines the surrounding landscape."

Although these poems set more toils for the unwary than do most of the others that are taught in high school, similar perils lurk in many non-Miltonic poems. Sometimes textbook annotations suffice to clear the way; textbook editors have become more and more helpful during the twentieth century. But, even with the annotations, some students will continue to misinterpret unless the class is guided by a capable and conscientious teacher.

It is to prevent gross misinterpretations that the paraphrastic approach is employed. It is not a lively approach and cannot employ a variety of techniques as the others can. But it does have value in clarifying meaning. Often it may be used as a preliminary to some other approach. Students must understand the words and the sentences in "My Last Duchess," for instance, before they can discuss it as a social document.

Miller and Slote, in *The Dimensions of Poetry*, point out that a poem may be summarized, paraphrased, or explicated, while they emphasize that the result of any one of these processes is by no means the same as the poem itself. A summary "captures and preserves only the bare substance of what is said in the poem, its nonpoetic part." They illustrate with a summary of this poem by Emily Dickinson:

> The Bustle in a House
> The Morning after Death
> Is solemnest of industries
> Enacted upon Earth,—
>
> The Sweeping up the Heart,
> And putting Love away
> We shall not want to use again
> Until Eternity.[11]

Their summary, "One of the most difficult of all tasks in life is the emotional adjustment following the loss through death of someone close," is, they say, "like the bruised rind of an orange from which all

[11] Reprinted by permission of the publishers from Thomas H. Johnson, editor, *The Poems of Emily Dickinson*, Cambridge, Mass.: The Belknap Press of Harvard University Press, copyright 1951, 1955, by the President and Fellows of Harvard College.

the golden juices have been squeezed." A paraphrase, in contrast, is longer, follows the original closely, and attempts to convey the full meaning: "On the day after the death of a beloved relative, the soberest activity in the home (the soberest, in fact, in the world) is the disposition of the affections which have lost their object and which will be superfluous until a spiritual reunion outside time is effected." Such a paraphrase is "like a black-and-white photograph of a brilliant masterpiece of art."

An explication, however, is less inclusive than either a summary or a paraphrase. It attempts to answer the hard questions about meaning, to show relationships among parts not obviously related. In the Dickinson poem, for example, why is the word "industries" used? Why "enacted"? How does one sweep up the heart? How can love be put away?

The point of all this, the point that the teacher must always remember in paraphrasing, summarizing, or explicating, is that the poem is an entity that cannot be replaced by something else. The paraphrastic approach (broadly enough defined to include summary and explication) may help to make clear, but the result must not be said to equal the poem itself.

The Analytical Approach

Just how much knowledge of poetic theory and terminology should be taught to high school students has long been a moot question. Is the architecture of the poem the important thing, or is it only incidental to something more important—the meaning and implications? Can meaning and implications be adequately taught if there is no understanding of the architecture? Some teachers expose students to every literary term that they themselves know, hoping that at least a few will stick; at the other extreme are a smaller number of teachers who call a poem a "story" and point out none of its distinguishing characteristics. And, in the middle, the majority of teachers introduce students to the poetical theory and terminology that seem to them most likely to be valuable.

Here the majority is probably right. The student must know something about poetic architecture in order to understand and appreciate, just as he can better appreciate the beauty of a cathedral if he knows something about naves, transepts, arches, and keystones. But minute metrical analysis is more the province of the professional poet or scholar than it is of the high school student who may soon be driving a truck or working in a laundry.

It is the whole poem that demands attention. Diction, figures of speech and other devices, sentence structure, and verse form are of significance only because of what they contribute to the whole. A "good" poem represents a happy blend of the thought and the poetic devices. The wrong device—inappropriate verse form, for instance, or an unwisely chosen simile—may spoil a poem. If Homer sometimes nodded, his descendants often do. Shelley, for example, wrote a serious poem about death, beginning,

> Death is here and death is there;
> Death is busy everywhere.

It is a bad poem because the meter does not fit the thought; if the subject were a rambling wreck from Georgia Tech the verse form would be more appropriate and the poem might be better. Wordsworth's occasional infelicities are notorious. In a poem about the curse laid upon a young man by a poverty-stricken old woman—a theme that Coleridge might have handled with consummate skill— Wordsworth begins,

> Oh! what's the matter? what's the matter?
> What is't that ails young Harry Gill?
> That evermore his teeth they chatter,
> Chatter; chatter, chatter still!

The prosaic "what's the matter?" is hardly fitting in a serious poem about a curse; the feminine rhyme, as in "matter" and "chatter," gives a humorous effect of the sort that Byron often intentionally attained and that we associate with Ogden Nash in our day; the repetition of "chatter" belongs in Tennyson's "Brook" but is out of place here; and the verse form no more fits the subject than does that of Shelley's poem on death.

A teacher should find these observations meaningful in his instruction because he ought to teach that a good poem is a unit in which all elements are in harmony. The metrical form, the similes, etc., are not merely surface decoration; they are intrinsic. A poet does not write a rough draft of a poem and then say to himself, "I'll add a few similes to increase the attractiveness." The similes are, instead, natural outgrowths of the idea or emotion that the poet is expressing. Neither does a true poet choose a particular word because it is euphonious or because it is the first one that comes to mind; he selects it because it is the one that best reveals the meaning and best conveys the mood.

In using the analytical approach, then, one does not pick to pieces, but one notes the contribution of each piece to the whole pattern. Students learn definitions of technical terms almost incidentally, through the class discussions. A student who has memorized the words "A metaphor is a figure of speech in which a term is applied to something to which it is not literally applicable" does not necessarily know what a metaphor is, but the student who has often talked about such expressions as "The wind was a torrent of darkness" and "The fog comes on little cat feet" probably does. This second student has examined the contribution of metaphors to individual poems and has understood the work that they do; he has recognized that they are implied comparisons; his experience with poetry has probably been much happier than that of the lad who was told to memorize dry definitions, or the one who was told to find and copy fifty metaphors from *Julius Caesar,* or the one who was left with the impression that poets sprinkle metaphors over their poems as a soda jerk sprinkles nuts over a sundae.

In a book that for decades has been read by British teachers of English (*English for the English,* Cambridge University Press, London, 1921), George Sampson warns against breaking into the mood of a poem by analyzing its parts:

What pleasure should we get from a performance of the C minor symphony if the conductor stopped the orchestra at every occurrence of the main theme to expatiate upon the wonderful significance with which Beethoven can invest a simple rhythmic phrase, or from a performance of the B minor mass if a choir were silenced while someone explained the harmonic effects that make the hushed close of the *Crucifixus* such a wonderful moment? It is delightful to have these beauties of musical language pointed out to us; but not while we are on the emotional plane of a performance.

If Sampson is right, a three-stage study of many poems would seem desirable. The first stage would involve one or two readings (at least one aloud) for the pleasure the poem can afford. Then would come any necessary paraphrasing, possibly a discussion of historical background, possibly some discussion of the author's purpose or point of view, and some analysis of the poetic techniques employed. After that, through one or two additional readings, the poem would be reassembled, so to speak; these new readings, with the light added by the second stage, should result in greater enjoyment than the first ones.

For further clarification of the matter of studying the architecture of a poem, in the second stage of the process just described, several aspects of "The Rime of the Ancient Mariner" may be briefly considered.

In the first place, the basic verse form used by Coleridge is the ballad stanza. For this poem, the ballad stanza is appropriate because the subject matter is akin to that of the Middle English ballads, which often stressed the supernatural. (It is probable that this stanza was widely used in late medieval times because it is versatile and because it is an easy form to compose, to learn, and to sing.) Sometimes, though, Coleridge departed from the pattern and included stanzas of five, six, or more lines. The reason is that the longer stanzas prevent the monotony that might result from constant employment of the ballad stanza in a lengthy poem.

The archaic diction of Coleridge's poem also contributes to the total effect. The ship leaves an unnamed country; the story takes place at an indefinite, unknown time. The language, therefore, should not suggest the here and now, but instead a vague "there" and an indefinite "then." Words like "stoppeth," "eftsoons," "swound," and "gramercy" remove the poem from 1798 and carry the reader backward two centuries, three centuries, or more.

The frequent repetition is deliberate and appropriate. You recall that when the ship was becalmed,

> There passed a weary time. Each throat
> Was parched, and glazed each eye.
> A weary time! a weary time!
> How glazed each weary eye.

Colerdige wanted to stress the weariness. How could it be better stressed than by repeating the word "weary"? Or how could the Mariner's loneliness be better emphasized than in

> Alone, alone, all, all alone,
> Alone on a wide wide sea!

Coleridge used alliteration for an equally specific purpose. As the south wind pushed the ship rapidly along,

> The fair breeze blew, the white foam flew,
> The furrow followed free.

The alliteration is more than "pretty"; it serves to hasten the line, to accentuate the speed of the ship. Consonantal alliteration often does this, whereas vocalic alliteration (as in "Alone, alone, all, all alone") tends to make a line move more slowly.

Personification—the sun as "he," the moon as "she," the storm blast as "tyrannous," Death and Life-in-Death, the articulate spirits of the sea, etc.—is more appropriate in this poem than in most. The setting is a vague period reminiscent of the Dark Ages, when many people believed that the physical forces of the world were conscious beings, often hostile to man. Moreover, it is human nature to employ a sort of reverse empathy and transfer our feelings to inanimate things; without thinking, we employ figurative expressions like "biting wind," "cruel sea," and "relentless sun." Shipwrecked men have been known to curse the sea as if it had plotted against them; travelers on a desert have looked upon the sun as a personal and implacable enemy. Coleridge's use of personification, then, is intrinsic in the situation he describes.

The similes and metaphors serve to clarify, to picture, to make the unreal seem real. "Mast-high" and "as green as emerald" show us the ice; the seaman's hailing of the albatross "as if it had been a Christian soul" demonstrates how happy the men were to see any living thing but suggests also the mysterious power of the albatross and the cruelty of killing it; "as idle as a painted ship upon a painted ocean" dramatizes the ship's complete lack of movement. Hardly can a more ghastly picture than that of Life-in-Death be imagined; yet the picture is composed largely of figures of speech:

> Her lips were red, her looks were free,
> Her locks were yellow as gold:
> Her skin was white as leprosy,
> The Night-mare Life-in-Death was she,
> Who thicks man's blood with cold.

In teaching "The Ancient Mariner," then, or any other poem in which it seems desirable to refer to poetic devices, it is desirable to help the students to understand the appropriateness of the meter, the diction, and the figures. Sometimes it is wise to talk about the organization of the whole poem, how each part fits, why each part is where it is. If students can be led to regard a poem as a unit to which each part contributes, their appreciation will be considerably increased.

In an extraordinarily useful article,[12] Howard Creed says, "The framework is significant: the guest, next of kin to the bridegroom, is on his way to celebrate a ceremony that fuses two people into one; but he is stopped to be taught that there is a more universal unity

---

[12] "'The Rime of the Ancient Mariner': A Rereading," *English Journal*, XLIX (Jan., 1960), 215.

than that of an isolated marriage, that all the world is one." In discussing imagery, Creed states,

I see no reason why an alert class, after being reminded that the Romantic imagination works best by moonlight, shouldn't be able to discover for itself which events in the poem happen under the moon, which under the sun, and whether or not any particular pattern of moon-sun imagery seems to be used. A simpler analysis, and one easily fitted into the fusion of the natural and the supernatural, can be made of the sequence of the vivid images as the voyage progresses: the natural images of the harbour (kirk, hill, lighthouse) giving way to the supernatural images of the polar sea (the skeleton ship, for instance) and then returning (lighthouse, hill, kirk).

Perhaps no two teachers would agree exactly concerning which technical terms ought to be introduced during the study of poetry. It would seem, though, that any technical term that is innate to the poem being discussed is appropriate, but that no term should be dragged in simply because the teacher happens to know it. Further, it seems reasonable to assume that a simile or an anapaestic foot is of no importance in itself, but attains significance only because of the part it plays in the structure of the poem.

In other words, no teacher should do what one teacher actually did: She could never remember the distinction between metonymy and synecdoche, but knew that both are figures of speech. Therefore, once each year she relearned their definitions and required her class to memorize them!

The analytical approach (which could as well be named the synthesizing approach) has merit when it is used to help students understand clearly how a poem is constructed, what function each constituent part performs. But, if it becomes merely a process of disassembly, it is almost valueless.

NON-FICTION

No extended discussion of the use of the six approaches with non-fiction is necessary; the teacher need only observe the principles already illustrated in considering fiction, drama, and poetry. Biographies clearly lend themselves to the historical approach, as do certain essays such as the *Tatler* and *Spectator* papers. Steele and Addison also provide splendid material for the sociopsychological approach, since they, along with Goldsmith, humanize the eighteenth century perhaps more than do any other writers. Essays such as the perennial favorite, Lamb's "Dissertation upon Roast Pig," and travel accounts such as Stevenson's *Travels with a Donkey* or some of Harry Franck's

Vagabonding stories lend themselves to the emotive approach. Almost any personal essay or biography may justify occasional use of the didactic approach. Francis Bacon, Benjamin Franklin, and possibly Thomas Huxley and a few others whose writings are sometimes taught in high school need to have their essays partially paraphrased before students can do much else with them. The analytical approach may be employed in the comparison of styles and techniques of various non-fiction writers; the personal essay, for example, may be used to demonstrate that the typical pattern is the reporting of observation and then the reporting of speculation upon what was observed.

The examples mentioned are all classics or near classics. For several reasons it is desirable to expose students to a number of these works of unquestioned merit. In the first place, the classics often have historical significance and thus help us to understand ourselves by clarifying our backgrounds. Second, they usually possess high literary merit. Third (to adduce an old argument), everyone should have an opportunity to share knowledge of our common cultural heritage—to know something about the best that has been thought and said. Fourth, superior students, at least, may use the classics as Matthew Arnold advised: as "touchstones" by means of which other pieces of writing may be judged.

But it is true that the non-fiction diet should not consist exclusively of classics. Teachers have the responsibility of paving the way for the reading their students will do as adults. A classroom contact with Bacon and Addison may influence youthful tastes somewhat, but as adults their chief non-fiction reading will probably be today's newspaper, this week's news magazine, and this month's digest or other popular magazine—not Bacon's essay or the *Spectator*.

Newspapers vary widely; some are ultrasensational, others ultraconservative, and the majority in between. Some are much more likely than others to contribute to the good of humanity. We may or may not agree precisely on the dividing line between good and bad periodicals, but the places where we draw our respective lines will probably not be far apart. Our students, however, may not have that critical knowledge unless we instil it in them. Because adults—somebody's former students—do not know or do not care, the sensationalizing newspapers and the most lurid of the cheap magazines flourish.

A partial solution is the teaching of a unit on newspapers and another unit, perhaps in a different year, on magazines. For this the sophomore and junior years appear most satisfactory, because the students on these levels are better able to read a large variety of materials and judge them with more discrimination than are their

younger brothers and sisters. Some teachers, though, have successfully taught such units in the junior high school.[13]

The usual procedure is to provide a number of newspapers or
magazines, varying in quality from worst to best. By reading and
by making detailed comparisons, students learn the strengths and the
weaknesses of the various periodicals. No teacher can expect to
convert an entire class to a sincere love of *The New York Times* and
Harper's, but he can expect to bring each student to a place somewhat
above his original level. And, if a student comes to a clear realization
that in an inferior newspaper he pays for distortion of facts, emphasis
upon the trivial, and omission of significant news, he is more likely
when he becomes an adult to purchase a fairly good newspaper.
Likewise, the student who by his own comparison has convinced himself that the lurid magazines are repetitious and inaccurate is likely
to buy something a little better at the newsstand.

In one unit of this sort, the teacher asked each student to bring to
class his favorite newspaper. The class discussed the points that they
believed intelligent people ought to know about newspapers and
made notes of the "Canons of Journalism" as named in Edgar Dale's
How To Read a Newspaper: responsibility, freedom of the press,
independence, sincerity, truthfulness, accuracy, impartiality, fair play,
and decency. The students evaluated the various newspapers in the
light of these canons: and compared them with *The New York Times*
and *Christian Science Monitor.* They noted and deplored the dearth
of "pitchers" and "jokes" and sports news in the latter two but were
impressed by the number of important national and international news
stories that were omitted from the papers they usually read. The
teacher says that, although she has no proof that any of the students
became confirmed in wise newspaper reading habits, she does know
that they began to have a new conception of the meaning of a newspaper, and to consider newspapers critically.

A magazine unit may be handled in a similar manner. An ingenious
variation, which brought satisfactory results when an Illinois teacher
tried it with a group of sophomores, involves emphasis upon the advertising. Students are shown that most magazines are simply media
for advertisers and that each advertiser aims at what he believes to be
the mental level and the interests of the readers. Nothing more
clearly demonstrates the low caliber of the pulps than their advertisements; just as a man is known by the company he keeps, so a magazine is known by the advertisements it keeps. These sophomores

---

[13] Newspaper and magazine articles may often add enrichment to any unit, of
course.

quickly saw how gullible people would be who would believe that they could "have a physique like mine in 90 days," "learn to throw your voice into a trunk," "play the piano in one month," "get a high school education in three months," "solve this easy puzzle and win $1,000." Since the sophomores did not want to be classified on such a low mental level, they agreed that these magazines were not for them.

Some teachers have planned units on travel books and modern biography, as parallels to units on newspapers and magazines. "Round-the-world trips," with each student responsible for one of the countries on the itinerary, have proved popular, as have units on "The Lands of Our Ancestors," "Europe Today," "Europe Yesterday," "Flying Carpets," "From Here to There in Fourteen Days," etc. A Missouri class studied biographies of nineteenth- and twentieth-century personages; separate committees specialized on scientists, statesmen, etc.; each student prepared an interesting report on some one person; there was a "Guess Who" program with five carefully prepared clues concerning each biographee; radio skits were presented to dramatize highlights; and the class tried to find concerning these great men and women "the source of their dynamic living" and "what they have discovered about life."

The brevity of this treatment of non-fiction should not suggest that essays, travel books, biographies, and other non-fictional materials ought to be slighted. They deserve a fairly large proportion of the class time because they are informative and stimulating and may possess high literary value. Only a few pages are here devoted to them, because the techniques of teaching them are essentially the same as those for other types of literature.

THE IDEA BOX

T. S. ELIOT ON TEACHING THE MODERNS

In "The Appreciation of Poetry" (*The Critic*, XVIII [April–May 1960], 78), T. S. Eliot warns against excessive analysis of modern poetry and against examinations based on such poetry. He suggests, though, that students may listen twice to a recorded poem and then write their interpretation of it and about the feelings or impressions it left with them.

"WHO KILLED POETRY?"

Mark Neville (*English Journal*, XLVII [March, 1958], 133) says that excessive emphasis on metrics and on prosodic (or prosaic!) analysis has given many students a distaste for poetry. The remedy: "Enjoyment, admiration, and sympathy are the stuff of appreciation."

THE FIRST POEM

In any unit containing a number of poems, it is especially important that the first poem be one that will interest and stimulate the class. This first happy experience will make discussion of the later poems easier and more satisfying.

"POETRY FOR NINTH-GRADERS"

August Franza (*English Journal*, XLVII [Dec., 1958], 575) and his ninth graders asked these basic questions about poems studied: "First of all, what is the 'sense' of a poem? What does the poem say? What does it tell us about? Secondly, what is the 'feeling' of the poem? What moods and emotions are conveyed to the reader? Thirdly, what is the 'theme' of the poem (if one can be determined)? What ideas is the author trying to get across? What is the significance of his poem? Finally, what is the 'form' of the poem? . . . Then we asked general questions. Does the poem make us aware of something we did not know before? Does it make us 'see' more clearly commonplace things we have taken for granted? Does it help us understand the complexities of human behavior? Has it introduced a new thought, idea, or vision we have never before considered?"

ON THE USES OF BAD POETRY

Harvey Firari (*English Journal*, XLVIII [May, 1959], 262) uses verses by Edgar A. Guest, by a local rhymester, and by himself in introducing poetry to his Culver, Indiana, classes of boys. Finding the flaws (while the teacher mildly defends these "poems") makes the boys more ready to applaud the truly poetic they encounter in better writers.

TO AROUSE INTEREST

One of the best ways to arouse interest in a poem is to help students see how it is related in some way to their own experiences and knowledge.

MYTHOLOGY IN MODERN LIFE

Mercury automobiles, Atlas tires, Jupiter and Thor missiles, Venus pencils, and the like may help students to see that remnants of Greek and Roman mythology still exist.

"COMPARING POEMS ON LIKE TOPICS"

Paul M. Wheeler (*English Journal*, XL [March, 1951], 154) stresses the values of comparing the thoughts of two or more poets writing on similar subjects, and concludes his article with a fairly long list of possibilities.

UNDERSTANDING LYRIC POETRY

"Students who have trouble reading lyric poetry with understanding often find it easier with this set of questions: Speaker? Listener? Situation? Mood?" (Elaine Clarke, Central High School, Grand Rapids, Mich.)

COLERIDGE'S PLAN

Some teachers use Coleridge's critical plan of finding the author's purpose, noting the methods used to achieve that purpose, and judging the success.

STATING THEMES

A comparison of two or more statements of the theme of a work may lead to understanding. One statement is accurate; the others, flawed. For example, for Browning's "My Last Duchess": "Fra Pandolf captured the grace and beauty of my last Duchess; although I regret her death, I shall now be honored to have the Count's daughter marry me." "My last Duchess showed too little respect for me and was not formal enough with others; now, if the dowry is sufficient, I shall honor the Count's daughter with my hand."

PICTURES IN POETRY

Read to your junior high school students a short descriptive poem, and ask them to draw something that they "see" in it. If some of them say that they can't draw, let them write a word picture.

METER

If you want to teach names of metrical feet, use names of your students to illustrate (e.g., iamb, Laverne; trochee, Wilbur; dactyl, Dorothy; anapaest, Antoinette; amphibrach, Louisa).

GREETING-CARD VERSE

Many students prefer greeting-card verse to poetry. Without attacking such verse, lead students to see the monotony and limitations of much of it—that, except for humorous verse, it almost invariably consists of a compliment, a wish, or a statement of appreciation.

A POETRY PARTY

Around the fireplace, students read short favorite poems and talk about them. Refreshments too, of course.

CHAUCER IN MODERN DRESS

In addition to writing parodies of parts of the "Prologue" to the *Canterbury Tales*, with modern characters replacing Chaucer's, students may enjoy preparing modern versions of some of the tales. For example, "The Pardoner's Tale" is the story of three hoodlums who hijack a liquor truck and, when each attempts to secure the profits for himself, all three are killed.

USES OF LITERARY RECORDINGS

1. Occasionally play the recording of a poem or a part of a play before the class reads it, especially for a "mood piece," in which emotion or mood should be understood from the beginning.

2. Sometimes students may read silently, following the text while the record plays. Thus eye and ear reinforce each other.

3. Oral reading by the class, in unison with the record, is good for descriptive or mood poetry.

4. Often study should precede the playing. As the class listens, it may watch for the reader's interpretation of particular passages to discover previously unsuspected meanings or to help settle possibly controversial points.

5. Sometimes a record should be played for sheer enjoyment, without class study of the selection. "Easy" verse or brief dramatic selections are particularly suitable. Seasonal poetry is often appropriate.

6. "Sing-along sessions" (especially ballads and folk songs) are good fun.

7. Musical recordings related to literature (e.g., Tschaikovsky's "Overture" to *Romeo and Juliet*) may help to show links between two arts. Some historical records also provide good background (e.g., "The London Story: A Sound Portrait of London through the Ages," London LL839, with scenes from the time of Elizabeth I, the Great Fire of 1666, the Age of Victoria, the Blitz of 1940, voices of Churchill and Elizabeth II, etc.).

8. Caution: Always listen to a record before playing it for a class. Some ostensibly suitable selections may prove undesirable because of the quality of the recording, faulty interpretation, or frankness of language.

WHICH DID THE POET WRITE?

To help students observe a poet's careful choice of words and the probable reasons for his choices, Robert L. Stevens, of Arizona State College, suggests giving a class slightly garbled lines of a poem along with the original. If the lines are intermixed, as in the passage from Pope's "Essay on Criticism" below, students can decide which lines are the author's:

True ease in writing comes from learning, not chance	True ease in writing comes from art, not chance
As those move best who have learned to dance.	As those move easiest who have learned to dance.
'Tis not enough no harshness gives offense,	'Tis not enough that no harshness gives offense,
The sound must seem an echo of of the sense:	The sound must seem a mirror of the sense:
Mild is the mood when Zephyr lightly blows,	Soft is the strain when Zephyr gently blows,
And the smooth stream in smoother numbers flows;	And the smooth stream in matching meter flows;
But when loud surges lave the sounding shore,	But when loud surges lash the sounding shore,
The hoarse, rough verse should like the torrent roar;	The howling verse should like the torrent roar;
When Ajax strives some rock's vast weight to throw,	When Ajax tries some heavy rock to throw,
The line too labours, and the words move slow.	The rhythm alters, and the words move slow.

Problems in meter, diction, auditory appeal, alliteration, context, and total effect may be discussed through these few lines. (Pope wrote lines 3, 4, 6, 8, 9, 10 in the first column, and lines 1, 2, 5, 7 in the second.)

"INTRODUCING HOMER'S *Odyssey* IN HIGH SCHOOL"

Enid Olson (*Illinois English Bulletin,* Nov., 1957) describes these materials and methods used with the *Odyssey:* Tennyson's "Ulysses"; a student map of the eastern Mediterranean; individual reports on the *Iliad* and the Trojan War; guest lecture by a teacher who has visited the Mediterranean; committee reports on the people and the mythology of ancient Greece; filmstrips of Athens and of the story of Ulysses; much reading aloud from the story.

PROVIDING ADDED EXAMPLES

Students' understanding of some poems may be enhanced if they add other examples to those chosen by the poet. For instance, in "Each and All" Emerson says that the sparrow, the sea shells, and the girl became less attractive when removed from their natural surroundings. What other examples might he have used?

SANDBURG AS A DOOR OPENER

Though Carl Sandburg is not dramatic or philosophical or even lyric, his non-conformity appeals to the eternal—and inevitable and desirable—rebelliousness of youth and, hence, makes him a door opener to poetry. Michael Yatron, "Carl Sandburg: The Poet as Nonconformist," *English Journal,* XLVIII (Dec., 1959), 524.

"POETRY SHOULD BE HEARD"

Harlen M. Adams (*English Journal,* XLVIII [April, 1959], 206) offers brief suggestions for students' oral reading. Key points: (1) Provide first an explanatory introduction to clarify purpose; for instance, point out that Browning's wife had died shortly before he wrote "Prospice." (2) "A reader does not recite words but rather reproduces ideas and emotions."

WHICH MODERNS?

Sister M. Bernetta Quinn, O.S.F., recommends selected poems by these poets as especially suitable for reading by able high school students: Frost, Eliot, Yeats, Cummings, Sandburg, W. C. Williams, H. Crane, W. Stevens, Jarrell, Nims, Larkin, Thomas, Spender, Auden. "Modern Poetry and the Classroom," *English Journal,* L (Dec., 1961), 590.

A JUNIOR HIGH DISCOVERS POETRY

Eric W. Johnson's junior high students, in Germantown Friends School, arrive at these characteristics of poetry: "1. rhyme (not always) 2. rhythm (almost always)—meter 3. form—verses; rhyme and meter a part of form 4. emotion—expresses feelings usually 5. concentration—says a lot in a few words 6. figurative language—comparison." Mr. Johnson finds

Robert Nathan's "Dunkirk" a good opener, follows it with W. R. Benét's "Skater of Ghost Lake," then a group of poems with students assigned to discuss meaning, form, sound, feelings created, and memorable lines. Students also write limericks, couplets, and a poem each, and learn principles of oral reading. *English Journal*, L (Nov., 1961), 546.

FOLK SONGS AND BALLADS

In "An Approach to Poetry," *English Journal*, L (April, 1961), 274, Frederick E. Danker describes his use in a sophomore class of his compilation of eighty pages of American folk songs and ballads. Advantages of this type of verse: strong rhymes and rhythms, dialog, simple stanza forms, and concentration.

"I SEE AMERICA DANCING"

Boys in Brooklyn Technical High School enjoy a twenty-minute assignment parodying Whitman. Teacher A. S. Flaumenhaft supplies the first line, "I see America dancing." *Clearing House*, XXXVII (Oct., 1962), 96.

STUDENTS AND ROMANTICS: THE COMMON BOND

William E. Lucas, De Kalb, Illinois, emphasizes what the romantic poets and high school students have in common: a rebellious spirit, idealism, susceptibility to religious and philosophical influences, and interest in the natural world.

MY THOUGHTS AND A POET'S

Before her students read poems from their anthology, Sarah I. Roody had them write paragraphs that she planned to relate to the poetry. Each paragraph was an answer to a question such as "What do you think are the pleasantest things in ordinary daily life?" (Related to Brooke's "The Great Lover.") "Have you ever felt that you would like to be a champion of the underdog?" (Masefield's "Consecration.") For details and other excellent suggestions, see "A Bridge for the Poets," *English Journal*, XL (Nov., 1951), 492.

NINE ARTICLES ON POETRY

The entire March, 1957, *English Journal* was devoted to the teaching of poetry. The nine articles are unusually helpful.

POETRY AND MUSIC

1. You might devote an hour to a ballad party, with phonograph records, class singing, and possibly the presentation of an original ballad or two.

2. Anna Haig, Bronxville, New York, recommends having students find music and a painting that express the same mood as some poem. The student names the mood, describes the painting briefly, copies a few bars of the music, and quotes from the poem. In Cheraw, South Carolina, students keep a "poetry-picture" scrapbook, with appropriate pictures to accompany poems or excerpts from poems.

3. "I use the theory that the first poetry was sung and that great poetry

has the same elements as great music. I show how poetry is set to music and what patterns of rhythm are most readily adapted to music. I show how parodies are written. I read 'Boots' by Kipling to show the accented syllables. I read a few lines that I have written." (Elizabeth B. Barton, Clanton, Ala.)

4. Harold P. Simonson, in Puyallup, Washington, spends a week playing records and reading related poetry. Some of his pairings include Tschaikovsky's "None but the Lonely Heart" with Wilde's "Requiescat," Debussy's "La Mer" with Byron's apostrophe to the ocean in *Childe Harold*, Debussy's "Clair de Lune" with De la Mare's "Silver," Grofé's "Sunrise" from the *Grand Canyon Suite* and Grieg's "Sunrise" from *Peer Gynt* with Dickinson's "I'll Tell You How the Sun Rose" and G. B. Hoover's "Mountain Dawn." See "Music as an Approach to Poetry," *English Journal*, XLIII (Jan., 1954), 19.

5. Mother Melanie Doyle, O.S.U., in "Correlating Music Appreciation and American Literature," lists forty-four selections with appropriate accompanying music, for example, Franklin's *Autobiography* and Gershwin's "American in Paris." *Clearing House*, XXX (Jan., 1956), 305.

6. Use a drum in the classroom to show the beat in "The Congo" and other poems with a marked rhythm. (Marguerite Chamberlain, Franklin, N.H.)

ANALYSES OF POEMS

Beginning in the September, 1961, *English Journal*, the NCTE Committee on the Reading and Study of Poetry in High School has been presenting in alternate issues detailed analyses of modern poems suitable for high school study.

HELPS IN TEACHING SPECIFIC POETS

These articles (in the *English Journal* except where the designation *CE* for *College English* appears) provide insights useful in teaching some major poets:

Matthew Arnold. Friedrich, Gerhard, "A Teaching Approach to Poetry," XLIX (Feb., 1960), 75. (Especially on "Dover Beach.")

William Blake. Gleckner, Robert, " 'The Lamb' and 'The Tyger': How Far with Blake?" LI (Nov., 1962), 536.

Robert Burns. Fisher, Mary C., "Ayr Lines, Ceiling Unlimited," XLIX (Jan., 1960), 39.

John Ciardi. Southworth, J. G., "The Poetry of John Ciardi," L (Dec., 1961), 583.

S. T. Coleridge. Owen, C. A., Jr., "Structure in 'The Ancient Mariner,' " *CE*, XXIII (Jan., 1962), 261.

E. E. Cummings. Mills, Ralph J., Jr., "Poetry of Innocence," XLVIII (Nov., 1959), 433.

Ray, David, "The Irony of E. E. Cummings," *CE*, XXIII (Jan., 1962), 282.

T. S. Eliot. Smith, Grover, Jr., "Getting Used to T. S. Eliot," XLIX (Jan., 1960), 1.

Robert Frost. Cook, R. L., "The Stand of Robert Frost, Early and Late," XLVIII (May, 1959), 233.

John Keats. Slote, Bernice, "Of Chapman's Homer and Other Books," *CE*, XXIII (Jan., 1962), 256.
Karl Shapiro. Southworth, J. G., "The Poetry of Karl Shapiro," LI (March, 1962), 159.
Wallace Stevens. Doggett, Frank, "Wallace Stevens and the World We Know," XLVIII (Oct., 1959), 365.

TO BUILD AN INTEREST IN BIOGRAPHY

1. Start with biographies of living men and women. Then pick comparable figures of the past.
2. Allow considerable freedom in the choice of biographies.
3. Let students compare problems faced by famous people with their own problems.
4. After discussing a number of biographies, help to straighten out chronology by playing the game "Who could have known whom?" For example, could Washington have known Lincoln?
5. Study famous friends (David and Jonathan, Damon and Pythias, Tennyson and Hallam, etc.).

BOOKS ON ADVENTURE ARE RESPECTABLE

Kon-Tiki, says Gorham Munson in the December, 1954, *English Journal,* set a new standard for books of true adventure, and later authors have been trying to reach the same level. Munson lists a number of titles, which you can supplement by use of the NCTE reading lists.

FRIENDS FROM NON-FICTION

"At the beginning of the study of a nonfiction unit I like to gather all available books and turn the class loose. At first there is a tendency to change books frequently, but soon they settle to concentrated reading. Ten minutes of each period is used to exchange ideas from and enthusiasms for books. At the end of the wide reading time we make lists of new friends we've met through reading. Sometimes this résumé takes the form of one student's introducing a newly acquired friend-through-reading to the class as though the subject of the biography were to address the group." (Esther Urie, Hartford, Vt.)

ORGANIZATION OF NON-FICTION ARTICLES

Nell Doherty, Las Vegas, New Mexico, High School, gives her students outlines of difficult articles to be read by the class. This procedure helps their reading and also assists them to see the value of organization.

MAGAZINES

1. *Reader's Digest* may be obtained by schools at special rates. Supplementary materials prepared for using the magazines in the classroom are available. Study guides for *Harper's* and a few other magazines may also be obtained. *Scholastic* publications are used in many classes.
2. To arouse interest in magazine articles, some teachers ask their students to prepare signed bulletin-board lists of articles they recommend, with brief annotations. Individuals or groups may make a careful study

of certain magazines. The teacher and members of the class may occasionally read aloud excerpts from articles they have especially liked.

3. Have students examine a number of magazines to determine which ones they would like to have later in their own homes.

4. In Greenwich, Connecticut, Hardy Finch's students learn to read magazine articles critically by (1) reading a controversial article and then having a panel find and present the arguments on the side not favored by the author, (2) examining the editorial policies of a magazine, (3) studying the author's competence to write authoritatively on the subject he has chosen.

5. It is useful to discuss with students the characteristics of "pulp," "slick," and "quality" magazines and have them apply the criteria to magazines they know. To be granted: (1) Occasionally an excellent story or article appears in a pulp; (2) the slicks frequently have good fiction and non-fiction; (3) not everything in a quality magazine is necessarily first rate, and quality magazines are usually harder to read; (4) a few magazines do not fit neatly into one of these categories.

6. Ruth Hughson's Princeton, West Virginia, sophomores spend about three weeks in reading digest-type articles, writing summaries of some they like, giving talks based on the articles, and (in connection with a study of punctuation) discovering that punctuation "rules" are really only generalizations summarizing how authors really punctuate.

NEWSPAPERS

1. Have students compare a newspaper such as *The New York Times, Christian Science Monitor*, or *St. Louis Post-Dispatch* with one of the scandal-sheet sort, answering such questions as: "What is emphasized in headlines and major news stories?" "Are stories biased?" "What do the editorials emphasize?" "What kinds of feature stories are included?" "Does the paper appeal more to emotions or to reason?" Criteria for judging newspapers should result.

2. A helpful book: Edgar Dale's *How To Read a Newspaper*.

"THIS I BELIEVE—ABOUT THE ESSAY"

Jerome Carlin answers four objections to teaching the essay: It's dull. It's difficult. It's archaic. Its form is hard to analyze. He makes a convincing case for more teaching of essays. *English Journal,* LI (Sept., 1962), 403.

WHY NOT TRY *Walden?*

In "*Walden,* Neglected American Classic," Leo A. Bressler argues that, because Thoreau was a rebellious spirit, he has built-in appeal for able young people. *English Journal,* LI (Jan., 1962), 14.

SATIRE

For lucid interpretations of the satire in *Gulliver's Travels* and the works of Dr. Bernard Mandeville, see two articles by James A. Preu: "The Case of the Mysterious Manuscript," *English Journal,* LII (Nov., 1963), 579, and "Private Vices—Public Benefits," *Ibid.* (Dec., 1963), 653.

8

COMPOSING IS THINKING

THE ENGLISH TEACHER AS A TEACHER OF THINKING

"The Common Thread of Education"

In 1961 the Educational Policies Commission of the National Education Association and the American Association of School Administrators issued a statement called "The Central Purpose of American Education." Without contradicting or denying the importance of the earlier-annunciated Cardinal Principles (health, worthy home membership, vocational competence, effective citizenship, worthy use of leisure, ethical character, and command of fundamental processes) the Commission made this statement: "The purpose which runs through and strengthens all other educational purposes—the common thread of education—is the development of the ability to think."

In elaborating upon this idea, the Commission made several statements of particular significance to teachers of English:

To be free, a man must be capable of basing his choices and actions on understandings which he himself achieves and on values which he examines for himself. He must be aware of the bases on which he accepts propositions as true. He must understand the values by which he lives, the assumptions on which they rest, and the consequences to which they lead. He must recognize that others have different values. He must be capable of analyzing the situation in which he finds himself and of developing solutions to the problems before him. (p. 4)

Psychological studies increasingly reveal unsuspected potential for growth in the development of human beings. (p. 14)

Each pupil is unique. He is different in background, in interests, moods, and tastes. This uniqueness deeply affects his learning, for he can react to the school only in terms of the person he is. No two pupils necessarily learn the same thing from a common learning experience. (p. 16)

Also, there is a highly creative aspect in the processes of thought. All the higher mental processes involve more than simple awareness of facts; they depend also on the ability to conceive what might be as well as what is, to construct mental images in new and original ways. Experience in literature and the arts may well make a larger contribution to these abilities than studies usually assumed to develop abstract thinking. (p. 18)

Facts, yes; but "more than simple awareness of facts." The English teacher perhaps has a better opportunity than any other teacher to inculcate this more than simple awareness, this ability to think. Fortunately, teachers of English do not have the sole responsibility. All other teachers share it. Parents share it. Every voluntary move made by a student during the day gives him practice in thinking. Everything that he hears, tastes, sees, feels, or smells gives him material for thinking and possibly a stimulus for thinking. His waking day, every day, is spent in gathering and, to a lesser extent, in using the wherewithal to think. But the English teacher has a unique opportunity to help him use the wherewithal.

What the English Teacher Can Do

Robert Frost said that he once saw a teacher who would plink pupils' heads with a finger and tell them, "Think." They didn't. They needed to be shown what thinking is. In Frost's words, thinking is "just putting this and that together; it is just saying one thing in terms of another. To tell [students] that is to set their feet on the first rung of a ladder the top of which sticks through the sky."

Putting things together is much more than describing sentence structure, Frost explained: "We will give them the forms of sentences and, if they have any ideas, then they will know how to write them. But that is preposterous. All there is to writing is having ideas. To learn to write is to learn to have ideas." [1]

Helping students to have ideas—or to realize that they have ideas—and helping them to put ideas together: those are the main contributions that English teachers can make to the development of thinking.

We have already discussed—indirectly or directly—ways of looking thoughtfully at literature. In each of the approaches to literature we have recommended putting things together. The historical approach puts together a selection and relevant background; the sociopsycho-

[1] From "Education by Poetry."

logical, a selection and human characteristics; the emotive, a selection and emotional reactions; the didactic, a selection and the author's purpose; the paraphrastic, a selection and other ways of expressing its ideas; the analytical, a selection and the author's techniques. We have not said "memorize facts." We have not said "Forget everything else you know, and look at this short story as a discrete entity." Instead we have said "Associate. Compare. Contrast. Agree or disagree. Tell why. Reason. Think."

In teaching literature we ask students to consider the thoughts, emotions, and experiences of other people. In teaching composition we ask them to deal with their own thoughts, emotions, experiences. Many or most of these, of course, are derivative, secondhand; but they in some way have become the students' own. We ask students to put together parts of their background—be it observation, reading, daydreaming, venture, or adventure. In composition they put the parts together and draw conclusions about the meaning of the pairing, the assemblage, the concatenation.

In the rest of this chapter we shall look at specific ways in which students may put things together in the form that we call a composition, and in following chapters we shall see that sentence structure, grammar, diction, and even such "mechanical" matters as punctuation and spelling may be taught as exercises in thinking and not as rote memory. But first let us list a few of the day-to-day activities, related or unrelated to composition, that may make an English class a constant exercise in thinking.

Adding to Students' Knowledge. To put things together, we need things to put together. All teachers, and everyone else whom students encounter, inculcate knowledge, often without the students' awareness. Selecting carefully what he should teach, the English teacher may add richly to the store of raw materials of thought.

Asking Frequent Questions Involving Reflective Thought (putting the raw materials together, solving problems). Able teachers encourage students to be *homo cogitans* and not merely *homo sapiens*. The thought questions they ask are not huge and amorphous, like "What seem to you to have been the trends in English literature in the last 300 years?" Rather, they are pointed questions that guide thinking, questions like "Besides the love of nature, what qualities do these two poems by Frost and Wordsworth have in common?" or "Why is 'because' better than 'and' in this sentence?"

Adapting Thought Questions to the Level of the Class and of Individuals. Thinking ability must be developed. Capable teachers address less

difficult questions to young classes and slow students, more difficult
questions to older classes and bright students. The young do become
more mature; even the slow sometimes become less slow. Patience
and sympathy are two of the strongest weapons in a teacher's arsenal.

**Having Students Occasionally Work Together in Groups for the Solution
of a Problem.**   Highly valuable is practice in the give and take and
in the compromise essential to problem solving in a democratic nation.

Opposing Merely Emotional Reactions.   The word "Republican" causes
some persons to emit sparks of fury; the word "Democrat" can hardly
be spoken by some others without an implied "damn." "Poetry" to
some students connotes long hair and effeminacy; perhaps "football"
to these same students always suggests something praiseworthy. To
city students, "rural" refers to "hayseeds and hicks." To rural students, city people are "smart alecks." Mere bigness often seems a
virtue. Since Bigg High has a larger enrolment than Possum Trot
High, Bigg must be a better school; since *Luscious Lucifera* is a best
seller, it must be a "great" book.

Opposing Either-or Thinking and Other Fallacies.   People tend to set
up false dilemmas: Either this must be true or that. Often a conclusion at neither extreme is the true one; sometimes a conclusion entirely
different from those proposed by the either-or advocates is justified.
The intelligent teacher helps his students to see through false dilemmas, to search for other solutions. Similarily, he recognizes and attacks such common fallacies as begging the question, ignoring the
question, hasty generalization, and *post hoc, ergo propter hoc.* He
helps his students to become alert to the propagandists' frequent employment of fallacious reasoning.

Avoiding Aimless Discussion.   There should be a goal in each class or
group discussion. Usually, at least tentative conclusions should be
drawn.

Practicing.   If one learns to do by doing, one learns to think by thinking. Each class period in English, whether devoted to Alexander
Pope or to the comma, should be an intellectual experience—if possible,
an intellectual adventure—in which every student has a share.

THE CONTENT OF COMPOSITION

Good Field, No Hit

A teacher of college freshmen says, "The greatest weakness of freshman themes is not usage errors, misspellings, and punctuation lapses;

too many students do not have anything to say." [2] A secondary school English teacher also stresses the need for emphasizing content: "Composition begins with the need to say something; it does not and cannot begin with the workbook, the spelling exercise, the vocabulary drill, the sentence diagram, the identification of speech parts, or even the ingratiating study of the nature of language." [3]

Every teacher of college freshman English has his own version of this story: A bright-looking girl named Shirley enters his class. Her IQ is above average, and her high school English grades were mostly A's. She makes almost no mistakes in her compositions—misspells no word, seldom mispunctuates, never fails to choose the appropiate form of an irregular verb. But the instructor has to give her C's, D's, and F's on her themes. He calls her in for a conference. "Your writing is accurate," he tells her, "but accuracy alone is a negative virtue, since it means only freedom from errors. You do not say anything in your themes; you do not show that you have thought about the subject or that you can think about it. All that you do is repeat clichés. And you don't even organize the clichés! You jot them down in whatever order they come to your mind. I would suggest . . ."

Since Shirley is an eighteen-year-old college freshman, it is a bit late—and extremely painful—for her to start learning to think. Her high school teachers could have saved her from the seeming brutality of her college instructor. Thought-provoking assignments, stimulating discussions, questions that require reflection as well as recall, gradual weeding out of merely emotional responses, emphasis upon content as well as mechanics, insistence upon a point of view toward composition subjects—these in her high school days would have made her college career happier and more successful.

In baseball a player who makes few fielding errors but also has a low batting average is laconically described, "good field, no hit." Often nothing can be done for him. The thousands of Shirleys, female and male, could be described similarly by their English teachers. But most of them can be helped, especially in finding something to say in their compositions.

What a Subject Is

Professor Bertrand Evans describes what is, alas, a too nearly typical theme written by a student who has escaped from high school and

[2] Clarence Derrick, "What Do You Expect?" *English Journal*, XLIX (Feb., 1960), 104.

[3] Carl G. Wonnberger, "Writing—a Way of Life," *English Journal*, XLVIII (Feb., 1959), 66.

found his way into college. His first composition, the student is told, is to be on "My Home Town." He outlines the composition: Introduction—Name, Location, Size; II. Recreational facilities—Skiing, Swimming, Fishing, Hunting, YMCA; III. Educational facilities—Grade schools, high school, libraries; IV. Source of income—Farming, Industry, Business; V. Conclusion. He writes the paper, with a sentence or so on each of the subtopics, and hands it in.[4]

So what's wrong? The student has written about his home town, hasn't he? That was the assignment, wasn't it? The student has written, but he has not composed, Professor Evans would reply. He had a *topic*, but he didn't have a *subject*. A topic is the name of something, anything: hobbies, Aunt Sara, atomic energy, bricklaying, my home town. A subject, in contrast, says something: Hobbies are overrated; Aunt Sara is a miser; atomic energy can become man's greatest boon; bricklaying requires skill; my home town is an exciting place in which to live.

A subject, then, demands thinking—putting together. It requires more than a listing of facts. It necessitates a selection of facts, an interpretation of them, a validated conclusion drawn from them. The writer puts things together and tries to see what they mean.

Another way of saying this is to say that a subject demands proof. The student writing about his home town wasn't proving anything. The writer of an article in your favorite magazine, in contrast, is trying to prove a point: British doctors think highly of socialized medicine; this year's Broadway plays are unusually poor; etc. Even description attempts to prove something, for instance, that the "beautiful blue Danube" is now neither blue nor beautiful, or that a room is tastefully decorated. Narration tries to prove something: An adventuress (Becky Sharp) may bring much grief to good but relatively simple persons; mass production may harm the lone artisan of high integrity (Galsworthy's "Quality").

The statement of subject involves a word or expression that may be called either "ambiguous" or "controversial." The italicized words in these sentences are examples:

Making a willow whistle is *easy*.
Automobiles are *safer than ever*.
My cousin is a *mathematical genius*.
My home town is an *exciting* place to live in.

Adequate development of a subject requires that the ambiguity be clarified, or that the weight on one side of the controversy be shown

[4] "Writing and Composing," *English Journal*, XLVIII (Jan., 1959), 12.

to exceed that on the other. What, for example, is a mathematical genius? What does my cousin do that shows he is one? Some persons believe that my home town is dull. What is the proof that it is really exciting?

Teachers normally assign or suggest topics, not subjects. That is as it should be, for a student should find his own point of view rather than accept a hand-me-down from his teacher or anyone else. But teachers should help students to see how they can transform a topic into a subject. The way to do it is this: Ask yourself, "What do I believe about this topic? What do I want to prove about it?" Put your belief into the form of a short simple sentence. Check the sentence to make sure it includes one expression that is ambiguous or controversial. It is this expression on which you will focus your attention in most or all of your composition. You now have a subject.[5]

Compositions written about subjects rather than about topics are inevitably idea-centered. The teacher and his classmates may disagree with what a student attempts to prove, but, if frank discussion is customary in the classroom, "Teacher and students respect one another's thinking, hence feel free to discuss both the point of view expressed and the words and arguments and illustrations used to advance it," as Helen F. Olson has said.[6] Miss Olson points out that "In an idea-centered classroom, attention is centered on identifying the main meaning or thought which a student wishes to convey and then on developing that meaning logically and interestingly."

Students *do* have something to say. Each of them has had experiences, has read a little, has heard and seen much, and has formed opinions worthy of expression and careful scrutiny. But many of them have never learned that they can find something to say that will interest someone else.

Suitable Topics for Student Writing

Topics, then, are to be converted to subjects before a student writes. But what kinds of topics?

No definitive answer exists. Some teachers argue in favor of personal topics; some, in favor of literary topics; others say that anything

[5] Two *English Journal* articles that elaborate on the points made in this section are "Teaching Students To Organize," by Robert Saalbach, XLVII (Nov., 1958), 505 and "Compositions—Write 'em Right!" by Victor Pudlowski, XLVIII (Dec., 1959), 535. The specific theme plans in both articles are fine for beginning writers; if long continued, however, they would result in colorless, wooden writing.

[6] "What Is Good Teaching of Composition?" *English Journal*, L (April, 1961), 239.

related to the current unit is appropriate. Some advocate expository topics only, but others like description, narration, argumentation. Short stories and poetry are considered suitable by some teachers, not by others. Disagreement exists about the desirability of the so-called research paper, journalistic topics, current events, papers related to the work of other courses. In some schools students choose most of their own topics; in others, printed lists are used. Some schools insist on a planned sequence, but others, in effect, draw topics out of a hat.

On the assumption that planning is better than planlessness, here are brief descriptions of the planned procedures of a number of schools.

Writing about the junior high schools of Pittsburgh, Lois Grose, Senior Supervisor of Language Arts, says,

Although the trend is toward increasing emphasis on expository writing, I believe that at the junior high school level boys and girls do their most effective work in writing about personal experiences and their own reactions to the world about them. For most of them the abstract has little interest; the desire to express their own experiences and feelings has great motivating power.

Miss Grose also recommends "the very practical forms of writing which pupils will use as adults": newsy personal letters, business letters, minutes, and notes for a report, as well as the use of controlled sources for a reference paper. Interested students should have the chance to write verse, short stories, or dramatic sketches.[7]

Clarence Hach, of Evanston, Illinois, recommends a sequence like this, covering both topics and compositional forms:

Seventh grade: friendly letters about personal experiences; thank-you-notes; narrative paragraphs; simple expository paragraphs; brief reports based on reference reading; instead of book reports, brief compositions retelling a single incident, reacting to a character, or evaluating the outcome.

Eighth grade: review; descriptive paragraphs; narrative paragraphs; expository paragraphs; certain types of business letters; friendly letters; reports; unstereotyped book reports; much writing on topics of personal interest.

Ninth grade: review; expository paragraphs developed by example, incident, reasons, comparison, contrast; descriptive paragraphs emphasizing sensory impressions and consistent point of view; answers to examination questions; two-paragraph expository themes, followed by 250–300 word expository themes.

[7] "Teaching Writing in the Junior High School," *English Journal*, XLIX (Feb., 1960), 89.

Tenth grade: review; various methods of developing an expository theme; argumentative or persuasive paragraphs, followed by longer themes of argument; how-to-do-or-make expositions; writing with quotations; adding color and the personal touch to writing; report writing on both reference topics and literature; more practice in writing examination answers; formal paraphrase of literature; comparison of books.

Eleventh grade: review; précis; 500–800 word informational essays; 1,000–2,000 word reference paper; extended definitions; more practice with writing examination answers; much writing about books.

Twelfth grade: review; expository papers on cause and effect; essays of opinion; themes of formal analysis, e.g., of ideas in literature; criticism of books, plays, television programs, concerts, etc.; a long reference paper.[8]

The English Language Arts in the Secondary School (NCTE, 1956) recommends much writing on matters of personal concern by junior high school students, followed by imaginative stories to release emotions; articles of opinion, with facts to substantiate; formal reports, usually related to the literature being read; practice in writing examinations; letters, as realistic as possible; "service writing" such as announcements, advertisements, minutes, formal requests; elective work in writing, such as courses in creative writing or journalism. Since the NCTE volume puts considerable stress on thematic units, much of the writing it recommends would be related to the subject matter of the units chosen, and, hence, the topics would to some extent be dictated by the units.

Teachers in schools that have produced the NCTE Achievement Award winners and that, therefore, may be supposed to have unusually good English programs were asked in a questionnaire what kinds of topics their students in grades ten, eleven, and twelve write on frequently. The responses were as follows:

Kind of Topic	Number Responding
Literature	620
Science	197
Social studies	334
Art	65
Music	64
Personal interests	622
Other	169

Especially significant in these answers is the evidence of balance in the kinds of topics assigned for composition. The "personal interest" topics are useful for motivation, yet limiting students' writing to such topics is

[8] "Needed: A Sequential Program in Composition," *English Journal,* (Nov., 1960), 536.

unwise because much later writing, in college or in business or industry, will have to be on non-personal, objective topics.[9]

From such practices and others that could be named as illustrations, we may draw some generalizations about the kinds of topics deemed especially suitable. First, although there are repetitions and overlappings, carefully planned English programs utilize a progression of topics. Second, the topics that appear best for junior high schools are those emphasizing personal experience and observation, though tentacles reach out toward impersonal reports and objective evaluations. Third, for the senior high school years the stress on personal topics is considerably reduced. In the table above, for example, personal topics have a frequency of only 30 per cent; note that literary topics have almost as high a frequency.

The kind of writing that for want of a better name is usually called "creative" merits special mention. (Actually any writing may be creative, whether it is expository, narrative, or what have you. Creative writing is writing done by a creative person.) Until the late 1920's most high school writing tended to be factual and interpretive essays. Then the pendulum swung, aided by a big push from two influential volumes by Hughes Mearns, *Creative Youth* and *Creative Power*, which contained many examples of excellent, picturesque, imaginative writing by children of secondary school age. A creative-writing fad resulted, lasting into the 1940's. After World War II came a counterreaction. Colleges complained that some of their freshmen wrote excessively flowery language and that many of them could not organize an exposition that demanded any arrangement other than chronological. The pressures of science and of education for science seemed to demean the importance of creative writing. Many school administrators were not interested in it. Demands for more attention to the three R's filled newspaper columns. Hence, the amount of attention to the writing of verse, short stories, and the like declined.

Not everyone agreed that the shift was wise, though. The head of the English department in the influential New Trier High School in Winnetka, Illinois, argued vigorously, ". . . 'creative' writing well taught requires planning, and form, and emphasis—in fact, all and more than is required in expository writing. I would not abolish expository writing, to be sure, but I plead for more attention being returned to the 'creative' approach." [10] A school principal joined in:

[9] J. N. Hook, "Characteristics of Award-winning High Schools," *English Journal*, L (Jan., 1961), 9.
[10] R. Stanley Peterson, "Once More to the Well: Another Look at Creative Writing," *English Journal*, L (Dec., 1961), 612.

"Without wishing to decry in any way the importance of being able to write clear, logical expository prose, I strongly suspect that a proper mixture of the two produces better expository prose, in part because a change of pace does help and in part because young people can learn a good deal about their use of the language from creative writing, including both the short story and poetry." [11] From other rooms came other voices. Today we appear to be moving in most schools toward a moderate amount of creative writing, both for its own sake and for the influence it may exert upon other writing. The precision of diction characteristic of good creative writing, the lightning flash of its imagery, its economy in words, and its human quality make it useful in sharpening and brightening any kind of composition.

THE PARAGRAPH: COMPOSITION IN MINIATURE

Reasons for Emphasizing Paragraph Construction

In the early elementary grades, pupils dictate sentences to the teacher about their experiences. She writes them on the board or prepares an "experience chart" to be used in the teaching of reading. A little later the pupils laboriously write their own little sentences. Gradually they begin to hitch sentences together, as well as to compose more elaborate sentences. They learn that several consecutive sentences may be about the same topic. By the time they are in the fifth or sixth grade most of them can put together, though in a relatively unsophisticated fashion, a number of statements on any topic about which they know enough.

Most entering junior high school students, then, possess basic knowledge of paragraphing. What they usually do not know are the methods of organizing and developing paragraphs and the ways to make them unified, coherent, and emphatic. The junior high school is the logical place to begin this instruction for most students, in order to make their handling of paragraphs more nearly mature and in order to strengthen the thought processes that may result in good paragraphs.

If instruction were confined to sentence structure at this time, students would be faced with a swarm of minutiae without readily apparent purpose or relationships. If it were confined to long composi-

[11] Cleveland A. Thomas, "Fostering Creativity in High School English," *English Journal,* LI (Dec., 1962), 625.

tions (e.g., two or three pages), fewer pieces of writing could be required and students would consequently get less instruction in organization and development. A paragraph is a convenient, "bite-sized" element of instruction.

Much of the composition instruction in grades seven, eight, and nine, then, may focus on the paragraph; occasionally, as a foretaste of things to come, students may be asked to prepare several interrelated paragraphs. Instruction in sentence structure, usage, and diction is woven throughout the year's work. Lois Grose of Pittsburgh, in the article previously mentioned, says, "By the time our boys and girls have finished junior high school they should be able to write a clearly developed paragraph which says something worth while, is correct in mechanics, and shows some variety in sentence structure." In grades ten, eleven, and twelve, assignments may often call for the development of a single paragraph, though the frequency of multi-paragraph compositions should be considerably increased.

An analogy exists between teaching composition and teaching wood-working. The shop instructor in a junior high school generally chooses for student projects whatnots, magazine racks, and other medium-sized articles, not jewel boxes or dining room tables. The polished sentence, like the skilfully made jewel box, requires much practice and experience. The whole composition, like the table, is too large for much experimentation and revision. But the paragraph is neither too large nor too small, and it may be fairly well constructed even though there are flaws in the component sentences.

The Need for Organization

Teaching good paragraph construction assists in the teaching of straight thinking. Straight thinking is organized, methodical thinking. The vague half-thoughts that come to our minds as we stroll down the street may be mildly entertaining, but they have no pattern, no destination, no future. The paragraphs that the untutored student writes are likely to be as chaotic and unstructured as are our thoughts while strolling.

Again and again each person is faced with big or little problems. He needs to marshal evidence and reach a decision. He needs to persuade someone else to follow a course of action. He needs to present information. He is required to relate an incident with clarity. Daily, hourly, he needs straight thinking, organized thinking.

The English teacher can help students to organize their thoughts.

The traditional methods of organization, proved by time, are the ones he must teach. He may be inventive in his ways of teaching them, but the methods of organization need not be invented. They have existed as long as man has thought consecutively.

Principles To Be Stressed

The three old rhetorical principles of unity, coherence, and emphasis must be taught. Of unity your students will have some notion, for they will have learned in elementary school, as we have seen, to write down several sentences on the same topic. What they probably will not have learned is the distinction between topic and subject (pages 230–232). Consequently, in a paragraph on "Bicycles" there will be a string of statements, all obviously on bicycles, but not making a definite point. Part of the job of secondary teachers is to help students to write, not about "Bicycles" but about "Swinthorne bicycles are best" or "Observing traffic rules will make bicycle riding safer." Such focusing of the subject, with writing that includes only those points pertinent to the subject, results in unity.

To achieve coherence takes much practice and hard thinking. Basically it results from following a pattern in arranging the parts. The methods of organizing that students should have practiced at least by the end of the junior year are these:

1. Chronological (the order of time; most common method of organization)
2. Spatial (the order of space; used most often in description, to show where objects are in relation to one another)
3. Inductive (proceeding from specific examples to a generalization based upon them)
4. Deductive (starting with a general statement and then illustrating, proving, or applying it)
5. Easy to difficult
6. Least to greatest (order of climax)
7. Reasoning from cause to effect or effect to cause.

Simple diagrams may sometimes be used during discussion of any one of these methods of organizing. Chronological organization may be shown by an arrow:

PAST   →   PRESENT

Inductive organization looks like this:

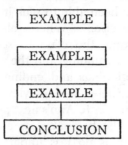

The preceding diagram, turned upside down, shows deductive order:

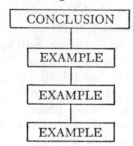

Least to greatest looks like this:

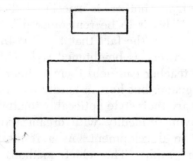

Easy to difficult may be represented by a series of stickmen, the first standing on one foot, the second turning a somersault, the third turning a cartwheel.

Emphasis is attained partly through position. Jo Ann, let us say, has written a paragraph that is unified and coherent but still weak because the most important point is buried in the middle. The teacher reads the paragraph aloud, gets some favorable comments from the class, and then begins fishing. "What is the most important thing that Jo Ann had to say?" Varied replies come from the class, and at last the one the instructor wants. Then he asks, "Do you recall where this statement was made?" Someone remembers that it was in the middle. "Would we have been able to pick it out more easily if it had been stated somewhere else?" "Where else could it have been stated?" The teacher wants the class to see that the positions of greatest emphasis are the beginning and the end. He accentuates the importance of strong beginnings and endings by references to short stories, *Reader's Digest* articles, and movies. A week or so later he returns to the matter again. In Jo Ann's next paragraph he may be able to praise the strength of the beginning or ending.

Emphasis by proportion is no less important. This means simply that a writer gives more space to a highly significant point than to an insignificant one. In this book, for example, it would be faulty emphasis if 100 pages were devoted to the comma and 20 to the teaching of literature. Many students, however, will spend five sentences on a trifle and one clause on a major point. The cure: an appeal to common sense. The teacher must help his students to realize that a major point, because it is major, needs to be restated, illustrated, and expanded much more than a minor one.

Other means of attaining emphasis are of smaller value. One of these is the use of mechanical devices, especially underlining and exclamations; some students may have to be warned not to employ these devices too frequently. Another is specific indication of the importance of a point: "This is to be remembered." "This is especially significant." "Let me stress the fact that . . ." A third device, usable by superior student writers, is heightened style. Most students have only one style. The teacher can help them to improve diction and to employ vigorous language, but he can hardly teach average or below-average students to vary their style noticeably to attain planned effects.

In addition to having difficulty with organization, many students encounter problems in development. As a result they hand in extremely skimpy paragraphs. The chief methods of development, which may appear in a paragraph either singly or in combination, are the following:

1. Supplying details
2. Using examples
3. Using comparison or contrast
4. Expanding a definition
5. Presenting causes or effects
6. Offering logical proof

Knowing these six and having used them, a student finds it less difficult to discover something to say. Often, for instance, after writing a statement to the effect that the Grand Canyon is an impressive sight, a student does not know what to say next. If he has learned to use details, however, he can support his generalization with appropriate comments on the ever changing colors or the long burroback ride from rim to river. (Students' papers more frequently suffer from lack of details than from any other cause.) If he has learned to use comparison and contrast, he can effectively develop the idea that the twenty-two miles of Manhattan could be almost hidden away in one small stretch of the Grand Canyon. If he has learned to present causes and effects, he can say something about the thousands of years of erosion that resulted in the canyon.

In developing a paragraph, as in developing a sentence or a long composition, relevance is a major consideration. Students need to be trained to ask themselves, "Is this detail (this example, this bit of evidence) relevant to what I am trying to do?" "In this paragraph about the Grand Canyon, is it relevant to mention the car trouble we had?" An understanding of relevance may make your students much more efficient writers when later they are faced with adult writing responsibilities. The author of this book has read thousands of business letters. Over and over he has found that irrelevance is a major flaw, a flaw that often leads to lack of clarity and that always wastes the time of both writer and reader. If, for example, a company has filled an order improperly, the customer is not interested in a detailed explanation of what went wrong. That is irrelevant. What the customer wants to know is what the company is doing to rectify the mistake. Teaching your students to include only the relevant is an important contribution that you can make toward efficiency in adult communication.

Inductive Procedures

No informed teacher would say to a class, "*Unity* means sticking to the subject. *Coherence* means arranging the parts in some sensible order. *Emphasis* means stressing the most important part. For tomorrow each of you should hand in a paragraph about trees. Be sure that the paragraph has unity, coherence, and emphasis."

Only a slight improvement is this: "*Unity* means oneness. It is derived from the Latin *unus,* meaning one, and is related to such words as *united* and *union.* In paragraph writing *unity* means that a paragraph should be about only one topic. For tomorrow each of you should write a unified paragraph about trees."

Much better, though slower, is an inductive buildup of an understanding of unity. The specific steps can be quite varied. For example, the class may examine a number of teacher-selected non-narrative paragraphs, attempting to summarize each in a single sentence —a simple sentence if possible. They thus gain the understanding that a paragraph normally concerns only one topic. Or the teacher can present for criticism a paragraph that he has found or written and that treats two or more topics. As a follow-up he can present another paragraph—about trees, let us say—that is on one topic but rambles in its discussion of the topic, perhaps combining remarks on pine trees, maple trees, apple trees, banana trees, trees in winter, and trees in summer. Then a contrasting paragraph can be read that makes a specific point about trees, for example, "Exactly what makes sap flow as it does still puzzles scientists." Still another inductive procedure would be to look at the content of a number of student-written paragraphs and have the class analyze why some are better than others. One recurring reason will be that some paragraphs stick to the subject, making one single point clearly.

One of the advantages of such an inductive procedure is that it makes the students partners in discovery. Instead of being handed information or statements of principle, they think them out for themselves. This leads to a second advantage: They are more likely to remember and apply what they have reasoned out than what they have merely been told. College students and other adults may be able to proceed from a generalization to its application, but less mature people usually need to build from examples to the generalization. When students, under guidance, have written a number of paragraphs and discussed a number of paragraphs, they are ready to synthesize their observations and talk about unity as a familiar concept.

Coherence, emphasis, and the various possible methods of organizing and developing a paragraph may likewise be taught inductively, mainly through the use of sample paragraphs (written by themselves or others), which the students analyze with particular questions in mind. Thus September classes may spend fifteen minutes or so of class time each day for a few days, writing things about themselves for the information of the teacher. A student may write about his chief ambition, the other people in his home, the person he admires most, the book he likes best, what he enjoys thinking about. Each time the teacher will provide guidance: suggesting ways of focusing the paragraph, offering a pattern of organization by listing specific questions to be answered, commenting on effective emphasis obtained by means of position and proportion, and commenting publicly on qualities that make this or that paragraph "especially good" such as good use of details. All this helps to prepare for the generalizations to come later about coherence, emphasis, development, and so on.

Teaching about topic sentences may serve here as a final illustration of inductive procedures. From a group of paragraphs, the teacher selects two or three that happen to have clearly stated topic sentences. So far, let us assume, he has not mentioned topic sentences in class. He reads one of the paragraphs to the class. "What makes that paragraph especially clear?" He may get several partially true answers before he gets the one he wants—that one sentence states definitely what the paragraph is about. He rereads the paragraph, stressing the topic sentence, showing how it binds together the whole paragraph. Then he reads one or two other paragraphs that contain topic sentences, and has the class pick them out. He does not insist that every student have a topic sentence in every paragraph, but he does leave the impression that topic sentences are often valuable. A few days later, he reads and has students comment on other paragraphs containing topic sentences, or he distributes copies of paragraphs and asks students to supply topic sentences for them. Soon the topic sentence is taken for granted as a useful device, whereas, if he had begun by saying, "You should usually have a topic sentence in your paragraph," students would have been as uncomprehending as if he had said, "You should manufacture some lymphocytes in your lymphatic glands daily."

The Paragraph in Narrative Writing

The narrative paragraph deserves separate consideration because its characteristics are different from those of exposition, argumentation, and description. It is less likely, for instance, to have a topic sentence, though such a summary as "Tuesday morning was hectic" is possible. It may rely more on action words than other paragraphs do. And, by virtue of being narrative, it is almost always chronological in organization. Some fiction writers such as William Faulkner and Robert Penn Warren write long paragraphs; others, like Hemingway, prefer short ones.

Some students erroneously conclude, however, that no rules at all exist for narrative paragraphs. It is wise, therefore, to teach that a new narrative paragraph is usually required in these circumstances:

1. With each change of speaker
2. At the end of each significant bit of action
3. When attention is switched from one character to another

4. When an important new character, setting, or emphasis is introduced
5. If the material differs in some way from its context (e.g., several sentences of description inserted in a story)
6. If the particular type of reader being addressed may need the psychological relief of a break on the page (e.g., a young reader needs more breaks than a sophisticated adult)
7. If dramatic effect will be heightened (i.e., short paragraphs, if not used excessively, tend to be more dramatic than long ones) [12]

These observations show that narrative paragraphs possess a degree of unity. Coherence may be illustrated through examining their steady chronological progression; and emphasis, through noting points that are stressed and the writer's choice of language.

PUTTING PARAGRAPHS TOGETHER

Similarity of Paragraph and Composition

If the paragraph is emphasized as the basic unit in teaching the contributions that unity, coherence, and emphasis make to straight thinking, the task of helping students with longer compositions is not difficult. A good piece of writing has these qualities, whether it is 10 or 10,000 words long.

The whole composition differs from the paragraph mainly in being larger. If a paragraph develops an idea, then a whole composition develops a larger idea. The same point could be expressed by saying that the whole composition develops an idea, and each paragraph develops one phase of the idea.

How Many Themes?

Despite such similarity, students do need practice in writing longer compositions, partly because greater space is essential for expressing some ideas and partly because practice is essential for the successful interlocking of paragraphs.

The guidance and evaluation of extensive written work, though, if carefully performed, require much time and thought. For that reason, the NCTE and various state organizations of English teachers have recommended that administrators and school boards work toward an English class load of no more than four classes per teacher

---

[12] Adapted from J. N. Hook, *Hook's Guide to Good Writing: Grammar, Style, Usage* (New York: The Ronald Press Company, 1962), p. 315.

and a maximum of twenty-five students per class. But, in these days of large enrolments and too few classrooms, many administrators admittedly have difficulty in reducing the load to such a figure, even though they realize that the request is justified. English teachers, nevertheless, should without whining keep before the public the fact that they cannot do their best work if they are so heavily loaded that their work week is fifty or sixty or even more hours.

All English teachers should require as much writing from their students as can be effectively supervised and evaluated. Those teachers who are fortunate enough to have a reasonable load should require considerable amounts, for students learn to write by writing, not by filling in blanks in workbooks.[13]

No specific number of themes can be stipulated for each year. In general, though, students in junior high school should write many compositions of one paragraph and a few of two, three, or more paragraphs. Sophomores and juniors should also write some one-paragraph themes and perhaps a dozen to eighteen longer ones. Seniors should write still more, and among their compositions should be at least one library theme of 1,500 or more words. Each piece of writing needs to be adequately motivated; students' problems need to be anticipated; and the finished product should be carefully analyzed.

The Need for Prevision

Grading of composition work is time-consuming, undeniably. It is one of the biggest of the chores that fall to the English teacher. The grading may not be painful, however, under certain conditions. If the teacher has helped the students to plan, and if he has attentively overseen their labor, the result need not be a mass of red when he returns it. That in itself may give some slight pleasure. But the real glow of happiness and pride comes when he sees proof that Dick is at last using his head, that Marilyn has thought one subject through, that scatterbrain Harold has for once put the horse before the cart, that shy Pearl has dropped her shyness long enough to defend a positive belief. Two or three such discoveries in one evening afford deeper pleasure than almost any movie.

The late Lucia Mirrielees used the term *prevision* for a process that may make such moments of pleasure more numerous. Prevision refers

---

[13] Frank Heys, Jr., questions "The Theme-a-Week Assumption," stating that having his students read a greater than usual amount improved their writing more than did writing practice (*English Journal*, LI [May, 1962], 320). Though more experimentation is necessary to prove the point, it may be true that superior students in particular may make writing gains through reading.

to the very desirable practice of helping students with their compositions before they write them and to some extent while they are writing them. Through prevision, teachers can make sure that students are ready to write a particular kind of theme, can anticipate many of their difficulties, and can partially supervise the writing.

Prevision involves choice of subject, motivation, and help in removing obstacles.

Choice of subject has already been discussed (pages 232–236). It is especially important that students do have subjects, not just topics, on which to write. A dramatic improvement in content sometimes results from simple insistence upon this distinction.

Motivation is increased, too, if subjects are carefully selected. There must be a reason for each assignment, and students should be helped to see the reason. A teacher of English should never teach anything that he himself does not consider valuable, and he should never teach anything without letting students see at least part of the value that it has.

Choosing theme subjects becomes somewhat easier if one keeps the preceding sentence in mind. It automatically excludes such a topic as "Pea Green" (which a teacher once did actually assign—500 words on "Pea Green"!). The teacher asks himself the question, "Would this subject have demonstrable value for this particular class?"

The words "demonstrable value" imply that the subjects chosen should require purposeful writing. A theme is not to be written for the sake of writing a theme. It is to be written to convey connected thoughts to interested readers. In a September class a teacher asks students to write about themselves so that he may best plan the course to meet their needs. In October classes students are writing to inform one another, to exchange information about their reading, their ideas. In November and later classes they may be writing to have opinions evaluated, arguments weighed. Sometimes they write to entertain (a perfectly valid purpose). They write letters—real letters to be mailed, if at all possible. They write answers to examination questions so that the practice will help them next week when they face essay examinations in various courses. They write to clarify for themselves and their classmates some of the material being studied in a unit. They write a poem to search for economy and precision in words or to express a striking image.

When composition subjects do not grow from a class unit, one good plan is to specify a certain kind of topic but to let the student make his own choice within the given area. For example, there may be a good reason for having a class write "How to . . ." themes. Not everyone should be asked to write on "How To Make a Kite"; each student may choose for himself the process he wants to explain. Before the writing, teacher and class will discuss the pattern of organization, the use of transitions, and anything else that the majority of students may need.

Sometimes the entire class may cooperate on a writing project. In a high school where the author taught, the sophomore class wanted to find out as much as it could about the birds of the area. Committees set to work and apportioned the tasks. Everyone did some of the searching and writing, one committee served as editors, more artistic students provided illustrations and a binding, and typing students typed the edited copy. The result was an attractive book, proudly presented to the library. At the end of the year, one of the students remarked, "I learned more from working on the bird book than I did from all the rest of the course."

One quality that students need to develop is accurate observation. Stevenson, in his *New Arabian Nights,* has a character exclaim, "I would have [observation] a piece of education in all schools! . . . Where is the use of eyesight and articulate speech if a man cannot observe and recollect? . . . Cultivate this art in future. . . . You may find it of momentous service." The teacher sometimes asks the question "Why do we have eyes?" and then issues a challenge, "How well do you observe? Can you see anything so clearly that you can put it down on paper exactly? If you roll a piece of paper into the shape of a tube and look through it out the window at one spot for thirty seconds, can you write down exactly what you have seen without looking again? Your eye is like a camera, and words are like film. Can you make a word snapshot?"

For the same purpose, the author once borrowed a technique often used by psychologists. He asked two senior girls to learn to act out a prepared script. At a prearranged time, while the junior class was in session, the two seniors burst into the classroom, rushed over to a wire basket containing some papers, seized a letter, and began arguing and almost fighting over it. The teacher finally quieted them and ushered them out of the room. Then he explained to the juniors that the incident had been staged to test their powers of observation. Each was to write an account of exactly what had occurred, including the conversation. Needless to say, when they compared their accounts with the copy of the script followed by the two girls, they were amazed at the discrepancies. This incident paved the way for several fruitful assignments.

In general, when theme subjects have once been chosen and when students clearly understand what they are to do and why, the teacher still needs to remove as many obstacles as he can. For instance, if the theme will probably entail the use of conversation, he may review quotation marks. If certain words will almost certainly appear, he may make sure that everyone can spell those words. If a particular method of organization is most probable, he discusses that method. If the theme will require note taking, he talks about the qualities of good notes. If footnotes are needed in the senior research theme, he illustrates their uses and form. In other words, he tries to anticipate the problems the students will encounter and to demonstrate the solutions. The students thus learn and apply. The learning is itself motivated because it is put into meaningful context.

Work with transitions may require special attention in prevision. With young students the term *bridge* may be preferable to *transition*, since it helps them to visualize the connecting function. The employment of bridges is an aid to clear thinking. It trains students to get into the habit of asking themselves, "Just how is this statement (or this paragraph) related to the preceding one? Is it an added illustration; is it an apparent contradiction; is it related in time; or what?" They then choose the appropriate transition: "in addition," "on the other hand," "next," "while this was going on," "because he was unhappy after his father's death," etc. Sometimes the teacher may offer some rather dramatic examples of the need for transitions. For instance, "Jess is a star football player. He scored five baskets last night." With transitional elements added, these sentences make sense: "Jess is a star football player. He showed that he is versatile, though, by scoring five baskets in the basketball game last night."

Still another help in prevision is having much of the actual writing done in the classroom. There the students will have access to dictionaries and other reference books, and will be able to avail themselves of the teacher's aid. In some schools, in fact, nearly all writing is done in this laboratory fashion.

Finally, practice in proofreading is important for prevision. Geneva Hanna suggests these steps:

1. To learn to attend to what is actually written, not to what the author intended to say
   A. *Hear* (verbalize) wrong words, omission of words.
   B. Read word for word.
   C. See stops and pauses and misspelled words.
2. To learn to listen for meaning—as a stranger listens
   A. First, be sure the meaning is there.
   B. Second, if the meaning is not there, revise the material.[14]

[14] "Proofreading, a Panacea," *English Journal*, LI (Oct., 1962), 482.

As a goal for all students, though realizing that its full attainment will be possible for only a limited number, teachers may keep in mind (and perhaps share with students) the following description of good student writing, published in the Advanced Program Syllabus of the College Entrance Examination Board in 1958:

The core of training in composition is . . . the frequent writing and careful revision of substantial themes on subjects sufficiently mature to challenge both thought and linguistic powers. These themes should be distinguished by superior command of *substance,* thoughtfully and interestingly presented.

A good student writer will demonstrate a high level of proficiency in *organization,* combining clear sentences in well-shaped paragraphs and arranging these in an order clear to the reader as well as to himself. . . .

However, a neat pattern of paragraphs is not in itself proof of, and can never be a substitute for, sound and compelling *logic.* . . . [The student] is careful to support general statements with specific proofs; he distinguishes between causes and effects, between subjective reactions and objective judgments; and he has cultivated the ability to select fresh rather than hackneyed illustrations.

A good composition exhibits a feeling for style, displaying both *precision* and *fluency.* An able student will make use of the varieties of English sentence structure. . . . His vocabulary will be distinguished not so much by its extent as by its exactness and appropriateness.

It should go without saying that a student in an advanced course will have mastered the *mechanics* of writing. His command of the conventions of spelling, capitalization, and punctuation will be firm; his syntax will be clear and accurate.

Outlining

The question of having students make outlines should be raised here. Some teachers insist that every theme, long or short, be outlined in detail before it is written. Others say that following a strict outline makes writing too mechanical and inflexible; they often add that, when they have required students to hand in a theme and its outline, the students have admitted that they wrote the theme first.

Perhaps the answer can be suggested by two analogies. Recently a man wanted to construct a sturdy frame to hold his outboard motor when it was not in use. He took a hammer, a saw, some boards, and some nails and hammered something together. But, as it was weak and shaky, he took it apart and started over. This time he made a rough drawing of the way the completed frame should appear. The result was much more satisfactory. Simultaneously a friend of his was building a garage. The friend did not proceed without a plan or with only a simple sketch but had a carefully drawn plan to guide him.

The short theme, of two or three paragraphs, is usually more successful when it is based on an informal outline, consisting perhaps of only a few points jotted down in logical order. The longer theme, however, such as the senior research theme, requires a more elaborate outline simply because the theme itself is more complex. One man wasted a few minutes by trying to build a simple frame without a plan, but his friend might have wasted several days if he had tried to build his garage in the same way.

Many teachers find the following procedure satisfactory. Before a student begins writing, he jots down in topic form the various things that he could include. If he knows definitely what his main idea will be, he crosses out the topics that do not contribute to that idea. If he still has not decided upon the central idea, he looks at the topics and tries to decide what he can make of them. Then, with the central idea chosen, he arranges the topics in the way that is most logical and effective. This arrangement of topics constitutes an informal outline.

The more formal outline, to be used for a long theme, has one big pitfall for students, but training in avoiding this trap has value in improvement of thinking. The students' difficulty comes in distinguishing the relative importance of points, in deciding which are coordinate and which are subordinate. If they are not helped, students are likely to write something like this:

I. George Washington was born in 1732.
   A. He was born in Virginia.
   B. He went to elementary schools.
      1. Then his brother got him a job as surveyor.
   C. His young manhood was filled with adventurous exploits.
   D. One of these was his defeat of the French at Fort Duquesne.
      1. Another was his serving as commander of Virginia's forces.

This is not an outline but a hodgepodge. Point I does not summarize the points below; A is not equal in importance to B, C, and D; B1 is not actually subordinate to B; D and D1 should both be subordinated to C.

Hodgepodges may best be prevented by working out sample outlines as a class. Since competent outlining requires considerable maturity, only advanced and able classes should be exposed to a discussion of the more subtle points. Even a slightly below-average senior class, however, should be able to construct an outline without the glaring defects of the partial outline given above.

Evaluating

A few pages back, the teacher was facing a pile of themes. Let us now return to see how he is getting along.

If he used prevision, his red pencil should not yet have been reduced to a two-inch stub. Mistakes he finds, of course. Some he marks; others he ignores for the time being. He marks errors that have been adequately discussed in class; points that have not yet been taken up he usually does not check. In a paper filled with errors, he marks only the most serious, those that should be eliminated first. To show Cedric (IQ 86) all his infractions at one time would be to leave him feeling helpless and beaten, but to show him exactly what his gravest faults are (and a way to correct them) would be to give him hope. Cedric must learn only one or two things at a time. Paul, a bright boy, makes no elementary errors. Should the teacher, then, leave Paul's paper entirely free of red and give him the feeling that it is perfect? No, because his writing can be improved. Therefore, the teacher makes some specific suggestions to him—suggestions that Cedric could not even understand. These suggestions pertain to matters that have not been discussed in class, that may not be discussed until next year. When the teacher reads Paul's composition, he thinks, "This is excellent. What does it lack, though, that an ideal article on the subject would possess? What would a professional author do that Paul has not done? How much of this shall I tell Paul?" The teacher helps Paul to use profitably the intelligence that he has; he does not hold him to Cedric's pace.

In other words, as the teacher sits with pencil in hand, he has one of his best opportunities to provide for individual differences. All students in the beginning have the same needs in composition, but some master the minimum essentials more quickly than others. At present, Cedric needs especially to work on the minima, Paul on something else, Wilma on something else. Each paper is part of a growing mind. The teacher wants to help each mind to grow as straight and as strong as it can. What he is doing with his pencil is much more than marking misplaced commas, fragmentary sentences, misspelled words, and incoherent paragraphs. He is feeding minds, shaping minds.

There is a wise philosophy of grading expressed in this comment by Luella Cook:

In recent years the marking of papers with red pencil has become for me chiefly a memorandum for myself. Less and less am I troubled by the errors that I find—these are already committed—and more and more concerned with what lies behind them and how one may forestall them in future writing. And so I have come to make a distinction between errors that are a careless failure to put into operation what one already knows and errors that arise from lack of knowledge or imperfect control over meaning. The first can be handled with a minimum of teacher effort. Students can be taught to edit their own and their neighbor's papers for careless errors, checking their finished copy against a "check list" made up of items agreed upon by class and teacher as understood. And teachers can refuse to accept a paper which has not been edited or edited carelessly. On this level, accuracy is merely a matter of discipline. . . . The second type of error can best be handled, I think, by making each set of papers the basis for a study of sentence structure and correct usage [and straight thinking, it may be added.] [15]

William J. Dusel has analyzed four methods of evaluating compositions.[16] The first, and least time-consuming, consists of marking a few of the most obvious mechanical errors and affixing a grade. The second, which requires a little more time, involves marking all mechanical errors, writing one or two negative comments such as "Weak opening sentence," and giving a grade. The third has the teacher himself writing in all the corrections he thinks desirable, attaching a grade, and writing "Recopy this and turn it in on Friday"; this takes about as much time as the second method. The fourth—the procedure that Dusel recommends—requires about two and a half times as many minutes per paper as the first method. It involves attending to ideas and not only to mechanics, commenting on something good in the paper, making suggestions for improvement, and giving a grade. Dusel correctly points out that students whose papers are evaluated by any of the first three methods are likely to learn comparatively little.

Some teachers favor two grades, one for content and one for mechanics, but there is no overwhelming evidence that two grades are better than one. Whether the teacher gives one grade or two, he has to consider these items on the debit and credit sides:

[15] "Fundamentals in the Teaching of Composition," *English Journal*, XXX (May, 1941), 360.
[16] "Determining an Efficient Teaching Load in English," *Illinois English Bulletin* (Oct., 1955), 6–13.

Debits	*Credits*
Below-ordinary content	Reasonably stimulating and fresh content
Lack of unity, coherence, or emphasis (crooked thinking)	Unity, coherence, and emphasis (straight thinking)
Infelicitous diction	Reasonably apt use of words
Errors in sentence structure, grammar, spelling, and mechanics (only those previously studied)	Some especially good sentences; accuracy in grammar, spelling, and mechanics

As the teacher balances the books, an especially large debit item may more than equal two credits, but, on the other hand, a large credit may cancel two debits. The A theme usually possesses, to a fair degree, all the elements on the credit side; the B theme may lack one of these but have no very noticeable debits; the C theme has a fairly even balance; the D theme has little to recommend it; and the F theme is weak in several respects and not very strong in any.

These debits and credits are, of course, composed of relative terms. "Reasonably stimulating and fresh content" in a senior theme is not the same as "reasonably stimulating and fresh content" in a freshman theme. The instructor expects a maturity in the senior paper that he could hardly hope for in one written by a freshman. Likewise, he excuses in a freshman theme certain errors that he would consider serious in a senior paper.

A somewhat different check list for evaluation has been suggested by the NCTE Committee on High School-College Articulation:

Content—Is the idea worth writing about? Does the student know what he's writing about?

Structure—Is there a clear statement of thesis? Does the theme follow an appropriate logical pattern? Is there adequate evidence to support the thesis? Is each paragraph clearly related to the thesis? Is there adequate transition within and between paragraphs? Is the ending adequate? Are the main points emphasized and the minor points subordinated by proper sentence and paragraph structure?

Diction—Is the level of language appropriate to the subject, the audience, and the writer? Is the wording exact and free from clichés, jargon, and deadwood? Is there a proper balance between denotation and connotation? Is the wording concrete? [17]

When the grade has been written, the teacher still must affix a comment—not merely "Good" or "Poor." Ida Jewett has stated that every comment should be measured by the "five S's: Sound, Significant, Stimulating, Specific, Suggestive." [18] Ponder those five words for a

[17] *English Journal*, L (Sept., 1961), 410–11.

[18] Miss Jewett also suggests that teachers who put marks like "Gr," "P," etc., on students' papers should in addition use some symbols of praise such as "Ilt" = I like this.

few moments. If comments possess those five qualities, they will be genuinely helpful. Most comments will have the five S's if they follow a simple formula—singling out one or two things for praise and then making one or two suggestions for improvement. Please note the phrasing: "suggestions for improvement," not "adverse criticisms."

After a student has had his paper returned to him, he should be expected to revise it. If he does not do so, he will glance casually at the grade and the comment, throw the paper into the wastebasket, and in his next composition make exactly the same mistakes. Careful revision, when it involves an understanding of why each correction is made, can prevent later repetition of the same errors. This fact should be made clear to the class, who otherwise will look upon revision as a penalty rather than an opportunity.

Revision consists only of writing the necessary corrections, either between the lines or on the back of the page. It is perhaps not necessary to have a student rewrite a whole composition unless it is so poor in organization that the student will profit from thinking through the subject again and writing a new version.

If an English teacher has such a large number of students that he cannot give as much personal attention to evaluation as he would like, he may make some use of student help. Groups of three or four students may occasionally work together, reading and discussing and suggesting ways of improving themes that they themselves have written or that students in another group have written; each member of the class will be in one of these groups, which may meet simultaneously. Unless the class has had experience in group work, the teacher must make careful preparation. The first time, relatively simple tasks will be given each group, but the tasks may gradually grow more complex and the responsibilities, greater. It is most important that the groups understand precisely what is expected of them.[19]

A number of schools now use lay readers to evaluate many student-written compositions. These readers are usually college-educated housewives who are interested in working with student writing and who can pass appropriate tests. Arguments for and against use of lay readers are presented in articles listed in The Idea Box (page 263). Most English teachers agree that, ideally, class load should be small enough to permit each teacher to grade his own students' papers but

[19] For details, see Loren V. Grissom, "Student Leadership in Evaluating Compositions," English Journal, XLVIII (Sept., 1959), 338. For additional suggestions on evaluation, see Eric W. Johnson, "Avoiding Martyrdom in Teaching Writing: Some Shortcuts," English Journal, LI (Sept., 1962), 399. For more on the theoretical basis of evaluation, see T. A. Koclanes, "Can We Evaluate Compositions?" English Journal, L (April, 1961), 252.

that, if such a situation does not exist, carefully selected lay readers usually do a good job and make possible the requirement of larger amounts of writing than would otherwise be feasible.

Conclusion

By the last semester of the senior year, if such a program as that outlined in this chapter has been followed, students should be able to write expositions that "hang together" and give a feeling of forward movement toward a definite goal. They will know a few of the technical terms that relate to writing, but, more important, they will be able to write with reasonable clearness. If they go to college, it is unlikely that 'their professors will say of their papers, "The facts are there but scattered around as if a whirlwind had passed along." Whether they go to college or not, they will have learned something of lasting value.

The superintendent of a large school system said at a meeting of English supervisors,

I have trouble in finding teachers who are keenly interested in teaching composition. When I ask a young prospective teacher, or even an experienced one, what branch of English she likes most, the answer is almost always "English literature" or "American literature." Although I recognize how important it is that our youngsters become discriminating readers, I should be very happy if I could find teachers who are equally interested in making them into discriminating listeners, discriminating speakers, discriminating writers, and discriminating thinkers.

All present knew that the superintendent was right. Teaching literature is commonly regarded as the enjoyable part of English teaching, the last luxurious forty winks in the morning, the happy lunch hour, the leisurely dinner with polite waiters and sparkling crystal, the after-dinner music, the theater or the opera. And teaching composition is considered drudgery, long hours of sweaty toil, dirty grubbing with pick and shovel, chopping through underbrush, laboring in unhealthful swamps where the deadly common fault blooms and the fearsome sentence fragment casts its grotesque shadow.

And so the teaching of composition may be. It may indeed be drudgery. But whether it is or not depends upon the point of view. If composition teaching means only hunting for maggots and termites, it is not a pleasant task. But if it means aiding the development of thinking power, if it means providing the students with tools that they can employ throughout their lives for their own advancement and that of others, there is no more rewarding work than the teaching of composition.

THE IDEA BOX

GET-ACQUAINTED WRITING

1. In "Anecdotal Autobiographies," Robert Lambert and Dorothy Mack explain how they enliven autobiographies by insisting on a central point of view, limited coverage, and development by appropriate anecdotes. *English Journal*, XLVIII (Dec., 1959), 528.

2. "Students write one-paragraph themes, each student describing some other member of the class. When themes are read, everyone tries to guess which student is being described." (Elaine Clark, Central High School, Grand Rapids, Mich.)

MORE ABOUT THINKING

Give students occasional exercises in "balancing the books." For instance, propose the problem of the student who wonders whether he should take a job after school hours; have the class members make needed assumptions, line up in parallel columns the arguments pro and con, weigh the importance of each, and reach a conclusion.

SUBJECTS FOR WRITTEN WORK

1. Usually, the closer the subject, the better the result. Sometimes let students write about historical incidents, landmarks, or houses of their town.

2. Have students jot down their ideas for themes in a part of their notebook reserved for that purpose.

3. The majority of theme subjects should ordinarily be related to other work of the course. According to Robert Pooley, these subjects should arise from genuine needs or interests of the students—topics that stimulate them to thought and feeling.

4. Occasionally have students write explanations of how a story made them change their minds, how environment made the characters what they were, how a fictional portrayal helped teach an understanding of living people, or how a personal problem may be solved by finding a parallel in fiction.

5. Albuquerque (New Mexico) High School uses subject matter of other departments for theme subjects in English, whenever practicable.

6. James C. Britain, in Seattle, uses "Magic Words" as thought starters for student writing—a different word each week. Both imaginative and factual papers result. Often the words anticipate a literary selection. Typical magic words: "vehicle," "equinox," "constitution," "abalone," "Djibuti," "cul-de-sac," "patina," "facsimile." "Magic Words," *English Journal*, XLI (Nov., 1952), 493.

7. "You Are in a Tight Spot," James Warren tells his Georgia students.

"The how, when, where, why is up to you. Try to communicate with the outside world. Describe your predicament and ask for help." *Clearing House*, XXIX (Dec., 1954), 227.

8. Elizabeth Pilant provides such theme starters as "Did that burn me up!" "That time I thought I was a goner." *Clearing House*, XXV (Jan., 1951), 290.

9. "I Encourage Students to Cultivate Their Hates," says Edgar Logan, meaning that he invites them to use their writing to let off steam. *Clearing House*, XXVI (Nov., 1951), 160.

10. Students' own problems, ideas, hopes, fears, experiences are inevitably the basic stuff for their writing. Let them write what they know and occasionally go outside that to what they imagine.

11. After juniors in Charles Reich's class in Port Washington, New York, have read the four stories in Steinbeck's *The Red Pony*, in which the unifying theme is Jody's learning of basic, universal things, they are given this writing assignment: "Look back into your earlier years to discover an incident or moment when you first became aware of some basic truth—the more staggering, the better. The discovery may be of a factual or a philosophical nature. Emulate the Steinbeck style in a composition by using as much vivid, sensory, connotative detail as possible to describe your discovery." ("Study Questions for *The Red Pony*," *Exercise Exchange*, April, 1962, p. 4.)

EXERCISES IN LOGIC

1. Help students to differentiate opinion from fact. For this purpose, discuss statements like these: (1) Our basketball team lost twenty games and won five this season. (2) Our basketball team had a poor season. (3) Our coach is not a good coach. (4) Lack of student support cost us several victories.

2. Statements of opinion may be accepted if agreement is reached on the meaning of key terms and if those terms are measurable. For instance, in (2) above, if everyone agrees that "poor" refers to losing over half the games, the opinion may be accepted. But what if preseason predictions were that the team would win no games at all? Help students to see that some statements of opinion cannot be proved, for example, "Chocolate cake tastes better than angel food."

3. Have students distinguish between hypothesis and reality. If an engine stops, the hypothesis may be that it is out of gas. But the flat statement "The engine is out of gas" does not represent reality; the engine may have stopped for another reason.

4. Discuss inductive thinking: reaching a conclusion or generalization on the basis of a number of bits of evidence. The classic example: Came home at night. Flipped light switch—no light. Another—no light. Other houses dark. Clock is stopped. What has happened?

5. Discuss deductive thinking: applying a generalization to a specific instance and reaching a conclusion. For example, test "He's an Italian, so he must like spaghetti" by the syllogism "All Italians like spaghetti. He is an Italian. He likes spaghetti." (The first statement, the major premise, is probably not true.)

CONSIDER THE GENERALIZATION

1. Discuss with students such hasty generalizations as "I knew I couldn't pass algebra. I failed in the very first test." "Plane travel is unsafe. Every few days you read about a crash." "Let's pick some mushrooms. The Smiths pick them every spring and never get sick from them."

2. Louis Zahner illustrates the pitfalls of generalizations with a student's sentence, "Long books are dull." He asks the student: "On what specific firsthand particulars is the generalization based? Are there enough? How does this statement differ from 'This book is rectangular in shape'? Upon what grounds may value judgments (*dull*) be based? How long, exactly, is *long?*" May 'long' refer to the way a book seems, not just the number of pages?" After such discussion, the student rewrites: "The longest story I ever tried to read was X, and it didn't interest me. I didn't finish it." E. J. Gordon and E. S. Noyes, eds., *Essays on the Teaching of English* (New York: Appleton-Century-Crofts, Inc., 1960), p. 13.

FOR CLARITY OF EXPOSITION

1. Have each student write a paragraph explaining to a "greenhorn" how to perform a simple task that can be demonstrated in class, for example, how to tie a shoelace or how to put on lipstick. The student reads his paper slowly while a volunteer greenhorn attempts to follow instructions, being careful not to do anything not included in the paragraph. If the instructions are inadequate, they must be revised.

2. As a variation, students prepare instructions for drawing a simple, unnamed object such as a fork, spoon, table, or chair. While one student reads, others, at the board, try to draw according to his directions.

3. Another variation, especially good for oral explanations, is to have several students prepare moderately intricate diagrams, comparable to this:

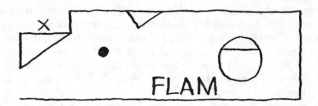

A student takes a diagram prepared by another and tells a third student, who is at the board, how to draw the diagram.

4. Have students explain, as to a complete stranger, how to get from the school to various places in the community. The class may object to inaccuracies or to anything that would puzzle the stranger.

TIPS FROM THE PROS

1. Saul Pett, Associated Press feature writer, offers advice most students need (*Illinois English Bulletin,* Nov., 1960):

"Without a viewpoint, the writer's separate little facts, his quotable quotes, his stubborn statistics, his bouncy biographical data, his clever alliterations, his flashy touches are all so much trivia, strung together without purpose, without shape, without effect.

"Don't tease me unless you can deliver, baby. Don't tell me the situation was dramatic and expect me to take your word for it. Show me how it was dramatic and I'll supply the adjective. You say this character is unpredictable? When, where, how? Give me the evidence, not just the chapter headings."

2. Margery Allingham, English novelist, says, "I write every paragraph four times: once to get my meaning down, once to put in everything I left out, once to take out everything that seems unnecessary and once to make the whole thing sound as if I had only just thought of it."

3. *Writers at Work* (New York: The Viking Press, Inc., 1958), edited by Malcolm Cowley, consists of informative interviews with sixteen American, British, and Continental authors including Forster, Thurber, Wilder, Faulkner, and Warren. The questions are incisive; the responses, revealing. Especially suitable for able upperclassmen.

4. Chapter 16, "Work Habits of Professional Writers," in J. N. Hook, *Writing Creatively* (Boston: D. C. Heath & Co., 1963), adds to the information in Cowley's book.

DEVELOPING A PARAGRAPH

1. In Pittsburgh's Schenley High School some teachers follow the practice of taking a couple of student-written paragraphs that are unnecessarily general and then rewriting them with enough detail to make them vivid. The contrasting paragraphs are then examined by the class, so that students learn how they can expand and brighten a generalized, dull statement.

2. Useful in teaching paragraph development are exercises in which students merely list all the details they might include if they were writing a paragraph. Give them such topic sentences as these: "Christmas morning is a hectic time at our house." "No cats are better than one cat." "Washing a car is easy if one prepares for the job."

A second step may consist of deleting the items that do not harmonize with the others.

IMPROMPTU THEMES

In college most students will have to do considerable writing in class, under pressure. It is kind to give them some practice in the upper high school years.

PRÉCIS WRITING

In many schools précis writing is employed to help teach organization. The theory is that a careful précis will not only aid students to understand difficult material but will also show them how the author organized it. Then they may employ similar organizational patterns.

ORGANIZATION

1. Ask students to write single sentences explaining what their purpose might be if they were writing on specified topics. For example, Advice to

a Practical Joker: "My purpose would be, through presenting an account of a joke that caused an injury, to discourage practical jokes that may be harmful."

2. To keep students reminded of the need for a plan, some teachers ask them to indicate at the end of a composition what type of organization they used.

3. Anna Haig, Bronxville (New York) High School, has her students arrange, in coherent order, scrambled paragraphs and also scrambled outlines of two degrees of headings. "These exercises must be made up by the instructor—laborious work," Mrs. Haig comments.

4. "We can clarify thinking on the relationship of sub-topics and main topics if we insist upon a more specific statement than 'The sub-topic is *related* to the main topic.' Pupils should understand that the sub-topic is *part* of the main topic. When they have had many illustrations of this relationship they can see why a certain sub-topic is illogical and can correct the error." (Margaret Mosher, Roosevelt High School, Chicago.)

5. Help the students to see that a good topic sentence does not merely name the topic, but also suggests how the topic is developed. Poor: Pinochle is the game I wish to discuss. Better: Pinochle is an easy game to learn but a difficult one to play well.

6. Mimeograph pairs of paragraphs. One paragraph in each pair will be notably deficient in unity, coherence, or emphasis; the other, on the same or a similar subject, will be especially strong. Ask students to compare the two and to analyze the weaknesses and strengths.

"MOTION PICTURES AND WRITTEN COMPOSITION"

William L. Parkins, Jr. (*English Journal*, LII [Jan., 1963], 31), describes a plan for having several compositions written about selected full-length films such as *The Grapes of Wrath* and *Intruder in the Dust*. A check list employed by lay readers in the Vancouver, Washington, school is also included.

LET'S PLAY EDITOR

Gordon R. Wood, of the University of Chattanooga, points out that, though it is the students who need practice in editing their writing, in actuality it is the teachers who get this practice. Instruction in what an editor looks at and how he works may help students to edit their own work. A copy editor from a local newspaper may be willing to present a lecture.

"RESEARCH" PAPERS

1. *Research* is too high-flown a term for what high school students can do. *Reference paper, library paper,* or *source paper* may be a better term. Debate has been raging over whether such papers belong at all in high school with those in favor perhaps having stronger arguments. For both sides, see "Dear Principal," by W. Arthur Boggs, *English Journal,* XLVII (Feb., 1958), 86 (opposed); "Dear Instructor of College Composition," by Will C. Jumper, *English Journal,* XLVII (May, 1958), 289 (in favor);

"Some Further Thoughts on Research Papers," by Katherine Burton, XLVII (May, 1958), 291 (mildly in favor).

2. A Chicago teacher recommends as a subject "The Historical Basis for Characterization of _____ in _____." His example is characterization in *Abe Lincoln in Illinois,* but the topic could be adapted to other literary works based on history. Carlisle L. Rast, "The Beginning Research Paper," *English Journal,* L (Oct., 1961), 469.

3. Some teachers help students select "research" questions answerable by intense scrutiny of only one literary work, for instance, for *Hamlet,* "Why Hamlet Delays in Killing Claudius." For description of one example of this approach, see Doris Benardete, "An Experiment in Primary Research," *English Journal,* LI (Oct., 1962), 487.

4. Librarian Evelyn Cornish offers helpful suggestions for teachers whose students will write term papers. Among them: (1) Make sure that material for approved topics is available. (2) Help students to limit topics. (3) Teach note taking. (4) Require handing in of rough draft and notes before the finished paper. (5) Stress the content, not fancy covers, clipped illustrations, etc. *Clearing House,* XXXV (Jan., 1961), 287.

5. The choice of subject is of major importance. A subject is good if (1) it interests the student, (2) material from at least four or five sources is available, (3) it is not too large and general and vague. "Aviation" is a poor subject; "Before the Wright Brothers Flew" is better. See Robert L. Coard, "The First Research Paper," *Clearing House,* XXX (Nov., 1955), 140.

6. To reduce plagiarism, discuss and illustrate proper use of sources and quotations. Some teachers have students' notes handed in with the themes.

7. Emphasize that an encyclopedia is only a starting point.

8. With upperclassmen, at least one theme should have all the paraphernalia: working bibliography cards, note cards, footnotes, bibliography.

YALE'S "DAILY THEMES"

In the famous "Daily Themes" course at Yale ("daily" means Monday through Friday) seven slogans, introduced one by one at intervals of some weeks, lead to improvement in description, narration, and characterization: (1) Individualize by specific detail. (2) Vivify by range of sensory appeal. (3) Clarify by point of view. (4) Use the indirect method (i.e., show, don't tell). (5) Characterize by speech and gesture. (6) Use words for their connotations. (7) Unify by a single impression. (Richard B. Sewall, Yale University.)

TOO MANY DAFFODILS?

Earl Hillbrand (New York State Council of Teachers of English *Newsletter,* Oct., 1958) satirizes choice of theme topics in these imagined words of a boy repeating the seventh grade: "I even write out the bills and send letters to the farmers about what their hogs and beef cattle brought at the stockyards. I only made three mistakes in 17 letters last time, my aunt said, all commas. She's been through high school and reads them over. I wish I could write school themes that way. The last one I had to write was on 'What a Daffodil Thinks of Spring,' and I just couldn't get going."

EVALUATING ONE'S OWN PARAGRAPHS

After a number of student experiences in writing of expository para-graphs, draw up with the class a set of criteria for evaluation (though ad-mitting that some paragraphs such as transitional or narrative ones need not conform). Among the criteria may be statements about unity, coher-ence, emphasis, transitions, and, as always, accuracy in mechanics. With such a list of criteria before them, students may occasionally evaluate their own or classmates' expository paragraphs.

COOPERATIVE REVISION

Edward J. Gordon's students see stars when their compositions are re-turned. Each asterisk represents an unclear sentence. Students copy these sentences on the board and clarify them with the help of their classmates. If the asterisk is used with discretion, this can be a valuable learning device.

GUIDE TO REVISION

Henry Fitts, of Winchester, Massachusetts, provides for his students a list of about thirty questions that they should try to answer as they revise the first draft of a composition. The questions are grouped under the headings of "looking over the job as a whole" (e.g., are the points in the best order?), vocabulary (e.g., is every word the best word for the job it is doing?), sentence structure (e.g., is the meaning of every sentence ab-solutely clear?), and style (e.g., are there any clichés that should be re-moved?).

COMMENTS DO HELP

In a controlled experiment, Dr. Ellis B. Page found that greatest aver-age improvement was made by students whose teachers commented rather specifically on test papers; next largest improvement, by students whose papers carried such comments as "Excellent!" or "Let's raise this grade!"; and smallest improvement, by students who received only a grade with no comment.

NO GROUNDS FOR DIVORCE

"Just as I am convinced that the study of grammar can do no good di-vorced from the practice of writing, and as I am convinced that the study of vocabulary apart from the text of good books is only a perverse occupa-tion, so I believe that writing dissociated from reading neglects its richest source of material and inspiration." Bertrand Evans, "Composition and Lit-erature," *Educational Forum*, May, 1960.

FRUSTRATION

Carl Wonnberger, on the basis of thirty-two years of secondary teaching, says that even slow students can learn to write: "The trouble . . . is that too many students are frustrated in their English study and begin to think of English as a formal discipline instead of a functional tool for man and the aspirations of man, that they get lost in verbal calisthenics, identification of 'speech parts,' the memorization of definitions that do not define, the filling in of blanks in workbooks, diagraming, and doing all manner of things that have no possible justification in the study of language and the development of sound language habits." *Michigan English Teacher,* March, 1961.

FROM JETS TO THE "ONE-HOSS SHAY"

Robert Arends, in the Winter, 1959–60, *Kentucky English Bulletin,* recommends choosing a sequence of topics leading gradually from poor students' immediate interests to something more remote, for instance, (1) a comparison of jet airplanes with older airplanes; (2) the invention of the first airplane; (3) Leonardo da Vinci's projected airplane; (4) transportation through the ages; (5) references to modes of transportation in literature, as in, for example, Holmes's "Deacon's Masterpiece," Dickinson's "Railway Train," or Shapiro's "Buick."

LAY READERS

For information about use of lay readers, and arguments pro and con, see these *English Journal* articles: "The Composition-reading Machine," by Sally van Schaick, XLIX (April, 1960), 237 (pro); "A Candid Opinion of Lay Readers," by Virginia M. Burke, L (April, 1961), 258 (chiefly pro); "Lay Readers in the High School Composition Program," by Paul M. Ford, L (Nov., 1961), 522 (pro); "Some Questions on the Lay Reader Program," by Paul H. Krueger, L (Nov., 1961), 529 (con); "Some Answers to Some Questions on the Lay Reader Program," by Harriette B. Kolker, LII (Jan., 1963), 51 (pro).

DRUGSTORE FOR SENTENCE AILMENTS

In a small high school, Jane Z. Carroll has a file of "pharmaceuticals," which are exercises to be completed by students who have committed specific errors in compositions. For details, see "A Plan for Meeting Individual Differences in Composition and Reading," *English Journal,* XLVIII (Nov., 1959), 466. *Individualized English,* sets of materials available from the Follett Publishing Company, provides such exercises.

STUDENT REACTIONS TO WRITING

West Virginia high school students were polled to get their reactions to the way theme writing was taught them. They advocated more writing(!), definite directions, choice of topics, understanding of grading system, use of models, much writing in class, help in writing poetry, chance to read classmates' themes. Among their dislikes: lack of explanation of a grade, failure to recognize plagiarism, overemphasis on serious subjects, lack of discussion of what makes a good theme. A valuable article. Lorena A. Anderson, "Ways and Means in the Teaching of Writing," *English Journal,* LI (Dec., 1962), 621.

FRIENDLY AND BUSINESS LETTERS

1. Classes may enjoy writing Christmas letters of appreciation to their parents—possibly *before* Christmas.

2. Some teachers have students write a letter to parents, telling what they have learned during the semester.

3. The Junior Red Cross will help teachers locate other teachers whose students want correspondents. The International Friendship League in Boston will supply foreign addresses.

4. Students in Natchez, Mississippi, wrote to students in other towns along the river. This plan may be varied according to local conditions. For instance, Danville, Virginia, may write to Danville, Illinois, or students in mountainous territory may write to students on the plains.

5. As sauce for the gander, one teacher writes an error-filled letter to be corrected by the class.

6. One teacher collects advertisements about free or inexpensive materials. Students write for any that they want.

7. Some teachers have students write letters to radio stations, praising good programs, criticizing bad ones.

8. A Massachusetts teacher prepares slips outlining situations for letters. Boys draw slips from one pile; girls, from another. Each student writes the letter called for by his slip, for example, "Ernest Nash, your good friend, has just received permission to invite you for a week's visit to the family camp in the White Mountains." Betty Leach, "Assignment—Social Letters," *English Journal*, XLVIII (Sept., 1959), 336.

9. Letters of appreciation to prominent persons or organizations (national, state, or local) make a good assignment. Each letter should be specific—not just "I like you."

10. The "five C's" of business letters: "Clear, Courteous, Concise, Complete, and Correct."

11. The biggest problem in letter writing in school is that of motivation. Try to make each assignment as realistic as possible.

STUDENT FOLDER

Many teachers keep folders of student writing, for their own reference and that of students. Some permit inclusion of only carefully revised work. Some use the folder as a motivating device, with no writing to be filed except that which teacher and student have agreed is especially good. Shirley Carriar, in the March, 1961, *English Journal*, recommends having students take home their folders near the end of the year, for parental inspection.

"IDEAFORM" THEME PAPER

This theme paper, prepared and sold by the NCTE for student use, features a useful check list to make easier and more effective evaluation.

LABORATORY PERIOD

Some Baltimore schools use a laboratory period for individual and group guidance in improving writing. See "A Realistic Pattern for Writing Assignments," *English Journal*, XLVI (Feb., 1957), 89.

In Barrington, New Jersey, a voluntary laboratory gives help to those requesting it. Small groups, especially of college-bound or foreign-born, write there almost daily and secure other special aids. See Grayce F.

Salerno, "An English Laboratory in Action," *English Journal*, LII (Jan., 1963), 37.

PLAGIARISM

Clues to possible plagiarism, but not definite proof, are these, says Richard Braddock (*Iowa English Bulletin*, Dec., 1959): (1) Much better than usual writing; (2) smooth writing with careless spelling, punctuation, or omissions; (3) content with which the writer probably would not be familiar; (4) writing that does not match the assignment.

To forestall plagiarism, Braddock recommends (1) frequent writing assignments, with about half done in class; (2) requiring submission of a rough draft with the finished out-of-class paper; (3) avoiding assignment of the same topics year after year; (4) clarifying what plagiarism is and why independent writing is important. (N.B.: The most frequent plagiarism probably involves copying from the encyclopedia or a similar source. Teach students how to copy honestly, giving credit as professionals do.)

GIMMICKS IN GRADING

1. Sometimes, try for a month or so to mark only *good* things in student writing, ignoring all errors, bad sentences, etc.

2. Have a class or a group evaluate some papers by listing in parallel columns for each theme "Strong Points" and "Weak Points."

3. As a once-a-year device, have "state's attorneys" and "defense lawyers" analyze papers.

4. Don't be afraid of humor in your written comments, but beware of satire, irony, sarcasm. Don't be afraid to praise, but avoid overuse of that colorless word "interesting."

5. Bar or line graphs may show students' progress in selected phases of writing. Time-consuming to construct, though, unless you teach students to keep their own graphs up to date.

6. Since a teacher tends to become either more or less liberal as he proceeds, it is wise to grade answers to question 1 in A–Z order, question 2 in Z–A order, etc.

GRADING STEP ESSAYS

Graders of STEP essays of the Educational Testing Service have been instructed to place 50% of the emphasis on quality of thought, 30% on style, 20% on usage. Sheets like the following are checked for each paper:

1. convincing	:____:____:____:____:____:____:____:	unconvincing
2. organized	:____:____:____:____:____:____:____:	chaotic
3. thoughtful	:____:____:____:____:____:____:____:	superficial
4. broad	:____:____:____:____:____:____:____:	limited
5. specific	:____:____:____:____:____:____:____:	vague
6. fluent	:____:____:____:____:____:____:____:	stilted
7. cultivated	:____:____:____:____:____:____:____:	vulgar
8. strong style	:____:____:____:____:____:____:____:	weak style
9. correct writing forms	:____:____:____:____:____:____:____:	incorrect writing forms
10. conventional grammar	:____:____:____:____:____:____:____:	substandard grammar

MANUSCRIPT PREPARATION

If your school does not have definite rules for manuscript preparation, you and your classes may work out a set to be followed in English work.

GROUP WORK IN IMPROVING WRITING

1. Marie Bullock, P.S. 80 in Buffalo, has her pupils help in planning, and uses working groups to carry out the plans. Membership in each group may be determined by sociograms, but results are as good if pupils are merely asked to form groups of no more than five or less than three.

2. In Newark, New Jersey, Grayce Foley's juniors divided into groups and produced a much needed handbook for Barringer High School.

IN FAVOR OF CREATIVE WRITING

A study by Nita M. Wyatt, reported in *The University of Kansas Bulletin of Education,* XVI (Nov., 1961), 13, and in *Educational Leadership,* XIX (Feb., 1962), 307, revealed that sixth grade children "wrote sentences of greater length and used a greater variety of vocabulary in compositions based on derived [i.e., imaginary] experience than they did in compositions based on real experience."

DESCRIPTIVE WRITING: A PLANNED SEQUENCE

Sister David Marie, Burlington, Wisconsin, suggests instructional and writing sequence for description, in "Specific Objectives in Composition," *Wisconsin English Journal,* V (Oct., 1962), 17. The major steps:

1. Informative description, an objective report (e.g., describing for the cleaners a dress for which the claim check is lost)
2. Somewhat more imaginative description, written from a single physical point of view (e.g., a flower garden or the inside of a room)
3. Description requiring change of physical point of view (e.g., outside and inside of a house, or going around on a Ferris wheel)
4. Description with a dominant impression (e.g., loneliness, peace, drabness, gaiety, fear, or disorder)
5. Description of the physical appearance of a person
6. Development of one basic character trait
7. Blending of external and internal characteristics of a person ("A loud, brazen individual and a reserved, retiring person would probably not dress alike.")
8. Suggesting character rather than stating it (may be combined with 7)
9. Using setting to reveal character (e.g., a girl's room or even a loose-leaf notebook)
10. Describing from several mental points of view (e.g., "Describe the prom from the point of view of a girl who is going, of one who hasn't been asked, of the mother of a girl who hasn't been asked, of a faculty member, of the janitor."

LITERARY WRITING

1. Years ago a superintendent said, "The teacher who is well rounded out with personal experiences in poetry, music, art, love of nature, and

love of the beautiful—whose soul is in tune with the best things in life—
will find a good response from pupils in creative expression."

2. What the child writes is less important than what the writing does for
the child.

3. In the teacher's file should be a gradually growing accumulation of
the best writing done by his students. A student who is asked to make a
copy for the file is motivated to do still better work. The teacher may
choose appropriate material to read to his classes or may keep the file
open for their browsing.

4. Each student keeps a journal of his observations, thoughts, emotional
reactions, etc. They are not graded, not read by other students, but are
read frequently by the teacher. For details, see Eleanor Brown, "Creative
Expression via Student Journals," *English Journal*, XXIX (Sept., 1940),
582, and Florence Guild, "Maintaining a Creative Atmosphere," *English
Journal*, XXXIX (March, 1950), 154. More recent is Ruth E. Reeves's
"The W in RWS," *English Journal*, XLIX (April, 1960), 520.

5. The British author of *Creative English*, Gordon Taylor, offers this
advice about describing places:

"1. Select the dominant feature.
2. Be clear about the time, weather and season.
3. Express as indirectly as you can the effect the place has on you.

"The *indirectly* is important. Present your sense data, and allow it to
produce its own effect on the reader."

6. Despite the usual admonitions to students to write on what they know
at first hand, Neal R. Edmund has found that in creative writing classes
the results are somewhat better and the vocabulary more varied when
students write on what he calls "derived" experience rather than "direct."
Clearing House, XXXIII (Nov., 1958), 163.

7. Euclid, Ohio, Junior High School has ninth graders describe a scene
before and after a disaster. As a later assignment, each student introduces
a character into this scene and develops him through presenting his reaction to the disaster.

8. Barbara Hadley's juniors studied main ideas of American short
stories, and each drafted a main idea for his own story; studied characterization and wrote character sketches; studied plot and outlined his own;
and then spent five days writing stories. "Short Story Writing in Senior
High," *English Journal*, LI (Jan., 1962), 49.

9. Virginia Craig suggests having students write "omitted" chapters to
accompany books they have read. For example, for *Treasure Island*, the
first interview between the doctor and Ben Gunn; for *Ivanhoe*, a new first
chapter, "Father and Son," introducing Cedric and Ivanhoe.

10. During the year, each student may make a "magazine" containing
his various writings.

11. Let your best class, if it wishes, prepare an anthology of original
verse or fiction.

12. In a unit involving reading *King Arthur and His Knights, The Once
and Future King,* and *A Connecticut Yankee,* eighth graders each chose
one Arthurian character and wrote an adventure for him consistent with

the sort of person he was. Eleanor K. Friedman, "Studying King Arthur in the Eighth Grade," *English Journal*, LI (March, 1962), 200.

13. A systematic program in creative writing is described by Lois Josephs, *English Journal*, LI (Oct., 1962), 468. Students write first objective descriptions, then subjective descriptions, creative exposition, a research paper, character sketches, simple accounts of personal experiences, and finally a short story.

14. Euclid Junior High School in Ohio has a schoolwide hokku contest each year. In the seventh grade it is used to introduce the idea of form in literature. (In the eighth grade, the "blues form" is taught, and able students also experiment with tankas, cinquains, triolets, and free verse.)

15. In writing poetry, start with the image or the emotion or the idea, then search for the form that will best express it. Every poem and every part of a poem is a picture; the form is the canvas and the paint, the medium for transmitting the picture.

16. Often, through revision, a good poem can be made better. For before-and-after examples, see Wilson Thornley's "Developing the Creative Process in Poetry," *English Journal*, XXVIII (Sept., 1949), 375. The teacher's share in revision of poetry is asking questions, not prescribing.

17. Lawrence Garrett, in his Denver junior high school, starts his students writing poetry by assuring them that only a few lines are enough, rhyme is unnecessary, and no profound thought is required. "We *do* want a play of the imagination, a fresh comparison, a humorous or serious reflection upon some point of interest or concern to the writer." "The Writing of Poetry," *English Journal*, XXXIX (Jan., 1950), 20.

18. Ralph Potter, in an Evanston, Illinois, senior class, begins with a daily sentence or two, on a card, describing a sensuous impression actually experienced. Then come limericks, then parodies, then serious quatrains and cinquains, then "object poems" and "character poems." The results are often amazingly good. "On Teaching the Writing of Poetry," *English Journal*, XXXIX (June, 1950), 307.

19. After all students contributed orally to the creation of a class short story, Norma Porter's eighth graders read some stories to see what "made them interesting" and then tried writing individual stories. "Fiction Writing—Eighth-Grade Style," *English Journal*, XLVII (May, 1958), 292.

20. To observe how poets make use of "sense words," Oakland's budding versifiers read de la Mare's "Silver" for sense of sight, Poe's "Bells" for sound, Morley's "Smells" for smell, and Elinor Wylie's "Velvet Shoes" for touch, B. Jo Kinnick reports. "Creative Writing," *English Journal*, XLVI (Feb., 1957), 86.

21. Your advanced students may profitably examine Thomas Wolfe's definition "Fiction is fact, rearranged and charged with a purpose." In Superior, Wisconsin, Joseph Schmidt's students start with that definition and proceed by extracting from their own experience the material for short stories. "The Short Story," *English Journal*, XLI (Dec., 1952), 536.

22. Paintings may sometimes be the inspiration for students' short stories. They tell the imaginary story behind the painting, or the story of one of the persons or objects portrayed.

23. Selma Bishop says that good creative writers often have IQ's of 95 to 106, are dreamers, aren't good in spelling and mechanics, and are some-

times called "dumb" by other teachers. "What I've Learned About Creative Writers," *Clearing House*, XXV (Oct., 1950), 89.

24. Students may be asked to clip a news story concerning a large number of people, for example, "Thousands Homeless as Floods Strike." The assignment: Pick out one person involved, and build a story on what happened to him.

25. Marianne Marshall's seventh graders use inconspicuous little newspaper stories as the starting points of narratives, or sometimes a concrete object (an apple for every student!), pictures, music, or a story begun but not finished by the teacher. "Helping Seventh Graders To Spot Plots," *English Journal*, XLVII (Nov., 1958), 507.

26. In Miami, Mabel Staats gets good results by having students work hard on just one paragraph of a short story—an opening paragraph of five to ten sentences that will indicate setting and main character and will arouse readers' interest to a high pitch. "Continued Next Week," *English Journal*, XLIX (Feb., 1960), 112.

27. "Most of our great stories are simple," Tom Person tells students, who tend to complicate needlessly. ". . . most of writing lies in the selection of details and the selection of right words to present those details," says this professional writer. Many helpful suggestions are in his ". . . So Proud You Could Pop!" *English Journal*, XLIX (Nov., 1960), 520.

28. In *Julius Caesar*, what might have happened had Brutus stayed for Antony's oration? Donald Noble advocates having students write on such "iffy" questions. "Rewriting the Great Plots," *English Journal*, L (Dec., 1961), 628.

29. Ruth Stroud ("An Approach to the Writing of Poetry," *Illinois English Bulletin*, Jan., 1962) has her students start with original comparisons. She asks, "What are the bare trees with a star caught in the branches, the full moon, the falling snow, the stop light, the shivering corn stalks, the cat blinking his wisdom at the fire, the bull dog with a haughty look?" Then each student chooses and amplifies his best comparison: ". . . you must extend your simile or metaphor so that the image will become more and more vivid. . . . The search will be for the right word, the words that laugh and cry, or mutter and mourn."

9

GRAMMAR(S): A RATIONALE

SOME VARIETIES OF GRAMMAR

Professor Harold B. Allen, a University of Minnesota linguist and a past president of the NCTE, has in various speeches and articles described four major varieties of English grammar. To avoid favorable or unfavorable connotations, he has labeled them as simply Grammars A, B, C, and D.

Grammar A dates back chiefly to the eighteenth century, in the work of such writers as the British Joseph Priestley and Robert Lowth and the American Lindley Murray. This grammar treats English as if it were Latin or at least Latin-derived. It uses terminology based upon Latin and tends to regard Latin as an ideal language of which English represents a debased form. One of the functions of a grammarian, then, is to prescribe ways in which English may come closer to "purity." Through the exercise of his reason, a grammarian should evaluate each construction, determining whether it is "correct" or "incorrect." Then he should lay down rules for all users of the language to follow.

This grammar is the one generally labeled "traditional." It has provided the basis for most instruction in the language for the past two centuries. Such instruction involves classifying words as parts of speech; classifying groups of words as phrases, dependent clauses, or independent clauses; and judging the rightness or wrongness of each locution or syntactical structure.

Grammar B concerns itself with the history of English and its relations to other languages. Many nineteenth-century grammarians, especially in Germany, explored Middle English, Old English, the related Teutonic tongues, and eventually the other members of the vast Indo-European family of languages, of which English is but one of a few dozen descendants of an ancestral tongue. Modern English, these grammarians found, is a sister of German, Dutch, and the Scandinavian languages, and a cousin (in one degree or another) of the Romance languages, Russian, Iranian, and a number of others. The work of the historical grammarians was brought to a climax by the great Danish scholar Otto Jespersen, whose huge grammar (1914) is based upon sound historical scholarship.

Historical grammar has had little impact upon instruction, except in scattered places. Here and there a unit has been taught on the history of English, or a brief lecture has been given on the relationships between English and other languages. But in general the work of the B grammarians, when known to teachers at all, has been accorded respect but not put to use. Perhaps the reason is that historical grammar *seems* irrelevant in the constant battle against "I done it."

Grammar C derives from the twentieth-century work of Leonard Bloomfield and various others such as C. C. Fries, Bernard Bloch and George L. Trager, and Henry Lee Smith. Their first assumption is that study of the spoken form of the language is especially important, since written language is based upon that spoken. Secondly, they believe it desirable to separate form from meaning in describing language: It is possible to analyze grammatically "The wolders adeled tadful poggy" even though four of the words are unknown; it is good to do so because connotations and idiomatic problems do not get in the way. Thirdly, C grammarians believe it is their function to describe the language, not to prescribe or to label "right" or "wrong": a scientist, they argue, studies houseflies without judging the rightness or wrongness of houseflies' behavior. (This does not mean, for example, that the C grammarians advocate "ain't"; they certainly do not use it. But they find that "ain't" exists, and therefore they have a responsibility to describe the conditions in which it exists.)

Behind such labels as "linguistics," "structural linguistics," or "descriptive linguistics," Grammar C has aroused tremendous interest among teachers, especially since the early 1950's. The interest has been much greater so far, though, than the utilization. In 1960, for example, Charles Alva found that "Structural grammar is being used to varying degrees by almost four per cent of the approximately 4,000 teachers of English in the public high schools of California."[1] Today

[1] "Structural Grammar in California High Schools," *English Journal*, LII (Dec., 1960), 607.

the proportion would be higher, but Grammar C has certainly not yet swept the country.

One of the reasons is that the grammar still best known to most teachers is traditional grammar; that is the only grammar with which they really feel comfortable. Another reason is that the C grammarians have gone off in various directions, often disagreeing among themselves on basic questions as well as details. A tradition-oriented teacher asks, "How can I teach something in such a state of uncertainty and flux?" Still another reason is that many teachers, through either intuition or reason, share the doubts expressed by an extraordinarily broad-minded and well-informed student of grammar, Charlton Laird.

In "Structural Linguistics: Notes for a Devil's Advocate," [2] Laird questions several "assumptions" of the structuralists. He argues that the best approach for analyzing language is not necessarily the best for teaching it: "Structural study is certainly important, but most truths have only limited uses, and structural study rapidly becomes so complicated that only the specialist can deal with it." Laird also doubts that we have "a sufficiently reliable understanding of linguistics in English so that we can formulate a practicable pedagogical statement." He questions the common belief that the best way to improve the use of the native tongue is the study of grammar, *any* grammar, and he doubts that there is any single method of teaching or any content most suitable for children of all ages. He concludes, "I should say that structural study is now so important that every prospective teacher of English should have a course in it; we cannot be sure, however, that it should become the central approach in mass education except on an experimental basis and with careful preparation."

The leading pioneers of Grammar D are Noam Chomsky and Zellig Harris, with Robert Lees, Robert Stockwell, Owen Thomas, and Paul Roberts among those making notable contributions to theory and popularization. Whereas C grammarians are interested in a sound mechanism for describing English sentences, D grammarians concern themselves with the ways in which we generate new sentences. Both believe that English relies upon a relatively small number of sentence patterns to achieve its purposes. The C grammarians describe these patterns; the D grammarians, who build upon the work of C, attempt to show how "transformations" are made from "kernel sentences" to variations of those kernels. Grammar D presents, with attempted mathematical precision, the exact rules that govern the construction of

[2] *College English*, XXIV (Nov., 1962), 93–97.

sentences. Thus, to explain the transformation of the active voice "John admires sincerity" into the passive "Sincerity is admired by John," Chomsky uses the formula $NP_1 - V - NP_2$ for the active, and shows that the rule for forming the passive is $NP_2 - is + Ven - by + NP_1$.[3]

Such formulas frighten English teachers, many of whom have unhappy memories of something that looked similar and was called algebra. Partly for this reason and partly because generative or transformational grammar is relatively new, Grammar D has as yet had very slight influence upon the schools. Yet, at least in theory, its impact should be considerable, because classroom teachers ought to be particularly interested in helping students to construct good sentences, and the construction of sentences is also the goal of the D grammarians.

These brief summaries of Grammars A, B, C, and D suggest only in general the divergences. Some grammarians do not fit neatly into any category; others have shifted allegiance from one category to another. And, within any category, the differences between viewpoints may be considerable. The enlightened traditionalism of Professor Ralph Long is certainly different from the rigid prescriptivism of Lindley Murray; the structuralists have varied emphases to which they attach such designations as *phonemics, ethnolinguistics,* and *dialectology,* and those working in the same subdiscipline often quarrel among themselves; generativists Harris, Chomsky, and Lees also have their scholarly disagreements.

What is the high school teacher to do, faced with such wealth, or diversity, or turmoil?

"A PLEA FOR PLURALISM"

Professor James Sledd believes that grains of truth are present in all four of the chief varieties of grammar, and that teachers should be informed about all of them:

We do not want just one book or one syllabus—we want many books and many syllabi, taking a variety of positions. . . . And we do not want teachers who have been falsely indoctrinated with the idea that by learning a single grammatical system they have learned enough to teach grammar. We should give prospective teachers, not a course in English grammar, but a course in English grammars. Institutions which teach the traditional schoolroom grammar should not be despised, since that grammar is not

[3] *Syntactic Structures* ('S–Gravenhage: Mouton & Co., 1957), 43.

totally false or misguided and since future teachers will have to live with it and probably teach it. But teaching the traditional grammar is just a beginning. We should also teach [in college] one of the scholarly non-structural books like Curme's one-volume *English Grammar* or Jespersen's *Essentials*. These works provide much more information about our language than most of their structural rivals do; they preserve methods and insights which the structuralists wrongly abandoned; and though Chomsky has somewhere said that they are more like the inputs to a language-learning machine than like real grammars, such inputs have their value for our language-learners. Respect for tradition, finally, does not forbid us to live and work in the twentieth century. We should certainly teach our future teachers some one of our structural grammars, and as soon as we have the necessary competence and the necessary materials, we should introduce them to transformational analysis. Our aim should be not only an understanding of each system in itself, but at least an elementary comparison and evaluation of them in both theoretical and practical terms.[4]

It is well known that English teachers ought to be omniscient. Since they cannot—even about the fraction of one per cent of the world's knowledge contained in the study of English grammar—a general knowledge of all the grammars and a detailed knowledge of one may afford the least unsatisfactory compromise. Such a compromise appears especially sensible in light of the increasingly frequent prediction that the grammar of the future will be a blend of the four, with Grammar A supplying most of the terminology, B the historical background, C the patterns for analysis, and D the comparable patterns for synthesis.

A suggestion concerning some useful books about each of the four grammars may be helpful. Either Curme or Jespersen (the books mentioned by Sledd) will provide basic information about traditional grammar; Ralph Long's *The Sentence and Its Parts* and the Hook-Mathews *Modern American Grammar and Usage* offer more up-to-date but less detailed descriptions. For history of the language, either Albert C. Baugh's *A History of the English Language* or the more recent Stuart Robertson–F. G. Cassidy *The Development of Modern English* is invaluable. So far, the best introduction to structural linguistics is a high school text by Paul Roberts, *Patterns of English*, but it should be supplemented by such a book as C. C. Fries's *The Structure of English* or W. Nelson Francis' *The Structure of American English*. Paul Roberts, who switched from Grammar C to Grammar D (after first being a Grammar A man), also is the author of a high school text on generative grammar, *English Sen-*

---

[4] "A Plea for Pluralism," *College English*, XXIII (Oct., 1961), 19–20.

tences; so far his is the only easily readable book on the subject, though some generativists regard it as impure. More thorough books than Roberts' and more comprehensible ones than Chomsky's *Syntactic Structures* are gravely needed and no doubt will soon appear. Finally, though it is pre-generative in date (1953), an amusing, provocative, and insightful introduction to language study is Charlton Laird's *The Miracle of Language.*

The teacher who has mastered the basics of the four grammars through study of such books, and who has mastered most of the details of Grammar A, C, or D, is prepared for most classroom situations in which instruction in grammar is required. He will probably place major stress on the grammar he best comprehends, and that is as it should be. Professor Laird once wrote,

Still I cannot help reminding myself that a superior teacher can teach almost anything successfully, but that no teacher can thrive in a system he does not understand and trust. . . . If the Ford or any other foundation has money they do not know how to spend, I suggest that they import an engaging and learned Kwakiutl Indian and ask him to teach English with Kwakiutl grammar; if he is a truly superior teacher I would predict for him a considerable degree of success.[5]

THE ROLE OF GRAMMAR IN THE ENGLISH CLASSROOM

Let us assume that you, a high school teacher of this decade, have acquired basic information about the four grammars and a reasonably thorough understanding of one. What should be the place of grammar in your teaching?

If we consider that the task of the English teacher is the threefold one of giving instruction in language, composition, and literature, and if we regard the three parts of the objective as equal, it would appear that about a third of a class's time should be devoted to the study of language. The three components are, of course, not independent: Language and composition are taught at least partly together, as are language and literature, and literature and composition.

The mistake of the past, though, has been to equate language and grammar. As a result, in many American classrooms, half or more of the time was spent on sentence analysis, drill on word forms, memorization of declensions and conjugations, and workbook exercises *ad nauseam.* To such work was added some study of spelling, punctua-

[5] "The Parts, or Vestigial Remnants, of Speech," *College English,* XVIII (April, 1957), 337.

tion, and capitalization. These activities constituted the whole of the language program—sometimes the whole of a semester's or even a year's English program.

But language is more than grammar, spelling, punctuation, and capitalization. It is also usage (the locutions currently employed for various purposes and by various groups), semantics (word denotations, connotations, and social impact), vocabulary development, and linguistic history. It is the study of the words and sentences used by some of the best writers of English, and the study of the words and sentences written by Sam Sophomore.

Language study clearly deserves the one-third of a class's time allocated to it by those who accept the tripod theory of the English curriculum. Grammar alone, being only one of the components of language, does not. In most British schools no more than a sixth of total English class time is given to the study of grammar, but the study of language goes on all the time, whether a class is reading Tennyson or preparing to write a letter.[6] Does the writing of the British child suffer because he is deprived of months of grammatical study? A subjective reaction, based upon the author's reading of several hundred unselected compositions by British secondary children and his reading of uncounted thousands of American school compositions, is that the British student, on the average, writes somewhat better than does his American contemporary. Not greatly better, but somewhat. A multidimensional language program seems in all ways preferable to one that concentrates on grammar alone.

Our first conclusion about the role of grammar, then, is that there should not be too much of it. It should be regarded as only one important segment of the language third of the total English program.

A second point is so obvious that it should not have to be made. Yet it must be, for many presently employed teachers violate it. *Students should not be taught untruths about their language.*

Here is a place where knowledge of more than one grammar is especially useful, for Grammar A is shot through with untruths and partial truths, and some versions of Grammar C are so given to exaggeration that the tag "untrue" is not entirely undeserved. In traditional grammar, for example, at least in its prescriptive form, such labels as "right" and "wrong" give a false impression of language. Custom, not morals or mathematical certitudes, determines which forms are currently in good repute. Until less than a century ago, for

---

[6] The estimate of one-sixth was made by the author when he spent a semester visiting a considerable number of British schools of all sorts; it was confirmed by representatives of the British Ministry of Education.

instance, "The house was building" was labeled right, and "The house was being built" was considered wrong. Today's custom strongly prefers the latter. But, *sub specie aeternitatis*, is either right, either wrong?

Another example of the untruths of traditional grammar lies in some of its definitions. "A sentence is a group of words expressing a complete thought," for instance, is untrue because a sentence is not necessarily a group of words and because a whole paragraph, chapter, or book may be necessary to express a complete thought—if such an expression is ever possible. If an adjective is "a word that modifies a noun or pronoun" then "upstairs" and "here" in "the man upstairs" and "the man here" must be adjectives, as must "brick" and "rose" in "brick house" and "rose garden."

The structuralists are guilty of other kinds of untruths. They exaggerate (at least for purposes of pedagogy) the importance of phonology: It is doubtful that they can point to any consistent improvements made in the language of a native speaker of English by long sessions of phonemic transcription. The structuralists also mislead when they divorce meaning from form. Certainly sentences like "A mertin oogles a floob" do illustrate a point about language, but since the chief purpose of language is to convey meaning, an exclusive concern with form is at best unwise.

The generativists have not been with us long enough to be guilty of many untruths, although some of their enthusiasts approach the boundary by making claims that cannot yet be verified. Neither a teacher nor a student should be led to believe that any system of grammar will ever lead to linguistic salvation. English grammar is basically simple, but its ramifications make it immensely complex. The "sentence trees" used by some generativists help to reveal this complexity even while they are intended to simplify; they are actually only a variant but still elaborate form of sentence diagram.

A third principle to keep in mind is this: *Teach what the students need most.* Teachers of a (hopefully) bygone day assumed that what students need most is the ability to take sentences apart and label the pieces. Some structural linguists, through overemphasis on what they call "immediate constituents," do the same kind of useless hacking.

Growing roses is not the same as chopping up rose bushes and analyzing the parts under a microscope. Growing sentences is not the same as dissecting sentences. One reason why many students have failed to learn to write good sentences is that their teachers have not understood the difference between growing and dissecting. Day after day, month after month, students are required to take apart someone else's sentences—analyzing, naming, underlining, encircling, diagraming—with only an occasional opportunity to write their own sentences, their own paragraphs. Nowhere outside the English classroom will they ever have to repeat such analyses. Yet they will be using sentences throughout their lives.

A high school sophomore once described dramatically what has gone on in too many classrooms:

"WHY I HATE GRAMMER"

It is a hot day (to hot for school) At the front of the room, a voice drones as I sit sleeply and try to listen. Suddenly the voice swackes "Dean, sences you are so wide-awake, you may take apart the next sentence." A few laght as most have to much spring-fever to even listen. Stranulessly I decompose the sentence. At last the terrifing task is done. I relexe again. "Dean, you are intirely wrong. Now do it right" the voice growls. Wearly I try again and again and again. Oh woe! Again I'm wrong. Again I try. Oh how I wish I was dead. "Dean won't you ever learn anything. Come in after school until you learn your grammer. Fibbly I protest. But to no avail. Now you know why I can't stand grammer.[7]

Clear understanding of the most important grammatical terms is important, mainly because these terms are convenient shortcuts, just as are the names of the parts of an automobile or the names of the elements in chemistry. The good chemistry teacher, though, does not stop with having his students memorize the periodic table. Discussions center on what happens when various elements are brought together, and laboratory sessions demonstrate the effects of the combinations. The good English teacher does not stop with having his students memorize facts about parts of speech and their roles in sentences. He has the students compose sentences, not just "decompose" them. A combination of analysis and construction, with greater emphasis on the construction, affords the best way of improving students' sentences.

The third principle, teaching what the students need most, also implies that instruction especially adapted to corrective procedures is desirable. This part of the principle is developed in the final section of this chapter.

A fourth principle makes it possible to regard as an advantage the fact that we at present possess more than one English grammar: *Choose from each grammar whatever is most helpful in clarifying a point.* Here are a few examples:

[7] Quoted in J. N. Hook, " 'Stranulessly I Decompose the Sentence,' " *Clearing House*, XXVI (Sept., 1951), 25.

1. In teaching phrases and clauses used as adjectives and adverbs, follow the generative concept that these are merely elaborations of kernel sentences, to be added in accordance with specific procedures.

2. In teaching punctuation, occasionally employ structuralists' findings concerning juncture and its relationships to commas and semicolons or periods.

3. In using either structural or generative linguistics, remember always, with the traditionalists, that meaning is important.

4. In using Grammar A, C, or D, refer frequently to Grammar B for light upon why we use certain forms or constructions. For instance, Grammar B can help us to understand why we say "you were," not "you was"; why we say "do," "did," "done"; why "be" is the most complex of our verbs; or why word order is especially important in modern English.

5. In teaching recognition of parts of speech, as they are defined by traditional grammar, use the structuralists' information about "signals" that help one to identify a word as a noun, a verb, etc.

6. Use the structuralists' designation "determiner" for words like "the," "these," "my," and "four" to distinguish this group from adjectives that describe and that can be compared: "tall," "good," etc. Use the structuralists' designation "intensifier" for words like "very" and "rather," which differ from adverbs like "soon" or "carefully."

Fifth, this principle: *Teach as much as possible about sentence structure by encouraging thought, rather than by the study of anybody's grammar.* A grammatical "rule" is a statement of an abstraction, and abstractions are difficult for many children or adults to grasp. But often a few moments of thought will clarify a point that a grammatical rule would only muddy, especially for the less able student.

For example, consider the dangling modifier. A text says, "Each participial, gerundial, or infinitival phrase should be so placed within a sentence that its relationship to the word it modifies is immediately clear." A student groans, audibly or secretly, when he reads that; he may have no inkling of its meaning. But assume that the teacher says, "What's funny about this sentence? 'Kicking and screaming, the mother carried her little girl to the bathtub.'" Another example follows, and another, and still more. Then the teacher draws a statement of the generalization from the class, in students' own words, maybe something like this: "We have to be careful about where we put phrases with -*ing* words or infinitives, or we may seem to be saying something we didn't intend."

As another example, consider the choice of a verb with a compound subject. Once more the textbook may have a complex rule or set of rules. The teacher who stresses thinking may proceed in some such way as this: He writes on the board a sentence like "George and Mary _____ here." "How many persons were here?" he asks. "Two." "Then should the verb be 'was' or 'were'?" Soon he moves on to "Either George or Mary _____ here." "How many persons were here?" "One." "Then should the verb be 'was' or 'were'?" Eventually he reaches "Either the man or the boys _____ here" and "Either the boys or the man _____ here." He takes the students with him each step of the way. They think each item through for themselves and arrive inductively at the heart of the "rule." Other examples of such inductive teaching appear later in this chapter.

Finally, *a school should develop a sequential program for instruction in grammar.* If homogeneous grouping is employed, the sequence may differ from track to track.

Professor Robert Pooley has recommended one workable sequence, though modifications may be needed for very slow or very able students. His recommendations may be outlined as follows:

Grades 1-6 *Recommended*:

No formal grammar
Casual references to such terms as *sentence* and *subject*
Emphasis on good usage habits; much writing

Grades 7-9

Emphasis on the grammar of simple sentences
Subject, verb
Predicate adjective, predicate noun, before teaching direct object
Simple adjective and adverb
Compound subject, verb, and complement
Phrase modifiers
Indirect object, "a special kind of modifier"
Adverbial clause as modifier

Grades 10-12

Adjective clause, noun clause
Stress on subordinate elements
Expansion of sentence patterns
Emphasis on skilful use of phrases
Parallel structure
Intensive practical review, with analysis of own writing, in Grade 12 [8]

Have a Sequence

---

[8] The outline is based upon Pooley's "What Grammar Shall I Teach?" *English Journal,* XLVII (Sept., 1958), 327–33.

Not everyone would agree that Professor Pooley's plan is ideal, especially for very bright students. The important consideration, though, is that it does represent a sequence, something that has long been lacking. It steers teachers away from the futile attempt to teach almost everything every year, an attempt which too often leads to mastery of very little.

In summary, grammar does have an important role in the English classroom. However, it should by no means be regarded as the whole of the language segment of the English program. It should be taught honestly and selectively; its presentation should take advantage of the contributions made by differing breeds of grammarians; it should encourage students to think more than to memorize; and it should be presented according to a planned sequence.

TEACHING SENTENCE STRUCTURE

The first job in teaching sentence structure is to make sure that all students can assemble in written form a noun and a verb in the pattern that is called a sentence. Children have been *speaking* sentences since they were two or three years old, but the transfer from speech to writing has been inadequately accomplished by many who enter high school and some who enter college. Failure to understand exactly what a sentence is results often in undesirable fragments or run-together sentences.

Teachers have made the structure of sentences appear more complicated than it actually is. The work of the structural linguists has revealed that most English sentences follow relatively few patterns, although there is not yet complete agreement on the classifications. A study that uses more traditional terminology than that of the structural linguists shows that 92.1 per cent of modern American printed sentences fall into only five basic patterns or combinations. These five patterns, and their frequencies of occurrence, are shown in the table on page 282. The minor patterns, accounting for a very small percentage of the total, are typically questions, imperative sentences, or sentences in which one or more of the parts are placed in an abnormal position (e.g., "This offer he refused," which alters Pattern II, changing the order to object-subject-verb).

Pattern	Basic Example	Examples with Modifiers	Frequency of Use as Sole Pattern	Frequency of Use Combined with Another Basic Pattern
I. Subject-verb	Women applauded.	The *women* who were standing in the aisles *applauded* vigorously.	25.1%	5.3%
II. Subject-verb-object	We ate hamburgers.	Sitting in the car, *we* sadly *ate* the *hamburgers* that were all we could afford.	32.9%	5.9%
III. Subject-verb-predicate nominative	Husbands are mice.	Too many *husbands* in this town *are* mere *mice* that fear to venture out when the cat is around.	10.5%	2.7%
IV. Subject-verb-predicate adjective	Helen is beautiful.	*Helen*, who spends almost no time in beauty parlors, *is* nevertheless strikingly *beautiful*.	10.1%	3.7%
V. Expletive-verb (predicate adjective)-subject	a. There are traitors. b. It is easy to swim.	a. Unquestionably *there are traitors* in our midst. b. *It is* probably *easy to swim* such a narrow stream.	4.3%	0.9%

SOURCE: J. N. Hook and E. G. Mathews, *Modern American Grammar and Usage* (New York: The Ronald Press Co., 1956).

Paul Roberts' structurally oriented book *Patterns of English* recognizes four "very common" sentence patterns, as follows:

Noun	Verb		1 ↔ 2		Birds sing.
Noun	Verb	Adjective	1 ↔ 2	3	Birds are beautiful.
Noun	Linking verb	Noun	1 ↔ 2L	1	Canaries are birds.
Noun	Verb	Noun	1 ↔ 2	1	Canaries eat worms.[9]

Roberts also mentions "statement patterns with *it*," "statements with subject after the verb," "question patterns," and "request patterns," as well as patterns in which two nouns follow a verb.

In Roberts' later book *English Sentences,* which was the first book-length attempt to translate generative grammar into high school terms, ten numbered patterns are described, as shown below. In the formulas, D means determiner, N noun or noun equivalent, V verb, Adv adverb, Adj adjective, V-b the verb "become" or "remain," V-t transitive verb, V-g a verb like "give" that can take an indirect object, V-c a verb like "consider," V-e a verb like "elect." Parentheses mean that the element may be present but need not be.

One:	(D)	N	V	(Adv)			Birds sing.
Two:	(D)	N	V	Adj			Birds seem beautiful.
Three:	(D)	N	V-b	(D)	N		The boy became a man.
Four:	(D)	N	V-t	(D)	N		The man shot the wolf.
Five:	(D)	N	V-g	(D)	N	(D)	N	The man gave his son a car.
Six:	(D)	N	V-c	(D)	N	(D)	N	My uncle considered me a fool.
Seven:	(D)	N	V-e	(D)	N	(D)	N	They elected my brother their president.
Eight:	(D)	N	be	Adv			The boy was here.
Nine:	(D)	N	be	Adj			The lions were hungry.
Ten:	(D)	N	be	(D)	N		Ambrose is my friend.[10]

The *"there* transformation" Roberts regards as a derivative from a basic pattern. Thus "There is a man here" (There be D N Adv) is a transformation of Pattern Eight: "A man is here" (D N be Adv).

The point of all this, whether you accept a modified traditional, a structural, or a generative approach, is that English sentences are basically simple. Once students thoroughly understand basic sen-

---

[9] Paul Roberts, *Patterns of English* (New York: Harcourt, Brace & World, Inc., 1956), pp. 70–73.

[10] From pages 27–46 of *English Sentences* by Paul Roberts, copyright © 1962 by Harcourt, Brace & World, Inc., and reprinted with their permission.

tence elements, they are ready to go on to the arrangement of modifiers of those elements.

A good beginning in teaching sentence structure to a junior high class is to have someone suggest a name—possibly "George." Write the name on the board, and then ask the class to tell, in one word, a number of things that George does or did. On the board appear several sentences like these: *constructing:*

Two word sentences

George walks.
George escaped.
George plays.

Then ask for a name that does not indicate a person or place. Perhaps "table" is suggested. The first procedure is repeated. (Students love to use their ingenuity in finding interesting word combinations.) [11]

Table stands.
Table collapses.
Table disappeared.

After a few more two-word sentences have been composed, but before the edge wears off the fun, explain briefly that they have been building sentences and that every sentence must have the two parts that they have been making up. These two parts are the subject and verb. The students identify some of the words on the board as subjects and verbs.

The next day, spend part of the time in an alternate procedure. *S V* Begin by writing a verb on the board, perhaps "break." Then the students supply subjects that could be used with that verb: "dishes," "windows," etc. After that, a student suggests another verb, and the rest of the class furnishes appropriate subjects to go with it.

Before much time has elapsed, you will need to prevent formation of the idea that only nouns may serve as subjects. Therefore you *Pronouns* introduce pronouns as subjects. A little later, you will use gerunds, infinitives, and possibly clauses as subjects, although you will not insist that their technical names be remembered.

The next step is to introduce predicate adjectives, and then predicate *Pred. Adj. &* nouns. On the board write: *Pred. Nouns*

[11] Lucia Mirrielees, in *Teaching Composition and Literature* (rev. ed.) (New York: Harcourt, Brace & World, Inc., 1952), offers the excellent suggestion that vocabulary building be sometimes combined with sentence building. Students should be encouraged, she says, to find appropriate, colorful, specific verbs to use with given subjects, for example, "cow—meandered—trotted—loped."

An astronaut is
Tom Sawyer was

Ask the class to think of words that can describe an astronaut ("brave," "healthy," etc.) and words that can describe Tom Sawyer ("mischievous," "intelligent," etc.). Point out that the words they have supplied are called adjectives and that their purpose is to describe the subject. Later, use a similar procedure, except that this time students will supply names that tell what someone or something is. Thus they can complete "I am" by adding "a boy," "a student," "an athlete," "a citizen," and so on.

If structural or generative grammar is used, pattern descriptions like those illustrated above may be employed. Assignments may consist of composing original sentences illustrating the patterns so far discussed.

Direct objects come next. Ask students to complete sentences like "Hunters shot," "Jim caught," "Helen made." After a number of illustrations, explain that the words being added are called direct objects and that many verbs that show action can take objects. Get more examples from the class.

Members of the class may now do a little dramatizing to fix the principles in their minds. Bill is asked to come up to the front of the room and lift the unabridged dictionary. "What did Bill do?" "He lifted the dictionary," someone says. On the board write, "Bill lifted dictionary." Then ask for volunteers to act out sentences of their own; the class must guess the sentence being acted out. *[handwritten: act out sentences]*

Procedures like this may seem exceedingly childish, and it is true that they would be in the junior and senior years. But remember that, although junior high students have been speaking sentences of some sort since they were about two years old, they have rarely paid much attention to sentence structure. The knowledge they are gaining now is basic; later improvement in sentence structure is dependent upon learning these fundamentals. When Bill lifts the dictionary, he is making a sentence come to life; the students can visualize the sentence and can understand its components. Dozens of variations of such procedures can be worked out by resourceful teachers.

Later on, you will guide the attention toward compound subjects and compound verbs: *[handwritten margin: noun compound s.]*

Sandra and George hurry.
Sandra laughed and shouted.
Sandra and George climbed and climbed.

Someone may ask whether "and" is part of the subject and verb. A good answer is that words like "and," "but," "although," "to," "under," etc., are connectives, which join parts of sentences. They are the glue that holds parts of sentences together.

Aux. Verbs &
main verb

Verbs consisting of more than one word are also considered at about this time: "It was raining," "Charles has been defeated," etc. The only explanation needed now is that verbs often have more than one part and that any verb to which the suffix -*ing* has been added must have a helping verb to make a sentence. That is why such a group of words as "The girl shaking like a leaf" is not a sentence.

modifiers:

Later come the modifiers. On the ever useful blackboard write a "sentence" such as "Woman drives car"—or else elicit a subject-verb-object combination from the class. Then say, "Let's add something to this sentence. Who can tell something about the woman?" Ask similar questions about "drives" and "car." Perhaps a sentence like this results:

> The swankily dressed woman skilfully drives her long, graceful car into the palm-fringed driveway.

Underline the subject, verb, and object to emphasize that the sentence is still the same. Call the additions "modifiers," and do not bother as yet with distinctions between adjectives and adverbs. Say that modifiers describe something and show how it differs from other, similar things. Since the students have built the sentence, they realize that "the swankily dressed" describes "woman," that "her long, graceful" describes "car," and that "skilfully" and "into the palm-fringed driveway" modify "drives."

More sentences are built. Some of the modifiers suggested are single words, some phrases, and some clauses, but you need not yet point out any technical differences among these. The concept of modifying must be completely clarified before such distinctions are drawn. Practice in building word, phrase, and clause modifiers of various elements in specific sentences should come later.

Complications

Synthesis
precedes analysis

Not until these preliminary steps have been taken do you turn to textbook material on sentence structure, unless the text contains exercises in the building of very simple sentences. Modern research has demonstrated that starting with sentence building (synthesis) brings much better results than starting with sentence analysis. The procedure of analysis, however, does offer a valuable follow-up. Students see that sentences written by others contain the same ingredients as those that they have been writing. To make the study less bookish, they examine sentences in newspapers and magazines as well as in their text.

At this point, several complications are sure to arise. The first is that Frances finds a sentence like this: "Down the street rushed the boys." She says that "Down the street" or possibly "Down" or "street" is the subject. You politely disagree, saying that almost always the subject does come at or near the beginning, but that in one sentence in about twenty the subject comes elsewhere. "You can always tell what the subject is by thinking about the sentence for a moment. We have seen that the subject always does something or has something said about it. Now, in your sentence, who does the rushing?" "The boys." "Good. So 'boys' would be the subject. Where did the boys rush?" "Down the street." "Then 'Down the street' is really a modifier of 'rushed,' isn't it? . . . I can think of another sentence where the subject comes last: 'After dark, in came Tom.' What is the subject there? . . . Who can think of another sentence in which the subject does not come near the beginning? . . . Can you decide why we sometimes construct our sentences in this way?"

The second complication arises when Larry finds a sentence fragment such as "Never again" or "On the contrary." Explain that these are not sentences, because they do not have subjects and verbs. Add that writers sometimes use fragments for various purposes, just as people do in talking:

> "Where to?"
> "Gym."
> "Why?"
> "Big game today."

"Sentence fragments are a kind of shorthand," you say. "They are occasionally acceptable, although in writing and speaking most people generally use complete sentences because the complete sentence can be more easily understood."

Lily finds a compound sentence and thus unearths a third complication: "The fire burned all night, but the damage was not great." She wonders whether a sentence may have two subjects and two verbs, whether it can really be two sentences written as one. Tell the class that such a combination can and often does make a sentence. Then or later, point out that the second part of such a sentence is preceded either by a semicolon or by "and," "but," "for," "or," "nor," and possibly "yet" or "so."

Frank wonders about such a sentence as "Because they had no money left, the boys hitchhiked home." Here, also, are two subjects and two verbs. Ask, "Why did the boys hitchhike?" "Because they didn't have any money left." "Then the first words in the sentence are a modifier, aren't they? They do not make a sentence, but simply modify 'hitchhiked.' We often have similar groups of words that serve as modifiers." By using this approach, you do not say that the clause is a sentence, and thus you forestall students' tendency to punctuate dependent clauses as sentences.

As each such complication arises, teacher and class explore it, give further illustrations, clarify the difficulty, and build additional sentences in accordance with the new pattern. They examine the positions of modifiers and the changes in meaning that modifiers make. They notice that some modifiers may be moved into other positions without changing the meaning but that for other modifiers only one location makes sense; thus they learn to look at their own sentences from the standpoint of clarity, since lack of clarity most often comes from faulty placement of modifiers. They learn simultaneously, in such a sentence as "The enthusiasm of students at the games is contagious," that the number of the verb is not affected by the presence of modifiers. Other principles of usage they develop as they go along, and always they construct their own illustrative sentences to reinforce their understanding.

Students do not learn all there is to know about sentences in a couple of weeks or a couple of years. No one knows everything about sentences. But you as teacher return again and again to the attack on "ol' debbil Ignorance." You vary your approach. You may, for instance, give the students a list containing perhaps five verbs, eight or ten nouns, and eight or ten modifiers; the students are to make five sentences, using only these words and having no words left over. Or you may have a contest to see who can write down in three minutes the most verbs—or the most interesting verbs—that can be used with "chair" or some other subject. A variation is to find as many objects as possible to be used in a sentence such as "Harold forgot   ." Another instructive "game" is to give students a sentence skeleton of three words and ask them to find a suitable one-word modifier for each of the three, or a phrase modifier or a clause modifier.

The procedures being described differ in two important ways from traditional ones. The first difference is that students compose many sentences instead of spending most of their time in analysis. The second is that the teacher steadily uses inductive tactics. The deductive approach, in contrast, begins with telling the students what the rule is and then continues by having them analyze or correct sentences. *The English Language Arts in the Secondary School* says,

The inductive method (discovery of a generalization through the study of many specific illustrations) should for the most part be used in introducing a new grammatical point. Although there is nothing wrong with stating a grammatical principle first and then illustrating it, a more effective procedure, usually, is to have the student find for himself from the analysis of a number of carefully prepared sentences the principle for which he has need. The important point here and elsewhere in the teaching of grammar is that the student shall not be tempted to memorize a statement instead of developing a clear concept.[12]

A little imagination can convert a classroom into a place where learning is exciting and enjoyable. Dozens of devices like those just mentioned may be employed. Your goal is always a serious one: You want students to learn and to apply what they learn. But you know that they may have fun while they are learning and that you can have fun with them.

Teaching the Complex Sentence

Although we may assume that the members of your class have learned to recognize subjects, verbs, objects, and modifiers in most sentences, they are not through with these fundamentals but will return to them again and again—sometimes incidentally, sometimes directly. You are aware that most human beings, thirty minutes after they have "learned" something, have forgotten 50 per cent of what they "learned"; complete retention comes only with frequent repetition and review. But reviewing may often be accomplished while students are building upon earlier foundations.

Junior high school students, and many older ones, tend to overuse the simple and compound sentence, one of their favorites being the seemingly endless "and . . . and" type. The sentence form is more than the garb of thought; it is an indication that the relationships of the ideas have or have not been clearly defined. For the expression of many ideas the complex form is best; because it shows most clearly the relative importance of two or more facts and the way in which those facts are associated.

Your procedure is to add to the varieties of glue that students use to join their ideas. You write two sentences:

> The game was over.
> We went home.

[12] New York: Appleton-Century-Crofts, Inc., 1956. Pp. 376–77.

Comment that these seem childishly short, and ask someone to make these two sentences into one. That seems easy. The answer comes immediately:

> The game was over, and we went home.

Accept that answer and write it on the board, but add that there are other ways of combining the two sentences. If no one can think of any, ask, "When did we go home?" "After the game was over." That sets a pattern, and more variations are suggested:

> When the game was over, we went home.
> Before the game was over, we went home.
> Because the game was over, we went home.
> Although the game was over, we went home.
> If the game was over, we went home.

Ask whether all of these sentences mean the same thing. Everyone can see that they do not. Then comes a key question, "Which of the sentences is least definite in meaning?" What you want the students to see is that "and" is often less exact than "after," "because," "although," etc. In other words, help students to realize that "and" is not the only nor always the best kind of sentence glue.

Notice that you have focused attention first on what is being said and second on how it is said. The old procedure, proved unprofitable by the experience of uncounted thousands, was to concentrate on the form. "A complex sentence is so and so," said yesterday's teacher. "Here is an example of a complex sentence. Now open your books to page so and so, and pick out all the complex sentences in Exercise umpteen." Students did learn to identify complex sentences but often did not realize clearly that they should and could use them. They got no practice in building them.

Students are taught the forms of independent and subordinate clauses, prepositional phrases, verbals, and appositional expressions. They are then adjured to use these forms to "vary sentence structure." The results of this time-honored approach (however cleverly adorned it may be) are well known. The learning of the forms provides some leaden hours. And at the last there is little evidence that the hard-earned grammatical lore makes any difference. In the glorious heat of composition out come the old ineptnesses; sentence structure is not "varied" after all. In short, just as the principles of harmony and boat-racing learned as rules are with difficulty carried into practice, so a philosopher's-eye view of language is but slimly connected with expression.[13]

[13] Arthur Minton, "Grammar Makes Sense," *English Journal*, XXXVI (Jan., 1947), 26. Minton delightfully discusses changes in meaning or emphasis that arise when students consider possible variations in "Jack and Jill went up the hill" and other sentences, or pairs of sentences.

One swallow does not make a drunkard, nor does one complex sentence make a habitual user of complex forms. So you and the class work out various combinations of sentences. Usually the sentences to be discussed arise naturally out of topics that the class is considering. Sometimes, though, you provide basic sentences; often these are suggested by members of the class. Occasionally students may try to find as large a number of logical connectives as they can for a given pair of sentences. Perhaps each student makes a list of as many connectives as he can think of, and students compare their lists in class.

The task of teaching the increased use of intellectually mature sentences is by no means completed. The next step comes in the paragraphs, letters, and themes that students write. From these you select excessively short sentences and straggling compound sentences and present them to the class for revision. You also choose particularly good sentences and offer them for class praise. Little by little each student sees that what he and the others have been talking about applies to *his* writing. *He* can make his ideas more clear to others if he uses the right kind of sentence glue. Slowly he grows in his ability to express himself. His sentences show ever increasing understanding of the relationships between ideas; that understanding is reflected in his subordination of the unimportant and in his placing of emphasis upon the most significant.

Diagraming

The beloved Columbia professor the late Allan Abbott used to tell his classes that he had learned in secondary school to diagram sentences but that "the chief adverse criticism of the themes I wrote in college freshman English was faulty sentence structure." Although some teachers, and therefore many textbooks, still include instruction in diagraming, there is hardly an iota of evidence that such instruction leads to improved student-written sentences.

Very simple diagrams may be used in class to clarify some elements of structure; for instance, an arrow may point from a modifier to the word it modifies, or a brace may enclose the parts of a compound subject or the words that compose a phrase or a clause. But assignments requiring students to diagram are seldom justified, and *never* justified when they necessitate expenditure of much time in determining what kind of line goes where and at what angle.

The formulas of the structuralists and the generativists are equivalent to diagrams and are subject to the same abuses. If they are employed only to identify the parts of someone else's sentences, they can be very wasteful of time. But when they are used on occasion to help students construct sentences of their own in accordance with specified patterns, they may throw light on some structures.

Terminology

It is noteworthy that structuralists and generativists, after experimenting with various terms and grammatical symbols, have returned as nearly as they can to traditional terminology. For some of their designations, however, such as *juncture, morpheme, determiner, intensifier, kernel,* and *string,* the older forms of traditional grammar had no precise equivalent. Other traditional terms the new grammarians may define in somewhat different ways.

All schools of grammarians would agree, though, that it is the grasp of concepts that really matters—not the ability to parrot terms. After the concept has been mastered, its name should be attached as a convenient label.

A precise list of terms to be mastered depends upon the type of grammar being stressed. In traditional terminology, the concepts embodied in the following names appear basic: *sentence, subject, verb, predicate, modifier, phrase, clause, noun, pronoun, adjective, adverb, preposition, subordinating* and *coordinating conjunctions, interjection,* and *appositive.* To these should be added, from the structuralists or the newer traditionalists, *pattern, determiner,* and *intensifier;* perhaps the useful concepts represented by the terms *form classes* and *function words;* and possibly some of the terms relating to phonology such as *phoneme, stress, pitch, juncture,* and *intonation.* From generative grammar, *kernel* and *transformation* are useful supplements to traditional terms. In describing sentence types, some teachers prefer the familiar *simple, compound, complex, compound-complex, declarative, interrogative, imperative, exclamatory;* others like better such pattern designations as *SV* and *SVO,* or such pattern numbers as those listed earlier in this chapter. The total number of terms to be mastered by the end of high school is no more than twenty-five or thirty.

The real problem is less "What terms shall I teach?" than "What concepts shall I teach?" The best answer to the latter question is rather simple: Teach concepts that your students can understand, and concepts that can demonstrably help them to write better sentences or make acceptable choices where questions of usage are concerned. If you can demonstrate conclusively, for instance, that your students must know about transitives and intransitives to write good sentences, you should teach those concepts; otherwise you should not.

Assignments

Whenever possible, out-of-class composition work should be connected writing of paragraph length or longer. There will be times, however, when you feel the need of reinforcing what you have been discussing in class; such reinforcement may come from having students prepare sentences to illustrate a particular point or to practice a construction they have been discussing.

Suppose, for example, that you want the class to practice using word, phrase, and clause modifiers. Make the assignment specific and challenging, not something like this: "Write ten sentences containing word, phrase, and clause modifiers." This assignment would be better: "Here are ten verbs: 'muttered,' 'upset,' 'shrieked,' 'galloped,' 'flew,' 'pursued,' 'undermined,' 'dived,' 'forgot,' 'escaped.' Around each of these verbs you are to build a good sentence that might be fitted into an exciting story. Be sure to use enough words to make us see clearly what kind of person or thing you are talking about, and exactly what is done and how it is done. For instance, . . ."

From such an assignment, you will get plenty of word, phrase, and clause modifiers. Part of the next class period may profitably be spent in reading, commenting upon, and revising the results. This work, in turn, may lead to an assignment that is a modification of the first.

More and more, textbook writers are creating exercises that help students to construct sentences and not just analyze them. If you have a voice in choosing a text, such exercises are among the things for which to look. Although exercises in analysis are necessary and desirable, a text that stops with analysis is not likely to lead to good sentence construction.

Programed Instruction

Today interest in programed instruction is high. In such instruction, students work independently, at their own speed, on series of "frames" that build toward mastery of a concept. Linear programs move methodically, frame by frame, from something simple like "Birds fly" to much more difficult concepts. Branching programs, rarer and more complicated than linear ones, send the student to elementary explanatory frames when he makes a mistake.

"Teaching machines" and programed textbooks both make use of the frame technique. Both simple and expensively elaborate machines have been manufactured, but a number of studies have shown that a programed text or a simple machine is as effective a teaching device as a costly electronic gadget.

Regardless of format and equipment, a poor program brings poor results. Some of the first programs devised for English merely stressed identification and hence were not at all superior to the conventional workbook. Of late, some attempts have been made to prepare programs that are intended to aid sentence building.

An ideal program in grammar and usage involves diagnostic tests to discover each student's particular needs. The student is then assigned series of frames on which he can work independently to overcome his defects. Mastery tests follow and are the only part given a grade. The program can also be used in connection with theme correction, the student being assigned the exercises his compositions reveal to be especially needed. In other words, a good program offers a splendid opportunity to provide for individual differences among students.

It is still too soon to say how extensively programed instruction may be used. The alert teacher will want to watch for reports on its failures and successes.

Conclusion

Slowly the sentences grow. In good soil they grow faster and stronger than in poor. Within your classes you have sand and clay and rich black loam. From the poor soil you expect less, quantitatively and qualitatively, than from the rich; but in each you plant good seeds, you cultivate painstakingly, you try to harvest the best crop that the soil can produce. All that you can ask of each student is that he do his best. With Robert Browning, you are aware that

> All service ranks the same with God:
> If now, as formerly he trod
> Paradise, his presence fills
> Our earth, each only as God wills
> Can work—God's puppets, best and worst,
> Are we; there is no last nor first.

IMPROVING SYNTAX AND CHOICE OF WORD FORMS

The Honest Approach to Syntax and Usage

For years many students have heard "bad English"—solecisms, barbarisms, improprieties, and badly constructed sentences. Bad Eng-

lish is fed by home, playground, street, and perhaps the places where
many of your students will be employed. It may be the language of
their heroes. It is heard more minutes per day than is your language.
It springs eternal to the human tongue.

Considerable improvements (meaning a closer approach to your
kind of language) will occur only if the student *wants* to improve. As
Professor Allen F. Hubbell has said,

An individual's linguistic usage is among other things the outward sign
of his most deep-seated group loyalties. If the usage of the group or groups
with which he identifies himself is not that of Standard English, the schools
are not likely to have much effect on his practice. For the blunt fact is
that only if his loyalties shift will his grammar change. In a democratic
society, the schools have an obligation to make a knowledge of the standard
language available to everyone. And teachers have an obligation to make
this instruction as interesting and meaningful as possible. They should not
be surprised, however, if the nonstandard forms of English continue to
flourish. They are hardy growths and will be with us for a long time to
come.[14]

The time-dishonored method of having students memorize rules
may as well be forgotten. No more successful has been the constant
use of the labels "wrong" or "incorrect" or the admonition "Watch
your grammar." (One boy said, "My grammar ain't goin' nowhere.
How come I gotta watch it?")

Some classes and some students are eager to bring their usage into
closer conformity with what we smugly call "standard." These are
usually the students with cultured parents or with parents who wish
they were cultured. Less frequently they are intelligent students who
are eager to surmount what they have come to recognize as the
handicaps of their environment.

But thousands of students have never been convinced (and perhaps
can't be) that the language you want them to use really is the language they should use. They will not be convinced by such essentially
dishonest statements as "This is the only right way to say it" and "Successful people are always careful of their language."

The honest approach to a don't-care class takes some such form as
this: "I'm not going to pretend that using 'good English' will ever
make you rich or successful. I know a hundred persons whose
English seems worse to me than my own does but who have a lot
more money than I'll ever have. And I'm not going to pretend to
you that one way of saying something is always right and that other

[14] "Multiple Negation," *Inside the ACD,* X, No. 1 (Oct., 1957), 3.

ways are always wrong. We'll look a little at history of the language and discover that ideas of right and wrong in English have changed from century to century. I can't tell you that people won't know what you mean if you say 'I ain't got nothin'.'

"But I can say this to you: Sometimes it will be important to you to make your meaning so clear that nobody can possibly misunderstand you. Sometimes you will write letters that may affect your future. Sometimes you will talk with people who will be sizing you up for an important job. Some of you will go to colleges where it is simply taken for granted that you use language in the ways that happen to be socially approved in this century; if you don't, out you go.

"So what we're doing is learning about the language that many of today's leaders, in all kinds of work, consider most clear and most acceptable. It is something that will be useful for you to know and that *may* make a difference in your future, though I can't say for sure. I'll not say that 'haven't any' is better than 'ain't got none,' but many important people today think it is better, and for that reason I'll say we ought to use it."

Individualizing Instruction

Your objective is to help students become successful in their verbal communication. But "success" is a relative term. The highly intelligent senior is not successful unless he has learned to think straight and express his thoughts with clarity, vigor, and color. But the less capable senior may be considered successful if he can think fairly straight and express his thoughts with clarity only. In other words, teachers need to motivate each student as much as possible and help each to reach the highest level possible for him. To expect all students to reach the same goal is to expect the impossible. What you can do is attempt in various ways to give each student what he particularly needs.

The first essential, of course, is to discover what each does need. Tests of sentence knowledge exist in great plenty, but unhappily most of these are tests of ability to recognize and to apply nomenclature, rather than tests of constructional ability. Your best indication of individual needs will be found in the sentences, paragraphs, letters, and themes that students write and the sentences they speak.[15]

One suggestion for meeting individual differences was offered earlier and may be briefly repeated. In grading papers, individualize the

---

[15] For an elaboration of this point, see pages 251–255.

corrections and comments. Marvin, you discover, especially needs help with fundamentals of verb usage, Ruth with word order, Tom with pronouns. Try in your grading to help each of them overcome his or her personal errors.

Having marked a paper, you may ask students to do some additional work to overcome their individual troubles. For instance, if the reference of some of David's pronouns is vague, give him some sentences to clarify. If Ellen has written too many "and . . . and" sentences, give her some appropriate work. Each student can be given a follow-up assignment that will benefit him. This device has the added value of discouraging carelessness, since careless errors will lead to more work.

The small-group plan may also be used. Four or five students are troubled by "set" and "sit." Let them meet with Beverly, who understands these verbs, and make up a number of sentences containing different forms of "set" and "sit." Simultaneously, other groups may work on other problems.

Sometimes a large part of a class, but not all, needs work on a stumbling block. Instead of wasting the time of students who you are sure do not need this instruction, allow them to read or to do some other constructive work.

Individual conferences are extremely valuable. However, until English teachers' class loads are reduced, they cannot be held so frequently as is desirable. Most English teachers, nevertheless, are generous in giving of their time after school and during their few free hours, and they often find that a little individual encouragement or attention brings big returns.

Combating the Most Persistent Errors in Syntax and Word Forms

When the word "error" is used here, it is in accordance with the preceding paragraphs. An error is a construction or a usage that results in a reduction of clarity or that is not socially approved at the present time.

The sentence errors that are most difficult to eradicate are the undesirable fragment, the run-on sentence and the related comma fault, excessive coordination, faulty subordination, dangling modifiers, faulty word order, faulty parallelism, and pronounced incoherence or lack of logic. Among the parts of speech, most problems arise with verbs and pronouns, but confusion of adjectives and adverbs also causes trouble. Here are some suggestions for reducing the incidence of such errors.

The Undesirable Sentence Fragment. The way to prevent the use of the undesirable fragment has already been suggested. Teach the students what a sentence is, emphasizing that it must usually have both a subject and a verb. The two most common types of unacceptable fragments are (1) the dependent clause punctuated as a sentence, and (2) a group of words with a participle instead of a finite verb. If the students have been shown clearly (as suggested on page 288) that most dependent clauses are modifiers, they can understand that these groups of words are not sentences even though they contain subjects and verbs. Show the students how they can join the clause to the sentence to which it is related. If they have understood the principle that a verb with an -*ing* suffix must always have a helper, they are unlikely to try to use such words as main verbs. When they do so, remind them of the need for a helper. Ask them, "Would you say, 'I running'?"

In an article filled with specific suggestions, Kellogg W. Hunt suggests substituting nonsense words to make clear that a fragment is a fragment:

> In years later after the foons wamped it can stand as the answer to a question or the beginning of a statement, but students quickly see that it is only a fragment. Whether or not it is a complete thought, it is an incomplete structure. The student's original was, *In years later when the Italians conquered it.*[16]

Some rather bright student will probably ask the old question "Why can't we use sentence fragments? Professional writers do." You will give the old answer that professional writers sometimes *consciously* use sentence fragments for the sake of varying their style. It is the unconscious use that is to be condemned. Tell your inquiring student that you have no objection to his using occasional sentence fragments if he will put a star in the margin to show that his use is intentional and not a blunder.

The Run-on Sentence and the Comma Fault. The run-on sentence consists of two or more sentences run together without punctuation. The comma fault is the same, except that a feeble comma tries in vain to hold the sentences apart. These mistakes, like undesirable fragments, may be prevented by teaching what a sentence is and giving adequate opportunities to construct many sentences with proper ter-

---

[16] "Improving Sentence Structure," *English Journal*, XLVII (April, 1958), 209. The entire article is worth studying. See especially the discussion of the use of nonsense words in attacking run-on sentences, on pages 209–210.

minal punctuation. (The comma fault is discussed further in Chapter 10.)

Excessive Coordination. This is the "and . . . and" or the "so . . . so" sentence, in which ideas are strung together as if they were beads of equal size. The remedy is instruction in the complex sentence, which makes possible the subordination of the less important ideas.

Faulty Subordination. The complex sentence, though, has pitfalls of its own. Used effectively, it can make writing precise. When one is writing a complex sentence, the chief principle to remember is that the main idea should be in the main clause, the less important idea (usually a modifier) in the other clause. Not being clearly aware of this principle, students sometimes write, "It was about five minutes after the storm started when lightning struck the house." This is not necessarily a poor sentence; perhaps the intention is to clarify the time when lightning struck. In most contexts, however, it would be poor, because the fact that lightning strikes a house is normally more important than the minute of striking.

The remedy is once more an appeal to logic. Students can readily understand that the main idea should be in the main part of the sentence. Focusing their attention on this point, give them additional practice in changing two simple sentences into one complex sentence.

A second pitfall is the "house-that-Jack-built" construction. This consists usually of a string of adjective clauses each modifying a noun in the preceding clause: "This is the dog that worried the cat that killed the rat that . . ." It may also consist of a string of loosely related adverbial clauses: "Dad agreed because he wanted me to go because he thought I needed the experience because . . ." The name "house-that-Jack-built" may help both to clarify the nature of the error and to laugh it out of existence. Assisting the student in seeing the underlying relationships of the parts of the sentence may lead to a satisfactory revision.

Student-written sentences illustrating either excessive coordination or faulty subordination afford excellent material for class discussion and the sentence manipulation that is often highly productive. Duplicate the sentences; write them on the chalkboard; or show them with an overhead projector.

Dangling Modifiers. Sometimes the dangling modifier is a "howler": "After failing in geometry, the principal had a talk with Stuart." "Standing on the peak and looking into the valley below, his heart pounded at the beauty of the scene." Usually, though, it is more prosaic: "By getting tickets early, it was possible to have a good seat."

When you find a dangling modifier in a theme, remark that it reminds you of a sentence you once read. On the board write a "howler." (A few gems are in The Idea Box, page 315. You should have a rather extensive collection.) Show the class why the howler does not make sense, and then show them that the sentence under discussion fits the same pattern, even though it may not be funny. Get the class to make the corrections. Show them that there is usually more than one way to place modifiers for clarity but that sometimes a modifier can be in only one place in a particular sentence. Write down a few more howlers or look at some examples in the textbook. The class corrects these. You comment that these expressions are modifiers that have nothing to modify; they are men without a country. To clinch the point, you write a few verbal phrases like these:

> Upsetting the bucket,
> While living in Spokane,
> To make a kite,

Ask the students to finish each of these sentences. Have them test each sentence by noting whether the modifier has something that it can logically modify. Someone is almost sure to write, "While living in Spokane, it was very rainy." Let the class help the writer of this sentence see that "it" was not living in Spokane.

Kellogg Hunt, in the article previously cited, makes this suggestion:

I can give them this: *Puffing and panting, the womble was woobled at last.* In place of the first nonsense word, students will substitute words for people, for animals, for a number of things that can puff and pant. But when I substitute what a student wrote, they reject it with a laugh. I write on the blackboard, *Puffing and panting, the top of the hill was reached at last.* They see that tops of hills don't really puff and pant even when they are being reached. They see this far more clearly when I substitute nonsense syllables than when I lecture to them on dangling modifiers.

Faulty Word Order. In English, more than in almost any other language, word order is important. The reason is that most English words do not have distinctive endings to show how they are used in the sentence. Consider, for example, "The dog killed the rat." In other languages—Latin, for instance—the word order in that sentence could be changed somewhat without affecting the meaning. But in English, if we say "The rat killed the dog," the meaning is entirely different; or, if we say "Killed dog the rat the," there is no meaning.

Most problems in word order arise in the placement of modifiers. It is well to admit to the class that some sentences are very difficult to write. For example, try these: "Seated in front of her were several men whose heads only she could see." "Carol is the girl in the hallway with blue shorts." When one happens upon a sentence like one of these, often the best solution is to start the sentence in an entirely different way.

Students, however, often write sentences in which only a shift in word order is needed for clarity. As always, stress the fact that in writing and speaking we are trying to express our thoughts clearly, so that others can understand us. Perhaps your students have written sentences like these: "I pulled the heavy fishing line up on the bank on which I found only a tin can filled with mud." "Sally encouraged him vigorously to fight back." "Ted was arrested before his intended crime was committed by the police chief." Using terms like *attributive adjectives, appositional adjectives,* and *squinting modifiers,* you *could* talk for hours about the placement of adverbial and adjectival modifiers. The results will probably be better, though, if you have the class apply simple logic: "Where was the tin can that was filled with mud? . . . How can we make the sentence say that?"

Faulty Parallelism.   Not at all rare, but difficult to overcome, is the habit of writing sentences in which grammatically equivalent elements are stated in different grammatical forms. For example, a student may write, "The dictionary shows us how to pronounce a word, its meaning, and where it originated." You should probably not object to that sentence if an average ninth grader wrote it, but an average eleventh or twelfth grader ought to be able to do better.

There are four situations in which parallelism is needed: (1) in a series, (2) in comparisons, (3) with linking verbs, and (4) with correlative conjunctions. The last two cause little difficulty and may be ignored in high schools. But a faulty series, like the illustration above, and a faulty comparison such as "I like baseball better than to run races" demand attention.

Concentrate first on the series. On the board write, "The dictionary shows us the . . . of a word." Ask, "What does the dictionary show us about a word?" Someone says, "Pronunciation," and you write that and inquire what part of speech it is. Write *n* above it. Ask what else the dictionary shows, and soon you will have a series in which, as you help the students to see, all the words are nouns. Get them to construct another series of nouns, then a sentence with a series of adjectives, another with a series of phrases, and another with a series of clauses. Series of gerunds or infinitives may also be used, although the technical names of these may be mentioned only casually. Perhaps eight or ten students may write on the board other sentences containing series.

At some later time, consider parallelism in comparisons. Write, "I like baseball better than track." "I like to play baseball better than to run races." "I like playing baseball better than running races." Help the students to see that the underlined parts are the things being compared and that within the same sentence they are stated in the same form. Comment—but do not write—that "I like to play baseball better than running races" would not be logical because the things being compared are stated in different forms. From the class get other comparisons requiring parallel construction.

Able students will enjoy observing how master writers employ parallelism for specific effects. The novels of Alan Paton offer especially good examples.

Pronounced Incoherence or Lack of Logic. An experienced teacher recognizes this error, even though its forms are myriad and even though it is usually accompanied by all the other errors in the book. Here is an example from the examination paper of a high school sophomore: "Juluis Cesar went forum and soothsayer sayed be wear Idies of March he didn't and died (got killed." This student needs almost everything. The only encouraging sign is that he does have subjects and verbs (plenty of them) in his sentence.

With as poor a student as this, you may as well face the fact that sentence polish is for him eternally impossible. Indeed, you may feel like adopting the traditional tactics of a coach whose team loses most of its games—work on building character. (Not a bad idea, really.) You will have succeeded with this boy if he becomes a respectable adult citizen who can write sentences like these: "Please send me one claw hammer. The catalog no. is X1905. I enclose three dollars ($3.00)."

If you have a boy like this in your class—either you do have or you will have—stress the fundamentals of sentence structure. Encourage him to write short sentences. Although he may be a sophomore or junior, your goal is to bring him up to a sixth grader's level. Praise him when he writes a five-word sentence that is clear. Let pairs of students sometimes revise their papers together; this boy, and others, will profit from the experience. Help the boy to see that careless omission of words is like careless omission of clothing or careless assembling of a motor. Show him how easy it is to misread something like "Julius Caesar went forum." Remind him that he doesn't talk like that; suggest that he write as he talks.

Errors in Verbs. Although the English verb has only a few forms, the fact that there is more than one form causes difficulties. Of these difficulties, the most frequent are those involving number. Students often use plural verbs where singular are needed, and vice versa. Here are the principles of verb agreement that cause most confusion:

1. A verb agrees with its subject even though other words intervene. (The cause of his misfortunes *was* his wife.)

2. The expletive "there" is not a subject; in a sentence introduced by "there," the subject often follows the verb. (There *are* four ducks.)

3. These pronouns take a singular verb: "anybody," "anyone," "each," "either," "everybody," "everyone," "neither," "nobody," "no one," "somebody," "someone." (Each of us *has* his own opinion.) "None" may be singular or plural, depending upon the intended meaning.

4. In an "either . . . or" or "neither . . . nor" sentence, the verb agrees with the nearer subject. (Either the employer or the men *are* at fault. Either the men or the employer *is* at fault.)

5. The number of the verb is not affected by expressions introduced by "as well as," "in addition to," or "together with." (Johnson, together with three friends, *was* in the studio.)

6. A collective noun takes a singular verb when it is regarded as a unit, but a plural verb when the members are thought of separately. (The band *is* playing. The band *are* putting away their instruments.)

7. In a clause introduced by "who," "which," or "that," the verb is singular if "who," "which," or "that" refers to a singular word, but otherwise the verb is plural. (This is one of the DRESSES THAT *have* been pressed. This is the only ONE of the dresses THAT *has* been pressed.)

Confusion is also caused by the fact that both the plural of a noun and the third person singular of a verb end in *s.* Therefore, "thinks" looks plural to many students.

Students need not be asked to commit to memory these principles. Memorizing them, except on the part of bright students, would lead to verbalism, not to application. But if the teacher knows the seven chief sources of confusion, he can proceed more intelligently toward a solution.

The seven principles have one thing in common—that the verb should represent the same number as the subject. That is the point that you need to hammer home, over and over. Each of the principles is only a variation on the theme. So, when Jennie writes, "Clark, as well as his mother and father, were disappointed," you ask her what the subject is. When she says "Clark," your next step is obvious. Or, when effervescent Effie writes, " 'Tobermory' is one of the best short stories that has ever been written," ask her what is the subject of the last clause. "That," she answers. "What word does 'that' stand for?" you ask. Perhaps she doesn't know. You make for her a little drawing like that shown as Fig. 9. "All these little circles represent excellent

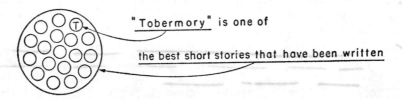

"Tobermory" is one of

the best short stories that have been written

Fig. 9.

stories that have been written," you say. " 'Tobermory' is one of the best of all the stories that have been written. 'That' refers to stories. Since we would say 'stories have,' we need to say 'that have.' . . . Now try this sentence: . . ."

Errors in tense usually involve an undesirable shift: "As I was walking down the street, a stranger steps up to me and says . . ." Technical names of the tenses are not needed. Ask the students whether they would say, "The sun was shining, isn't it?" or "The moonlight is bright, wasn't it?" Then point out that, when we begin a sentence with a verb that shows past time, we should continue using past verbs unless there is good reason for making a change.

Advanced students may be told about the "eternal present," represented by such a sentence as "Columbus proved that the world *is* round." Explain that, although that sentence begins with a past verb, the world still *is* round, and, therefore, we use the present verb.

The only one of the three moods that causes trouble is the subjunctive. Although the subjunctive is employed much less often than formerly, it is still used in four chief ways:

1. After "if," when the statement is not true (if I *were* you)
2. In expressing a wish (I wish I *were* rich.)
3. After certain verbs such as "ask," "require," "recommend", "suggest," "propose," "demand" (I ask that you *be* ready. She proposed that he *be* initiated.)
4. In certain idioms (Heaven *forbid; far *be* it from me; if need *be*)

Numbers 3 and 4 need not concern most high school students. In fact, in number 3 there is a strong tendency to substitute this form: "She proposed that he *should be* initiated."

Numbers 1 and 2 can better be taught by drill than by theory. One teacher has each of her classes drill for one minute a day on a dozen phrases or short sentences containing troublesome expressions (not only the subjunctive): "between you and me," "there are two," "if I were you," "I wish Admiral Byrd were here," etc. The drill consists simply of having the class read the phrases aloud in unison. After the same expressions have been read every day for several weeks, they become fixed in students' minds. The theory of the subjunctive is so complicated that few students can understand it, but most can learn through drill to use "were" rather than "was" in contrary-to-fact statements.

The principal parts of verbs are often troublesome. Our language would be much easier to use if the past participle of a verb were always identical in form with the past tense. But about fifty of our verbs have different forms for these two parts.[17] These verbs cause more trouble than all the others. It is because of their peculiarities that Bert says, "I've already ate," "He had rode all day," and "He done it."

Bert and his classmates may be helped in a number of ways. Perhaps the best is sentence building, taught by means of any of several devices. For example, you may write five of the troublesome verbs, perhaps "draw," "eat," "fall," "freeze," "speak." Ask for a sentence with "draw." Someone volunteers, "I can draw a picture." You accept that and say, "Suppose that you did the drawing yesterday. How would you express it?" When the correct answer is given, write the sentence to the right of the one with "draw." Then say, "Suppose that you have never done any drawing. How can you use a form of our verb to say that?" When an answer similar to "I have never drawn" is given, write the sentence. Proceed similarly with the other verbs. Above the second column print NO HELP WANTED. Above the third column print HELP WANTED, explaining that these verbs always require a form of "have" or "be" as a helper.[18] Call "be" the Lone

---

[17] The most commonly used of these verbs are "become," "begin," "bite," "blow," "choose," "come," "do," "draw," "drink," "drive," "eat," "fall," "fly," "freeze," "give," "go," "grow," "know," "lie" (recline), "ride," "rise," "run," "see," "shake," "shrink," "sing," "sink," "speak," "steal," "spring," "swim," "take," "throw," "weave," and "write."

[18] *English Journal*, XXXVI, 191.

Ranger verb, which keeps popping up in disguise and helping out other verbs.[19] On the board you have three columns like these:

APPLICANT	NO HELP WANTED	HELP WANTED
I can draw.	I drew a picture yesterday.	I have never drawn.
I fall very often.	I fell on the ice.	I have fallen.

To enliven the illustrations, sometimes have the students make up as picturesque a sentence as possible, using each of the last two forms of each verb.

It takes no great ingenuity to invent simple little games to help junior high school students learn principal parts. For instance, after twenty or thirty of the difficult verbs have been studied, the class may be divided into teams. The list of "eligible" verbs is placed on the blackboard. A member of Team A asks a question of a member of Team B, using one of the verbs. The Team B player must answer the question in a complete sentence using a different form of the same verb, for example, "Did you ever freeze your feet?" "No, I have never frozen my feet." Then B questions A. Each team's score is the number of answers in which the verb is used correctly. In addition, the answering team scores if the questioning team misuses the verb in the question.

Upperclassmen are likely to have trouble with only a few of these verbs. If several in the class have trouble with the same one (as they will with "lie" and some others), devote some class time to that verb. Otherwise, the corrections may be made largely on an individual basis.

Errors in Pronouns. The chief pronominal errors may be classified as *faulty reference*, *wrong case*, and *shift in person or number.* These terms may be used as convenient handles with sophomores, juniors, and seniors, but more attention should be paid to the thing than to its name in the earlier years.

Faulty reference is objectionable because it leads to temporary misunderstanding. Show this fact by referring to such sentences as these once found in students' papers: "After calling the dog, William placed a newspaper in his mouth and sent him to deliver it." "Dr. Kanley told Jim that he was likely to lose his arm if he did not succeed in what had seemed to him a minor operation." "Other factories are those where workers make pants, which cover several city blocks." "Margaret had a cat, Maizie, of which she was very fond. Sometimes she would come purring around her and beg her for her saucer

19 *Ibid.,* XXXIII, 501.

of milk; she always fed her several times a day." Sentences like these dramatically demonstrate the need for making sure that the meaning of each pronoun is readily understandable.

Practice in building sentences containing pronouns is, of course, desirable. Writing in which pronouns naturally appear in meaningful context is best but may be supplemented. One device is to have students write fairly long sentences in which they refer to two or three specified persons, animals, or things and employ at least three pronouns; for example, the sentences may include the following nouns: lawyer, dentist, doctor; employer, employee; man, dog, rabbit; living room, kitchen, house.

The indefinite "they" causes a special problem in pronoun reference: "They have many oil wells in Oklahoma." Simply ask, "Who are they? . . . Does the sentence show who they are? . . . How can you revise the statement?"

Errors in case, like all other errors, should be foreseen and prevented whenever possible. The one major source of difficulty comes in the use of two pronouns together, or in the use of a noun and pronoun together. Eighth grade Fred, who would never say "Me did it," sometimes says "Him and me did it." His older sister Freda, who would not say "Mother sent I," thinks she is speaking correctly when she says "Mother sent Mary and I." Recently a reputable sports announcer said "It's a jump ball between Smith and he"; it is unlikely that this announcer would say "between they."

Try to prevent such errors by having students build sentences.

I won → He and I won → Bill and I won → May, Bill, and I won.
He asked me → He asked John and me → He asked her and me.
This is for me → This is for you and me → This is for her and me.

Show that the form of a pronoun that appears with another is the same as if it were used by itself. Then, when an error is made, go back and review.

Do not worry if your students say, "It's me." This form is regarded as established.[20] "It's her," "It's him," and "It's them" are still a few feet outside the pale of respectability, but they are rapidly approaching it. Please do not feel that this represents a degeneration of the language; it simply shows that language is still changing as it always has changed. It was once good English to say (possibly with altered spelling) "Him was given the money," "He has never said nothing," and "This was the most unkindest cut of all." Has the language be-

---

[20] See, for instance, Bergen Evans and Cornelia Evans, A *Dictionary of Contemporary American Usage* (New York: Random House, Inc., 1957), p. 294.

come worse because people now express themselves differently? Would you want to go back to the old forms? The reason for the victory of "It's me" and the coming victory of "It's him" is that the English sentence typically follows the subject-verb-object pattern; therefore, speakers and writers tend to make most sentences adhere to this pattern.

It is desirable to tell students such facts of sentence life in connection with expressions like "It's him." Explain in simple words why "It's he" has long been regarded as the only acceptable form. Explain why the change is occurring. Tell the class that some people still are shocked when they hear "It's him," and that, for bread-and-butter reasons, it may be desirable for the students (as it is for you) to continue saying "It's he" for a while longer. Give them other examples of the way that the language has changed, and explain why it has changed and is changing. Part of everyone's cultural background should be at least a slight knowledge of the history of the language he uses daily.

If there is nothing that your students need more than information about "who" and "whom," or when they ask questions about these words, explain that, when they are in doubt, they should consider only how the word is employed in the clause to which it belongs. For example, in "Who is there?" "who" is the subject. In "Whom does she expect?" "whom" is the object of "does expect." In "Give it to whomever the president designates," "whomever" is the object of "designates" (not of "to"). But in "Give it to whoever calls," "whoever" is the subject of "calls," and the whole clause is the object of "to."

Unlike some of the idiosyncrasies of case, consistency in number and person of pronouns should be carefully taught to all students. Undesirable shifts like these are common: "Does everybody have their hats?" "Each of them is (are) doing their best." "Whenever you write humorously, a person must be sure that their humor is not just plain silliness." [21] Some teachers have reached such a point of desperation in trying to get students to treat "everybody" as a singular that they have forbidden its use, telling the students to use "everyone" instead. College freshmen have sometimes admitted that they thought "everybody" was a "bad word."

One of the reasons for the existence of the faulty "everybody . . . their" construction is that English lacks a third person singular common gender pronoun. In this book the author had to choose between

[21] Here is a puzzle for you and perhaps for your class. How do you answer the question "Is everybody here?" If you say, "Yes, he is," it sounds ridiculous, because several people are here. But, if you say, "Yes, they are," you are guilty of shifting the number of the pronoun. (Bergen Evans and Cornelia Evans, *op. cit.*, p. 164, say that *they* is the usual choice.)

"he" and "she" to refer to an English teacher, or else use the clumsy "he or she" or the ungrammatical "they"; with masculine arrogance, the author chose "he." The student who says, "Does everybody have their hats?" is facing a similar problem when he addresses a mixed group. If he says "her hat," he seems to be ignoring the boys; if he says "his hat," he neglects the existence of girls' chapeaux. So he compromises and says "their."

Talk over matters like this with your classes. Admit that the language is not perfect, but remind them that capable speakers and writers do follow certain conventions such as saying "Does everybody have his hat?" Let the students see how illogical and confusing a sentence may be when shifts are made from "you" to "one" to "they," etc.

Adjective-Adverb Confusion. In the junior high years students learn through building sentences that some words modify nouns and pronouns, and that different words modify other parts of speech. Gradually the terms *adjective* and *adverb* are applied to these two kinds of words, so that the sophomore finds it natural to call "true" an adjective in "a true account," and "truly" an adverb in "truly surprising."

Students never make the mistake of saying "a truly account" or "true surprising." Their errors in adjectives and adverbs almost invariably take one of these three forms:

1. Adjective to modify a verb which precedes it (She plays the piano *good.*)
2. Adjective to modify an adverb or adjective (I studied *real* hard.)
3. Adverb to modify a noun, after a verb representing one of the five senses (The honeysuckles smelled *sweetly.*)

The cure is a commonsense explanation followed by extensive opportunity for practice. The explanation for number 1 might go something like this: "Are you trying to say that it is a good piano? . . . Then what is it that is good? . . . The playing? Do we use a word like 'good' to modify a verb? Should we say 'She plays good' or 'She plays well'? . . . Right. Now tell us whether you would use 'good' or 'well' in these sentences: . . ." More practice, of course, follows later.

Error number 2 may be treated similarly. Number 3 is more complicated, because sometimes an adverb is used to describe a verb of the senses. Compare these sentences:

> I felt happy.
> I felt carefully through the darkness.

In the first sentence, "happy" describes I; in the second, "carefully" tells how the action of feeling was performed. Your older students and the bright ones in the younger classes will be able to understand this reasoning.

These mistakes by no means cover the whole realm of possible error. Just as botanists discover a few previously unnoticed plants every year, so English teachers sometimes find a sentence with an error of a sort that they have never before seen. But the preceding discussion describes most of the weeds that you will find in your composition garden. The others, the rare specimens, can often be prevented from sprouting at all; when they do sprout, they can be eliminated by using the same tools and sprays that are used on the common errors.

Are You Sure It Is a Weed?

Time and again, because of personal prejudice or lack of information, English teachers attack as errors perfectly acceptable constructions, which any reputable grammarian or linguist can demonstrate to be fully established in educated usage. Thus George Curme devotes more than three solid pages to quotations containing split infinitives—sentences written by such authors as Wordsworth, Arnold, Pater, Carlyle, Browning, Clemens, Doyle, Galsworthy, Cather, and Sinclair Lewis. The normal location of a preposition is at the end in such a sentence as "Where did he come from?" and no one but a pedant would say or write "From where did he come?" Please do not have students correct nonexistent errors!

An English teacher has too many important responsibilities to waste time in pulling weeds that turn out not to be weeds after all. To identify a weed, rely upon the help of modern scholars, not upon hearsay, not upon the drugstore self-help manual, and not even—alas!—upon what some of your own high school and college teachers told you.

THE IDEA BOX

GRAMMAR IS A MAP

"The professional grammarian is the mapmaker who charts all the known roads of the English language; grammar is the map; the teacher is the driving instructor who chooses the most useful roads recorded on the map and teaches them to his students. Ultimately the students develop their own judgment and read the map for themselves. The mapmaker does not say . . . , 'You must use this road and no other.' He says, 'Here is the map of the roads,' and he may, by the red and black lines on his map, indicate which are most used and which are in best condition." E. J. Gordon and E. S. Noyes, eds., "What About Grammar?" *Essays on the Teaching of English* (New York: Appleton-Century-Crofts, Inc., 1960), pp. 44–45.

A DAY'S ENGLISH

To provide motivation, some teachers have students list all the uses they make of language in one day, from hearing Mother's "Time to get up" to the last "Good night." Presence of both formal and informal English may be noted.

HISTORY AND PHILOSOPHY OF THE LANGUAGE

Throughout your teaching you may emphasize the historical aspects of the language. This is really a type of motivation, as it shows the students *why* a given practice is followed.

NATURALNESS OF EXPRESSION

Encourage students to write naturally. Let them know that your purpose is not to inhibit their writing but to help them observe the generally accepted decencies of usage and to help them make themselves clear. Not "fine writing" but clear writing is the goal.

GRAMMAR "AN INTEGRAL PART"

"Students begin by writing paragraphs. Errors are pointed out, the grammar involved is studied, and the errors are corrected. Grammar is not segregated from the written or spoken word but is studied as an integral part of all written and spoken work." (Paul Hassett, Menomonie, Wis.)

MOTIVATION

1. A text formerly used at West Point pointed out that an order not written with perfect clarity or an order misinterpreted might cost lives.

2. During World War II, Secretary of the Navy Knox stated, "I would go so far as to say that the ability to use clear, concise, and forceful English underlies and reinforces efficiency in any and all branches of the Naval Service." And Secretary of War Stimson declared, "In war, as in peace, the ability to report facts and to express ideas clearly is an important attribute of the leader in every field of action."

3. Joseph W. McGovern, lawyer and a member of the New York State Board of Regents, has said, "A lawyer should not merely be logical and orderly in this thinking but he must be precise in his use of language. . . . To the extent that the lawyer achieves clarity and accuracy in [his] work of setting down the thoughts of other persons, he succeeds; otherwise he fails." *English Record*, XIII, No. 1 (1962), 3.

4. "An English teacher should be as enthusiastic over things in which the student is naturally interested as he is in the subject in which he is trying to interest the student. The boy who is interested in wrestling has much more respect for the nonrestrictive clause or transitive verb if his

English teacher can appreciate the scissors hold or the halfnelson." (Harold R. Hansen, Menomonie, Wis.)

THE TRADITION

In a vigorous attack on the rule-bound tradition of teaching language, Francis Christensen says, "by its very nature, the school tradition is a school for conformity, generally a dull conformity," and it "does harm by widening the distance between spoken and written language." "Between Two Worlds," *Word Study*, XXXVIII, No. 1 (Oct., 1962), 6.

WHY IS GRAMMAR SO ENTRENCHED?

Robert L. Tresize answers the question in the *Michigan Education Journal*, April, 1962: (1) Many persons regard study of grammar as good for "moral fiber"; (2) it is a symbol of authority; (3) grammar exercises are easy to mark, but progress in using English is hard to evaluate; (4) grammar is easier to teach than good writing; (5) themes take more time to grade than do X's in blanks.

ANY PRESCRIPTIVE GRAMMAR?

Albert Marckwardt, though a "modern" grammarian, says that as long as we must teach large numbers of students from homes in which "standard" English is an unknown tongue, "we shall have to employ prescriptive grammar to a degree. We must see to it that we use it in as enlightened a manner as possible." ("Grammar and Linguistics in the Teaching of English," *Illinois English Bulletin*, Oct., 1958), 4. Perhaps this means that we should not equate the double negative, for example, with sin or even with crime but only with a social misdemeanor that, like other social blunders, may be expensive.

SHOULD WE WRITE AS WE SPEAK?

To attain fluency in writing, some students should be encouraged to write approximately as they speak, including details they would normally include in conversation. However, Gordon R. Wood, University of Chattanooga, has advanced the hypothesis that some college freshmen write too much as they talk. He says that the written expository paragraph conforms to the principles of oratory. Hence he recommends discussion of essential differences between informal and formal presentations, paralleling differences between conversation and oratory.

"SHOW 'EM AND LET 'EM COPY"

In wartime an oververbal teacher was trying to tell a recruit the principles for adjusting the barrel of a machine gun. No success. A combat veteran took over. "Look, Mac, this way," he demonstrated. The recruit understood at once. Said the combat veteran to the teacher, "If we tried to explain *how* everything works, we'd never win a war. Show 'em and let 'em copy." A group of New England teachers point out that people learn most of their grammar and usage by imitation, too. E. J. Gordon and E. S. Noyes, eds., "What About Grammar?" *Essays on the Teaching of English* (New York: Appleton-Century-Crofts, Inc., 1960), p. 35.

WORDLESS COMMUNICATION

Edward T. Hall's *The Silent Language,* a paperbound Premier Book, discusses such things as gestures and facial expressions as devices of communication. Since these differ from culture to culture (e.g., clapping hands is not universally a symbol of approval), this kind of knowledge is of value to a traveler. Moreover, it helps students to understand more clearly that spoken language too is tied to the mores of a people.

ANOTHER ANALYSIS OF PERSISTENT ERRORS

Professor George Horner reports (*North Carolina English Teacher,* Feb., 1959) that entering North Carolina freshmen have particular difficulty with organization, understanding of sentence patterns, subordination, wordiness, irregular verbs, verbs with *each of* and *one of* phrases, *there is* and *there are,* agreement of verb and delayed subject, pronoun case as in *us boys,* expressions like *would of* and *could of,* apostrophes, and punctuation of quotations, non-restrictive elements, and compound-complex sentences.

REMEDIAL AND DEVELOPMENTAL GRAMMAR

Some students need grammar to remedy such faults as verb disagreement, faulty pronoun case and reference, or dangling participles. All, however, need it to effectuate greater variety, flexibility, and clarity of sentence structure. To give remedial drill to students who need only the second kind of help is time-wasting.

"SOME STRUCTURAL AMBIGUITIES"

Highly valuable is Norman Stageberg's article (*English Journal,* XLVII [Nov., 1958], 479) describing and illustrating twenty linguistic situations that often result in ambiguity, for example, adjective plus noun in possessive case plus noun: *a dull boy's knife;* *more* or *most* plus adjective plus noun: *give more realistic details;* noun plus noun plus noun: *cream cheese cake.*

"A GRAMMATICAL AUTOBIOGRAPHY"

For reviewing grammar, Don M. Wolfe recommends assignments requiring statements about the student's self, expressed in prescribed form. For example, "List ten ambitions in infinitive phrases." "Use a series of participial phrases, with objects and modifiers, to summarize a personal experience." "Write (a specified number of) sentences about money, each starting with 'although.'" "Write eight or ten sentences about your personality, each beginning with a prepositional phrase and ending with a predicate adjective, such as 'At home I am usually talkative.'" *English Journal,* XLIX (Jan., 1960), 16.

INDIVIDUALIZED STUDY

Individualized English provides a method by means of which each student can learn to overcome his own problems in usage, sentence structure, punctuation, and mechanics of writing. Thus, the whole class need not be retaught something that only a few students need. *Individualized English*, consisting of specially designed program cards, along with diagnostic and mastery tests, is published by the Follett Publishing Co., Chicago.

"LEARNING TO THINK AND TO WRITE"

Says S. I. Hayakawa (*College Composition and Communication*, Feb., 1962, p. 6), "The way to get students to think is to treat them as if they were capable of independent thought. The self-fulfilling prophecy will operate, and the students will start thinking." Hayakawa also recommends frequent periods in which students write rapidly and continuously for fifteen or twenty minutes, "without pausing, without taking thought, without taking pen from paper. If the student runs out of things to say, he is to write the last words he wrote over and over again over and over again over and over again until he can find other things to say. The paper is to be turned in unsigned—unless the student feels like signing it. . . . [There] will be tremendous improvement with about the third or fourth exercise" (p. 8).

USING A MODEL

"To help the students to understand and appreciate good sentence structure in a well-written essay, draw their attention to the various ways in which the author commences his sentences, his choice of specific words, and his use of concise, forceful English." (Eva Frost, Roosevelt High School, Chicago.)

POSTER DISPLAY

Try cartoons, stick figures, or other posters stressing the elimination of certain common errors. Student-made cartoons usually arouse most interest.

CORRECTING MONOTONOUS SENTENCE STRUCTURE

1. Read jokes with monotonous sentence structure, and have students rewrite them to make them more effective.
2. Have advanced students, in an occasional theme, write in the margin the part of speech or sentence element they have used to begin each sentence. If they have used the same one repeatedly, they can revise.

PRUNING

"A considerable part of revision is basically a matter of sentence pruning. Developing an alertness for unnecessary words will therefore automatically teach correct usage. A group of common faulty expressions (in sentence setting), can be economically studied as a unit. E.g., this (here), have (got), sort of (a), (had) ought, (in) back of, could (not) hardly, off (of), remember (of), made (out) of, opposite (to), (on) last Sunday, take (a) hold, started (in), amount (up) to." (Braintree, Massachusetts, High School.)

GAMES FOR JUNIOR HIGH

1. The baseball game is a favorite. Have two teams. A right answer to a question on grammar (or something else) is a single; a wrong answer is an out.

2. In the old game of adverbs, one student (It) is sent out of the room. Others decide upon an adverb to act out. When It returns, class members do what It says, for example, "Go to the blackboard in the manner of the adverb," "Make a face that suggests the adverb," etc.

THE "WHY" OF PARTS OF SPEECH

✓ Have students try to write a story, using only nouns and verbs. Then they see the reason for other parts of speech.

IF YOU USE CROSS-OUT EXERCISES

Have the students think of the reason first and *then* cross out the incorrect expression.

USE OF BLACKBOARD IN TEACHING SENTENCE STRUCTURE

✓ Frequently, copy students' sentences on the board and ask, "How may this be improved?" (Not "What is wrong with this?")

"NEVER AGAIN" LIST

Some teachers have students keep a list of errors that they resolve never to make again.

HOWLERS

✓ Use sentences like these to show your students how ridiculous a dangling modifier may be; "Sitting around the campfire, he told us the story of his life." "Standing on my tiptoes, the horse was barely visible." "After ringing violently for a couple of minutes, the door finally opened." "While laughing aloud, his teeth fell out." "Sailing toward the plate, the batter said that the ball looked as big as a balloon."

STUDENT OBSERVATION

Students can learn much about usage by observing conventions in the articles they read and in the speech of television announcers, assembly speakers, etc. Each member of a class may be asked to make notes for a week on a particular item—"It was he" vs. "It was him," "went" and "gone," etc. Then he prepares an oral or written report, giving examples and drawing conclusions.

REDUCING TIME FOR STUDYING SENTENCE STRUCTURE

In a controlled experiment, teachers in Eugene (Ore.) High School found that as much improvement in writing resulted from ten hours of class time on sentence structure as from thirty hours. The time-saving system was "a procedure in which all sentence structure items were taught only as the result of errors made in weekly themes which students wrote in connection with a literature unit." One comparison group spent all its time in studying sentence structure; another, in studying sentences and writing a weekly theme. Silvy Kraus, "A Comparison of Three Methods of Teaching Sentence Structure," *English Journal*, XLVI (May, 1957), 275.

WHICH SENTENCE IS BETTER?

"School spirit is when somebody gives up something he wants to do to cheer at an unimportant football game." "School spirit is loyalty to the highest ideals of the institution." Louis Zahner prefers the first, because "The content is the precious cargo; start with it, find and teach its appropriate form. . . . Our job is to wed form and content." So, says Zahner, we praise the fullness of an idea, condemn the empty words of a platitude, and thus we build the desire to say well what is worth saying. You'll not want to overlook "The Teaching of Language," *English Journal*, Nov., 1955, 443.

MOVABLE MODIFIERS

Dorothy Dakin, in the Puget Sound Council *English Notes,* suggests using cards on a flannel board. Print on cards the parts of a sentence such as *"The leaves of the trees rustle/when the wind blows/in the forest."* Move the parts around to note possible positions of modifiers and resulting changes in meaning or emphasis.

GROUP WORK IN CORRECTING SENTENCES

1. David Leek, in Glendale, California, mimeographs poor sentences from student papers and turns them over to student committees for discussion and correction. "Committee Study Improves Writing," *English Journal*, XXXIX (Oct., 1950), 455.

2. Try having small groups discuss and suggest improvements in selected poor sentences from your students' themes.

FACTS ARE NOT ENOUGH

Professor William Paulk, West Carolina College, says that he is happy when a student can tell him facts about Whitman's life or about the metrical scheme of a sonnet but that he is disturbed when a student cannot understand "Out of the Cradle Endlessly Rocking" because he does not comprehend the grammatical structure. Hence he pleads for more attention to poets' use of inverted patterns, elliptical sentences, and the like. *North Carolina English Teacher,* April, 1960.

PARALLEL CONSTRUCTION

Margaret Lamon, of Siena High School, Chicago, demonstrates parallel construction and introduces students to this useful rhetorical device by writing a speech of Brutus (*Julius Caesar*) in this way:

"Romans
    countrymen
and lovers!
          hear me
             for my cause,
         believe me
            for my honor,
         censure me
            in your wisdom."

A more elaborate example of this procedure, based on Alan Paton, is in J. N. Hook, *Hook's Guide to Good Writing: Grammar, Style, Usage* (New York: The Ronald Press Co., 1962).

PARAGRAPHS BY FORMULA

To "backstop" and use grammatical knowledge, a teacher may occasionally specify the types of sentences to be used in a paragraph, for example, "(1) a sentence beginning with a clause of time; (2) a sentence using a participial phrase; (3) a sentence ending with a subordinate clause; (4) a sentence beginning with a phrase of time; (5) a sentence using parallel construction." Don't expect polished results at first, warns Armand Burke in *English Record*, XIII, No. 2 (1962), 29.

LEVELS OF USAGE

1. Draw up groups of sentences like these: "She has an appointment with James to attend the dance." "She has a dance date with Jimmy." "She's agonna go to the hop with Jimmy-boy." Ask the class to discuss which sentence they would probably use, which they might use in certain circumstances, which they would never use seriously, and what alternative version they might prefer.

2. An exercise involving reader's point of view as well as levels of usage is to ask students to write three versions of the same letter, for instance, "You have been involved in a minor automobile mishap. Write about it to the insurance company, to your father or mother, and to your closest friend." Other possibilities: an autobiography to go with an application to a college, and an autobiography for a new pen pal; instructions for making something, addressed to a child and addressed to a how-to-do-it magazine.

AN INTRODUCTION TO LINGUISTICS

The May, 1963, *English Journal*, devoted to linguistics, provides an excellent introduction to the theoretical bases and applications of both structural and generative grammar. An easy book on structural grammar is Paul Roberts' *Patterns of English* (New York: Harcourt, Brace & World, Inc., 1956). The same author's *English Sentences* (New York: Harcourt, Brace & World, Inc., 1962) offers a simplified form of generative grammar.

THE ROLE OF GRAMMAR IN THE CLASSROOM

Robert C. Pooley, in *Teaching English Grammar* (New York: Appleton-Century-Crofts, Inc., 1957), presents an exceptionally clear history of the teaching of grammar, along with a specific discussion of grammar's present and potential role in the English classroom. This book, as well as Pooley's earlier *Teaching English Usage* (New York: Appleton-Century-Crofts, Inc., 1946), must have a place on your bookshelf.

GRAMMAR IN COLLEGE PLACEMENT TESTS

Many teachers still hold misconceptions about college placement tests. Neither College Entrance Examination Board tests nor the tests given by individual institutions place emphasis on the ability to classify grammatical constructions. What they *do* stress is ability to distinguish poor constructions from good ones; those institutions that require compositions also emphasize the ability to compose coherent sentences in thoughtful, coherent paragraphs.

10

IMPORTANT DOTS AND CURLS

WHY BOTHER ABOUT PUNCTUATION?

A Brief History of Punctuation

When written communication was still in its infancy, neither spaces nor marks separated words or sentences. The result was comparable to this:

NEITHERSPACESNORMARKSSEPARATEDWORDSORSENTENCESTHERESULTWASCOM
PARABLETOTHIS

After some centuries, great benefactors of the race (unfortunately unknown, so that we cannot pay them the homage they deserve) began using spaces between sentences; still later, other ingenious men put spaces between words.

In ancient Greece the practice began of using a very few marks as added signals to the reader, usually telling him that he had reached the end of a thought. The Romans continued the practice. Medieval scribes developed ornamental letters that became our capitals, and they used dots or lines that became our periods.

The man chiefly responsible for systematizing punctuation (has he a statue anywhere?) was Aldus Manutius (1450–1515). An Italian, he founded the famous Aldine Press, edited Greek manuscripts, and invented italic type. But his greatest contribution was the formulation of principles upon which sentences and parts of sentences may be marked off for clarity—principles that writer and reader both interpret in the same way. Most of our uses of commas, periods, question marks, semicolons, and colons follow his precepts.

There have been changes since Manutius, and even today punctuation cannot be regarded as permanently fixed. The nineteenth century sprinkled punctuation marks like black pepper on a page. The twentieth century tends increasingly toward few marks and insists that each be clearly justifiable. The eighteenth and nineteenth centuries were periods of much oral reading; numerous commas and other marks suggested desirable vocal pauses. Today little material is read aloud, and a multiplicity of punctuation marks would slow down the silent reader.

No Aldus Manutius has yet completely clarified the principles for modern Americans. Some marks such as the period at the end of a complete statement are obligatory. Others such as the comma before "and" in a series are optional. As teachers we need to insist upon the obligatory and to discuss the pros and cons of each option, realizing that usages in punctuation, like usages in words, can never be pinned down to simple and permanent codification as right or wrong.

Five Axioms

To teach punctuation intelligently, a teacher should understand five things about it.

Axiom 1. *The purpose of punctuation is to help a reader understand a writer's meaning.* When writer and reader both understand that ! shows strong feeling (almost a shout), writer uses the mark to help to indicate the feeling, and reader sees it and says to himself, in effect, "Aha! Strong feeling! This is almost a shout!" Similarly with the other marks. "Men work together," says Robert Frost, "whether they work together or apart." Writer and reader work together even though miles and years separate them.

You will recall that, when Bottom and his fellows present "Pyramus and Thisbe" in *Midsummer Night's Dream,* Quince mangles the prologue by putting periods in the wrong places:

> . . . All for your delight
> We are not here. That you should here repent you,
> The actors are at hand. . . .

Theseus comments, "This fellow doth not stand upon points." Lysander elaborates, "He hath rid his prologue like a rough colt; he knows not the stop. A good moral, my lord: it is not enough to speak, but to speak true."

Quinces are not merely sixteenth-century phenomena. Joe Quince and Marjorie Quince are in every American high school classroom.

They know not the stop, and as a result they often do not speak or write true.

To help them, lead them to see what happens if punctuation is lacking or is out of harmony with the principles generally accepted in our age. Have them imagine, for instance, that no punctuation marks or capital letters existed. (Capitals have a function similar to that of punctuation marks.) Give them a little paragraph like that following, and ask them to time themselves to find how long it takes each of them to understand it thoroughly.

i am enjoying my stay in st petersburg where i have a room one with a glorious view of the bay in the grandvilla hotel where did you tell me that you stayed when you were here in the manor house was it that is where louella and i ate dinner friday morning and noon meals we usually take in our own hotel

After the students have timed themselves, have them insert the needed capitals and punctuation and time themselves again. Most students' time will be cut at least in half.

Then raise the question "Suppose each of us punctuated to suit himself; what would the effect be?" Hand out another paragraph without capitals or punctuation, and ask each to punctuate it, not according to rules he has already learned, but letting his imagination roam. He may use X's, for instance, or circles, or check marks, or anything else he chooses; he may capitalize at random. Let the completed papers circulate for a few minutes, so that students can see what would happen if we had no common agreements about what punctuation to use where.

Axiom 2. *Most punctuation marks are written substitutes for intonation.* When we speak, the things we do with the voice tell a listener a great deal. He hears that one group of words is a statement, another an exclamation, another a question; that a phrase is attached to a preceding part of a sentence rather than to a following part; that the White House (the President's mansion) is meant and not just any white house. He has unknowingly learned in childhood the principles of juncture and intonation that linguists have described scientifically, and he uses these principles in interpreting the spoken word.

The reader, however, does not hear a speaking voice. Hence, he must rely upon the visual symbols that have been developed as substitutes. The symbols are less than perfect, but, if they were nearly enough complete to reflect all that the voice does, they would be too complex to learn with any degree of ease.

Not all marks are substitutes for intonation. Some such as the punctuation in the formal parts of a letter are simple matters of convention.

Axiom 3. *Variations in the punctuation of a sentence may result in difference of meaning, lack of meaning, or difference in emphasis.* Here are examples of difference of meaning:

> Henry said his teacher was ill.
> Henry, said his teacher, was ill.

> She brought thirty-five dollar bills.
> She brought thirty five-dollar bills.

Too much punctuation, too little punctuation, or misplaced marks may make a sentence almost meaningless. Examples: "When, after the first, snowfall—of the season, he brought out his, old, pair of skis; his lovely, worshipful, bride, was lost (in admiration), because, he could move, at all, on those, clumsy things." (Only two marks are needed.) "Old elephants like old men, cherish memories, and relive their days of glory." (Insert a comma after "elephants" and delete the comma after "memories.")

Differences in emphasis are revealed in these sentences: "The candidate spoke well, but he carefully avoided local issues." "The candidate spoke well. But he carefully avoided local issues." (The second version puts more stress on the second idea.)

Axiom 4. *A rule of punctuation is only a statement about what at present is customary practice.* "Right" or "wrong," then, means only that a mark in a particular context is or is not used in accordance with current custom, or that it aids or reduces clarity and the smooth flow of a sentence.

The misuse of a mark, therefore, may be only a social blunder like using the wrong spoon. Yet, like other social blunders, it may have both social and economic consequences. No one can say how many carelessly written social letters have caused misunderstanding, heartache, and the cooling of friendship. No one can say how many persons have failed to get or keep positions they wanted, or to gain advancement in their chosen professions, because their writing was sloppy in spelling, punctuation, or other mechanics. No one knows how many legal cases have depended on the interpretation of a clause that would have meant something quite different if a comma had been inserted or omitted.

Nor can anyone estimate the dollars-and-cents cost of faulty punctuation. The story is told of a father who wired what he intended as a refusal of his daughter's request for a fur coat: NO AMOUNT IS TOO MUCH. The lack of a stop after NO cost him several hundred dollars. The federal government once passed a bill saying that "all foreign fruit, plants" should be admitted duty-free. The intention was to say, "all foreign fruit-plants." Before the error could be corrected, two million dollars in duty had been lost. In July, 1962, the federal space agency sent its first probe toward Venus. It failed, at a cost of eighteen million dollars. The reason for the failure: a hyphen missing from an equation.

In summary, a writer's and a reader's mutual understanding of current conventions of punctuation may lead to clear communication and sometimes may save money.

Axiom 5. *Punctuation cannot make a bad sentence good.* Some students appear to believe that they can correct almost any writing fault by slipping in an extra comma or two. Thus, one student wrote, "Flying just beneath the low-hanging clouds I saw a V of wild geese." He tried, unsuccessfully of course, to remedy the faulty structure by placing a comma after "clouds." The only cure possible for that sentence was redrafting.

OBLIGATORY AND OPTIONAL PUNCTUATION

Obligatory Punctuation

Some principles of punctuation afford virtually no choice. These should be taught as established conventions followed by all careful modern writers. The following list includes the chief of these, exclusive of certain formularized practices in letters, footnotes, bibliographies, and other writing not involving complete sentences.

Terminal Punctuation

1. Period after a sentence making a statement
2. Period after a command or a request, even though phrased as a question ("Will you please close the door.")
3. Question mark after a direct question
4. Exclamation mark after a sentence expressing strong feeling
5. Comma after a sentence quoted within a sentence, unless a question mark or exclamation mark is required ("'That is all,' she said. 'Is that all?' she asked.")

Divisional Punctuation

1. Semicolon to separate complete statements within a sentence when "and," "but," "for," "or," "nor," "yet," or "so" is not used

2. Colon to separate a formal list from the rest of a sentence
3. Quotation marks around quoted sentences or parts of sentences; comma after "he said," or colon if the statement is very formal
4. Single quotation marks around a quotation within a quotation
5. Comma to prevent momentary confusion ("Whatever is, is right.")
6. Comma to separate consecutive modifiers of the same type ("The angry, snarling dog pursued him relentlessly, endlessly.")
7. Comma to separate pairs of items ("His meal consisted only of bread and milk, and tea and lemon.")
8. Comma to separate items in a sequence ("Refer to Act I, scene i, line 14.")
9. Comma or dash to separate words used for effect ("Long, long ago he should have decided—decided to make the climb.")
10. Dash to signal an abrupt change in structure ("When he was—Don't drive so fast!")

Parenthetical Punctuation

1. Comma to inclose non-essential clauses ("Grady Blue, who played left tackle, was injured.")
2. Commas to inclose non-essential phrases if clarity will be enhanced ("A bookcase, laid flat on the floor, occupied one corner.")
3. Commas to inclose non-essential appositives
4. Dashes or parentheses to inclose strongly interruptive elements
5. Brackets to inclose interpolations in quoted material

Optional Punctuation

The University of Chicago's *A Manual of Style* says of the comma, "There are a few rules governing its use that have become almost obligatory. Aside from these, the use of the comma is mainly a matter of good judgment, with ease in reading as the end in view." What is true of the comma is true in varying degree of the other marks also. Punctuation is an art and not a science.

In a number of situations, of which the most important are listed below, a writer may choose between one mark and another or between one mark and none. Sometimes clarity will dictate one choice or the other, or sometimes the emphasis will be changed by the presence or absence of marks, but often the choice is completely free. It seems wise to indicate and permit this freedom to students; if they follow the obligatory usages, they should not be condemned if they depart from the teacher's or the textbook writer's preferences in the optional ones, although they should be consistent in their own choices. (Some preferences of the author of this book are indicated later.)

1. Comma optional before "and" in an *a*, *b*, and *c* series ("The flag is red, white, and blue. Or . . . red, white and blue.")
2. Commas optional in an *a* and *b* and *c* series ("The ground was hard and cracked and sun-parched." Perhaps more emphatic: ". . . hard, and cracked, and sun-parched.")
3. Commas or question marks in separating two or more parallel questions in the same sentence ("When will she have time for shopping, for cooking, for keeping house? Or ". . . for shopping? for cooking? . . .")
4. Comma optional before "and," "but," "for," "or," "nor," "yet," or "so" in a compound sentence
5. Comma optional to set off an introductory adverbial clause
6. Comma optional to set off an introductory word or phrase
7. Commas, dashes, parentheses, or sometimes no marks, with interpolated phrases ("He may, or may not, win the election." "He may—or may not—win the election." "He may (or may not) win the election." "He may or may not win the election.")
8. Comma optional to indicate omission of one or more words ("Hyperbole refers to exaggeration; litotes, to the opposite. Or ". . . litotes to the opposite.")

Two Modes of Presentation

The usual method of teaching punctuation is to devote some lessons to terminal punctuation, some to the comma, one or two to the semicolon, and so on. This procedure has the advantage of affording a systematic overview of the specific uses of each mark.

A second method is to teach punctuation along with sentence structure. When the class is studying the compound sentence, for example, the teacher helps students to learn the ways in which varying forms of the sentence should be punctuated. This instruction is timely and useful; it has the special merit of permitting the class members to practice the usage as they compose sentences requiring it.

Both of these procedures are to be commended, and both should be used at one time or another. Each may reinforce the other. The second procedure should always be followed when a particular structure is being introduced. The first is valuable for review or to tie loose ends.

The remainder of this discussion will consider the marks one by one, concentrating on chief uses and major trouble spots. It might with equal logic, though, consider the various structures that require punctuation and the obligatory or optional usages with each.

The Period

The most important of punctuation marks is the period. High school students seldom omit periods except through carelessness. As motivation this old jingle may be used; when capital letters and periods are properly inserted, it makes some degree of sense:

> A funny old man told this to me
> I fell in a snowdrift in June said he
> I went to a ball game out in the sea
> I saw a jellyfish float up in a tree
> I saw some gum in a cup of tea
> I stirred my cream with a big brass key
> I opened my door on my bended knee
> I beg your pardon for this said he
> But tis true when told as it ought to be
> Tis a puzzle in punctuation you see.

In junior high school, students usually get the idea that a comma is a versatile mark of punctuation. In fact, they consider it so versatile that they often substitute it for a period. Thus is born the hated comma splice, also called the comma fault and the run-on sentence. It is actually a failure to use a period. This error often persists through the senior high school and appears in thousands of papers written by college freshmen and even in those by upperclassmen.

Juliet to the contrary, there is something in a name. As long as one teacher called the error a comma fault or comma splice, he could not eradicate it. In the hazy way that all of us sometimes think, students apparently believed that a "comma fault" was a failure to use enough commas; as a result, commas and comma faults both increased remarkably, despite the teacher's hours of work. When he began to use the term "run-on sentence" for the same error, its frequency decreased somewhat. Then, somewhere, he discovered the name "Siamese sentence" for this unnaturally joined construction. The students, sharing the universal interest in so-called Siamese twins, grasped the meaning of "Siamese sentence" at once, and came to look upon such a sentence as a linguistic monstrosity. In a short time no more than one Siamese sentence appeared where ten comma faults had flourished. If you have students who put commas where periods belong, you may try referring to Siamese sentences.

A teacher in a Champaign, Illinois, junior high school uses a different device to help students determine whether a comma, semicolon, or period is the right mark. She tells them, "When you are writing a sentence, pretend that you are a back-seat driver and that the reader is at the wheel. You put in a comma to tell him to drive slowly, a semicolon to say that there is a child in the street so that he must almost stop, and a period to represent a stop sign." This device is, of course, only an inadequate rule of thumb, but it has the positive merit of reminding the writer that he is always responsible for helping the reader.

Some students use not too few periods but too many. They write, "Silas was very lonely. Although he enjoyed counting his gold every night." Correcting the habit of punctuating sentence fragments as sentences is not easy. Here, punctuation and knowledge of sentence structure are closely linked. The student who really knows what a sentence is does not write graceless, unintentional sentence fragments. The cure for this error is not to preach punctuation but to teach sentence structure.

Classes that learn about juncture in structural linguistics can use that knowledge in determining whether a comma will suffice or a semicolon or period is needed. Plus juncture /+/ helps a listener to recognize where one word ends and the next begins; the classic examples are "ice" /+/ "cream" and "I" /+/ "scream." Single bar juncture /|/ comes at the end of a group of words at a place where there is a slight pause but no change in pitch; it usually comes just after an accented word, for example, "The men in the barn /|/ were . . ." Double bar juncture /||/ involves a slightly longer pause and a slight rise in pitch, for example, "My uncle" /||/ who lived in Nebraska /||/ was . . ." Finally, double cross juncture /#/ signifies a still longer pause and generally a slight fall in pitch, for example, "The crowd left quietly" /#/ "The surprising defeat had left nothing for them to say" /#/

Usually plus and single bar junctures require no punctuation. The double bar normally indicates a comma. The double cross generally signifies a semicolon or a period. Students who have learned to distinguish the double bar juncture from the double cross juncture may apply that knowledge directly to the punctuation of their own sentences.

The Question Mark

In high school most omissions of needed question marks arise from carelessness. Sometimes, though, a student will use unnecessary question marks, as in "I wondered whether I should run now?" or "After our warm (?) trek through Maine last December . . ." The first error is caused by unawareness of what an indirect question is and may require five or ten minutes of instruction. The second is probably written by the same student who writes "Ha ha" or "Laugh now" after a joke; he is trying to make sure that his humor or irony is not overlooked. Tell him that, although the question mark is sometimes used to indicate uncertainty ("Chaucer, Geoffrey, b. 1340?"), it is not used to show that the writer is trying to be funny.

The Exclamation Point

Perhaps least troublesome of the punctuation marks is that denoting exclamation. Two cautions, though, must sometimes be given individual students: (1) Despite the practice of comic-strip artists, one exclamation point is sufficient after any ejaculation. Two or more exclamation points shout deafeningly in the reader's ear. (2) Like any other device for securing emphasis, exclamation points should not be overused. A long series of exclamatory statements tires out the reader; besides, the third or fourth exclamation is not nearly so emphatic as the first.

The Comma

The text that the senior class used had a section of thirty-five or forty pages devoted to comma uses. Most of the section consisted of rules and illustrations. The volumes used by the other classes contained the same section in abridged and slightly varied form. The then-inexperienced teacher [1] tried manfully to get his students to master all the rules, but it seemed that when they learned to set off non-restrictive appositives they forgot about transitional words, and when they remembered transitional words they forgot names in direct address. They did not learn very much about using commas, even though they could state the rules. One sophomore girl wrote, "Use commas to separate members of a series and use them also to set off non-restrictive elements because those are not really needed and use them between clauses in a compound sentence."

[1] His name: J. N. Hook.

The fault was the teacher's. He did two things that were entirely wrong. In the first place, he falsely assumed that knowing the rules and being able to apply them were synonymous. The result was mere verbalism; the students could parrot the rules but could not punctuate a sentence. In the second place, he taught each rule as an entity. He pointed out no similarities among the rules; indeed, he may not have seen any similarities. Each rule was there in its own little shell. The teacher was attempting to teach technical differences between herrings and sardines to students who did not yet know the differences between fish and mammals.

After that first painfully inadequate teaching, he gradually developed a simplified plan of teaching comma usage. He borrowed ideas from so many places that he cannot say for sure that any part of the plan is original. But he found that it does work.

The heart of the plan is a reduction in the number of comma rules. The rules may be reached inductively, and should certainly be taught inductively in the high school class.

What do the following sentences have in common?

> Just opposite a tall building was in flames.
> To cope with these people must be energetic.
> Mary Howard was here, but he has gone.
> Her crying spell over the girl went home.
> If James is sure there can be no mistake.

In each of these sentences, a comma is needed to prevent momentary misreading. Insert commas after "opposite," "these," "Mary," "over," and "sure." Comma rule number 1: *A comma may be used to prevent a possible misreading.* If a sentence is poorly constructed, of course, punctuation alone cannot make it clear.

Now to develop the second comma rule. Once more, what quality do all these sentences share?

> Oh, I didn't know that.
> The lesson being finished, Sandra was happy.
> He insists, I should warn you, that his employees be punctual.
> Yes, I agree.
> After that, Mother, went to a show.
> Helen, above all, is meticulous.
> In March, 1958, he announced his candidacy.
> Portland, Oregon, has a splendid school system.
> "You see," he said, "I was once wealthy."
> Dorothy, who is my sister, was at the station.
> Dorothy, my sister, was at the station.
> These five answers, however, possess varying degrees of correctness.

In each of these twelve sentences is one element that is not essential. The element may add interesting or relevant information, but it is not really needed. If you read any of the sentences without the part set off by commas, the meaning of the sentence may be reduced, but it is not changed. For example, "I agree," means the same as "Yes, I agree." "Dorothy was at the station" means the same thing as "Dorothy, my sister, was at the station."

Thus comma rule number 2: *A non-essential part of a sentence should be set off with one comma if it comes first or last in the sentence and with two commas if it comes anywhere else.*

You notice that this rule does not make a separate issue of restrictive and non-restrictive clauses. It seems that the term *restrictive* is never completely clarified for any except the brighter students. The others can echo definitions and attain 90 per cent success in workbook exercises involving identification of restrictive and non-restrictive elements, but their own punctuation of such elements remains shaky. Therefore, non-restrictive clauses may simply be called non-essential clauses. They thus fall into the same category as "however," "oh," words in address, and other non-essential elements. When students write a sentence such as "Henry, who is two years older than I am, led the way," they recognize that the clause is not essential and set it off with commas. When they write a sentence such as "People who lack loyalty are traitors," they see that the clause is needed and, therefore, omit commas.

Now, to develop comma rule number 3. What do the following sentences have in common?

> The tall, straight soldier entered.
> The soldier was tall, straight, and young.
> We hunted pheasants in the cornfields, in the patches of long grass, and near the pond.
> The old man asked who we were, what we wanted, and why we had knocked on his door.
> Helena started to answer the question, but Hermia interrupted her.

Each comma in these sentences separates adjoining ideas that are stated in the same form and that serve the same purpose. In sentence 1, "tall" and "straight" are both adjectives describing the soldier. In 2, "tall," "straight," and "young" are adjectives modifying "soldier." Sentence 3 has three prepositional phrases used as adverbs modifying "hunted." Sentence 4 contains three noun clauses used as objects of the verb. The last sentence consists of two equal clauses.

Comma rule number 3 might be stated thus: *When two or more words or groups of words are similar in form and function, they should be separated by commas.* If students are sufficiently advanced to understand the expression "coordinate elements," the rule might be stated like this: *Use commas to separate coordinate elements within the sentence.*

There are two corollaries to this rule. One is that, in an *a, b,* and *c* series, the comma before "and" is optional. It seems preferable to have it there, but, since many reputable publications omit it, one cannot insist upon it. The chief reason for preferring the comma before "and" is that some sentences may be misread if it is left out, for example, "Charlotte, Lucille and Alice called today." It is difficult to say whether that sentence means that two persons called or three. A comma after "Lucille" would make it clear that three persons called. A second reason for the preference is that the comma distinguishes a true series from a false one:

> That tall, ugly, and unpainted house is my home. (True series; comma before "and.")
> That tall, green and white house is my home. (False series; no comma before "and.")

The teacher's personal preference, however, should not carry much weight. If students still omit the comma before "and" in a series, it should not be considered an error unless the class has agreed to consider it incorrect.

The second corollary is that sometimes words appear to be the same in form and function when they actually are not. For instance, consider "four tall trees." "Tall" modifies "trees," but "four" modifies "tall trees"; it does not tell how many trees there were, but how many tall trees. Similar expressions not requiring commas are "large brick building," "the first heavy snowfall," and "blue silk dress." Show students that they can usually test whether or not they need a comma between two such words by inserting "and" between the words. If the "and" makes sense and seems a natural expression, a comma is required; if it does not, a comma should not be used. "Four and tall" trees would be almost meaningless; therefore, no comma. "Tall and straight soldier" makes sense; therefore, "tall, straight soldier." A second test is to invert the order of modifiers. "Brick large building" is un-English; so is "silk blue dress." But "straight, tall soldier" is satisfactory. When the modifiers survive the test of inversion, they are truly coordinate and should be separated by a comma. Structural linguists, by classifying "four" and "first" as determiners, "tall," "large," "heavy," and "blue" as adjectives, and "brick" and "silk" as nouns, show an accurate grammatical reason for the needed punctuation. Coordinate adjectives ("tall, straight soldier")are separated by commas, but determiners and adjectives ("four tall tress") or adjectives and nouns ("large brick house") are not.

These three comma rules summarize the multitudinous rules sometimes found in textbooks, except for those dealing with such formalized matters as the punctuation of parts of a letter. They are statements of general principle; they use no difficult terminology. A student need not know forty definitions or memorize twenty rules.

You may have a legitimate complaint at this point. "The text we use doesn't simplify rules like this. Won't it be confusing to students to tell them one thing in class but have them read something different outside of class?"

Although reduction of the number of rules is a feature of many present-day texts, let us suppose that your text cites thirty rules for the comma. Instead of having the students learn the thirty rules, let them see that all thirty are simply subdivisions of the three basic principles. Teach the thirty as specific illustrations, and insist only that the students understand thoroughly the big three. Thus, when your sophomores read the rule that a non-restrictive appositive should be set off by commas, help them to see that "the Father of Waters" is non-essential in "The Mississippi, the Father of Waters, flows past St. Louis." It thus comes under the second principle. Students may study the other examples of the non-restrictive appositive and see that they fall into the same category. They contrast these non-essential words or phrases with "Mark Twain's novel *Huckleberry Finn* is more profound than his *Tom Sawyer*," noting that *Huckleberry Finn* is not set off, because it is essential rather than non-essential; the sentence would lose its meaning without those two words.

One of the curses in the teaching of punctuation, especially the teaching of commas, has been excessive verbalization. Teachers have insisted that students learn rules by the bookful, and have given them good grades if they could repeat the words. But the parroting of words is by no means proof of comprehension or of ability to apply. Punctuation may be taught much more effectively if every teacher emphasizes (1) that a writer should always have a reader in mind, asking himself, "How can I punctuate this so that even a stupid or a wilfully stubborn reader will understand?" (2) that a small number of rules, thoroughly mastered, will be enough to guide the writer to punctuate almost any sentence, and (3) that where legitimate options exist, students may be permitted at least whatever freedom the editor of the *Atlantic Monthly* would grant them.

Quotation Marks

Junior high school students readily grasp the fundamentals of using quotation marks but seldom are mature enough to understand and remember the intricacies. As with any other mark of punctuation, the first step in teaching is to let the students see why quotation marks are used. Trick sentences may be employed to advantage:

> The author said the reader was an ignoramus.
> "The author," said the reader, "was an ignoramus." [2]

Paragraphs that are confusing until quotation marks are inserted will also be valuable.

Most junior high school students can learn to use a separate paragraph for each speaker, put quotation marks around what each speaker actually says, and indicate the break around such inserted elements as "he said."

The intricacies such as the punctuation of several paragraphs spoken by the same person and the punctuation of a quotation within a quotation may best be left until the sophomore year or later, except when a class or some bright students ask questions about such intricacies or show that they have mastered the more fundamental processes. Always it is best to teach technicalities in response to a need felt by the students themselves. For example, the students may be preparing to write a composition that is almost certain to include considerable dialog. Before they write, they may be shown what is standard practice in using quotation marks in various situations.

Let your students know that the relative placement of closing quotation marks and other marks of punctuation is simply a matter of convention. Americans have adopted one set of conventions; the British, a different set—just as Americans refer to "car," "hood," and "gasoline," while the British say "motor," "bonnet," and "petrol." We Americans place periods and commas inside closing quotation marks, and colons and semicolons outside. But we let logic, not an arbitrary rule, determine whether the question mark and the exclamation point go inside or outside. The British usually let logic determine the placement. Examples of American usage follow.

[2] *English Journal*, XXXXIII, 560.

"I agree," said she.

Steinbeck wrote "The Red Pony"; he did not write "The White Rabbit."

He recited a couple of lines from "To a Mouse": "The best laid plans of mice and men/Gang aft agley."

"Who's there?" he asked.

Did he say, "Five more"?

"Watch out!" she shouted.

What a "concobberation"!

The Semicolon

Although bright youngsters in junior high school may master the chief use of the semicolon—to separate two rather closely related ideas each expressed in sentence form—usually the tenth grade is the best time to put emphasis on this useful mark, with review and much additional practice in the eleventh and twelfth grades.

Miss Eunice Helmkamp has described an excellent inductive procedure.[3] She asks her students to bring to class six sentences containing semicolons. The sentences are to be taken from contemporary printed material, but not from advertising, poetry, headlines, and the like. Each sentence is to be written or pasted on a 3- by 5-inch card. In class she tells the students that a semicolon is sometimes like a "weak" period, sometimes like a "strong" comma, and she reads examples to illustrate what she means. The students examine their own sentences to see how the semicolons are employed. They discuss their sentences in groups or with the class, copying some of them on the chalkboard to clarify various points. As a class, they attempt to formulate their own rules. One class came up with these:

A. Use a semicolon when the ideas in sentences are so closely related that a period would make too distinct a break between them. Sometimes the second sentence may contain a word which states the relationship between the two ideas. Typical relationship words: *besides, nevertheless, similarly, also, then, furthermore, instead, however.*

B. Use a semicolon between items in a series if the items contain commas, or if they are long and complicated.

C. Use a semicolon before the conjunctions *and, or, but, for, nor* in a compound sentence if the sentence is long and involved, or if there are other punctuation marks within the sentence, or if you wish to give special emphasis to the last part.

The students' examples on the cards are tacked under *A, B,* and *C* on the bulletin board. When one of the students comes up with a

[3] "Semicolons in Action," *English Journal,* XLII (Oct., 1953), 391.

sentence that does not appear to follow one of these rules, such as "Broadway has its Lunts; London its Oliviers," the class and teacher examine it. They find, for the example given, that the second half is a complete sentence with a verb implied and that, hence, it fits under Rule A.

The advantage of such a procedure is that it shows students that semicolons are not just things they study in school. Their "research" and their active thinking will enable them to remember much more easily than if they had just listened to a lecture by the teacher or studied a textbook discussion. Textbook practice exercises may clinch the understanding.

One caution is necessary. Some college freshmen who have half-learned the use of the semicolon write, "Although it was raining hard, we decided to drive on; since we were already late." Pressed for an explanation, these students say, "In high school the teacher said that, when there was some other punctuation, we should use a semicolon between clauses." The caution, then, is this: Stress the fact that the basic use of the semicolon is to separate clauses that could stand alone as sentences. The clause "since we were already late" cannot. If a sentence has a long and involved series, especially if the elements in the series contain commas, then a semicolon is justified between the elements, as in this example: "We spent spring weekends at Aunt Jane's, either in her town house or at the lake; long summer days with Uncle Judd, who owned a small farm; fall Saturdays, which seemed much less pleasant, at home." The semicolon is primarily a mark to be used in compound or compound-complex sentences; simple or complex sentences almost never need it unless a series is involved.

The Colon

The colon is not a troublesome mark. In junior high school, its use after the salutation of a business letter should be taught. Mention that this use is only a matter of etiquette, like shaking hands. Everyone expects it of us, and we are considered queer if we do not follow the general practice. Ninth graders may also learn that the colon is used before a formal list. Tenth graders may learn the other uses of the colon: before a formal quotation, between biblical chapter and verse, and between hours and minutes (8:24 A.M.). Your bright seniors can understand how a colon may introduce a follow-up statement for which a preceding independent clause has made the preparation: "A novelette is not a small novel: it is an art form with characteristics all its own."

You may want to tell students that the colon is a very formal mark of punctuation, that you associate him with white ties and tails, and that he is never found in boisterous surroundings. And when someone asks why a semicolon is not half a colon, since "semi-" means half, you may answer simply that the word "semicolon" is now a misnomer and that in present American usage there is no relationship between the colon and the semicolon, although originally the semicolon was intended to indicate a shorter pause than that shown by the colon.

The Apostrophe

Perhaps the apostrophe and the hyphen should be treated in the chapter on spelling, since both are spelling devices, used in single words, rather than punctuation marks, which separate parts of sentences. Convention, however, places these marks with punctuation. It might be interesting to experiment in order to see whether any improvement would be noticeable if all misuses of apostrophes and hyphens were marked "sp" instead of "P."

After reading a good many reams of student themes, the author has come to the conclusion that the number of times the apostrophe is omitted just about balances the number of times it is used unnecessarily. If we could only teach students to put apostrophes in the right places . . .

Here is what some of them do: They omit apostrophes in possessives, misplace them in contractions, insert them to form possessives of personal pronouns (especially "it's" for "its"), and insert them to form all sorts of plurals. Many of the errors are due to students' carelessness; others are caused by poor teaching.[4]

The first step is to let students see that apostrophes are too important to be neglected. Have them pronounce these words:

shed   were   wed   shell   well   as   is

(If the school board doesn't mind, you can add "hell" to this list.) Then insert an apostrophe in each word, and have someone pronounce them again:

she'd   we're   we'd   she'll   we'll   a's   i's   he'll

---

[4] There is a little agitation, especially in England and in avant-garde American writing, to do away with the apostrophe as an unnecessary mark. However, in some contexts, at least momentary confusion arises when it is omitted.

Motivation, all-important motivation, consists often only of letting them see why!

Junior high school students should learn and practice the two most common uses of the apostrophe. With the students' help, build on the blackboard a rather long list of words in which apostrophes are used to show omission of letters. The words above (except "a's" and "i's") will be included, and also words like "o'clock" and numbers like "'66" (meaning 1966). Be sure to stress that the apostrophe always goes into the place where the omitted letter or letters were taken out. By emphasizing that fact, you can prevent monstrosities like *were'nt* and *ar'ent*.

Tell the seventh, eighth, or ninth graders that the second use of the apostrophe is related to the first. Several hundred years ago some people believed that the proper way to show possession was to use the noun with the pronoun "his." Instead of writing "Henry's shoes," these people wrote "Henry his shoes"; likewise, they wrote "the king his crown," etc. When they pronounced "Henry his shoes" rapidly, however, the "hi" could hardly be heard (let the class try it); the result sounded like "Henrys shoes." "The king his crown" sounded like "the kings crown." So, many people wrote, "the kings crown." Here they ran into difficulty, because "kings" might mean two kings, or it might indicate possession. Someone then got the idea of using an apostrophe to show that the "hi" had (supposedly) been left out. In that way the form for the possessive originated.

It seems best to teach possessives by having students write the words in phrases—"king's crown," "woman's hat," "Edward's watch," etc. Doing so may prevent the tendency to use the apostrophe in such a sentence as "Two kings fought for the crown." It is also best to be sure that students master singular possessives before they go on to plural possessives. Many a ninth grader has been confused because he was told about "kings' subjects" before he had really learned "king's subjects."

In teaching plural possessives, teachers have found the following procedure successful: Start with simple plurals. Ask the students to spell the plurals of such words as "dog," "raven," "lady." Put these in one column, and for a second column have students spell the plurals of irregular words such as "man," "woman," "ox." (With advanced classes, words like "sister-in-law" and "alumnus" may be included.) Then, after each plural noun, write, with class help, the name of something that noun might possess, as "dogs noses." Ask the students how the possession could be made clear. Someone in the class will say that an apostrophe should be used after the *s* in "dogs." Go down the first column, inserting an apostrophe after each final *s*. Have the students copy the list of phrases in their notebooks, because the act of writing will tend to make the principle stick.

Then turn to the second column. The problem is different here, because these plurals do not end in *s*. Show the students that these irregular plural possessives are formed by adding an apostrophe and *s*. Have them copy this second list.

The next day, dictate a number of phrases from both lists, and add a few others for additional practice. Repeat a few days later, and repeat after that until perfection has been attained. Vary the phrases sufficiently that rote memory will not suffice; it is the application of the principle, not memory of a few phrases, that you want. Students who make two perfect scores in succession may be excused from later drills.

Possessives of words like "Jones" cause particular trouble. Unless a student asks the question, probably Mr. Jones should be ignored until the sophomore or junior year. Teach "dog's nose" and, sometime later, "dogs' noses," but let Mr. Jones take care of himself. When he finally demands your attention, tell the class that "Jones" ("Dickens," "Burns") is a regular noun; let them use "Jones's" as the singular possessive, just as they would write, "Smith's." (Actually, either "Jones'" or "Jones's" is acceptable; what you want to avoid is "Jone's.") The plural may also be taught as a regular plural, like "churches." If your juniors learn to write "the Joneses' automobiles," you have done a good job of teaching.

Students tend also to write "her's," "your's," "our's," "their's," by analogy with "dog's, etc. Some teachers, after their students have made such an error, review the forms of the personal pronoun, stressing that "hers," "yours," "ours," and "theirs" are personal pronouns. "No personal pronoun," they say, "ever takes an apostrophe. Nobody would write 'm'y' for 'my,' or 'hi's' for 'his.' There is no more reason for apostrophes in any other personal pronouns." The same reasoning applies to the possessive "its," although that word is used as a possessive adjective rather than as a pronoun. A simple injunction: "Never write 'it's' unless you can substitute 'it is' or 'it has'; the possessive form is always 'its.'"

The Hyphen

Junior high school students should learn the use of the hyphen to divide a word between syllables at the end of a line and to separate compound numbers. Show them that the hyphen at the end of a line prevents misreading in such a sentence as this:

. . . He climbed up the flag

staff.

Let them see also that there is a reason for the hyphen in compound numbers. Call their attention to the sentence already cited on page 322: "She brought thirty five dollar bills." Help them to see that the placement of the hyphen makes a difference of $115.

Encourage the use of the dictionary when students must divide a word at the end of a line. Show them that failure to divide between syllables sometimes leads to impossible or ridiculous pronunciations: flagst-aff, packthr-ead, thoro-ugh, etc.

In the senior high school, when you come to the matter of hyphenation of compound adjectives and nouns, you will need to explain that the practice of hyphenation changes. Tell them about "basketball." When Dr. Naismith invented the game, he called it "basket ball" because a ball was thrown into a peach basket. As the game became better known, the two words were felt to be closely associated, and were written with a hyphen. Today we consider the two words as a unit—"basketball." The same thing has happened in "football" and "baseball." That is, a word may be written as two words in one period of time and with a hyphen in another; it may be written with a hyphen in one decade and solid in another. Advise students to refer to the dictionary when they are in doubt whether a compound noun should be hyphenated (although dictionaries frequently do not agree). Tell them about the expensive hyphens mentioned on page 323.

Let them see that words linked together to form single adjectives need to be hyphenated except when the dictionary indicates that they are written solid. Call to their attention the difference between "strange looking glass" and "strange-looking glass," between "man made mistakes" and "man-made mistakes," and between "man eating tiger" and "man-eating tiger." Dictate a number of expressions such as "a never-to-be-forgotten moment," "an old-time dance," "a quick-as-a-flash retort."

Parentheses

Juniors and seniors, and sometimes younger students, may be introduced to the mysteries of parentheses. These marks are used in rather formal writing to indicate the insertion of material that has no structural relation to the rest of the sentence. Teach inductively, using numerous examples. For instance,

> I am enclosing a check for three dollars and twenty-seven cents ($3.27).
> These questions (page 47) remain unanswered.
> William Shakespeare (1564–1616)
> His reply (it was delivered in a speech in New Haven) aroused much controversy.

College teachers are sometimes rightfully distressed because somebody, somewhere, has taught students to inclose in parentheses words or groups of words that are to be disregarded. Material in parentheses is *not* disregarded. If a student wants to show that something should be omitted, he should neatly draw a single line through it.

The Dash

Dashes are useful in writing that is not very formal, and are occasionally found even in formal writing. The teacher must not advocate frequent use of dashes, though, or some student may become a dashomaniac. Some college freshmen at the beginning of the year use no mark of punctuation except the dash. Reading the first page of their first compositions leaves the instructor completely breathless.

The chief use of the dash is to indicate an abrupt break in thought or construction. For example,

> When I was—there's a skunk, George!
> This machine—another one like it is over there—is a combine.

It may also be used to indicate hesitation:

> I—I doubt it.   (Tell the students to put a dash right between the *I's*.)

Finally, the dash may set off an introductory appositive or an appositive loosely attached at the end of a sentence:

> Sympathy and willingness to make haste slowly—these are two requisites for any teacher.
> He did possess something that was superior—his teeth.

It is advisable to have students use two short marks or one rather long mark for a dash, to distinguish it from a hyphen. In typing, they must use two hyphens, as the standard typewriter keyboard has no dash.

The dash is not an important mark of punctuation. If your students do not know the more useful marks, do not spend time on the dash. You may want to explain its use to your more capable students, but you can let the others ignore its existence.

Brackets

If your seniors write a research paper, they may need to know about brackets. These marks have a more limited use than any others. Contrary to popular superstition, they are not alternative forms of parentheses. Brackets are used primarily to inclose one's personal comments or corrections when one is quoting from someone else:

> The senator continued: "Our state now leads the nation in production of butterfat. [Applause] We now . . ."
> "When Rhodes died in 1901 [actually 1902], he left six million pounds to the public."

A second use, very rare, is to represent parentheses within parentheses:

> The new state (the boundaries of which [see map, p. 647] had recently been ratified) still had no constitution.

Italics

It is conventional to underline titles of books, magazines, newspapers, plays, and motion pictures, and to place quotation marks around titles of short stories, poems, chapters, and articles. Nothing subtle or abstract is involved here. Junior high school students of even below-average intelligence may be led to follow this convention.

The other uses of underlining (italics) are less important; some, indeed, seem on the way to the discard pile. Although numerous texts still say that names of ships, trains, airplanes, and pullman cars should be italicized, not all editors of magazines and books, and probably no editors of newspapers, now follow this rule. Perhaps a casual mention of the principle might be made to the college-preparatory seniors, but the point is not worth stressing.

The use of italics to indicate a word referred to as a word, a letter referred to as a letter, etc., is more defensible than the preceding use and is more widely observed. "She left an *o* out of *sophomore*"

may be slightly more clear than "She left an o out of sophomore."
"He said that the *when* was misplaced" is easier to read than "He said
that the when was misplaced." Therefore, unless there are more
fundamental things to present, this use of italics should be taught.
(An alternative, used in the present text, is to inclose in quotation
marks any word referred to as a word, with the exception of technical
terms, which are italicized.)

Caution is necessary in teaching the use of underlining for emphasis. Too many students make a vice of underlining. Some seem to
reason that, if one underlining creates emphasis, two underlinings
should create more. In the paper of one student some words were
underlined five times, and an applicant for a secretarial position once
double-underlined every sentence in her letter of application because
she wanted the letter to be emphatic. (She did not get the job.) The
sane approach is to tell—and show—the students that a little underlining goes a long way and that too much underlining for emphasis
detracts from a piece of writing.

Students like to know the relationship between underlining and
typesetting. When a printer sets copy, he will set in italic type anything underlined once, in small caps anything underlined twice, in
capitals anything underlined three times, and in boldface anything
underlined with a wavy line.

Capitalization

As remarked at the beginning of this chapter, capitalization is
closely related to punctuation. It is a signal to the reader, just as
a punctuation mark is. It tells the reader, "Here is the beginning of
a new sentence, or here is a proper noun or something comparable to
a proper noun, or here is some kind of title."

The seventh grader will already know that he needs a capital to
start a sentence, that he should capitalize the pronoun "I," and that
he should capitalize names of persons and places. Beyond these
things, his knowledge of capitals will probably be sketchy. More
than likely he will use too many capitals rather than too few. Some
high school compositions have a slightly German look because most
of the nouns are capitalized.

A week spent on capitalization in any grade is likely to be three
days wasted. A few of the principles will stick, but, since there are
twenty or more capitalization rules, many will be forgotten. A better
technique is to take up individual questions about capitalization at
the time when the need is present. Learning thus becomes purposeful.

For example, suppose that the students are going to write a paper on the football prospects of their school. The teacher will anticipate the kinds of capitalization they will need and talk over the matter with the class. The composition will have a title. Which words do we capitalize in titles? There will be references to this high school and perhaps to other schools. When do we write "High School" and when do we write "high school"? Teacher and class will provide illustrations, and the principles will probably be remembered because they are presented at a time when the students feel a need for them.

Similarly, when one writes a letter, one usually refers to one's relatives. So, before the students write a letter, they talk over the question of when we capitalize "Mother," "Aunt," etc., and when we do not.

The capitalization errors most frequently made by students are in names of relatives, seasons, directions, and school subjects. Difficulty is the reason; students' stupidity is not. To the young student, capitalization looks hit and miss. Sometimes people do capitalize "Uncle," "South," and "Algebra," and sometimes they do not; but whichever he chooses, it seems, is wrong. Poets get by with capitalizing "Winter," but Miss Demeanor tells him that he must not do so. The apparent contradictions do not make sense.

Statistics on the "holding power" of schools are often interesting, but they do not reveal enough. It would be interesting if statistics were available to show how many students drop out of school because capitalization or the federal judiciary system or quadratic equations do not make sense. It would be equally interesting if other statistics were available to show how many students stay in school because one teacher can explain things so that they seem reasonable and understandable and worth knowing.

Why are "Uncle," "South," and "Algebra" capitalized part of the time? There is the key: Why? Consider these sentences:

> But, James, I haven't any money.
> But, Uncle, I haven't any money.
>
> He lives in Alabama.
> He lives in the South.
>
> I am taking Algebra 1.

In the first pair of sentences, "Uncle" is used as a proper noun, the equivalent of "James." In the second pair, "South" is a proper name, including Alabama and other states. In the last sentence, "Algebra 1" is a proper name; it does not refer to algebra in general but to this particular algebra course.

But sometimes these words are not used as substitutes for proper names:

> My uncle came for a visit.
> We walked south two blocks.
> He enjoys studying algebra.

In these sentences, "uncle," "south," and "algebra" do not refer to proper names. That can be proved, at least in the first two, by trying to substitute a proper name. Most persons would not write:

> My James came for a visit.
> We walked Alabama two blocks.

Let them see why! If one teaching technique is of greater importance than any other, it is probably that one—let them see why.

FOR TALL PEOPLE ONLY

When the young man began teaching, very fresh from a year of graduate school, he was taller than he is now—much taller. He was so tall that he had his head in the clouds.

A wise old professor had told him and others in his class that getting educated consists of learning limitations, their own limitations and those of others. The young man did not believe it. He rather doubted that he had any serious personal limitations, and he was reasonably sure that humanity was on the verge of a more golden Golden Age. He knew what his contribution to that age would be. He was going to make all his students into Lovers of Literature; he was going to imbue them with a desire for nothing less than the Good Life; he was going to inspire them to write sentences filled with Rhetorical Fire. He gave little thought to such trivialities as commas, semicolons, capital letters, and spelling. His eyes were above cloud level.

The first papers that his students wrote reduced his stature considerably. From a typical freshman came, "I like to go Swiming and to hunt Frogs with my Father in the Summer that is of corse." And from, alas, an almost typical senior, "My father is engaged in the profession of Dentisty, someday I hope to become a dentist too." Rhetorical Fire, he decided, would have to wait.

During the rest of the first year, his stature continued to shrink. The juniors did not share, and apparently could not be induced to share, his enthusiasm for Melville. How, he wondered, could they become Lovers of Literature if they were not Lovers of Melville? The sophomores got lost in the fourth act of *Julius Caesar.* The Good Life, fortunately, seemed to be faring reasonably well, although he found himself becoming a little less certain of its ingredients.

He went back to the wise old professor and told him his troubles. "That is what often happens to English teachers," the professor said. "During the first year they discover that they and everyone else have limitations. You have found that in nine months you cannot turn a hundred or so average boys and girls into polished writers or into worshipers of Santayana. This is a crucial time for you. Like every English teacher who becomes disillusioned during the first year, you have an important decision to make. You may go on teaching 'the finer things' exclusively, in the hope that something you teach will make an impression. Some English teachers choose that alternative. Or you may start at the level where each class is—or even where each student is—and try to help the students grow, try to help them get ready for 'the finer things.' Some of them will grow so much that eventually they may outstrip you or me. Others, because of their limitations, will never be able to comprehend the more esoteric uses of punctuation, will never be able to write a coherent compound-complex sentence, and will never feel at home even with a Sinclair Lewis novel.

"I hope that you choose the second alternative, that of helping the students to grow," the professor went on. "Patience is what you need, patience to let nature work, patience to irrigate and to cultivate. People grow slowly, like oaks. Asparagus grows quickly, but soon goes to seed. We want human oaks, not human asparagus."

"But the things many of these youngsters need seem so petty, so insignificant," the young man said. "I feel as if I'm wasting my time and theirs when I spend so long on these minutiae. Why, I'd have to spend hours on teaching elementary reading and on spelling and capital letters and commas and writing of simple sentences. It would take hours, months, years."

"Precisely," said the wise old professor.

THE IDEA BOX

THE PROBLEM ISN'T NEW

A grammar published in Boston in 1817, Daniel Adams' *The Thorough Scholar,* cites this sentence as an example of the importance of punctuation and spelling: "A man having gone to see his wife, desires the prayers of the Congregation." The intended meaning: "A man having gone to sea, his wife desires the prayers of the Congregation." (Quoted in *Purdue English Notes*, Feb., 1961.)

IMPORTANCE OF PUNCTUATION

1. Legend has it that the Czarina of Russia saw on the desk of Alexander III a note: "Pardon impossible; to be sent to Siberia." She changed the punctuation: "Pardon; impossible to be sent to Siberia." Louise Noyes, *English Journal*, XXXIV (June, 1945), 340.

2. As a motivating device, occasionally write on the board a tricky sentence for students to punctuate. For example, write, without punctuation or capitals, "Bill, where Henry had had 'had,' had had 'had had.' 'Had had' had had the examiner's approval." Louise Noyes, *English Journal*, XXXIII (Nov., 1944), 513. Or, "That that is, is; that that is not, is not. Is not that it? It is." Carl Miller, *English Journal*, XXXIV (June, 1945), 348.

3. Here are some old favorite examples, as well as some new ones, showing how punctuation may affect meaning:

> Woman! Without her, man would be a savage.
> Woman without her man would be a savage.
> Louise thinks her employer is attractive.
> Louise, thinks her employer, is attractive.
> Mr. Rice, the superintendent came in.
> Mr. Rice, the superintendent, came in.
> "Bill," called Ralph. "Come here!"
> Bill called, "Ralph, come here!"
> The tight-rope walker almost fell.
> The tight rope-walker almost fell.
> The net was made of four wire cables.
> The net was made of four-wire cables.
> She is there now.
> She is there now!
> She is there now?
> No man can be happy.
> No. Man can be happy.

The following make sense if properly punctuated:

The Indian Toti went off by himself to eat the rattlesnakes and the lizards squirming uneasily in the fragile box at my elbow rather spoiled my appetite.

Lord Wellington entered on his head a helmet on his feet a pair of well polished boots on his brow a cloud in his hand his favorite walking stick in his eye fire

The fight over the boys came home

While I was dressing my little brother came in

4. In *Ralph Roister Doister* (*ca.* 1553) Ralph had a scrivener pen this epistle to the wealthy lady he was courting:

> Sweete mistresse, where as I love you, nothing at all
> Regarding your substance and richesse; chiefe of all
> For your personage, beautie, demeanour, and wit
> I commende me unto you: Never a whitte
> Sorie to heare reporte of your good welfare.

His false friend, Merygreek, transmitted the message like this:

> Sweete mistresse, where as I love you nothing at all,
> Regarding your substance and richesse chiefe of all,
> For your personage, beautie, demeanour and wit,
> I commende me unto you never a whitte.
> Sorie to heare reporte of your good welfare.

5. Encourage your students to collect sentences in which mispunctuation would cause comic misreading.

"PUNCTUATING THE COMPOUND SENTENCE"

J. C. Gray teaches this formula: ; = (, + cc). (The cc means coordinating conjunction.) *English Journal*, LI (Nov., 1962), 573.

INTELLIGENCE AND PUNCTUATION

Although it can hardly be argued that poor punctuation and poor capitalization are signs of intelligence, a study by Nita M. Wyatt, reported in "Research in Creative Writing," *Educational Leadership*, XIX (Feb., 1962), 307, shows that bright sixth graders try more experiments, for example, in writing conversations or in writing complex sentence structures, and hence make more errors than do their classmates who are content with sentences like "I saw a woodpecker." Perhaps this suggests the unwisdom of simply counting errors in determining a grade. A student cannot fairly be penalized for a mistake in a construction not yet studied.

BLACKBOARD REMINDER

In some classes, part of the blackboard is reserved for reference purposes. Principles of punctuation, etc., that are needed most are kept there as convenient reminders for students.

DISTRIBUTING PUNCTUATION MARKS

Some teachers in junior high school occasionally pass out sentences with all necessary punctuation marks at the end. Students put the marks where they belong.

ELIMINATING "SIAMESE SENTENCES"

Lou LaBrant suggests that the "comma splice" is caused by a student's failure to supply the word necessary to relate the two clauses, and recommends helping him to supply that word. For example, "He breathed rapidly, he was nervous" needs a "because." "Teaching High-School Students To Write," *English Journal*, XXXV (March, 1946), 123.

PUNCTUATION IN BUSINESS LETTERS

Madeleine Sparks, in Westbury, New York, has her business seniors study punctuation in real business letters, analyzing the reason for each mark and checking their analyses against textbook rules. In groups of five, the students present their findings to the class. "A Practical Approach to Punctuation," *English Journal*, XLII (March, 1953), 158.

PUNCTUATION CHART

Here is a convenient summary of the most widely followed punctuation practices. You may want to prepare and post a chart based upon it or to duplicate copies for individual student reference. The amount of grammatical terminology has purposely been kept small.

A Simple Guide to Basic Punctuation

Pattern	Usual Punctuation	Example
1. A statement	Period at end	He went home.
2. A question	Question mark at end	Did he go home?
3. An exclamation	Exclamation mark at end	Run for your lives!
4. Any construction that may be misread without punctuation	Usually a comma	To overcome this, work is essential.
5. A series of grammatically equal items	Usually a comma or commas	(a) She writes novels, plays, and poems. (b) . . . a scrawny, underfed kitten.
6. Two complete statements connected by "and," "but," "for," "or," "nor," "yet," "so"	Usually a comma; sometimes a semicolon if there is much other internal punctuation	(a) Man proposes, but God disposes. (b) Although the day was cold, she felt warm, cheerful, and optimistic; but Harvey, who walked with her, was grouchy.
7. Two complete statements not connected by "and," "but," "for," "or," "nor," "yet," "so"	If written as one sentence, a semicolon between the statements	The squirrel scurried along the ice-coated wire; beneath it ran a dog, barking hopefully.
8. Introductory clause (not used as the subject) followed by a complete statement	Usually a comma after the clause; now tending increasingly to be omitted	While she played the organ, he washed the dishes.
9. At beginning of a sentence, words not necessary to basic meaning	Usually followed by a comma	Well, I can find time if I must.
10. Within a sentence, words not necessary to basic meaning	Usually a comma on each side; less often dashes, parentheses, or brackets	My father, who objected to cigar smoke, thought that a bit of snuff was all right.

11. At end of a sentence, words not necessary to basic meaning	Usually preceded by a comma	He made a poor impression on my father, who objected to cigar smoke.
12. After such words as "as follows" or their equivalent	Usually a colon	He ordered the following merchandise: one gross horsecollars, one dozen . . .
13. With quoted words	Double quotation marks around the exact words quoted	Helen exclaimed, "He was never in Ithaca!"
14. Preceding a quotation	Usually a comma	(See 13 and 15.)
15. Quotation within a quotation	Single quotation marks	Bert asked, "Who said, 'Whatever is, is right'?"
16. Titles of short literary works, etc.	Quotation marks	Poe's "The Raven"
17. Titles of books, plays, etc.	Underlining	For Whom the Bell Tolls

11

SPELLING: TRIAL AND TERROR

WHY WE'RE IN THE MESS WE'RE IN

Stuart Robertson and F. G. Cassidy remind us that "spelling was still, until late Middle English times, quite largely a field in which the individual might display whatever eccentricity he pleased."[1] True, a thirteenth-century monk named Orm had attempted to standardize spelling, at least to the extent of doubling consonants after short vowels, but Orm was the exception. Among Chaucer and his contemporaries one may find, for example, as many as a dozen different spellings for such a simple word as "day."

After Caxton introduced the printing press into England, however, pressures toward uniformity of spelling began to mount. Printshops, anticipating the stylebooks of today's publishing houses, began making arbitrary decisions about spellings; they prepared lists for the guidance of their compositors so that whatever came off their presses would be orthographically consistent. The lists were often in disagreement; even today dictionaries include hundreds of variant spellings and differ in their judgments of which is preferred.[2] The fact that the early printers were not highly literate did not help English spelling during the period of standardization. Neither did the fact that English was simultaneously undergoing the Great Vowel Shift, by which English pronunciation of vowels became different from the Con-

[1] *The Development of Modern English* (Englewood Cliffs, N.J.: Prentice-Hall, Inc., 1954), p. 332.
[2] Every teacher may be enlightened by the NCTE pamphlet *Variant Spellings in Modern American Dictionaries*, by Donald Emery, which includes an annotated list.

tinental pronunciations (the sounds now represented by *a, e, i, o, u* in English are very different from the sounds of the same vowels in French or German, for example). A further complication was added by Renaissance scholars who tried to make English spelling conform to Latin: They insisted on the *b* in "debt" and "doubt," for instance, even though the letter was silent even then, because *b* appears in the Latin ancestor; and, thinking mistakenly that the English "iland" came from the Latin "insula," they demanded that printers insert an *s*, making the word "island." Words ending in *-ation* and others equally out of accord with phonetic principles multiplied during these years of the fifteenth and sixteenth centuries.

As Englishmen increasingly wandered over the globe and transacted business hither and yon, words from more and more foreign languages were borrowed. Sometimes they were anglicized; sometimes they retained their original forms. The resulting problem is illustrated by Eva M. Tappan with reference to place names borrowed from Indian tongues:

> For they fastened a name to every nook,
> And every boy with a spelling-book
> Will have to toil till his hair turns gray
> Before he can spell them the proper way.

In brief, English spelling is inconsistent in two ways: (1) We represent a number of sounds by a single letter, and (2) we use a number of letters to represent the same sound. Thus, the letter *a*, according to Merriam-Webster, represents different sounds in "ale," "chaotic," "care," "add," "account," "arm," "ask," and "sofa." The sound called "long i" is represented by fourteen different letters or letter combinations in "aisle," "bayou," "aye," "stein," "geyser," "eye," "kind," "lie," "sigh," "coyote," "guide," "buy," "sly," and "lye." In some other languages such as Finnish, Spanish, and Russian a single letter usually represents a single sound; conversely, when one makes a sound, one knows what letter or letter combination to use in writing it. It has been estimated that the Russian language, which has 36 symbols for 34 basic sounds, is about 90 per cent efficient in its sound-letter relationships and that English, which has 379 symbols for 40–44 basic sounds, is about 20 per cent efficient. Such a disparity has implications for the teaching of reading as well as for the teaching of spelling. A Russian child may learn to read much more quickly than an English or American child because he need only sound out the letters to recognize a word. But an American child faced with "pneumonia" or "colonel" finds sounding of little avail. And, when he has to spell "psychology," an ear-justified spelling like "sikoloje" is red-penciled or even ridiculed.

Correct spelling, the mastery of inconsistencies, has become a status symbol of sorts. In nineteenth-century America, spelling bees flourished; the man or woman who could spell "syzygy" could win a prize even if he thought that syzygies were porcupines or petunias. Thorstein Veblen, in *The Theory of the Leisure Class* (1899), commented,

> As felicitous an instance of futile classicism as can well be found is the conventional spelling of the English language. English orthography satisfies all the requirements of the canons of reputability under the law of conspicuous waste. It is archaic, cumbrous, and ineffective; its acquisition consumes much time and effort; failure to acquire it is easy of detection.

Today a person misspells at his own peril. Spelling errors in a letter of application or an important report may result in unemployment. Employers seldom complain about a secretary's faulty sentences, which may not be very easy to detect, but they are loud in their wails about faulty spelling.

Through the centuries many persons have tried to reform our chaotic spelling. As early as 1573, John Barrett suggested simplifying by elimination of the letter *q* and of the letter *c* except in *ch* combinations. Two centuries later, Benjamin Franklin recommended a new alphabet. Noah Webster achieved some simplification, notably in reforming such words as "honour," "centre," "musick," and "plough," but he was defeated in his plea for "farewel," "crum," "wo," "ake," and "soop." Late in the nineteenth century the philological associations of Great Britain and the United States vainly sought a basis for simplifying. Andrew Carnegie proved, to his regret, that wealth could not effect the needed changes. When Theodore Roosevelt wanted to use simplified spelling in his White House correspondence, Congress threatened to withhold his appropriation. Slowly a few shortened spellings like "gram," "catalog," "quartet," and "traveled" have become accepted. Some newspapers have entered the campaign for simplified spelling. Groups of scholars and laymen have worked in various directions: some to simplify the spelling of only a few especially unphonetic words, some to respell virtually all words, and some to employ a new alphabet with a different letter for each of the forty-odd sounds of English. In his will, George Bernard Shaw provided funds for the development of a new alphabet; the winning entrant in the subsequent competition has gone almost unnoticed.

Upton Sinclair wrote an impassioned plea to President John F. Kennedy. Bills for reforming spelling have been introduced in Congress, and in 1949 the British Parliament narrowly defeated one such measure. In the early 1960's the British, followed by some Americans, experimented with the teaching of reading, using what they call the Augmented Roman Alphabet. Chicago businessmen are helping to support the Foundation for a Consistent and Compatible Alphabet, partly on the ground that a revised alphabet and mode of spelling would possess great economic value. The publisher of *Parents'* *Magazine* begs repeatedly for reform. The examples could go on and on.

The future of simplified spelling will not be bright unless three unlikely events are brought to pass: A workable basis for simplification must be found, powerful backing must be obtained, and human inertia must be overcome.

English teachers and their students, then, must go on making the best of a bad bargain. English spelling may be a poor thing, but 'tis our own. Maybe we can learn to chuckle at its idiosyncrasies, love it with its faults, even take pride in its uniqueness and unpredictability. Men have learned to do that with women.

MOTIVATION FOR SPELLING

You have heard the saying that one must be cautious in deciding what one wants, because one is likely to get it. If a student decides that he really wants to learn to spell, he is likely to learn to spell.

Here are several suggestions for motivation. None are infallible, but one will work with some students, another with others. A combination of the five should effect a wholesome desire to improve and to continue improving.

Building an Interest in Words

Help students to see that words are like people. Words have personalities—drab, shy, aggressive, colorful, scary, etc. Like people, too, they often belong to families: the Antes, Antis, Ocracies, Ations, and so on. The English language has been a melting pot for words as America has been a melting pot for people; just as it is sometimes interesting to find out a person's ancestry, so it is often interesting and informative to discover the ancestry of a word. (See Chapter 12 for further discussion of building interest in words.)

Demonstrating Why Spelling Has Become Standardized

You might have each of your students write three or four sentences on any subject. Tell the class that each is to spell all the words in any way that he wishes—the more original the spelling, the better. Write something like this as an example: "Hwenn thuh Inngglissh lannggwidge wuzz jungrr, itt wuzz vehree dyffruhnt phrumn thuh lannggwidge ovv 2da." Have the students exchange papers and try to read what their classmates have written. The time will not be wasted, for they will prove to their own satisfaction that, if each person spelled to suit himself, confusion and loss of effort would result.

Showing that Employers Value Correct Spelling

If you have the opportunity to find out what a few employers in your community think about spelling, make use of it, because nothing will impress students more than the point of view of influential local people. Collect a few pertinent real-life anecdotes about the stenographer who couldn't spell (and the one who could), the mechanic's trouble with "gas kit" and "gasket," the farmer who ordered clover because he couldn't spell "alfalfa," etc.

Making Correct Spelling a Challenge

Unless a student is determined to learn to spell, he will not do so. For some students the greatest challenge may come from awareness that bad spelling may cause failure at a job or in college. (Some evidence suggests that the greatest weakness of students placed in remedial English in college is poor spelling.) For other students the challenge may be to pride: "You aren't going to let twenty-six little letters get you down, are you?" One teacher made a friendly wager with a class, betting that the class could not make an average score of 95 per cent on a semester test. At stake were some special (and legitimate) privileges that the class wanted. The poor spellers were so much hounded and helped by their classmates that the average was 98 per cent.

Continuing Motivation by Praising Improvement

Graphs or charts to show individual or class improvement are often helpful. Praise of the student who has just overcome his habit of confusing "their," "there," and "they're" is beneficial, even though he still misspells a dozen other words in one paper. To tell a class that it is improving in its spelling brings better results than to say, "Your spelling is worse than that of any other class I've ever taught."

SELECTING THE WORDS TO BE TAUGHT

Word counts have revealed that about 1,000 words constitute the basic vocabulary of English. Many of these are used over and over: "a," "an," "the," "you," "of," "with," etc. If one were to take random passages of English writing totaling 100,000 words, one would find that about 90,000 of the words were these basic 1,000 employed again and again.

Commonsense, then, dictates that these 1,000 words are the ones everyone should know how to spell. The spelling bee of Grandfather's day placed stress instead upon long, difficult, and seldom used words. Sometimes the spellers learned the orthography of words they could not define or use. Today we emphasize spelling for use. Since few students will ever have occasion to write "catachresis," that word is not taught, but, since all will probably need "coming," "certain," and "choose," these are taught.

But, of the 1,000 or 2,000 or 3,000 most common words, not all cause spelling problems, at least for high school students. Words like "with," "sand," "window," and "understand" are almost never misspelled except through rank carelessness. It is wasteful to spend time on words already mastered. However, some of the frequently employed words do cause trouble. These are the "demon" words, like "its," "than," and "too." For instance, a group of twenty-five students who had just been graduated from high school, in writing that totaled about 110,000 words, misspelled 291. The only words misspelled more than once were "already" (2), "believe" (2), "convenience" (2), "doesn't" (3), "evidently" (2), "immensely" (2), "incidentally" (2), "indispensable" (2), "its" (5), "it's" (3), "nuisance" (2), "occasionally" (2), "preceding" (2), "receive" (3), "review" (2), "similar" (2), "strenuous" (2), "than" (4), "their" (4), "then" (2), "there" (3), "too" (9), "truly" (2), "woman" (2), and "writing" (2). For this particular group, then, 25 words accounted for almost a fourth of the errors. Mastery of a relatively small number of demons—100 or 200— may reasonably be expected to reduce spelling mistakes by half or more.

No two lists of demons are exactly alike. The 417 words in one list, compiled by Thomas C. Pollock, were found to account for 52.4 per cent of misspellings by college students.[3] Another list, prepared by Fred C. Ayer, is a composite based upon twelve spelling books.[4] The following list was compiled by Edna L. Furness and Gertrude A. Boyd on the basis of frequency of appearance on five carefully compiled lists including those by Pollock and Ayer. A student who can spell correctly all 231 of these words will not necessarily be a good speller, but he is unlikely to be a bad speller.[5]

[3] absence	bureau	[3] deceive	extremely
[3] accept	[5] business	decided	[3] familiar
accidentally	[3] busy	definite	[4] February
[4] accommodate	cafeteria	[3] definitely	[3] finally
acquaintance	calendar	definition	[3] foreign
across	campaign	describe	[3] forty
advise	cancel	[4] description	fourth
[3] affect	capital	desert	freight
[3] all right	captain	desirable	friend
already	[3] cemetery	despair	[3] fundamental
[3] amateur	certain	dessert	generally
analyze	changeable	[3] develop	genius
answer	[3] chauffeur	development	[3] government
anxious	[3] choose	[3] different	[3] governor
apparatus	clothes	disappear	[4] grammar
[3] appearance	coarse	[3] disappoint	guarantee
appreciate	[3] column	disapprove	handsome
Arctic	[3] coming	disastrous	[3] height
[3] argument	[3] committee	[3] discipline	humorous
arrangement	competent	divine	hungry
athletics	completely	[3] doesn't	[4] immediately
awkward	conceive	[3] effect	[3] independent
[4] beginning	[4] conscience	embarrass	interested
[3] belief	conscientious	emphasize	interesting
[4] believe	consistent	equipped	interfere
beneficial	convenience	especially	it's
[3] benefit	corporation	exaggerated	[3] its
[3] benefited	course	[3] excellent	knew
brilliant	courtesy	except	knowledge
Britain	criticism	[4] experience	[3] laboratory

[3] "Spelling Report," available from the NCTE. The list has been reprinted, with trouble spots indicated and with an additional list of 583 words, in J. N. Hook, *Hook's Guide to Good Writing: Grammar, Style, Usage* (New York: The Ronald Press Co., 1962), pp. 427–31.

[4] *A Study of High School Spelling Vocabulary* (Austin, Tex.: The Steck Co., 1945).

[5] "231 Real Spelling Demons for High School Students," *English Journal*, XLVI (May, 1958), 269–70. Reprinted by permission of the NCTE. "Words which appear on two lists are unmarked; words which appear on three lists are marked by the number 3; those in four lists, by the number 4; and those on five lists, by the number 5."

laid	original	received	[4] surprise
[3] leisure	paid	recognize	tariff
library	pamphlet	[4] recommend	[4] their
loose	[3] parallel	recommendation	[3] there
[3] lose	parliament	reference	they're
losing	pastime	referred	[3] thoroughly
magazine	peculiar	relieve	[3] to
maintenance	perhaps	religious	together
marriage	permanent	[3] repetition	[3] too
mathematics	persuade	respectfully	[3] tragedy
meant	physician	[3] restaurant	tried
minute	piece	sandwich	tries
mischievous	[3] planned	[3] schedule	[3] truly
misspell	[3] pleasant	[4] secretary	Tuesday
mortgage	possess	[3] seize	[3] two
naturally	[3] principal	[5] separate	typical
[5] necessary	[3] principle	shining	[3] until
nickel	[4] privilege	[3] similar	[3] usually
niece	[3] probably	[3] sincerely	valuable
ninety	professor	[3] sophomore	vegetable
[3] noticeable	pronunciation	speech	weather
nuisance	psychology	straight	[3] Wednesday
occasion	[3] quiet	studying	[4] whether
[4] occurred	quite	succeed	whose
occurring	realize	success	woman
omitted	really	sufficient	[3] writing
opinion	[3] receipt	superintendent	[4] written
[3] opportunity	[5] receive	surely	

If a limited list will cut spelling errors approximately in half, it is certainly worth teaching thoroughly. An English department may agree, for example, that a list like the one above will constitute the bulk of the spelling program for, say, the ninth or tenth grade, with perfection the goal for all students, and with each student to be excused from the basic spelling work once he has made a perfect score on the total list. (A tape recorder may pronounce the words, twenty-five or fifty in a group, and save the teacher's time.) In subsequent years, a small amount of review should be sufficient, and attention may be devoted to students' individual spelling problems that are unrelated to the common demons.

GROUP PROCEDURES

Although learning the spelling of a word is in the last analysis the result of individual effort, some group instruction may make that effort easier. In this section we shall look at what the teacher and class can do together; in the next, at what the student needs to be encouraged to do by himself.

Phonetics

You may have some students who do not know the usual sounds of letters. Although today's reading instruction in the elementary schools typically combines phonic and other approaches, some schools still exist in which students never learn to "sound out" words. A study made in Indiana revealed that students who have never learned phonetics have about a 50 per cent greater chance of being retarded in spelling than those who have received such instruction. Students who lack knowledge of basic sounds are likely to write some such curiosities as "brapoly" for "probably," or "furtst" for "forest."

If your students do need such training, spend a few minutes a day for several weeks with simple one-syllable words, grouping them as the "at" family ("bat," "cat," etc.), the "it" family, the "and" family, and so on. Give additional drill on the usual sounds of consonants, employing both real and nonsense words such as "bib," "bob," "bab," "beb," "bub." Move on to simple combinations such as "batboy," "hotrod," etc. Teach the blends: *sl, sp, st, ch, sh,* and the like. Next may come clarification of the effects of a final *e* or of a doubled letter, as in "fad" and "fade," "hug" and "huge," "hoping" and "hopping." All this is elementary work and is not very helpful with unphonetic spellings like "thought" and "psychology," but it does prevent some of the more ridiculous misspellings.

Pronunciation

Slovenly or otherwise inaccurate pronunciation may lead to misspelling. Class drill on frequently mispronounced words such as those in the following list may eliminate some spelling errors.

accidentally (Note AL.)	jewelry (Not joolery.)
Arctic (Note C.)	laboratory (LABOR.)
athlete (Two syllables.)	mischievous (Three syllables.)
attacked (Two syllables.)	perform (PER.)
barbarous (No I.)	perspiration (PER.)
cavalry (CAV.)	probably (Three syllables.)
diphtheria (Note PH.)	relevant (REL.)
diphthong (Note PH.)	remembrance (Lost E.)
drowned (One syllable.)	sacrilegious (Cf. sacrilege.)
February (Two R's.)	surprise (Two R's.)
film (One syllable.)	temperature (TempER.)
government (GoverN.)	tragedy (Not tradegy.)

Grouping of Words

Wise grouping of words seems desirable. Grouping means, for example, teaching several words ending in *ible* at one time, and words ending in *able* a few weeks or months later; *ent* words at one time and *ant* words at another; "prove," "move," and "lose" at one time but "smooth," "booth," and "loose" at another. Words with various common characteristics may also be grouped, for example,

define	imagine	sincerely	perform	already
definite	imaginable	merely	perforate	altogether
definition	imaginary	severely	perspective	almost
definitive	imagination		pertinent	
	imaginative			
	image			

Mnemonic Devices and Games

Associational devices in limited numbers may be helpful, but too many of them create more confusion than they dispel. The teacher may suggest to Tommy, who can never remember how to spell "separate" and "grammar," that Pa is in one and Ma in the other. When Linda leaves out two letters in "laboratory," she may be told that scientists *labor* there. Students may sometimes wish to originate their own mnemonic devices for a few words.

Games may occasionally be used for teaching spelling, but, when they are, they should be regarded just as educational fun and not as serious competition for grades. The old-fashioned spelling bee has little value except for good spellers. One variation of it, which partially overcomes this objection, is to have two teams standing. As soon as a player spells a word (or two words) correctly, he may sit down. The first team to have only three players standing is the winner. Another variation is to have everyone remain in the game, a point being given a team for each correct spelling. Words that someone has missed may be reintroduced later in the session, with two points awarded for the right spelling.

Prefixes and Suffixes

The spelling of words to which prefixes or suffixes are attached puzzles students rather often, giving them trouble especially in deciding whether or not to double a letter. Exercises like this are valuable:

dis	+ *agree*	= *disagree*
dis	+ *appoint*	= *disappoint*
dis	+ *satisfied*	= *dissatisfied*
smooth	+ *ness*	= *smoothness*
drunken	+ *ness*	= *drunkenness*
sudden	+ *ness*	= *suddenness*
immediate	+ *ly*	= *immediately*
final	+ *ly*	= *finally*
principal	+ *ly*	= *principally*

Inductive Teaching of Rules

The value of rules has been warmly denied and hotly defended. In the nineteenth century, some texts contained dozens of rules with hundreds of illustrations and scores of exceptions. At present, the consensus is that only a few rules are worth teaching and that those rules should be taught inductively.

Here is an illustration of teaching a rule inductively. The teacher writes on the board, "hate," "name," "arrange," "fate," and "like." He asks what all of these words have in common and gets the answer that each ends in a silent *e*. Then he asks students to spell "hateful," "namely," "arrangement," "fateful," and "likeness," and he writes these words opposite the first list, underlining the suffixes. "What would happen if we didn't keep the *e* in 'hateful'?" he inquires. The students explain that the *e* prevents confusion between "hateful" and "hatful" and between "fateful" and "fatful" and that one would tend to mispronounce "arrangement" if the *e* were not there. The teacher wonders whether the suffixes have anything in common and is told that each begins with a consonant. He calls for other words ending in silent *e;* the students find suffixes to add to words like "state," "late," "white," etc., but they notice that many words such as "dice," "while," and "please" do not take suffixes beginning with consonants.

At this point the teacher may pause to have the class formulate a rule that says that, when a suffix beginning with a consonant is added to a word ending in silent *e,* the *e* is retained. He may, however, first go back to the original list and ask the class to spell "hating," "naming," "arranging," "fatal," and "likable," which he writes in a third column. Here is something new, since the *e* has been dropped. A little judicious questioning reveals that the distinction between these words and the ones in the second column exists because here the suffix begins with a vowel. The teacher comments that there is a good reason for dropping the *e,* for, if one saw such a word as "fateal," one might have trouble in pronouncing it. More illustrations and then on to the formulation of a rule something like this: In adding a suffix to a word ending in silent *e*, retain the *e* if the suffix begins with a consonant, but drop the *e* if the suffix begins with a vowel.

One more step remains—mentioning the most important exceptions. On the board the teacher writes "singe" and tells the class that, for a good reason, this word is an exception. He writes, "singeing" and lets the class see that the *e* is retained here before a vowel. "Why?" he asks. Immediately someone sees that "singing" would be confusing. The teacher refers to "shoeing" and "hoeing," commenting that "shoing" and "hoing" would look like names of Chinese provinces. He may mention a few other exceptions such as "dyeing," "courageous," "notice-able," and "judgment."

Later practice does not involve the restating of the rule except to verify a spelling. At subsequent class meetings, though, the teacher does give much practice in adding suffixes to many words ending in silent *e*. Without such practice, the rule will have little value.

Four other rules are of particular worth. They may be taught inductively, several weeks apart, by following procedures similar to the one just described. These are the rules:

1. Words of one syllable ending in a single consonant preceded by a single vowel double the final consonant before a suffix begin-ning with a vowel ("lag," "lagging"; "plan," "planned").

2. Words of more than one syllable ending in a single consonant preceded by a single vowel double the final consonant before a suffix beginning with a vowel, if the syllable preceding the suffix is accented ("occur," "occurred"; "prefer," "preferring"; "repel," "repellent"; but "travel," "traveled," "traveling"; "preference").

3. Final *y* preceded by a consonant changes to *ie* before an *s* ("army," "armies"; "fly," "flies"; but "turkey," "turkeys"; "at-torney," "attorneys"—because a vowel precedes the *y*).

4. In the *ei, ie* combinations pronounced *e* as in "feel," *i* comes before *e* except after *c* ("believe," "receive"). The most com-mon exceptions are contained in this sentence: "Neither leisurely financier seized either weird species."

Teaching from Lists

In the junior high years some teachers devote part of each class period to spelling. The most common pattern is that of the weekly list of about twenty words. On Monday, a pretest is given, and stu-dents immediately study the words they missed. (If they miss none, they are excused from spelling for the week.) On Tuesday, they once more study the words they missed; Wednesday brings another test and more study; Thursday, more study; and Friday, a final test and study of any words still missed. The strong points of this procedure are that the test-study plan has been proved efficient and that each student works only on the words that he misses. Its weaknesses are those inherent in any plan in which the teacher uses the list approach; particularly, the words may not be the ones that these students need.

Ideally, each student should work each week on his own individualized list, but no teacher has time to draw up 100 or 150 tailor-made lists every few days. Here are some possible compromises:

1. Have each student keep a record of all words he misspells in any class. Each week he is required to add five of these words to the basic list assigned to the whole class. He studies these, and at testing time a spelling partner pronounces the five words for him.

2. Divide the class into two or three groups on the basis of spelling ability, and prepare separate lists. The poorest spellers concentrate on demon words; the others, on other useful words encountered in their reading.

3. Prepare weekly lists, half the words from the demon group, half from recently studied literature.

4. Sometimes have each student draw up his own list of "Words I Should Learn To Spell." In testing sessions use spelling partners.

Able classes in the senior high school may need no work with lists, although some students may need help. Bright students may be made to feel completely responsible for the correctness of their own spelling.

INDIVIDUALIZED PROCEDURES

Discovering One's Own Road to Success

Individual differences exist in methods of learning. What works well for one person will not necessarily work well for another. Let your students know that a speller may recall a word mainly by motor, auditory, or visual means. Some persons, in a sense, have spelling at their fingertips; once they have written a word, say, "existence," a few times, they can write it automatically, without thinking. Others remember with their ears: "Ex-is-tence," they say, perhaps exaggerating the pronunciation to remind themselves of the e after t. Still others have camera vision; when they encounter a new word, they take a "snapshot" of it, and when they need the word again, it flashes on a "screen" inside their heads: They actually "see" the word. And some persons combine two or all three of the methods. Having students think about their own techniques for remembering may assist them in making best use of their strongest assets without ignoring the other means of remembering.

Harry Shefter, in a popular paperbound book, *Six Minutes a Day to Perfect Spelling* (Pocket Books, 1954), advocates a five-step procedure in learning a word. His steps include the three techniques just described, and add some others: "SEE THE WORD" (i.e., look at it carefully, spotting its peculiarities and possible trouble spots); "THINK THE WORD" (i.e., associate the word with something that may help you to remember it: "She screamed 'EEE!' as she passed the cEmEtEry."); "FEEL THE WORD" (i.e., pronounce it carefully); BUILD THE WORD (i.e., relate it to other forms or to similar words: "beauty," "beautiful," "beautify," "beautifully," "beautification").

To increase independence in studying spelling among children in upper elementary grades, Howard Blake recommends giving them individual copies of questions they may find it useful to answer.[6] Blake's list consists of forty-three questions under the headings of phonetic analysis, structural analysis, meaning, and usage. Representative questions: "What other words can I write that begin like this word?" "What story, poem, announcement, report, letter, or instruction can I write using this word and others on the list?" Blake emphasizes that each child should select from the forty-three questions the ones that seem to him to be most helpful in studying.

An NCTE committee recommends this procedure:

In studying a word, a good procedure for a learner is, (1) to say each syllable distinctly and look at the syllable as he says it, (2) with eyes closed to think how the word looks, (3) to look at the word again to check his impression, (4) to write the word and check with the book, and (5) to repeat twice the writing and checking. If on any one of these five trials he misspells the word, he should copy it in his spelling notebook. Finally, he should write the group of words studied as a parent, brother, sister, or friend pronounces them for him.[7]

From an assortment of suggestions such as these, a student should through a little experimenting find what works best for him.

[6] "Studying Spelling Independently," *Elementary English*, XXXVII (Jan., 1960), 29–32.
[7] *An Experience Curriculum in English*, p. 259.

Characteristics of Good Spellers

Good spelling is not necessarily a mark of high intelligence. Rather, it is likely to be a result of certain attitudes and habits. These are described by E. W. Dolch:

. . . the "good speller" (1) checks his guesses, (2) proofreads for spelling, and (3) studies the spelling of new words, which means (a) he gets the exact pronunciation of each new word, (b) he asks if this sounding tells the letters, and (c) where it does not, he finds a means of remembering the exact letters at the difficult spot. He makes this rapid check in all subjects, in English, in history, in science, or what not. He habitually makes this check, and does it in a few seconds only.[8]

Programed Instruction

Interest in machine teaching or other forms of programed instruction has extended to spelling, and a number of new programs are emerging. So far, experiments have not revealed that programed instruction is superior to regular classroom instruction in its results, but it may have the advantage of making individualized work possible. The ideal program would first offer a number of diagnostic spelling tests, to be taken by all students. On the basis of this diagnosis, each student would then "do" the programs indicated as best for meeting his deficiencies. Posttests would reveal the extent of his gains, and periodic reviews would help him to retain the correct spellings. Although more experimentation with programing is needed, it may be safely said that spelling is one subject in which its promise is considerable.

SUMMARY

Improvement in spelling most often results from proceeding in these ways:

1. Motivate spelling.
2. Teach the words that most students will need.
3. Encourage students to find and master their own demons.
4. Suggest a variety of attacks on spelling problems.
5. Encourage visualization.
6. Teach correct pronunciation.

[8] "Teaching Spelling," *Illinois English Bulletin*, XXX, No. 6 (March, 1943), 5.

7. Teach phonetics, if necessary.
8. Encourage tracing, writing in air, etc., to build the "feel" of a word.
9. When practicable, present words in related groups.
10. Use a few mnemonic devices.
11. Teach the addition of prefixes and suffixes.
12. Teach only a few rules, always inductively.
13. When teaching a list, use the test-study procedure.
14. Use a few spelling games.
15. Give individual help when it is needed.
16. Encourage the dictionary habit for checking guesses.
17. Give plenty of practice in writing.
18. If possible, experiment with programed instruction.

THE IDEA BOX

"A COMMON-SENSE APPROACH TO TEACHING SPELLING"

This pamphlet, written at Ball State Teachers College, Muncie, Indiana, as a result of a study sponsored by the Eli Lilly Foundation, compares results of teaching spelling through the individualized approach, with each student concentrating on the words that trouble him most, and through a conventional use of word lists. Students following the individualized approach appeared to spell better at the end.

ANECDOTE FOR MOTIVATION

A motorist was arrested for parking beside a sign that said "No stoping." He was freed when he proved that he had not been "stoping," that is, digging for ore.

SPELLING "MUST" LIST

Let students agree upon a short list of words that must never be misspelled. This list may gradually be enlarged. Let students determine what would be a fair penalty if one of these words is misspelled.

LOGICAL ANALYSIS

Often a moment's thought will clarify a spelling; for example, "bookkeeper" has two *k*'s because it combines "book" and "keeper."

A HARD LOOK AT THE WORD

One of the spelling techniques recommended by Sister Josephina, C.S.J. in "Spelling: The Responsibility of Every Teacher," *Clearing House,*

XXXII (March, 1958), 393, is having students observe anything note-worthy in the meaning, root, prefix, or early history of each troublesome word.

SIMPLIFIED SPELLING

Minor simplification of spelling will do little good, yet a plan for a new alphabet such as George Bernard Shaw advocated would necessitate scrapping all our typewriters and linotypes, retraining their operators, and reteaching reading to everyone. We need a system in which each English sound will always be represented orthographically in the same way; with such a system, no teaching of spelling would be needed after the second grade, as is true in Finland even now. One workable (but not flawless) system was almost adopted in England in the late 1940's. Its characteristics are revealed in this verse from *The New York Times*:

> Mai hart iz sad fer litel wunz
> Hw uend dher uei tw skwl
> Tw lern dhe Inglish langgwidj
> Uith its totel lak ov rwl.

MNEMONIC DEVICES

> "You wouldn't believe a lie for a minute,
> But the word *believe* has a *lie* right in it."
> —Harriet Johnson (*Word Study*, Oct., 1946).

The princi*pal* is the students' *pal*.
The vil*lain* had *lain* in wait.
Give me a *piece* of *pie*.
Princip*les* are ru*les*.
Calen*dar*s give *dates*.
Gabri*el* is an ang*el*.

JUXTAPOSITION

Teachers in the English Department at Thomas Carr Howe High School, in Indianapolis, prepared a very useful spelling book for their classes. One of the features is juxtaposition of words with similar characteristics, for example, "define," "definite;" "imagine," "imaginable," "imaginary," "imagination," "imaginative," "image;" "diphtheria," "diphthong." See Thelma L. Cooley, "Spelling Attack," *Clearing House*, XXVII (Nov., 1952), 155.

SPELLING PARTNERS

Frank Dunn, Sayville, New York, Junior High School, has students work in pairs on their spelling chores. Mr. Dunn has three levels of spelling words for each grade, assigning to each student words on the level for which he is ready. "Multi-level Spelling Program," *New York State Education*, May, 1960, p. 22.

HOMONYM DOWN

To increase sensitivity to homonyms, Louise Swinney's tenth graders, in Elsinore, California, enjoy an occasional spelldown with homonyms.

The teacher pronounces a homonym; a member of one team spells it; and then a member of the next team must spell another version of it. The student may be asked to use in a sentence the homonym he has spelled.

SPELLING LESSONS VIA TAPE RECORDINGS

For an account of an experiment that showed that teacher time could be saved by use of recorded spelling lessons, at no loss in learning effectiveness, see the *Bulletin* of the National Association of Secondary-School Principals, January, 1959, page 49. The experiment was conducted at Westside Junior High School, Omaha, and is described by Mrs. R. E. Gibson in "The Tape Recording Experiment."

PROOFREADING

Proofreading exercises, requiring students to look carefully at every word, have some value. Even more valuable is insistence that students proofread their own written work. Sometimes their reading the work slowly aloud will help them to catch spelling errors they would otherwise miss.

TROUBLE SPOTS

Since usually a word has only one bad trouble spot (e.g., the sixth letter in *"existence"*), it is often useful to focus students' attention on that spot. For an extensive list, see Arthur I. Gates, *A List of Spelling Difficulties in 3876 Words* (New York: Teachers College, Columbia University Bureau of Publications, 1937).

STUDENT EXPERTS

"Call each student an 'expert' on a word that he misspells consistently. Whenever that word is used in class, it is the expert's responsibility to check the accuracy of the spelling. He must learn the word in order to check it, or he must find its correct spelling in a dictionary each time the problem appears." Many other interesting suggestions are included in Hardy Finch's "Memo to a High School Principal. Subject: Spelling," NASSP *Bulletin*, XXXIX (Sept., 1955), 62.

GAMES AND OTHER MOTIVATION

Robert L. Coard of Minot, North Dakota, lists for lowerclassmen the words his seniors misspell and issues the challenge "Can you outspell our seniors?" For other tactics, see Mr. Coard's "Spelling-Game Time," *Clearing House*, XXX (Sept., 1955), 9.

EXCUSING GOOD SPELLERS

Some of the best spellers may be excused from spelling work, with the proviso that they may at any time be called upon to demonstrate that they are maintaining their ability.

"DON'T SAY UNKLE"

This article by Mary Peavey and Nell Stillwagon, *English Journal*, XXXVIII (March, 1949), 150, recommends having students find pairs or groups of words that have similar trouble spots, for example, "sincerely," "merely," "seventy"; "perform," "perforate"; "already," "altogether."

GRAMMAR AND SPELLING

"Spell the noun form of *abominate*," says Herbert V. Ogden to his students, thus recalling some grammar as well as teaching spelling. Mr. Ogden also describes his classes' honor system for spelling in "Spelling Makes Friends," *English Journal*, XLI (Nov., 1952), 468.

GOOD AND SHORT

Crammed with excellent advice is Morton Botel's "How To Teach Spelling on the Secondary Level," *High School Journal*, XXXIX (Nov., 1955), 76.

12

WORDS, WORDS, WORDS

BUILDING VOCABULARIES

The Cardinal Principles of Vocabulary Building

In Sherwood Anderson's *Winesburg, Ohio* appears a teacher advising one of her former students who wants to become a writer. "You will have to know life," she says. "If you are to become a writer you'll have to stop fooling with words. . . . You must not become a mere peddler of words."

Her advice is good not only for would-be professional writers but for all who use language. Accurate understanding of words comes from experiences with the things and ideas for which words stand. To a farm boy, "cow" is a rich and meaningful word because the boy knows what cows are and has had much experience with cattle. But "wombat" is probably only a fortuitous collection of letters, unless the child has happened to see a wombat in a zoo. To the city child, "subway" is replete with associations. "Silo," however, if it means anything to him, is likely to suggest only a thumb-shaped projection that stands near farmers' barns; the city child knows nothing of silo filling, of the damp, green smell that silage has in midwinter, or of the way that silage is fed.

A word is nothing in itself. The word's power of suggesting is everything. Before a bomb hit Hiroshima, "atom" for most people was only a word encountered in a science class. But now "atom" suggests measureless energy, submarines, ships, interplanetary travel, destructiveness and human suffering, an unbounded source of good, the hope and the dread of mankind. A group of letters has assumed vivid meaning because all of us at least vicariously have had experiences in which that group of letters played a part.

Suppose that, instead of learning about "atom" as we did, we had been told in school that an atom is a minute particle consisting of a nucleus and a varying number of electrons. The richness of association would have been missing. We would have remembered "atom" long enough to define it in an examination and then perhaps would have forgotten it forever. Or we might have remembered the word and dragged it into the conversation some evening when chemistry was the topic of discussion; that is, we might have peddled the word, though for us it was empty of real meaning.

Word peddlers are persons like the one described by Sara A. Garratt in the New York *Sun:*

> I like the words *epitome,*
> *Digamma,* and *baleen.*
> I toss them off with nonchalance,
> But don't know what they mean.

Or they are like the high school senior girl who wrote,

In the celestial radiance of my maternal forebear's enigmatic smile, my *frater* and I puissantly and incessantly grew toward that apex of desiderata, adulthood as pleasurable as juvenility had been because of the incontrovertible fact of her existence.

(Teacher, puzzled, gave the girl an A.)

Word peddlers may be as harmless as this erstwhile senior probably is now. It is easy to picture her, a dozen years older, floridly introducing today's speaker to the Community Culture Club. But other word peddlers may be dangerous when they wrap little ideas in big words. They may be elected to Congress.

The long prevalent attitude toward vocabulary has been that the number of words learned is all-important. The slogan "Learn a new word every day" has too seldom been phrased, "Learn a useful new word every day" or "Learn what words really mean." In the merry or not so merry chase after new words, students have emerged with terms that not one in a thousand will ever need: "sphagnous," "oxytone," and "elasmobranch." Perhaps to these same students, "overture," "laxity," and "corroborate" are unknown, and "culture" and "democracy" are words that they mouth with little comprehension.

All available evidence points to the belief that vocabulary grows as alert children and adults encounter new experiences. Words do not exist in a vacuum and are not learned in a vacuum. The weekly list of twenty randomly selected words is almost a vacuum; tests a couple of months later will usually reveal that only a small proportion of previously unfamiliar words from such a list will be remembered. A thing and the name for the thing impress themselves simultaneously. Vocabulary and a spirit of inquiry grow together. The crippled child of illiterate parents, living on an isolated farm, without electricity, back in the hills, almost certainly will possess a meager vocabulary even if he is highly intelligent. Another child, whose homelife and school life are filled with varied activity and whose teachers have stimulated an interest in words, is likely to attain a resourceful vocabulary.

Vocabularies, like fingerprints, are never identical. They vary, partly because of differing experiences, partly because of degrees of intelligence, and partly because of the way words are regarded by the child's parents, peers, and teachers. Two children may share an experience and still not receive the same word dividends. In a chemistry class, for example, one student may learn early in the semester the meaning of "reagent," "catalyst," and "osmosis," but another for a long time may refer to "stuff that looks like water." After reading *Treasure Island,* one student may have vivid impressions of "schooner" and "coracle," while another still uses no more definite words than "big boat" and "little boat." The difference arises in part from variation in intelligence; bright students learn new words quickly, just as they do most other things. But it may arise also from interest or lack of interest in words. To some students, a new word is a challenge, something to examine, taste, experiment with, and use; to others, it is a thing to ignore. Some will employ the word to express themselves with exactness; others, unless they can catch the same spirit, will remain content with "stuff" and "deal" and other woolly words.

The two cardinal principles of vocabulary building may be summarized thus:

1. Rich vocabularies result from rich experiences, firsthand or vicarious.
2. Precise diction results in part from intelligence and in part from a keen interest in words as symbols.

Adding to Students' Experiences

Despite the shortcomings of television, it brings our students experiences and consequent knowledge that they might never attain without it. A fad for westerns brings information about mesas, buttes, and saguaros; a fad for courtroom drama clarifies the meanings of "plaintiff," "defendant," "habeas corpus"; a fad for doctor stories dramatizes a score or two of medical terms. More offbeat programs add information on a wide range of subjects, and with the information comes the relevant vocabulary. Radio, newspapers, and magazines, accessible now in almost every home, provide still more information.

Within the schoolroom, the films, kinescopes, filmstrips, and recordings that are now available are rich resources. English field trips to libraries, colleges, newspaper plants, museums, theaters, government buildings, and places related to literature may directly broaden experience. Pictures, maps, bulletin boards, and chalkboards may supplement experiences.

In short, more opportunities exist now than ever before for students to step outside the boundaries of home and school and to participate at least vicariously in the varied experiences of the human race. From these experiences are derived the words to describe them.

Alert teachers use such opportunities. Television, filmstrips, and the like are part of their teaching arsenal. So is a constant attempt to associate words with ideas, and ideas with things. Straight thinking involves accurate use of words. Through class discussion, students can have stimulating experience with ideas, particularly when the ideas are translated in terms of tangibles. Few students—indeed, few adults—can think in abstractions. Teachers can assist students to associate words, even abstract words, with things. In fact, if students do not make such associations, words will lack meaning. The child who can glibly quote the dictionary definition of "democracy" as "government by the people" knows less about the word than the one who has examined a specimen ballot, attended a town meeting, taken part in a mock political convention, and participated in student government. If you tell a child that a symphony is "an instrumental composition in sonata form for a full orchestra," his understanding will be less than if you make it possible for him to hear even part of a symphony.

Alert teachers stress the rich experiences afforded by literature. Although no one lives long enough to participate personally in even one-millionth of the experiences that life offers, each, through books, can participate vicariously in multitudinous activities—sharing in the observation, thoughts, emotions, and acts of thousands of other people near or remote in time and place. Literature, chosen wisely and read well, opens the floodgate of experience.

Increasing Interest in Words

"Here is your list of useful words for this week. Look each one up in the dictionary, copy its definition, and write a sentence containing the word. We'll have our test on these words on Friday." That is the traditional method of vocabulary building, which still has its practitioners. It is not valueless, particularly if the words listed really are useful. But it has its weaknesses. One is its puny motivation. Another is that a word out of context may be misunderstood. For instance, one youngster looked up "quaver" and found that it means "shake"; she had trouble in understanding why it is incorrect to say, "I quavered the tablecloth." Still another weakness is that most of the words are forgotten in a few months.

Better than the list approach or any other single approach is keeping an interest in words going constantly. This means that there is some talk about words in almost every class period—oblique references in discussion of literature, direct comment in study of composition, remarks about the language of a TV newscaster, and so on. It means that the teacher uses variety in his attack on the problem.

The trouble with much vocabulary building is that it is spasmodic, whereas it should be part of every day's work. It need not be labeled "vocabulary drill"; in fact, there will often be no drill involved. The teacher must be interested in, and well informed about, words. When questions arise that the teacher cannot answer, he and the class will search for the answers. In a story, a class found a woman characterized as a "mimosa." Neither teacher nor class knew the word. Upon looking it up, they discovered that it is another name for the "sensitive plant," which folds up when it is touched. When someone noticed that it is derived from the same word as "mimic" and "pantomime," the class tried to guess at the connection. They returned to the story to find why the author had used this word, and uncovered examples of the character's sensitiveness. Had the teacher merely said, "Look up the word," the class would have missed a wealth of associations. "Mimosa" itself is not a particularly valuable word, but the class discussion that arose from it threw light upon the story, added the useful words "mimic" and "sensitivity" to several students' vocabularies, and increased interest in words. In this teacher's class, such study of words is common; yet it does not smack of "drill."

The following paragraphs discuss several devices, traditional and otherwise, used successfully by teachers to build interest in words and to increase verbal precision. Others are in The Idea Box, pages 392–401.

The Dictionary. Students need help in order to learn to use the dictionary efficiently. From unhappy experiences, some students have come to regard the dictionary as a foe rather than a friend. The chief trouble is that many students have not learned to find a word quickly.

Using a desk dictionary, a student should be able to locate in about fifteen or twenty seconds any word that he can spell. (You, the teacher, should need no more than twelve seconds.) Teach students to know the alphabet thoroughly, to open the dictionary in about the right place, and to use the guide words. Give them numerous dictionary problems. Help them to analyze dictionary entries to see what a wealth of information each contains. (Most publishers of dictionaries supply free pamphlets containing dictionary exercises.)

Here are a few examples of worthwhile dictionary problems:

1. Why do Londoners sometimes call their policemen "bobbies"?
2. What three different kinds of animals are called "gophers"?
3. What is a corollary? How do the British pronounce the word?
4. Find definitions of "scale" referring to zoology, botany, metallurgy, and music. Use "scale" in sentences that will illustrate each definition.
5. How does the Gregorian calendar differ from the Julian?
6. What might you expect to see if you heard someone shout "Hoicks!" or "Yoicks!"?
7. Does your dictionary suggest that some meanings of "fix" are less formal than others?

Expansion of Meaning. It has been said that it is not more words that make an educated man or woman, but more meanings. With this in mind, classes have explored all the meanings of common words such as "like," "light," "name," "go," "tie," "fast," "start," "lie," "dream," and "beat." The result is at least a better understand of the versatility of words.

Learning from Words Previously Known. Sometimes it is possible to determine word meanings by associating them with other words. Thus the word "micrometer" is composed of elements already familiar in "microscope" and "meter" or "metric." A bright student may be able to put the parts together and decide that a micrometer is something to measure small objects. A valid criticism of this technique, though, is that the guesses may often be erroneous; the student may decide mistakenly that "micrometer" means a small measurement. The chief value of association with other words seems to be that meanings once learned may more easily be retained because of an awareness of similarities.

Learning from Context. "Whenever you come to an unfamiliar word, look it up in the dictionary." Too many teachers have given this advice, ignoring the fact that learning words via the dictionary is an artificial method. The six-year-old child may have a vocabulary of 20,000 words, even though he has never touched a dictionary; he learned the words by hearing them in context. The dictionary is valuable to verify a guess about a word or to define it when the meaning cannot be obtained from the context. But anyone should attempt first to determine the meaning by noting the surroundings of the word. For example, if a student does not know the meaning of "tractable" in the sentence "The children were more tractable than she had anticipated; in fact, only Joel was at all stubborn," he should follow the contextual clues before referring to the dictionary.

High school students enjoy being "word detectives." The teacher gives them sentences with one or more unfamiliar words and is careful to include clues to their meanings. He lists four or five other words from which a synonym is to be chosen. The following types of clues are suggested in *The English Language Arts in the Secondary School:*

1. The experience clue, which enables the students to draw on their own experience; e.g., their experience with crows enables them to define *raucously* in "A pair of crows called raucously."
2. The comparison or contrast clue, as in the example of *tractable* above.
3. The synonym clue, in which the sentence contains a near-synonym.
4. The summary clue: "He was completely *disheveled*. His hair was mussed, his shirttail was out. . . ."
5. The association clue: "He was out of it in an instant with the *agility* of a pickpocket."
6. The reflection of a mood or situation clue, as with the word *melancholy* in the first sentence of "The Fall of the House of Usher."
7. The previous contact clue: students' knowledge of the Emancipation Proclamation should help them to understand *emancipate.*[1]

Notebooks. A favorite device is to have students record, define, and copy in context the new words that they have learned. One teacher suggests that only one new word be put on a page; below the word the student pastes a picture illustrating or suggested by the word; under the picture he puts a definition and a sentence using the word. "Relaxation," for instance, may have a picture of a cat stretching lazily.[2] The value of the device is in the association of the word with something tangible.

[1] *The English Language Arts in the Secondary School* (New York: Appleton-Century-Crofts, Inc., 1956), p. 170.
[2] Harold T. Eaton, "Timely Teaching Helps," *English Leaflet*, XLV (Dec., 1946), 138.

Word Diaries. Some students may be encouraged to keep for a few weeks a word diary in which they record useful new words they hear or read, together with the context and an original sentence.

Synonyms and Antonyms. Able students enjoy discovering the fine distinctions that exist among near synonyms. "Distant," "far," and "remote," they discover, do not mean exactly the same thing, nor do "decadence," "deterioration," and "degeneration," or "dominant," "domineering," and "dominating." Less able students often fail to see the distinguishing points involved in such words, but even they can profit from discussion of the numerous specific synonyms for such words as "go" and "say." In French schools, teachers spend time in having students find the exact antonym of given words, the theory being that one does not actually know a word unless one also knows its opposite.[3]

Games. Word games are fun and, with junior high school students, may be played as rewards. Some classes have vocabulary bees, comparable to spelling bees. The teacher keeps a list of interesting, useful words encountered in literature or employed only incidentally in class. Students use these words in sentences or define them, as they wish. The teacher or an elected student is the judge, and three students, equipped with dictionaries, may be a court of appeal for dubious meanings. Possible variations of this game are endless.

Units. Short units, closely related to other work in oral or written composition, may stress words. A teacher in a vocational high school taught one unit based on the origin of the last names of his students, another on geographical names, and others on military slang, baseball slang, and Hebrew derivatives. Especially enlightening was a unit called "One Word Led to Another." Starting with the word "kilometer," the vocational students thought of two other words based upon either "kilo" or "meter," then two words based upon each of these two new words, and so on. They thus learned much about root words and families of words.[4]

[3] It is interesting to note that, in learning a word, one first puts it into the class to which it belongs, and later one distinguishes it from other members of the same class. The author once gave the word "erudite" in a multiple-choice test to eighty-seven recent high school graduates. Ten defined it as "rude," five as "rough," eleven as "polite," thirty-one as "well educated," and thirty as "ignorant." The last figure is the significant one, as these thirty students realized that the word referred to knowledge, but did not yet know whether it pertained to much knowledge or little. Even though they gave the opposite of the true meaning, they knew more about the word than did those who defined it as "rude," "rough," or "polite."

[4] Samuel Beckoff, "A Word to the Wise," *English Journal*, XXXIII (Jan., 1944), 23.

Another teacher thus describes his plan for short vocabulary units:

. . . one unit is called "Taking a Word Snapshot of Yourself." This unit utilized the pupil's interest in his own appearance and asked him to check words that described himself, such as the following: "burly," "ruddy," "prim," "prepossessing," "swarthy." The students enjoyed this exercise and at the same time learned words and profitably used the dictionaries. A second unit was a personality scale in which each student rated himself and others. Thus he enjoyed learning personality words, such as "punctual," "tactful," "veracious," "energetic," etc. A third unit asked them to tell stories to illustrate certain abstract words like "irony," "initiative," "philanthropy," etc. Other units with maximum appeal were based on describing scenes, malapropisms, puns, advertising, headlines, picturesque speech, mystery, etc.[5]

Derivations. Many words have fascinating histories. A few examples are "lunatic," "salary," "supercilious," "curfew," "pecuniary," "kindergarten," "familiar," and "boycott." Students enjoy discovering that "lunatic" comes from the Latin word for "moon," and that it was once believed that lunacy arose from being too much in the moonlight. When they know the derivation of "salary," they can see a connection with the expression "He's not worth his salt." Often they can learn words and history at the same time, as with the words "boycott" and "pecuniary." [6]

World Words. The English language has borrowed from dozens of other languages. A teacher stimulated the interest of one sophomore class by placing a large map of the world on the bulletin board. The students tried to find English words taken from the languages of as many countries as possible. The words were typed and fastened to the map in appropriate places. At the end of a month, few of the world's land areas were visible.

Roots and Affixes. Knowledge of the meanings of forty or fifty Latin and Greek roots and affixes will enable some students to add hundreds of words to their vocabularies. More important, it will show them relationships between words and help them to use words with greater accuracy. From the Latin *"audire"* (to hear) come such words as "audibility," "audible," "audience," "audile," "audiometer," "audi-

---

[5] Jay Greene, "Modernizing the Teaching of Vocabulary," *English Journal,* XXXIV (June, 1945), 343.

[6] The G. and C. Merriam Company, Springfield, Massachusetts, supplies free booklets giving interesting word histories. Another useful publication of this company (sent free to English teachers who request it) is *Word Study,* a periodical pamphlet with short articles on words. Random House, Inc., publishers of the *American College Dictionary,* will put you on their mailing list for *Inside the ACD.*

tion," "auditive," "auditor," "auditorium," and "auditory." From the
Greek "*chronos*" (time) are derived such words as "chronic," "chron-
icle," "chronogram," "chronological," "chronologist," "chronology,"
"chronometer," and "synchronize." Other especially useful roots are
listed in The Idea Box (page 395).

Programed Instruction. A number of experimental programs for individual learning are being developed. They make it possible for a
student to concentrate on groups of words least familiar to him. One
of the experimental programs, by Edgar Dale, of Ohio State University,
and Joseph O'Rourke, of Columbus, may serve as an illustration. The
student is given brief information about a root such as *spect*. Then
he faces a number of multiple-choice problems such as "Retro*spect*ion
means a. preparing for the future b. becoming worse c. a survey of past
time." He keeps the answer column covered until he has chosen his
response, which he may then check immediately. Following that, he
faces a number of "frames" devoted to words he missed. The frame
for "retrospection" explains the derivation of the word and requires
the student to write the parts of the word in three different blanks.
Still to be determined is the relative effectiveness of programed instruction and more conventional methods, but the promise of programing
appears excellent.

History of the Language. One of the best ways to build an interest in
words is to refer frequently to details of the captivating history of the
English language. Most people are more interested in life than in
death. Life involves change and development; death is immutable.
The English language is alive and has long been alive. It is still changing. Let the students know that it is alive, that changes in usage are
still occurring, that words are dying, that new words are being born.
One of the services that English teachers can render is to instil in students a wholesome, creative attitude toward language—the kind of
attitude that existed in Elizabethan times.

Information about how words enter the language is interesting. The
routes of entry, plus an example or two of each, are these:

1. Sheer invention (rare): *Kodak*
2. Compounding: *railroad, out-of-date, born*
3. Addition of affixes or combining forms to existing words: *unknown,
   newness, cigarette*
4. Functional shift (use of a word as another part of speech): to *ink*
   a contract
5. Back formation: *editor* → *edit*
6. Extension of meaning: the fifth *power* of a number

7. Figurative language: *lady's slipper, Red* (for Russian)
8. Use of initials (acronyms): *DDT, WAVE*
9. Conversion of proper nouns to common: *sandwich, volt*
10. Onomatopoeia: *fizz, pop, meow*
11. Telescoping: *brunch, electrocute*
12. Borrowing from other languages: *betatron, blitzkrieg* [7]

Study of what may happen to a word after it enters the language also deserves some time. Among a number of changes that may be considered are those in the following list, condensed from the same source as the above group:

1. Shortening: *taximeter cabriolet* became *taxicab* or *taxi* or *cab*.
2. Metathesis: *bird* was once spelled *brid; wasp* was *wæps*.
3. Generalization (broadening of meaning): *cupboard* was originally a board to hold cups.
4. Specialization: although *liquor* may still mean any liquid, it is generally specialized to refer to alcoholic beverages.
5. Elevation: *pastor* was once a shepherd.
6. Degeneration: *knave* (cf. German *Knabe*) once meant a boy; *hussy* was once any housewife.

WORDS AND THOUGHTS

Verbal Confusion

In the case of *Towney* v. *Eisner*, Justice Oliver Wendell Holmes stated, "A word is not a crystal, transparent and unchanging; it is the skin of a living thought, and may vary greatly in color and content according to the circumstances and time in which it is used."

Almost any word could be chosen to illustrate Holmes's statement. "Resolution" one normally thinks of as something praiseworthy, but New Year's *resolutions* one is likely to regard with contempt because they are often broken. "Clever boy!" may express approbation or sarcasm. Soil described as *fertile* in one region might be considered *poor* in another. In "The snail hurries," the meaning of the verb is not exactly the same as in "The rabbit hurries."

Because of such semantic difficulties, scrupulous writers and speakers often pause to define key terms, whereas unscrupulous or careless ones add disorder to confusion by adopting the tactics of Humpty-Dumpty, in *Alice in Wonderland*, whose words meant whatever he chose they should mean. Many arguments are caused not by difference

[7] Condensed from J. N. Hook, *Hook's Guide to Good Writing: Grammar, Style, Usage* (New York: The Ronald Press Co., 1962), pp. 101–2.

of opinion but by difference of definition or by failure to define.
Recently two reasonably well-schooled adults were discussing socialism.
One contended that it is good; the other, that it is bad. As the discussion progressed, it became apparent that one was thinking of socialism
as governmental ownership of utilities and that the other was thinking
of complete governmental control of all production and distribution.
Their discussion got no further than would an argument about the
best way to grow grain, when one person was thinking about oats and
the other about corn.

Some writers and speakers add still more to the confusion by hiding
their thoughts in a fog of words. "Gobbledygook" is the picturesque
name given to this kind of language by former Congressman Maury
Maverick, who said that it sounds like the gobbledy-gobbling of a
turkey cock, which usually ends in a gook. Here is an example from
a field manual for quartermasters, most of whom no doubt rapidly become gray-haired:

> Proper application of prescribed preventative maintenance measures
> must be a prime consideration in order to minimize replacements. Vehicle
> equipment of tactical organizations and that of administrative units and
> reserve pools should be interchangeable wherever possible in order that
> needed replacements for forward areas be cleared by inter-organization
> transfers to meet emergencies in which normal channels of supply would
> introduce delays.[8]

Connotation and Denotation

Words, then, sometimes fail to convey thoughts adequately. Often,
though, words convey more than their dictionary definitions. Professor
Pooley illustrates this fact in his comment on these five sentences:

> 1. I think I'll hit the hay.
> 2. It's time for me to turn in.
> 3. I believe I'll go to bed.
> 4. I think it is time to retire.
> 5. I shall withdraw to seek repose.

. . . Sentence 1. is intentionally slangy, appropriate only to intimate
circumstances when humor is the intent. Sentence 2. is still intimate, but
less slangy; it would pass as appropriate usage in the close family circle.
Sentence 3. is the simplest and most direct of the five forms; it is acceptable
usage in almost any circumstances. Sentence 4. implies less intimate circumstances; the word *retire* is a polite substitute for the blunt "go to bed."
This form would be appropriate to a guest in the home of relative strangers.

[8] Quoted in H. L. Mencken, *The American Language: Supplement I* (New
York: Alfred A. Knopf, Inc., 1945), p. 416.

Sentence 5. is stilted and artificial. The simple act of going to bed makes such elaborate wording slightly ridiculous. Yet there are people with a mistaken idea of elegance who would prefer sentence 5.[9]

In short, from the choice of words in sentences we infer not only a factual meaning but also some of the attendant circumstances and even the mood and character of the speaker.

Because words do carry connotation as well as denotation, they may cause emotional reactions. S. I. Hayakawa tells of two cities that in depression days gave aid to the needy. In one city, words like "relief," "poverty," "shiftlessness," "laziness," and "shame" accompanied the aid. The recipients became sullen, humiliated, and defeated; their children were ridiculed at school. The officials in the other city referred to the past services of those who were temporarily unemployed, spoke of the aid as a kind of insurance dividend, called giving the assistance a "straight business proposition," and referred to bright days ahead. The recipients squared their shoulders and set out energetically to seek work anew.[10]

Lee Deighton quotes from Galbraith's The Affluent Society a passage concerning the frequent substitution of new terms to indicate a period of economic difficulty. In the nineteenth century, "crisis" was first used for this purpose, but its connotations became so unpleasant (partly because of Karl Marx's term "capitalist crisis") that "panic" became the vogue word, perhaps because "panic" suggests short duration. In the 1930's, "depression" was used, but the Great Depression was so distressing that "recession" was its later replacement. In 1953–54 the recession had become a "rolling readjustment." [11]

By changing a single word, one may subtly move someone else to favor or oppose an action or idea. Suppose that a bill is before Congress. If one is neutral toward the bill, he says, "Congress intends to pass the bill." If one favors it, he says, "Congress promises to pass the bill." If one opposes it, he says, "Congress threatens to pass the bill." Likewise, if one favors something new, it is an improvement, but, if he dislikes it, it is an innovation. A judge who is one's friend sometimes receives gifts, but a judge whom one detests takes bribes. A statesman whom one likes is conservative, but a

[9] Robert Pooley, Teaching English Usage (New York: Appleton-Century-Crofts, Inc., 1946), p. 29.

[10] Language in Action (New York: Harcourt, Brace & World, Inc., 1941), Introduction. (This book and its revision, called Language in Thought and Action [1949], are perhaps the most readable on semantics.)

[11] "Developing Vocabulary," English Journal, XLIX (Feb., 1960), 82.

politician whom he dislikes is reactionary. Consciously or unconsciously, one allows the emotional overtones of words to affect his choice; usually unconsciously, listeners are influenced by these emotional overtones.

Two chief points are involved in the foregoing discussion. One is that a person often uses words inaccurately or unskilfully and therefore fails to convey the ideas present in his mind. The other is that one's words, through their connotations, may cause readers or hearers to react emotionally and to deduce from the statements more than the words actually say. In subjective writing (poetry, for instance) one consciously tries to rouse emotion, but in factual writing (such as a news story) one should use uncolored, neutral words. As Professor LaBrant has said, "There is immediate and profound need for teaching the citizens in our schools the power for good or for ill which is in that greatest of man's inventions, language." [12]

Later, her sister, Roberta Green, observed that some progress was apparently being made:

In almost any adult discussion which involves opposing or dissimilar attitudes, we are likely to hear phrases that suggest a groping for clearer means of communication than are customarily used: "Define your terms"; "That's only a generalization"; "It's all a matter of semantics." Although they may do little more for the immediate discussion than indicate confusion, such phrases suggest a growing realization that there are better ways of thinking and talking than the general public or even those in high places use.[13]

Translating Semantic Principles into Practice

Knowledge of semantic principles has increased remarkably since 1930, as more and more teachers have realized the need for teaching not only dictionary meanings but also the emotional implications of words and the fact that speakers and writers can influence people not merely by what they say but also by how they say it. Some teachers have studied such basic books as those by Korzybski, and Ogden and Richards, and simpler ones like Chase's or Hayakawa's.[14]

[12] Lou LaBrant, "Control of Language: A Major Problem in Education," *Bulletin* of the National Association of Secondary-School Principals, XXX (Feb., 1946), 49.

[13] "Teaching How Language Works," *English Journal*, XLVII (Jan., 1958), 25.

[14] C. K. Ogden and I. A. Richards, *The Meaning of Meaning* (New York: Harcourt, Brace & World, Inc., 1938); I. A. Richards, *Practical Criticism* (Harcourt, Brace & World, Inc., 1938); Alfred Korzybski, *Science and Sanity* (3d ed.) (Lakeville, Conn.: Institute of General Semantics, 1948); Stuart Chase, *The Tyranny of Words* (Harcourt, Brace & World, Inc., 1938), and *The Power of Words* (Harcourt, Brace & World, Inc., 1954); S. I. Hayakawa, *Language in Thought and Action* (Harcourt, Brace & World, Inc., 1949).

Others have found in the books by LaBrant and Thomas numerous ideas for teaching about what language does to us.[15]

Any teacher who wants practical, class-tested exercises in semantics will find scores of them in Cleveland Thomas' *Language Power for Youth*. The exercises suggested in the rest of this section are not from that source but are similar to some of the many varieties that Thomas recommends.

Teachers may profitably employ pairs of related sentences in order to make students aware of differences in connotation. For instance,

He is one of the homeless unemployed. (This creates a feeling of pity and possibly a desire to help the poor unfortunate.)
He is a tramp. (The word "tramp" suggests dirt, shiftlessness, and a possible tendency toward criminality.)

He is generous. (Generosity is considered a virtue.)
He is a spendthrift. (We usually do not like people who waste money.)

He is a holder of uncommon views. (This suggests that he is praiseworthy because of his presumably original thinking.)
He is a crackpot. (He holds uncommon views we do not like.)

He sauntered down the lane. (He is a pleasant, carefree chap.)
He sneaked down the lane. (He is a deceitful person, afraid to be seen.)

Study of headlines may also be valuable, especially when two or more newspapers are available for comparison. One paper may head a story DEMOCRATS BLOCK TAX CUT; another, DEMOCRATS SUCCEED IN HOLDING TAX LINE; another, CONGRESS DEFEATS TAX SLASH.

Students should certainly be familiarized with various questionable tactics commonly used to influence a course of action. (1) *Name calling:* using a bad label in order to make us oppose something or someone. "He is incompetent." "He is unprogressive." "He is a radical." "The plan is undemocratic." "He was involved in an underhand political deal." (2) *Glittering generality:* the reverse of name calling. "He fought bravely for his country." "She is a superior cook." "She was a ravishing beauty." "Old Dominion Virginia-cured

---

[15] For example, Lou LaBrant, *We Teach English* (New York: Harcourt, Brace & World, Inc., 1951); and Cleveland A. Thomas, *Language Power for Youth* (New York: Appleton-Century-Crofts, Inc., 1955). A convenient and useful summary of concepts to be taught is to be found in Dr. Thomas' *English Journal* article (XLIX, [March, 1960], 186–91), "Semantic Concepts for Secondary School English."

ham is tops." (3) *Transfer:* connecting a person, idea, action, or thing with something highly regarded. "In the well-run home, Nomar is as necessary as soap and water." "Doctors use Antamine." "Strike for Harry and for England!" "Hollywood indorses Glamour Hour." "The soap that lovely women prefer." (4) *Plain folks:* following the theory that what is "common" is best. Using the plain-folks approach, office seekers sometimes plow corn, have their pictures taken while they are drying dishes, sing hillbilly songs, quote Edgar A. Guest, and repeat the commonplaces that "plain folks" supposedly like to hear. (5) *Band wagon:* urging others to follow the crowd. "More people smoke Dromedary cigarettes than any other brand." "Be sure that your vote is included in the landslide of ballots for Adams." "Most thinking people prefer the *Herald.*"

The chief tests to apply to statements like these are two in number. Is there any evidence to support the statement? If the statement is true, does it matter? For example, consider "Hollywood indorses Purple Night perfume." Perhaps the advertisement names five actresses who have given or sold testimonials of the perfume's efficacy in hypnotizing men. Does that necessarily mean that "Hollywood indorses" the perfume? And even if it does, is Hollywood's indorsement a sufficient reason why Janet should use Purple Night?

Another teaching technique leading to straight thinking and to a correspondingly apt use of words is to make conscious attacks upon generalizations. "All generalizations are false—including this one" is more than an academic wisecrack; it points at the widespread tendency to generalize, to oversimplify. "Popular generalizations ('Women are fickle by nature.' 'All men are beasts.' . . . 'You can't change human nature!') can be broken down, and their degree of validity weighed." [16] Most students will unthinkingly accept such statements simply because they have heard them frequently. It is both provocative and wholesome, therefore, to have the class point out numerous exceptions that show that a generalization has only limited applicability. Once a pattern of attack has been established, students become less and less gullible in accepting statements of "allness." They begin to question whether all cowboys are noble and fun-loving, all gangsters ride in black sedans, all Swedes are big, blond, and stupid, all Jews are avaricious, all Europeans are musical, and so on. They may pursue the attack further to the point of definition. What is a Negro? If a man is one-thirty-second "colored," is he a Negro? In Sinclair Lewis' *Kingsblood Royal,* is Kingsblood, whose great-great-great-grandfather was black, a Negro? Is Kingsblood's

---

[16] Charles I. Glicksberg, "Methodology in Semantics as Applied to English," *School Review,* XLIII (Nov., 1945), 545.

daughter? In the light of recent studies concerning the races of man-kind, is any narrow definition of race permissible? A highly desirable broad-mindedness may grow from such analysis.

A variation of the approach is to analyze proverbs, which are, of course, generalizations. The purpose is not to prove that the proverbs are "wrong" but to show that exceptions do exist and that proverbs sometimes contradict one another. For example, "A stitch in time saves nine" is antithetical to "Don't cross the bridge before you come to it." Some teachers place two familiar proverbs side by side and have students decide whether they are similar in meaning, opposite, or unrelated.

Much of the work involving the study of language as symbols may be done incidentally, when the "felt need" appears. But some should be done directly. The purpose is to make students sharply aware of the nature of the language, its resources, its deficiencies, and the ways in which it can be employed effectively. Glicksberg has phrased it thus: "The primary purpose is to make the student aware of how he thinks, to relate his linguistic behavior to reality, so that he may in time achieve neurological control over his actions." [17]

It is constantly necessary to draw a distinction between objective and subjective writing. A factual explanation of how to change a tire should normally employ uncolored, unfigurative words. So should an objective statement of a candidate's qualifications for a public office. But a poem, play, short story, or personal essay may—indeed, must—be subjective, because it offers an interpretation of a facet of life, not a photograph. Shelley's "To a Skylark" is not a scientific, unbiased description of a bird but a frankly personal state-ment of admiration.

Failure or unwillingness to recognize a difference between the two types of writing leads to a confusion between factual and emotional or persuasive presentations and may reveal itself in such things as editorialized news stories or prosy imaginative writing. When a teacher fails to see the difference, he is likely to praise only vivid writing, even when straightforward prose is more suitable for the purpose. Miss LaBrant recounts this anecdote:

"The artist splashed his colors on the huge canvas," wrote a student. Later she substituted: "The artist was painting a picture, to be hung over our living-room fireplace. The face of my mother, almost life-size, pleased me by its likeness to her." Asked about the "huge canvas," she replied: "I have been taught to make things striking." [18]

[17] *Ibid.*, p. 547.
[18] Lou LaBrant, "The Words They Know," *English Journal*, XXXIII (Nov., 1944), 475.

Vivid writing has its place, but so has quiet presentation of facts. Both teacher and student should keep in mind the purpose of the writing, and choose words accordingly.

In subjective as in objective writing, it is necessary to choose appropriate words. In addition, since subjective writing is often figurative, it is also essential to select fitting figures of speech. Characteristically, a poor or untrained writer uses figures that are either trite, farfetched, or mixed: "The burning sun was hot as fire." "She tripped downstairs like a feather in the breeze." "That snake in the grass is barking up the wrong tree." Once a student combined all of the figurative vices by writing, "The sky was black as pitch, and it was raining pitchforks." It takes a creative mind (not necessarily an "educated" one) to originate an effective simile or metaphor, but even an ordinary mind can borrow someone else's tropes and use them effectively. The test of the quality of a figure of speech is always its appropriateness in the particular situation.

Students frequently have the impression that figures of speech are things that only authors employ, in order to vex and confuse readers. It is helpful to let them see that tropes, especially metaphors, abound and that there is good reason for their existence. When we refer to the arm or leg of a chair, the eyes of a potato, or the hands of a clock, we are speaking metaphorically. "Black looks," "a hangdog expression," "leaden sky," "carefree laughter," "raining cats and dogs"— hundreds of more or less common expressions are figurative. "Wheel" for "bicycle," "Washington says" for "government officials say," and "a volume of Wordsworth" are other examples of tropes in daily use. Slang is composed largely of figurative language.

Why use tropes? Primarily for picturesqueness, for persuasion, and for clarification. "The moon was a glistening white balloon, released by a careless child" is picturesque, but it also portrays clearly the appearance of the moon on a particular night. "He is like Hitler in his lust for power" tends to persuade us to detest the person described. Thoreau's comparison of the shape of Cape Cod to "a bended arm" enables us to visualize the Cape. Students enjoy finding illustrations of the employment of tropes for all three of these purposes. One class, divided into committees, concentrated on metaphorical language in slang, advertising, cartoons and caricatures, songs, editorials, and sports writing. They learned that the use of figurative language is not restricted to long-haired poets.

LEVELS OF USAGE [19]

Good English is appropriate English. At a baseball game, "Hit it over the fence, Joe" is better than "Smite the sphere vigorously, Joseph" simply because it is more appropriate. Yet, in countless classrooms the doctrine of appropriateness is ignored, and a mythical "correctness" is substituted—"correctness" usually meaning a pseudo-literary language.

Largely to blame for this misplacement of emphasis is the idea that levels of usage vary in desirability from literary English at the top to vulgarisms at the bottom. This ladder of levels—to which there are serious objections—looks something like this:

> literary English
> technical English
> formal English
> colloquial English
> localisms
> ungrammatical English
> vulgarisms and illiteracies

Most English teachers are cognizant of the large amount of scholarly writing concerning such levels, and, being near perfectionists, many strive to teach literary English as the goal toward which all should aspire. In the classroom, students are generally acquiescent. If the teacher wants them (horrible thought) to write, "Smite the sphere vigorously, Joseph," that is what they write. But at the ball game, at home, in conversations, in the writing of friendly letters, and in most other circumstances, they revert to their old habits. They are justified in doing so, for only literary writing demands literary language.[20]

---

[19] In writing this section the author has leaned heavily upon Arthur Kennedy's *Engish Usage* (New York: Appleton-Century-Crofts, Inc., 1942); Robert Pooley's *Teaching English Usage* (New York: Appleton-Century-Crofts, Inc., 1946); and especially John S. Kenyon's "Levels of Speech and Colloquial English," *English Journal*, XXXVII (Jan., 1948), 25.

[20] Professor Pooley (*op. cit.*, p. 24) says, "It is obvious that the literary level cannot be made a requirement for all students in schoolroom composition. It is too much the product of mental maturity and highly developed skill to be attainable by the average student, or indeed, by the average teacher. Therefore, while examples of beautiful prose should be given to pupils to study, and the few who are gifted should be encouraged to strive toward the development of a literary tone and style, the great body of school children should be expected to do no more than to cultivate the clear, direct English of communication, together with a feeling for the appropriateness of word and idiom to the purpose intended. Students in whom these perceptions have been engendered will always use 'correct,' adequate English."

Actually, as Professor Kenyon has pointed out, there are only two levels, standard and substandard. Kenyon does not mention slang, which, it would seem, is in a no-man's land between the two levels.

The rebuilt ladder, then, has only three rungs:

> standard English
> slang
> substandard English [21]

Let us start at the bottom in our consideration of the three.

Substandard English

Substandard English is that which is not idiomatic, is not in accord with the grammar and usage of cultivated people, or is limited to a particular geographical area. For instance, "I bought the dog off of Harvey" is unidiomatic. "We was," "this here dog," and "hadn't ought" would be used only jocosely by most people who consider themselves cultivated. "May I carry you to the dance, Lilybelle?" is a localism or provincialism, as is "make a bed down" in contrast to the standard "make a bed."

Substandard English, then, is not appropriate except in reproducing the speech of people who use that level of language. In students' English, it is underbrush that needs to be cleared away to let the trees grow. To the educated ear, it is ugly and often indicative of incompetence. Only a small proportion of the American population would be likely to vote in a presidential election for a man who said, "Us Republicans is agonna clean up this here mess that the Democrats has gotten us in." Most people would feel that, as the candidate's degree of mastery of his native language was so pitifully small, his mastery of the country's economic and political problems would be even smaller.

V. Louise Higgins sums up the matter succinctly for her students like this:

"If you speak this way, you go in the back door; if you speak *this* way, you go in the front door." I make it very clear that I neither built the house nor did I designate the doors. In this case, I am merely an agent showing off the real estate. I have the key to the front door, and once the student

---

[21] J. J. Lamberts suggests a different three levels: Hyperstandard, standard, and substandard. The hyperstandard label would be applied to usages that seem affected or unnecessarily elaborate, for example, "desire" where "want" is sufficient, "ablutions" for "bath," "domicile" for "home," "mortician" for "undertaker." "Another Look at Kenyon's Levels," *College English*, XXIV (Nov., 1962), 141–43.

has the concept of usage levels I have given him the key. The back door is always ajar.[22]

Slang

Slang has long been a controversial topic. In a study reported in 1925, the elimination of slang was listed as one of the chief goals of 193 teachers of English who answered a questionnaire. Since that time, though, the middle-of-the-road attitude of William Lyon Phelps has been widely accepted:

> Our slang's piquant as catsup. I decry it
> Not as a condiment, but as an entire diet.

More to the right of center are the *Oxford English Dictionary* definition and the comment of Greenough and Kittredge:

Slang. Language of a highly colloquial type, considered as below the level of standard educated speech, and consisting either of new words or current words employed in some special sense.

A peculiar kind of vagabond language, always hanging on the outskirts of legitimate speech, but continually straying or forcing its way into the most reputable company.

A slang expression may sometimes add picturesqueness to a sentence. Shakespeare, as is well known, frequently used Elizabethan slang, some of which has since become standard English. There is nothing inherently bad in slang.

Slang may be objectionable, however, on one or more of three counts. One is that it is a transitory language. Little of the slang prevalent in grandfather's day would be comprehensible to grandson. The "bop talk" of the early 1950's followed the "jive talk" of the 1940's into obsolescence. How completely slang or cant disappears is shown by H. L. Mencken, who quotes from the eighteenth century: "to fib the cove's quarron in the rumpad for the lour in his bung" (which means "to beat the fellow in the highway for the money in his purse").[23]

The second objection, sometimes called a virtue by those who like to mystify others, is that some people will fail to understand a slangy sentence. The third is that constant use of slang expressions (or any

[22] "Approaching Usage in the Classroom," *English Journal,* XLIX (March, 1960), 185.
[23] *The American Language: Supplement I* (New York: Alfred A. Knopf, Inc., 1945), p. 158.

others) tends toward mental debilitation on the part of the speaker and toward boredom on the part of the listener. A person who calls everything either "swell" or "lousy" gradually loses whatever power of discrimination he may once have had.

Students of a California teacher, Dennis R. Dean, compiled a dictionary of teen-age slang and reached two sorts of conclusions. First, they and their teacher decided, slang can be interesting and colorful, slang words are unusually difficult to define, and slang is the language of an in-group. Second, slang should not be used

> —whenever any written record is meant to endure;
> —whenever exact definition is necessary;
> —whenever communication is with an adult, person in authority, or non-member of the group;
> —whenever one wishes to use language that will command respect.[24]

It is both impracticable and undesirable to attempt to eliminate slang. It is desirable, however, to talk with students, as Mr. Dean did, about both the good and the bad aspects of slang—its piquancy and its weaknesses. The couplet by Professor Phelps quoted earlier in this section may well be a teacher's theme song in dealing with the problem of slang.

Standard English

The highest level of English is the standard. Included in standard English are literary, technical, formal, and colloquial language. No one of these is always "better" than another. Each may be "better" in some circumstances. What must be understood is that colloquial English is as good as literary, technical, and formal, and that there are many more occasions for employing colloquial English than for employing the other three.

Literary English is that used in subjective writing for the primary purpose of conveying emotional reactions. Thus Tennyson used literary English in most of his poetry because he wanted his readers to share his feelings; William Thackeray in his novels and E. V. Lucas in his essays used it for the same reason. Technical English is that which is appropriate in scientific, unemotional writing, for example, in a treatise on the swordfish family or in a monograph on the preterit in Old Norse. Formal English is that used when one's subject is serious but not technical and when one is addressing groups composed mainly of people who are strangers and who will probably

---

[24] "Slang Is Language Too!" *English Journal*, LI (May, 1962), 324.

remain strangers. Colloquial English is that used in discussing any subject with people whom one knows or expects to know fairly well.

All of these varieties of standard English, then, are useful. One is not superior to another, except in a given set of circumstances. The teacher should clarify the distinctions and should help the students to use the kind of standard English most appropriate to the time and place.

In creative writing of the highly subjective type, the writings of a few students may possess a literary tone. The reference paper or papers written usually in the senior year may be somewhat technical. Contest writing, much newspaper writing, business letters, and public addresses and debates usually demand rather formal language. But, most of the time, colloquial English is particularly appropriate— in friendly letters, in conversations and class discussions, on the athletic field and in the shop, and with the family, the teacher, and one's other friends.

Colloquial English is the natural English to use in a friendly, familiar environment. It differs only slightly from the formal; it makes use of contractions, nicknames, and a few words and grammatical constructions that would not appear in formal English. Thus "I'm," "Johnny," "squelch," and "Who did he select?" are colloquial, whereas "I am," "John," "subdue," and "Whom did he select?" are formal. John S. Kenyon stresses the fact that most words may be used either colloquially or formally and adds,

> Consequently, it is impossible to draw a strict dividing line between the colloquial and the literary or formal vocabulary—between colloquial diction and formal diction; the boundary consists rather of a very wide belt of words. The colloquial or formal character often depends as much on occasion and circumstances apart from the language as on the words themselves. Many whole sentences may be either colloquial or formal according to context and circumstances. . . . Sometimes only a slight sprinkling of words gives to a passage either its colloquial or its formal coloring.[25]

What brand of standard English should be taught in the classroom? "Unstiff formal" may be the best answer. V. Louise Higgins, in the article previously mentioned, makes the point by a useful discrimination between private and public language:

> The hallmarks of private utterance are that it is definitely limited and that the emphasis is on content, not form. It is language in most prag-

[25] John S. Kenyon, "Levels of Speech and Colloquial English," *English Journal*, XXXVII (Jan., 1948), 25.

matic form and we all use it with our families, our friends, in our note to the milkman. Public communication differs in that it is meant for a wider audience and that both form and content are considered. In our classrooms, we are dealing primarily with usage as it pertains to public utterances.

The "unstiff formal" usage is suitable for most of the public utterances likely ever to be required of your students. The few of them who become lawyers, scientists, writers, or the like will need later to make special adaptations of their language, but the "unstiff formal" provides an easy point of departure.

WORDS, WORDS, MERE WORDS

One of the masters of words, William Shakespeare, made some of the wisest remarks concerning these tools of mankind. Hamlet, buried in his grief, read only "words, words, words," because his troubles were much more intense than printed syllables. Claudius knew that unmeant, unfelt words are empty, that his prayers were vain because they were not sincere: "Words without thoughts never to heaven go." Troilus found in Cressida's letter "words, words, mere words, no matter from the heart." And Holofernes pointed at a general vice when he said, "He draweth out the thread of his verbosity finer than the staple of his argument."

Words, however pretty, however sonorous, can be no stronger than the thoughts behind them. We who teach words must always remember that fact, if we are not to divorce words from action. The Bible says, "A word spoken in due season, how good is it!" But it also asks, "Who is this that darkeneth counsel by words without knowledge?"

THE IDEA BOX

ACTIVITIES FOR WORD POWER

These are listed by Verna Hoyman among forty-five activities, as part of a long article on the teaching of vocabulary (*Illinois English Bulletin,* Nov., 1961): (1) Finding color words that give clues to a mood; (2) finding substitutes for overworked words; (3) finding words based on Greek myths, for example, "chaotic" (Chaos), "odyssey" (Odysseus), "vulcanize" (Vulcan); (4) finding in a magazine examples of trite subject matter, hackneyed words, poor diction; (5) pointing out words that are the expression of opinion in news stories; (6) writing a definition of an abstraction and developing it with a paragraph of concrete illustration; (7) appreciating the vivid language of the sports announcer; (8) choosing ten words that aptly describe the movements of animals; (9) writing an article, slanting it favorably, then rewriting, slanting it unfavorably.

MANIPULATING NEW WORDS

For a word to become an active part of a student's vocabulary, it must be used. Among useful manipulative activities: (1) give the antonym of the word; (2) ask a question using the word (e.g., "Is it *inevitable* that the Yankees will win the pennant this year?"); (3) compare the meanings of words (e.g., "Is a person who is *vigilant* ever *cowardly*?"); (4) supply another form of the word (e.g., "imply," "implication"); (5) name contexts suitable for the use of the word (e.g., "marauders" could be used for pillaging soldiers, for pirates swooping down on a coastal village, for some of the Danish invaders of medieval England).

THE EVIL OF OVERWRITING

A study of admittedly great non-fiction such as the best of Winston Churchill or of Rachel Carson may help both a teacher and his students to realize that the best prose is not flashy, not decorated with gingerbread, not cryptic, not flowery, and never—never—wordy.

THE EXACT WORD

1. Say to someone in the class, "Your name is Wilbur, isn't it?" "No, it's Ralph." Turn to the class. "Is it right for me to call Ralph Wilbur? No? Then it isn't right to call a _____ a _____, is it?"

2. Tell students of trouble sometimes caused by failure to choose the right word, for example, the ambiguous sign "Fine for fishing." (Dilla Tucker, Nampa, Idaho.)

3. Remind students that noted authors have often had to struggle to find the precise word; for example, Elizabeth Browning used to put pyramids of words in the margin while she wrote, and then would select the most appropriate one. Conrad and Flaubert sometimes sought the right word for hours. Mark Twain said that the difference between the right word and the almost right one is as great as the difference between lightning and the lightning bug.

4. Write a paragraph with numbered blanks replacing certain words. Below, write the numbers, with four or five suggested words for each. Students are to pick the word that best fits the context.

5. For a discussion of how students may be taught to differentiate among such words as "chagrin," "embarrassment," and "mortification," or "sedate," "staid," and "stuffy," see Jenny Cohler's "Say What You Mean," *English Journal*, XLIII (Feb., 1954), 84.

6. Discuss with able students the shades of difference in words generally considered synonyms, such as "wages," "salary," "fee," "stipend," "remuneration," "emolument," "honorarium," "dole." It is wise to have Webster's *Dictionary of Synonyms* available to check questionable distinctions.

7. Try a "Find a Better Word" exercise. Sentences illustrating misconceptions of words may be accumulated for the exercise, especially from students' themes, for example, "We should *mimic* noble men and women." "He *administers* a large restaurant."

TWENTY QUESTIONS

As an interest-rousing exercise, Isabelle Swatts's seniors in East Chicago, Indiana, play Twenty Questions to find the meaning of a word. A student acts as moderator. Too time-consuming for frequent use but a good motivator.

RELATED WORDS

Mabel Lindner, in Latrobe, Pennsylvania, has her classes study groups of words related to menus, to medicine, to plays and ballets that the class sees, etc. Frederic Baxter's West Bend, Wisconsin, students improve their vocabularies through newspaper study, finding that words in headlines are often defined in the news stories and that even the comics and the advertisements may lead them to new words or new meanings. Edgar Logan's sports-minded Detroit students are interested in colorful words related to boxing and other sports and are encouraged to use these "physical" words in their writing, thus getting away from colorless abstractions.

SOPHOMORES VS. "SAID"

Martha Pence's sophomores in Kittanning, Pennsylvania, found in their reading 567 substitutes for "said." Perhaps their reading benefited as much as their vocabularies.

GENERAL TO SPECIFIC

"Take a paragraph from a good writer and replace the specific words with general ones. Then let the students use colorful, vivid words to see how near they approach the writer's vocabulary." (Eva Frost, Roosevelt High School, Chicago.)

ENCOURAGING USE OF THE DICTIONARY

"I stimulate use of the dictionary by frequently using it myself, in class." (Elizabeth Barton, Clanton, Alabama.)

"LEVELS OF ENGLISH" PROGRAM

The roles of Formal English, Ordinary English, Slang, and Poor Usage may be played by students. They sing appropriate songs, and read appropriate compositions.

CLICHÉS

Read to your classes one or two of Frank Sullivan's often reprinted "cliché expert" articles, which appeared originally in the *Atlantic Monthly*. Some are reprinted in *A Pearl in Every Oyster* (Boston: Little, Brown & Co., 1938).

METAPHORS

1. Have students construct metaphors to describe things named by the teacher, for example, clouds passing over the moon. John Gray, "A Study of Metaphor," *English Leaflet*, XLVI (April, 1947), 53.
2. Have students match things that have something in common (*Ibid.*), for example,

(1) sand dunes	(a) happy laughter
(2) fog	(b) jet propulsion
(3) a calm pond	(c) roller coaster
(4) a sneeze	(d) a gray cat
(5) Benny Goodman's "I Got Rhythm"	(e) a freshly ironed handkerchief

3. Talk about the difference between a "*black* cat" (literal) and a "*black* look" (figurative). Other examples: "warm hands," "warm heart"; "roaring lion," "roaring fire"; "break my leg," "break my heart" (or "my word"). Have students use words like these both literally and figuratively: "sea," "root," "anchor," "hound," "crown," "tower," "mountain," "river."
4. Talk about favorable and unfavorable metaphors applied to people; for example, a girl may be a peach, a lemon, the apple of someone's eye. A man may be a fox, a pig, a snake in the grass, a mule, a sheep, a lion in battle, a jackal, or a sly or gay dog.

MRS. CLAY'S FRECKLES

"Mrs. Clay had freckles, and a projecting tooth," Jane Austen wrote. In eight words (or two brush strokes) she painted a portrait. Let your students try their hands at two-stroke portraiture.

A FEW WORDS WITH INTERESTING HISTORIES

abundance, accost, aftermath, aggravate, agony, ambition, assassin, astonish, ballot, bonfire, candidate, capital, congregation, curfew, deliberate, easel, enthrall, extravagant, fool, garret, halcyon, inaugurate, intoxicate, journey, milliner, panic, pedigree, prevaricate, remorse, tantalize, taxicab.

WORD ORIGINS

In a study of word origins, try giving students a short list of English words of Germanic origin for which they are to find English synonyms derived from Greek or Latin, and another list reversing the procedure. Among many possible pairs: "tongue," "language"; "friend," "companion"; "heavenly," "celestial"; "red," "vermilion"; "forgiveness," "pardon."

USEFUL ROOT WORDS

Besides knowing the meanings of the most common affixes, students will find it helpful to know the meanings of these roots: *aqua, audio, bene, corpus, credo, dominus, ego, facio, frater, jungo, locus, loquor, mater, mitto, multus, omnis, pater, pes, primus, pugno, scribo, socius, solus, totus, utilis, verto, video; aer, arche, autos, bios, chronos, cratos, grapho, homos, hydro, logos, metron, micro, orthos, pan, pathos, penta, philos, phone, polis, poly, pseudos, psyche, sophos, tele, theos.*

PREFIXES, SUFFIXES, AND ROOTS

1. Plan an exercise on this pattern:

benignant, well disposed   - - - *ignant*
homogeneous, of the same kind   - - - - - - *geneous*

Students are to supply beginnings to form antonyms of the words at the left.

2. Another exercise:

Word	Prefix	Root or Stem	Suffix	Meaning of Word
amorphous	*a,* without	*morph,* form	*ous,* having	having no form, shapeless
implacable	*im,* not	*placare,* to quiet, to appease	*able,* capable of	not capable of being appeased

Choose words whose meanings are made rather clear by their component parts. In the first exercise of this sort, leave the last column blank for students to fill in. In later exercises, leave the last four columns blank.

3. James I. Brown, University of Minnesota, talks about the numerous technical terms that students encounter. He then gives a twenty-item vocabulary test, students putting their answers under I:

			I	II
1. aberrance	1. deviation	2. entrance	1. _____	_____
	3. comprehension	4. precision		
20. endocarp	1. thick layer	2. inner layer	20. _____	_____
	3. outer layer	4. middle layer		

Then he hands out a list that gives only the meanings of the prefixes or initial combining forms, for example, *ab-,* from; *endo-,* within. The students take the test again, putting their answers in Column II. Since he has found that college upperclassmen average 66 on the first test and 92 on the second, his procedure dramatizes the importance of knowing the meanings of common prefixes and combining forms. ("Vocabulary Development," *Exercise Exchange,* April, 1962, 12–13.)

BOOKS YOUR CLASSES WILL LIKE

The Tree of Language, by Helene and Charlton Laird (Cleveland: World Publishing Co., 1957), is a delightful and yet scholarly book from which high school students can learn the story of their language, the reasons for its oddities, and the stories behind about 100 common words. *Words: Tricks and Traditions,* by M. Newton Friend (New York: Charles Scribner's Sons, 1957), is full of word games, puzzles, limericks, boners, palindromes, and the like.

VOCABULARY BUILDING THROUGH WORD ANALYSIS

Laura Dunklin describes a detailed plan including such exercises as this:

New word—"derision"
Sentence in which it appears: "This sports writer thinks the players deserved the derision of the crowd."

Analysis: *de*—down *ris*—laugh *ion*—act of
Original sentence: Martha, discouraged by her classmates' derision, gave up trying to learn to swim.
Synonyms: ridicule, scorn, contempt

"Developing Word Mastery," *High School Journal,* XXX (Jan., 1956), 233.

"CLEVER" DEFINITIONS

Occasionally let students try to make clever definitions like these: *Abuse:* "The refined substitute for fists when confronted by an argument which cannot be refuted." (George Dorsey) *Art:* "Usually what the most influential critics approve." (Charles Poore) *Elegance:* "A quality appropriate to the young man who presides at the button counter." (Elbert Hubbard) One class came up with these: *Home:* "Last resort." *Homework:* "Something to put off until you get done what you'd rather." *School bus:* "The only vehicle in which one can get run over while inside." *Pizza:* "A round dish, often used as a substitute for food." Carolyn K. Tuttle, "A Little Lexicography Is *Not* a Dangerous Thing," *English Journal,* LI (Dec., 1962), 648.

CHARGED WORDS

Have students clip attractive advertisements and note the reason for their appeal. They should observe especially the copywriter's use of words that appeal to emotion.

STYLISTIC PARODIES

Able students may sharpen their observation of style by attempting to imitate the sentence structure, typical word choice, and point of view of various authors. Let them try, for example, to write such a story as "Little Red Riding Hood" in the styles of Hemingway, Faulkner, Dickens, Addison.

SHOW; DON'T TELL

Provide a number of sentences that simply tell something, for example, "Rollie made a fine catch in deep center field." Ask students to rewrite them, showing what happened, for example, "At the crack of the bat, Rollie turned his back to the infield and raced toward the center field wall. As he reached it, he spun around and sprang high into the air. The ball struck the fingers of his glove and plopped into his bare hand as he fell to the ground."

THE IMPORTANCE OF CONTEXT

1. To dramatize for students the need for considering the meanings of words in context, have them compose sentences in which the context requires a specialized meaning, for example, "A goose is one bird from which you can get *down.*" Other words to suggest to the students who stare uncomprehendingly: "runner," "fly," "well," "corn," "boxer," "ring," "diamond," "gridiron," "flat," "light," "type," "base."

2. Discuss the prime meaning of certain words to various persons, for example, "pipe" to piper, plumber, organist, oil worker, Dad; "court" to a king, judge, tennis player, suitor; "log" to mathematician, sailor, woodsman.

PREDESCRIPTION

Two lessons precede Eric W. Johnson's assignment of a one-page description. One involves replacing certain words with "more interesting" and accurate words, for example, "The *nice* girl *went* into the *unpleasant* cellar." The other requires completion of comparisons or implied comparisons: "Their team came onto the field like _____" and "The strikers _____ into the stadium." Mr. Johnson helps students to see that *oozed* in the last blank implies a comparison, but that *went slowly* does not. "Stimulating and Improving Writing in the Junior High School," *English Journal*, XLVII (Feb., 1958), 68. (Read the whole article for excellent suggestions about teaching writing.)

WHAT IS EFFECTIVE ENGLISH?

According to Louis Zahner, "English is most likely to be effective if it is appropriate in at least five directions: to the purpose; to the subject; to the occasion; to the receiver; and to the speaker or writer." (E. J. Gordon and E. S. Noyes, eds., *Essays on the Teaching of English* [New York: Appleton-Century-Crofts, Inc., 1960], p. 14.) Test Zahner's statement with a class by taking a sentence such as "Football is an athletic contest requiring strength, skill, stamina, speed, and mental and physical alertness." Is that sentence effective if the supposed speaker or receiver is a small child? an uneducated elderly person? a person opposed to football? May it be effective if the occasion is a party? a speech contest? a literary discussion? an exciting moment in a game? May it be effective if the subject of conversation has nothing to do with athletics? Is it effective as a defense of football? as part of a poem extolling athletics?

SLANG

Classes enjoy analyzing current slang to find the implied comparisons that are almost always present.

ARCHAIC TO MODERN

Copy some sentences with archaic words (from Shakespeare, Spenser, the Bible, etc.) and have students substitute appropriate modern words.

WORD AUTOBIOGRAPHIES

Students may write autobiographies of words. As a variation, the class may guess the word described in the autobiography.

A JOURNALIST'S ADVICE

Sally Winfrey got good results from her Englewood, New Jersey, students by urging these rules of a journalist: (1) Make your sentences short. (2) Use the right word, especially the verb, to picture what you are telling. (3) Avoid weak words. If your sentences begin with strong words, you will save your reader time. (4) Avoid trite expressions as you would a puff adder.

THE RIVER OF ENGLISH

To clarify for students the historical development of the English language, picture it on the chalkboard as a river, with tributaries from many lands. For details, see J. N. Hook, "Footnote to 'A World of Words,'" *English Journal*, XLII (Sept., 1953), 334.

"WHAT LANGUAGE SHALL WE TEACH?"

Be sure to read this eminently sensible article by A. J. Walker of Georgia Tech. Professor Walker treads a happy path between the extremists who do not object to "I ain't got nothing" and those who deplore the language of everybody except themselves and Dr. Johnson. *English Journal*, Nov., 1953, p. 431.

THE FEAR OF RIDICULE

Sometimes students object to using the language that they learn is "correct." They say, "I'd get made fun of if I talked like that anywhere besides school." It is perhaps best to let such students know that you understand their dilemma, but to add that you are not urging them to use stilted, unnatural language; you are trying only to help them to learn to speak and write clearly and effectively. Tell them that, if they do not feel that they should use certain expressions in their homes and neighborhoods, they of course do not need to do so; but the knowledge is still worth having, because there will be times when they will be in different surroundings and will be writing or speaking to persons who will expect standard English.

COPING WITH GROSSLY SUBSTANDARD USAGE

Faced with many Detroit students who suffered from grossly impoverished cultural backgrounds and whose speech was much below standard, Ruth Golden conducted experiments and devised numerous exercises stressing practical applications. These are described in her *Improving Patterns of Language Usage* (Detroit: Wayne State University Press, 1960), available from the NCTE.

REDUCING WORDINESS

Laurence Perrine, Southern Methodist University, suggests "padding" a well-written paragraph by inserting in it "a number of favorite student devices for wordiness." Students are asked to squeeze out the excess words. They may then compare their new version with the original well-written paragraph. "A Class Exercise in Paragraph Revision," (*Exercise Exchange*, April, 1962, pp. 6–7.)

MOTIVATING VOCABULARY BUILDING

Remind your students that civil service tests and promotion tests used by some big industries often stress vocabulary, as do most college entrance examinations.

TRUE-FALSE

Prepare some true-false statements. Students are to correct each false statement and tell why the correction was made. For example, "Levitation" results when something is funny.

COMPLETION

Have students fill in a word that agrees with the thought expressed. For example, "The selection was played by a (group of five musicians)."

VOCABULARY GAME FOR JUNIOR HIGH SCHOOL

Give a word such as, "atrophy." Students try to think of all possible words of a certain type beginning with each of the letters in that word. For example, they may think of verbs of action or abstract nouns, or names of plants, etc.

ADDING TO SUFFIXES OR PREFIXES

Give a suffix or prefix and definitions of several words in which that affix is used, for example, suffix *-ment*: "a tomb" (monument), "an assertion" (statement), "a verbal disagreement" (argument). For a discussion of how one class studied prefixes and suffixes, see Helen F. Olson's "Affixes and Twelfth-Grade Vocabulary Building," *English Journal*, XLIII (Jan., 1953), 38.

SYNONYMS IN BLANKS

Give a definition and the first and last letters of a synonym, for example, "unfriendly: h __ __ __ __ __ e."

WORD CHALLENGE

Students bring to class words they have found in their reading, and challenge classmates to define or use them correctly. (Bar archaic, technical, and foreign words.)

WORD GRADATIONS

Have students supply word gradations, for example, "Freezing, _____, _____, boiling." "Amoeba, _____, _____, _____, man." "Sad, _____, _____, _____, happy."

Semanticists use similar ladders to show degrees of abstractness, for example, Hayakawa's "Bessie, Cow, _____, _____, _____, Wealth." They further show that the Bessie one person sees is not the same as the Bessie another sees.

SEMANTIC EXERCISES

1. Have students rearrange items in a list, from most general to most specific, for example, animal, cat, organism, tiger; fiction, "The Gold Bug," prose, short story. As an oral exercise, give a general word such as "vegetation"; a student makes it more specific ("plant"); others make it still more specific ("flower," "lily," "Easter lily," "the Easter lily in Carter's window").

2. Have students make referents of abstract words clear by writing an original one-sentence definition followed by a one-sentence example, for instance, "*Freedom* is the privilege of doing as one pleases, providing that one does not interfere with the privileges of others. I am free to drive down the highway but not down the middle of it."

3. Have students develop paragraphs of comparison and contrast, to show the similarities and differences in two words, for example, "famous," "notorious"; "prudence," "timidity"; "boldness," "bravery."

4. Discuss connotations of groups of words, for example, "acquaintance," "chum," "companion," "friend," "pal"; "antagonist," "enemy," "foe," "opponent," "rival"; "aroma," "fragrance," "odor," "scent," "smell," "stench."

5. Discuss whether such words as "horse," "steed," "nag"; "liberal," "left-winger"; "farmer," "agriculturist," "hick"; and "wise," "smart," "crafty" are neutral, favorable, or unfavorable in connotation. Have students compose pairs of sentences with the same basic meaning but different connotations, for example, "She gave us dinky little sandwiches." "She served delectable tea sandwiches."

6. Have students write paragraphs in which they explain the connotations that given words have for them, for example, "television," "Saturday," "football," "courtroom," "crash," "mathematics," "April." Or ask for both the denotations and the connotations of words: "pig," "date," "average," "childish," "antique," "tenement."

7. Use semanticists' subscripts (e.g., democracy$_{USA}$, democracy$_{USSR}$, automobiles$_{1935}$, automobiles$_{1956}$). Ask students to point out common elements (if any) in the things being discussed, and also the differences. Relate the discussion to the dangers inherent in such words as "all," "never," "everybody," "nobody," "always."

8. Let bright students try their hand at Bertrand Russell's game of formulating triads like these: I am slender; you are thin; she is skinny. I am firm; you are obstinate; he is a pig-headed fool.

9. Teachers at a Rhode Island College summer session suggested this team game for connotations: Students from each team take turns at the board. The teacher pronounces a word (e.g., "proud") and then says either "Positive" or "Negative." For "Positive," the students try to think of a word with favorable connotations, like "self-confident"; for "Negative," a word like "haughty." Other words for the teacher: "good," "rude," "radical," "rural," "bold," "dull-witted," "selfish," "horse."

10. Think of a specific house or piece of real estate. Write an advertisement intended to interest a possible buyer. Then write what an unscrupulous real estate dealer might tell a prospective purchaser if the dealer thought he could persuade him to buy a different, more expensive property.

NOTE TAKING

The South Molton School, Devon, England, early in the course stresses economy in words achieved through writing of telegrams, postcards, advertisements, headlines, and summaries of paragraphs. Later, its students practice taking notes that will capture the gist of an article. "There is nothing like note-making for dispelling foggy writing and foggy thinking," says A. Elliott-Cameron, *Times Educational Supplement,* December, 1958.

13

LISTENING CREATIVELY

When Daniel Boone strode along the faintly marked trails in the Kentucky woods, usually the only sounds he heard were the chirps of the birds and the rustle of leaves as a startled chipmunk scurried to safety. If Daniel or his contemporaries went into town, even there the sounds were subdued—the faint clop clop of horses on the dirt street, a few voices, perhaps a church bell.

But now sound engulfs us. Automobiles and trucks roar along a maze of streets and highways; airplanes drone overhead; voices are more numerous because people live closer together; television blares in every living room; and even deep in the forest we may meet a youth with a transistor radio.

Daniel Boone probably welcomed sounds. We have learned to shut them out, to ignore them, to insulate ourselves against them. Insulation is a protective device useful in its way. It is often an aid to concentration. Besides, if we were exquisitely conscious of every sound, we might, to parody Alexander Pope, die of a song in auscultative pain. But the trouble with insulation is that it shuts out both what is worthless and what is worth hearing.

In our sound-filled world we need a strainer over our ears, a strainer that will automatically exclude the sounds of no significance to us but allow the others to filter through to a responsive brain. In other words, we need to listen intelligently.

IN THE CLASSROOM

Listening Is Not Just Hearing

We listen approximately three times as much as we read, five times as much as we write, and one and one-half times as much as we speak.

Yet, until fairly recently, presumably because of the mistaken belief that effective listening is an innate skill, schools paid almost no attention to this important member of the communications family. In the 1950's, though, about 100 master's and doctor's theses were devoted to the nature of listening or to techniques for teaching it, and more and more elementary and secondary schools planned units in which instruction in listening was included.

Hearing and listening, we are increasingly aware, are not identical. Listening requires conscious effort, and it results in some kind of activity. One *hears* the sound of passing cars, and it leaves no impression; but one *listens* to find the source of a squeak in one's own car, and then one tries to do something about it. A fond mother *hears* the babble of children's voices, but she *listens* to her own child's voice and reacts appropriately.

Listening Creatively

It is this "appropriate reaction" that makes listening creative. In effect, we make a new decision each time we listen. We listen to a commercial for Breathless mouthwash and decide to buy or not to buy it. We listen to an appeal to vote for Joe rather than for Moe, and we perhaps find reinforced our decision to cast a ballot for Moe.

What we listen to we must evaluate and use. From those who address us we may learn how to look at the world about us, learn the unchanging verities, formulate a philosophy, and discover how to accomplish things, and why and when.

If for no other reason, creative listening is important in a democracy because it can help us to think straight about the issues that a democratic nation continuously faces. Essential to democracy is intelligent choice. There is no royal road to utopia—there may be no utopia—but we have to weigh the merits of each trail through the swamps and choose the least undesirable one. We have to distinguish between the weighed words of the scientific pleader and the weighted words of the spellbinder. Constantly we are faced with the necessity of evaluating and choosing—between two or more candidates, isms, methods, or proposed solutions.

The Objective of Classroom Listening

School is both a part of life and a preparation for later life. Since this is true, each classroom activity should have meaning and value for both the present and the future. Creative listening meets this demand, since for the student it does at least the following things: It

1. Adds information
2. Increases interests
3. Creates wholesome attitudes
4. Improves skills and techniques
5. Improves social behavior
6. Aids appreciation
7. Aids creative expression
8. Improves discrimination and critical thinking

The objective of classroom listening, then, is to build listening ability and habits to a point where maximum progress toward each of these outcomes may be made.

Techniques for Improving Listening

So much for theory. Now for some practical suggestions concerning ways in which students may be made into creative listeners.

Discussion of Listening. Students are usually amenable to reason, especially when they supply the reason. Therefore a class discussion on the why and how of listening may be valuable. It is hoped that the class will stress courtesy ("listen unto others as you would have them listen unto you"), purposefulness, accuracy, and responsiveness. Young classes may need to talk about physical requirements for listening, such as having desks clear, showing interest by posture and facial expression, and being patient when a speaker has difficulty. Discussions may be followed by having a volunteer committee construct a poster naming and illustrating the qualities of a good listener; this poster may be left for some time in a conspicuous spot as a reminder. If a student is adept at cartoons or caricatures, he may use his ability in order to laugh out of existence some of the faulty listening habits.

Suggestions on What To Listen for. Before playing a record in a music-appreciation course, the teacher generally suggests that the students listen for something in particular—the function of a certain instrument, the repetition of a theme, etc. This technique may be borrowed by the English teacher when he knows fairly well what to expect in an oral presentation. Once, for instance, when several freshmen were explaining how to make things, the teacher simply asked the class members to try to follow each explanation and be ready to ask questions if there was something they did not understand. When a junior was talking about the life of Walt Whitman, the teacher asked the class to listen for what they thought was the most interesting episode in the poet's life. It is surprising how much a very little guidance will increase the intensity of listening; surprisingly also, the understanding of the entire presentation seems to be increased when the students are supposedly concentrating on one item.

A variation of the plan, with the advantage of teaching the students some of the fundamentals of note taking, is for the teacher to read something interesting related to the material being studied. The students are asked to take notes on certain points mentioned in advance by the teacher.

Still another variation, suggested in *The English Language Arts in the Secondary School*, is to divide the class into groups, each listening for a different point:

Group 1 may be asked to listen for new ideas; *Group 2*, for familiar ideas aptly expressed; *Group 3*, for the speaker's plan of organization; *Group 4*, for effective ways used by the speaker to hold or to reclaim attention; *Group 5*, for quotable phrases or sentences; *Group 6*, for unsupported generalizations; *Group 7*, for clues to questions to be raised in the discussion period.

After the talk, each listening group is allowed five minutes to share within the group whatever was heard. One member is chosen by the five as their spokesman in the general discussion. What each representative brings out will help the entire class to see what can be done in purposeful listening. Discussion under the guidance of the teacher will also reveal how listeners can focus their attention and how they can school themselves to remember what they decide they want to recall.[1]

Note Taking. Although taking notes may be useful for all students, those who are planning to go to college will find it especially so, because they will almost certainly be subjected to lectures in college.

The teacher may help here by suggesting that the class try to write down not everything that is said but only the most important points, together with a pertinent example or illustration here and there. One teacher demonstrated the process by taking notes on an assembly address while her students made their own notes. She mimeographed hers, and the students compared what they and she had written down.

Quizzes. It is certainly a mistake to allow students to assume that they will be held responsible only for the material in the textbook. If class periods have any value, much of what is said in class is worth remembering. Examinations, therefore, may cover content presented in class in addition to that in the textbook.

Following Instructions. Any teacher can cite instances of students' failure to follow oral instructions. Probably any foreman could supply

[1] P. 262.

more illustrations. The school provides a worthwhile service if it offers much practice in following instructions.

Most such practice will come automatically from school activities. One teacher, though, dismayed by the fact that his students habitually did things the wrong way, held a discussion on the importance of following instructions. Then he gave oral instructions on a number of useful topics—how to open a new book, how to check a book out of the library, how to take notes on a 3- × 5-inch card, etc. He encouraged creative listening by having his students try to answer the question "Why?" after each step; for example, "Why is the page number of the reference included in the notes?" After completing each set of instructions, he had the students do what he had just explained. At a later class meeting he had each student give instructions for accomplishing some task that could be done quickly in the classroom, and other students carried out the instructions.

Understanding Organization. Let us assume that you have been unable to attend a lecture and that you want to find out what the speaker had to say. If you ask an acquaintance to tell you about it, the chances are perhaps even that he will say "It was good," "It was dull," "He speaks well," or "He talked about ——," but will be unable to summarize the lecture for you. Why? Because listeners are often unaware of the organization of a talk, and, having no mental outline to follow, they are unable to reconstruct it. They may have listened to every word, but if they have not understood the organization they will be able only to generalize or to refer to a point here and there.

Of double value to your students is listening to a speech or report in an attempt to understand its organization. The first value is that they can learn to give intelligent summaries of what they hear; the second, that they become increasingly conscious of the need for organization in order to assure clarity in their own speaking and writing. A procedure that may be employed is to review the possible methods of organization and to discuss ways of identifying the chief supporting points. A few comments on the use of transitions are apropos here. Then the students listen to the next assembly speaker, or to presentations by their classmates, and make analyses. Students who have been taught to listen for the organization of a talk tend to comprehend it rather well; they also tend to be highly critical of any rambling discourse.

Listening for Details and for Language Signals. In *Using Mass Media in Teaching English* (Albany, 1960) the New York State Bureau of Secondary Curriculum Development suggests using newspaper stories for two purposes. The first is to help students listen for details. A newspaper story, perhaps about a ball game or some other topic of great current interest, is read to the class. Specific questions, prepared either by the teacher or by students, are then to be answered, for example, "How many spectators were in the stadium?" The second purpose is to make students more aware of transitions, or language signals. After a discussion of such signals, the teacher reads from a newspaper the text of part of a speech. The class is responsible for noting such signals as those that anticipate new points ("next," "then," "finally," "another," etc.) and those that show other relationships ("however," "for this reason," etc.). Radio and television programs may sometimes be used for the same purposes.

Selecting Main Ideas. A natural outgrowth, indeed, a part, of the study of organization is the selection of main ideas. One procedure is to have students write papers of 150 to 200 words on such a topic as "What Our School Needs Most" or "If I Were a Czar of Television." After each paper is read, the members of the class try to reduce the main idea to one terse sentence. If the writer has not been clear, the listeners will not hesitate to tell him so.

A follow-up can be the reading of carefully selected passages from a current magazine, a newspaper editorial, or the work of a major writer. Once more the students try to reduce the material to a single sentence.

A college teacher presented well-organized lectures to his freshmen and asked them to find the main point of each. Before instruction in listening, only 27 per cent could select main ideas. After instruction, 50 per cent of the poor listeners showed significant improvement.[2] Boys, interestingly enough, seemed to be slightly better listeners than girls.

A prepared debate between two student teams affords a different kind of summarizing activity. Here the purpose is to list the arguments on both sides.

David Levinson suggests that students may profit from reporting on speeches in the way that a journalist would.[3] He points out that here a summary is not desirable; instead, students seize upon what appears most newsworthy.

A measurement of a speaker's ability to convey his main ideas is W. H. Ewing's speaking-listening index.[4] Ewing would employ the

[2] Charles E. Irvin, "Evaluating a Training Program in Listening for College Freshmen," *School Review*, LXI (1953), 25.
[3] "Reporting Speeches: A Writing Unit." *English Journal*, XLIX (Oct., 1960), 477.
[4] W. H. Ewing, "Finding a Speaking-listening Index," *Quarterly Journal of Speech*, XXXI (Oct., 1945), 368.

index as a measure of a speaker's success in conveying his thoughts to his audience, but it would seem to have value as a measure of listening ability as well. While one student speaks, the others write down what they believe is the theme of his speech and each of the chief supporting ideas. What they write is then compared with the speaker's own written statements of theme and supporting ideas. The formula for measuring the success of the speaker is this:

$$I = \frac{P + 2C}{.02\, N_1\, N_e}$$

I = index. P = number of partially correct statements by all members of the class. C = number of correct statements by all members of the class. N_1 = number of speaker's items. N_e = number of listeners. For example, a class of 30 has 64 partially correct statements and 58 correct ones; the speaker had 5 items.

$$\text{Index} = \frac{64 + (2 \times 58)}{.02 \times 5 \times 30} = \frac{180}{3} = 60$$

The speaker's index would be 60 (a fairly high figure).

But each listener could measure his listening ability by simplifying the formula to

$$\frac{P + 2C}{.02\, N_1}$$

Thus, if a student had two partially correct statements and one correct out of a possible five, his index would be

$$\frac{2 + (2 \times 1)}{.02 \times 5} = \frac{4}{.10} = 40$$

Consistent attainment of a listening index of 60 or above should be the goal.

Listening for Contradictions and Faulty Reasoning. In a discussion or an argumentative presentation, a speaker will sometimes contradict himself, although the contradiction may be well hidden. The classic example is that of the politician who comes out in favor of lower prices, higher wages, and larger profits.

Even more common than contradictions are flaws in reasoning, and the use of propaganda tricks. Advanced high school students may be taught to identify fallacies and tricks like these:

1. Begging and ignoring the question: talking about a related subject instead of the point at issue; talking about a person's strong or weak points instead of the facts or ideas actually in-

volved; arguing in a circle (e.g., "The Koran is the word of God. We know that, because it says so, and the word of God cannot lie."); appealing to the emotions instead of to reason; stating as a fact something that remains to be proved

2. False analogy: inadequate resemblance between the two things being compared

3. Hasty generalization: drawing a conclusion from too few examples

4. Faulty dilemma: submitting only two choices when more actually exist

5. *Post hoc, ergo propter hoc:* (after this, therefore because of this) assuming that, because one thing follows another in time, the later is based on the earlier (e.g., since the French Revolution was later than the one in America, the French people were necessarily inspired by the Americans)

6. Hidden major premise: failure to state the generalization upon which a conclusion is based (e.g., "Giuseppe sings well because he is an Italian" has the hidden premise that all Italians sing well)

7. Incompetent authority: using the opinion of someone who is not an expert in the field being discussed (e.g., "_____ _____ the movie star believes that we should declare war at once")

The purpose of keeping students alert for flaws in reasoning is not, of course, to make them hypercritical of one another. Rather, it is to help them as speakers to reason logically, and as listeners to be aware of the types of faulty reasoning against which they should be on guard.

Bringing in One's Own Knowledge. To listen creatively, one must relate what one hears to what one already knows. That means that one should classify it, compare it with related information or ideas, reject it if it seems worthless or false, and keep it if it appears valuable and true. The person with a well-ordered mind apparently files away his information so that whatever he wants can be quickly found. If, for instance, he learns that Venezuela produces much petroleum, he tucks that fact away snugly with what he already knows about Venezuela and about petroleum production. Sometime he will receive a stimulus that will call for this particular bit of information; he will then open the mental file, and there it will be. From another part of the file he may draw another fact; he will put the two together in the form that we call a thought—actually a creative response. In contrast with this possessor of a well-regulated mind is the person with a haphazard mind. He does not regularly relate newly acquired bits of information to anything else; as a result, they drop quickly from memory or else become so badly scattered that they cannot readily be recalled. This person also has a mental filing system, but he files nearly everything under the heading "Miscellaneous."

Teaching students to relate what they learn to what they already know is one of the biggest jobs in education. In a sense it is the topic of most of this book and of hundreds of other educational writings. Here are presented a few suggestions concerning ways of helping students to mesh the gears between their ears and their brains:

The "post-mortem" is probably the most useful device. A challenging assembly speaker should not be ignored in the English class that follows his appearance. Talk about what he said; question his statements of opinion and possibly his facts; let the class amplify some of his remarks, and seek parallel incidents from life or literature. When a student has made an oral presentation, the same procedure may be followed. The oral work will probably improve when the class knows that more comes from its efforts than a mark in a gradebook; student attention will be heightened; and the processes of thinking will be accelerated.

The search for parallels is particularly stimulating. Suppose that a class has heard a report on James Russell Lowell in which the emphasis was upon his versatility—poet, critic, humorist, essayist, editor, professor, speaker, and international diplomat. Questions like these should be raised: "What other poet was also a humorist?" "An essayist?" "A professor?" "What other writers have held high government positions?" "Who is the most versatile person you have ever heard of?" "What versatile people do you know?" Parallels to almost anything are endless—history does repeat itself infinitely—and recognizing parallels seems to help in the improvement of mental filing systems.

Similar to searching for parallels is supplying examples. The following illustration refers to a literary selection, but the same technique may be used after a talk. Van Loon, in his *Geography*, refers to prehistoric animals that "went about their daily affairs clad in the armor of a medieval knight." What were some of these animals? Other creatures, he says, have gone "into domestic service." For example? Man, van Loon goes on, has taken possession of the earth "by right of his superior brain and by the strength of his foresight and his shot-guns." What has man conquered by his brain? By foresight?

By shot-guns? This searching for examples helps students to listen more attentively, to straighten up their mental files, and possibly to include more examples in their own writing.

Three more devices may be mentioned briefly. (1) Supplying contrasts is desirable. Suppose, for instance, that a student has been explaining to a senior class how plays were staged in ancient Greece. Pointing out the contrasts between Greek and modern, or between Greek and Elizabethan, staging will be valuable. (2) Sometimes a statement by a speaker will recall a proverb or a famous quotation. Let the students think of it. (3) When a talk has been about a person—fictional or otherwise—a clever teacher may construct certain hypothetical situations and ask what that person would do in each situation. As illustrations: "What would Hamlet do if an enemy army invaded Denmark?" "What would Wordsworth do if he were living today and were told that he had to spend the rest of his life in New York City?" Questions like these lead students to bring together what they have heard about a person and what they already know about life.

Of all the aspects of creative listening, this relating of the known to the previously unknown is most important. It leads to minds that are awake, to critical response, and to retention of what has been heard.

Evaluation. If a debate like that suggested on page 407 is held, or if political candidates representing diverse points of view may be heard on radio or television, it is useful to have students evaluate the opposing arguments. After listing contrasting arguments in parallel columns, they may see which opinions have been refuted in whole or in part and may then compare the merits of the remaining opinions or arguments. Some students may tend only to count the points on each side, but they can soon be shown that one strong, unanswerable argument may be worth a half-dozen trivial bits of reasoning or evidence.

Often a class will conclude that neither side is right nor wrong, but that some compromise is desirable. When the students reach that stage, they have advanced far toward an understanding of one of the principles upon which democracy is based—the principle that alternative or compromise solutions are often the only practicable ones. Lou LaBrant, in *We Teach English* (New York: Harcourt, Brace & World, Inc., 1951) has pointed out vigorously that often a question has several sides, not just two.

"The important part of the listening and reading process is not the tape-recorder type of reception," says Sam Duker, of Brooklyn College. "The real emphasis should be on evaluative and critical listening and reading." [5] Dr. Duker points out that the poor listener is swayed unduly by a speaker's appearance and eloquence. "A person with a pleasing, dynamic, and outgoing personality may not have anything worthwhile to say, while another, who has a jarring personality, which makes it impossible for you to feel any sort of rapport with him, may have a real message for you."

IN FRONT OF THE RADIO OR THE TELEVISION

Educational Programs

Since the early days of radio, many schools have made extensive use of broadcasts. As early as 1923, Haaren High School, in New York, broadcast accountancy lessons; the WLS (Chicago) Little Red Schoolhouse program, which originated in 1924, in a short time had an audience of 27,000 schoolroom users. Through the intervening years many classes have tuned in on radio broadcasts intended specifically for classroom audiences. Educational television stations in many cities now transmit programs, many of them superbly planned and executed, watched by thousands of students and large numbers of interested adults. An airplane circles over Indiana, beaming television programs into the classrooms of five states. Kinescopes of hundreds of programs are available and can be used as motion pictures would be.

Some educators have worried about the possible spread and influence of educational television, fearing a monolithic educational system in which, for example, every ninth grade English class in the nation would tune in on the same lesson: "a million students on one end of a coaxial cable and Mark Hopkins on the other." Not only would such a system fail to provide for individual differences, but it could also tend toward indoctrination and thought control out of harmony with American ideas of democracy. The role of the teacher would be reduced to policing, supervising written work and physical activities, and giving grades. Fortunately, the likelihood that education will become so monolithic appears slight, but the danger does exist: Arguments on the grounds of economy and effectiveness will perhaps be heard increasingly.

Commercial television is also being used for educational purposes, though few programs suited to those purposes are available during

[5] "Basics in Critical Listening," *English Journal*, LI (Nov., 1962), 565.

school hours. As for the assignment of evening viewing, a Newton-ville, Massachusetts, teacher summarizes the difficulties:

. . . the enrichment provided by television was only sporadic; for adapting night telecasts to the day's recitation presents problems of preparation, content, and scheduling. Because I cannot preview, I am totally dependent on the study guides occasionally provided by a producer or a sponsor. Usually I must devote hours *after* the night telecast to planning classroom follow-up. Nor can I expect from the entertainment provided by commercial television the continuity, repetition, and progression that insure learning. . . . Even the opportunity to extend the viewing experience through reading the play is rare, for textbooks cannot be obtained on short notice. The demands made on our school library are heartening but symptomatic of interests generated and opportunities lost.[6]

As we shall see, commercial television may have its classroom uses, but they are more likely to be incidental than direct.

Teaching Discrimination

Comparatively few teachers ever bothered to teach discrimination in radio listening. If they had, perhaps the public would have clamored enough to effect some improvements. Now comparatively few teachers help students to be discriminating television viewers. As a result, much of television is still a "wasteland."

Hearing no roaring demands for quality, TV sponsors and producers (with praiseworthy exceptions) have filled the channels with visual adaptations of the same kind of stuff that was accepted on radio, and have added new varieties on the same level of immaturity. Hence the endless retellings of the same tale in the pseudowesterns, the sagas of suds, the annually changing fads for programs about detectives or lawyers or doctors or hillbillies, the ridiculous audience-participation and quiz shows; hence the depictions of life as it never was nor can be; hence, perhaps worst of all, the shallow stereotypes of characterization.

Teachers are usually inept reformers. They can effect no sudden improvements in TV fare. But, if they can teach what quality is, teach distrust of the tawdry and respect and liking for the meritorious, their students, becoming adults, may join in cries for more significant programs.

Here, sketched very briefly, are a number of devices for helping students toward higher standards for their listening and viewing.

[6] Miriam Goldstein, "Humanities Through Television," *English Journal,* XLIX (April, 1960), 250.

Some of these ideas may be combined in an "On the Air" unit, or some may be used as a change-of-pace activity between units. Probably each school system should agree to pay some systematic attention to TV and radio once in grades seven, eight, or nine, and once again in grades ten, eleven, or twelve, with emphases differing according to the ages of the children.

Analyzing Amount of Time Spent. To help both teacher and class discover how large a share of a 168-hour week is devoted to broadcasts, students and teacher may prepare a simple questionnaire on listening and viewing habits. The number of hours spent each week on different kinds of programs should be included. Students are often impressed when they realize that as much as a seventh or a sixth of the 168 hours may be devoted to broadcasts, as much as a fourth of their waking hours. The questionnaire may be supplemented by another, on the listening time of other members of the family or other adults.

Discussing "Getting Your Time's Worth." A logical follow-up of the questionnaire is a discussion of how large a role broadcasts *should* have in one's life. What does one sacrifice by staying glued to a set? What other activities are worthwhile? Why is time often called man's most priceless possession? What would be a sensible amount of time per week for broadcasts? We often hear about getting our money's worth. How can we decide whether we are getting our time's worth?

Preparing a Class List. Students may be asked to keep up to date a section of the bulletin board called "Worthwhile Programs." The personnel of the responsible committee should change frequently. Students may obtain information about future programs by writing to the networks.

Letter Writing. Individuals and classes may be encouraged to write thoughtful letters to both sponsors and networks. Some of these letters may be critical of programs that seem too shallow, too improbable, too stereotyped. Perhaps more should be letters of reasoned praise for good programs. Dozens of such programs have been taken off the air because the audience response was disappointingly small.

Discussing Changing Tastes. "When I was a child, I spake as a child, I understood as a child, I thought as a child; but when I became a man, I put away childish things." (I Cor. 13:11.) Children are constantly struggling to elude childhood; they look longingly toward adulthood. Discussion of programs they have outgrown may lead toward a desire for still more mature programs.[7]

Reading and Writing Reviews.   Some of the best newspapers have excellent review columns (which should be sharply distinguished from mere uncritical puffs). Weekly news magazines and some other magazines, especially *The Saturday Review,* contain columns of penetrating analysis. Some of these reviews will appeal only to your brighter or more mature students, but other students will often enjoy reading someone else's reactions to programs with which they are familiar. A natural sequel to the reading of reviews is the writing of them.

Summarizing Plots.   A good exercise in writing and in criticism is to have students summarize, in the fewest words possible, radio or TV dramas. A frequent summary may be: "Good guys beat bad guys." A virtue of this device is that it shows up the monotony of plot of many programs, especially those in a series; "Teen-ager gets into trouble and out," for example, is the plot of an amazingly large number of plays about young people. In contrast, although plots of good plays may be similarly capsuled, these summaries seldom are repetitive.

Estimating Probability and Truth to Life.   With a little training, students in both junior and senior high school can learn to pick out at least the glaring improbabilities in dramatic broadcasts. For instance, they can realize how unlikely it is that one man can be shot at week after week, year after year, and never suffer more than a flesh wound, or they can decide that sudden and complete reformations are questionable. Conversely, they can learn to recognize and praise those dramas in which the events might actually happen and in which the people act like people. Although in their study of literature they need to learn about "the willing suspension of disbelief," and although they need to appreciate fantasy for fantasy's sake, they should come to condemn, more or less vigorously, artistically unwarranted distortions of human portraits and the laws of chance.

Applying Literary Tests.   In their study of literature, students acquire at least partial answers to such questions as these: "What are the characteristics of a good story?" "Of a good play?" It is not unfair to apply the same or similar criteria to dramatic broadcasts, even though television drama is showing evidence of becoming a unique

---

[7] For an excellent discussion of the mass media and children's maturing, read Sarah I. Roody's "Effects of Radio, Television, and Motion Pictures on the Development of Maturity," *English Journal,* XLI (May, 1952), 245.

genre. Erwin Steinberg suggests a comparison of the techniques used by TV writers and writers of printed stories or stage plays, with particular attention to the demands made by limitations of time, space, or dramatic conventions.[8] In addition, classes may discuss non-literary characteristics peculiar to the medium, such as plausibility of the acting, excellence of the photography, or quality of the direction.

Reading Books on Which Broadcasts Are Based. A comparison of the book and its dramatization may be fruitful. Lively and informative discussions may result from such questions as these: "What important episodes or characters were left out?" "Why?" "What differences in characterization did you notice?" "Why were these changes probably made?" "What alterations were made in the arrangement of events?" "Why?" "What depth of meaning did you observe in the original but not in the dramatization, or vice versa?" "What other differences did you see?" "Was the ending the same in both versions?" Sarah Roody has pointed out that some movie and radio versions of *Pygmalion* end with Eliza Doolittle's marriage to Henry Higgins, although "Shaw considered that outcome most unlikely and wrote an epilogue for the express purpose of telling why such a marriage would have failed to attract Eliza in the first place or to satisfy her in the long run." "Which version, Shaw's or a later one, is preferable?" "Why?" "How does *My Fair Lady* (based on *Pygmalion*) end?" "Is this ending satisfactory?"

Showing Kinescope or Film Versions of Good Programs. More and more good kinescopes and film versions are becoming available for use in classrooms. Showing these, and discussing what makes them better than average, is worthwhile.

Writing Radio and Television Plays. Not only does this activity provide well-motivated writing experience, but also it sharpens critical acumen. As the students try to avoid the weaknesses to which they have learned to object, they become even more aware of those weaknesses. And, as they attempt to bring into their plays what they have learned to approve, they develop a keener appreciation of the professionals who succeed. Some of their efforts may be to create original dramas; others may involve the rewriting in play form of short stories studied in class. Both individual and group creations are possible. Some of the best work may be presented in assembly programs.

---

[8] "Television and the Teaching of English," *English Journal*, XLIX (Oct., 1960), 484.

Teaching the Power and the Responsibilities of the Mass Media. When twenty million or more persons watch the same program, the television writer and producer and sponsor may exert a strong influence on twenty million minds. The influence may be good or bad. In the control of the unscrupulous, television can contribute toward mental and moral bankruptcy, but fortunately the potential for good is no less. A nation addicted to the mass media must learn to question ceaselessly the integrity of the purveyors. Students in the senior high school can understand and should discuss the implications of the immense power the mass media have placed in the hands of a few hundred or a few thousand people.

Analyzing Speeches. *The English Language Arts in the Secondary School* says that, in listening to speeches intended to influence thought or to inform,

"Who is speaking?" students learn to ask. "Why? Under what sponsorship?" and "On what authority?" Ability to detect bias in point of view, unsubstantiated generalizations, or inferences inadequately drawn is particularly important in a land where freedom of speech gives equal rights to the informed and to the uninformed, to the straight and to the crooked thinker, to the sincere and to the insincere. Critical examination of what is heard is vital in today's world.[9]

Comparing Newscasters or Commentators. Anna K. Bloom, in Baltimore, helped her students to draw up a scorecard for judging newscasters and commentators. As a result, the students learned to prefer the solid to the sensational.[10]

Reporting Events. Students may profitably write or present orally, as if they were newscasters, descriptions of events that they have witnessed in person or on TV. This activity will give a better understanding of the problem real newscasters face.

Discussing Subjects Not Treated or Seldom Treated. Mature classes may find profitable discussion of the fact that the large network shows infrequently treat realistically such topics as race relations, unfair or unethical practices of employers, abuses by labor of its privileges, the fact that the white race is numerically a minority, and the like. "What are the reasons for such omissions?" "Are the omissions defensible?"

Encouraging Variety. Just as some students read only the sports page or the comic page in the daily newspaper, so some stick to the

[9] P. 229.
[10] "Taught, Not Caught," *English Journal*, XLIII (Oct., 1954), 367.

same monotonous radio and TV fare. Encourage them to shop around, to develop varied tastes. To choose the good, they must know both bad and good.

Developing a Class List of Standards. An important goal in any series of activities dealing with the mass media—in fact, *the* goal—is the creation of a set of standards that will guide students in the future. These standards cannot be teacher-prepared or teacher-imposed. They must come from the observations and the discussions of the students themselves. It is good to draw up a list of the major kinds of programs—drama, comedy, speeches, quiz shows, music, and so on—and have the class decide the characteristics of the programs to which they could conscientiously attach the label "Good."

Planning Units. In 1961 the NCTE published *Television and the Teaching of English*. This paperbound book devotes about seventy pages to "The Educational Significance of Television" and about fifty-five pages to "The Classroom Study of Television." Although the examples inevitably became dated very quickly, the basic information and suggestions remain valid. Among the recommendations are some on brief units isolated from the regular curriculum, brief units within the regular curriculum, and an extensive unit. The first kind of unit would make possible a planned discussion of important drama on television, such as a play by Ibsen. Before the production the class discusses topics related to the theme of the play; during the telecast they listen for answers to specific questions; and after the telecast they discuss these questions and others. In a brief unit within the curriculum, the teacher has the class read a play or story to be televised; the students then compare the printed and the televised version. A possibility for an extensive unit is summarized in this way: "An ambitious project for a class would involve the study of television programs as an expression of American life, a study that would extract from television plays, comedies, musicals, and commercials the values that television seems to find inherent in American life."

THE IDEA BOX

A STUDENT PANEL

Some teachers use panels in which students discuss the characteristics of good listeners.

CONTINUING A STORY

One student starts an original story and designates a second person to continue the telling. He designates a third, etc. No one may bring in anything that is incompatible with previous statements.

TECHNIQUES THAT BROUGHT RESULTS

Nettie B. Lewis, in Oklahoma City, brought her class from a listening test percentile rank of 35 in October to 57 in May. She used records, tape recordings, directions to be followed, and sometimes tricky exercises such as "If New York is west of San Francisco, write the word Chicago on the first line of your paper." "Listen, Please," *Clearing House*, XXX (May, 1956), 535.

RECORDINGS

1. A library of carefully chosen recordings may add to the enjoyment of literature as well as sharpen listening skills. Many excellent recordings are available at reduced prices to members of the NCTE. Numerous commercial companies also sell recordings.

2. Dorothy Dixon discusses effective use of disk and tape recordings in "Recordings Will Help," *English Journal*, XLV (Sept., 1956), 341.

A PLAN FOR TEACHING AUDING

Don Brown, of Redwood City, California, who prefers the term "auding" to "listening," advocates "speaking and writing assignments based upon auding experiences." For his discussion of the importance and the techniques of teaching auding, see his "Concepts and Practices in Teaching Aural English," *English Journal*, XLV (Dec., 1956), 540. Different plans are described in detail by Gertrude Elliff in "A Direct Approach to the Study of Listening," *English Journal*, XLVI (Jan., 1957), 20; and by Alexander Frazier in "Making the Most of Speaking and Listening Experiences," *English Journal*, Sept., 1957, p. 330.

LISTENING TESTS

The Brown-Carlsen *Listening Comprehension Test* (New York: Harcourt, Brace & World, Inc., 1953), measures immediate recall, following of directions, recognition of transitions, recognition of word meanings, and lecture comprehension. Educational Testing Service (Princeton, N. J.) has a newer (1957) listening test measuring plain-sense comprehension, interpretation, and evaluation and application.

A LISTENING GUIDE

Joseph Mersand (*Bulletin* of the NASSP, May, 1958) uses prepared guide sheets with a recording of Poe's "Cask of Amontillado." Students answer questions about the time of year, the name of the narrator, the kind of background music, etc.; they also summarize the story in 100 words or write a 50-word opinion.

EDUCATIONAL TV PROGRAMS FOR YOUR SCHOOL

Many 16-mm. educational TV programs, both films and kinescopes, on literary and other subjects, may be rented at modest rates from NET Film Service, Audio-Visual Center, Indiana University, Bloomington. A catalog is available.

PROS AND CONS OF EDUCATIONAL TV

The two strongest arguments in favor of educational TV are that it affords opportunity to expose students to an exceptionally able teacher who has ample time to prepare and that this teacher may employ expensive or difficult-to-obtain teaching aids and materials not available in most classrooms.

Students in Danville, Illinois, High School, however, after a semester of viewing air-borne television, objected on these grounds: can't take notes fast enough; can't ask questions; too easy to daydream; "If your attention wanders a second, you're lost"; no helpful discussion; too much outside reading; vocabulary too large; boring.

Teachers objected on these grounds: format too confining and inflexible; arbitrary time allotment; teacher a mere monitor, relegated to "warming up a TV dinner"; too much emphasis on lecturing, listening, note taking; inadequate provision for individual differences; curriculum, in effect, organized by "outsiders."

LITERATURE VIA TV

Bob Donaldson criticizes television teaching of literature on these counts: (1) teaching should involve more than telling; (2) TV does not provide for individual differences; (3) discussion and language practice are not provided by TV; (4) in large TV classes, too little written work can be required; (5) the TV teacher cannot be argued with; (6) TV tends to avoid the controversial; (7) students need to give, not just receive. *Newsletter,* Michigan Council of Teachers of English, April, 1959.

COMMERCIAL TELEVISION

In "Ten Uses for Commercial Television in the English Classroom," *English Journal,* XLVII (Dec., 1958), 566, James J. Brunstein offers varied suggestions including a dozen theme topics and a suggestion for a quiz program on matters of grammar and usage.

TELEVISION DRAMA

Television plays may provide a wedge for literary study, William R. Martin argues ("Television Drama in the Junior High School," *Speech Teacher,* X, Sept., 1961, p. 225.) Building upon the students' interest in "How does it end?" Mr. Martin would move to discussion of various components of a story and the way they lead to a resolution of the conflict. The discussion may turn to dialog, characterization, and "stage effects," all of which, except possibly the last, are pertinent in consideration of fiction and drama.

BEST TV AND RADIO BETS

Anita Willens ("TV—Lick It or Join It?" *English Journal*, XLIX [Dec., 1960], 639) tells of improvements in student choice of TV and radio programs brought about by weekly posting of suggested "best bets," with brief class discussion of some programs.

TV: A RUNG ON A LADDER

Build on students' interest in TV plays by taking them a few more steps up the literary ladder, Patrick and Mary Hazard urge ("What's TV Doing to English?" *English Journal*, XLVIII [Oct., 1959], 414). "If TV goes half-cocked on westerns, push Walter Van Tilburg Clark, A. B. Guthrie, and Francis Parkman for all they're worth. Use the unmotivated violence of mysteries and police films to explain the artistic integration of violence in the Greek tragedies, Elizabethans like Shakespeare, and moderns like Tennessee Williams."

14

IMPROVING STUDENTS' SPEECH

SPEECH ACTIVITIES FOR THE ENTIRE CLASS

Many large high schools and some smaller ones have departments of speech or at least separate courses in speech. In some, a semester or a year of speech is required. Others offer no courses with a "Speech" label.

The amount of speech training to be given within the English class depends upon whether all students in the school are required to take a speech course. If they are, a number of the activities described in this chapter may be minimized within the English class. But, if students need not take a separate course in speech, or if they have no opportunity to do so, the English teacher's responsibility is increased. Even if there is a speech requirement, many of the assignments in English should involve oral work.

For the purpose of this chapter, no separation between English and speech will be assumed. Methods of instilling valuable oral language principles and habits within English classes will be considered. Nothing will be said about the correction of serious speech defects such as stuttering, because that is the province of specially trained personnel.

Objectives

The intention in oral English is not to make platform speakers but to develop citizens who can participate satisfactorily in the everyday situations that demand spoken English. These situations may be. grouped roughly according to their frequency in adult life, as follows:

Group I, often needed. Conversation, telephoning, making introductions, giving directions, telling stories, reading aloud, informal discussions.

Group II, important but less frequently needed. Interviewing or being interviewed, making announcements, introducing a speaker, giving reports, following parliamentary procedure, defining, taking part in panel discussions.

Group III, possibly important for superior students. Giving book reviews, dramatizing, debating, platform speaking, after-dinner speaking, choral reading, reciting of memorized passages, participation in radio programs.

Group IV, needed for professional work. Techniques of salesmanship may serve here as a single example.

All students should be given enough practice to become reasonably proficient in the situations named in Groups I and II. Less emphasis need be placed on Group III, and none at all on Group IV, except when a particular student wants assistance.

Organizing Oral Work

A typical but probably mistaken procedure is to devote each Friday to oral work—talks of various kinds, panel discussions, dramatizations, and the like. The weaknesses of this procedure are that it interrupts whatever the class is doing and that it seems to point to a nonexistent dichotomy between English and oral English. It seems better to allow most oral work to grow naturally out of other class activities and to prepare short concentrated units for those phases that have no particular relationship to the other activities.

From the study of literature and composition arise many opportunities for oral work. Oral reading, class and panel discussions, reports, definitions, giving directions, dramatizations, telling of stories, choral reading, and recitation are natural outgrowths of the "regular" study. A good class discussion is actually a conversation, but diffident students may be given more chance to converse if the class is occasionally divided into small groups, each of which is to talk about one aspect of the work. Telephoning, making introductions, and conversation may well be combined as part of a courtesy unit. Other short units may be devoted to the interview, parliamentary procedure, and additional speech activities that do not grow readily out of the work in literature and written composition.

The Role of the Teacher

To develop students who can speak well, the teacher himself must be a reasonably competent speaker. That does not mean that he should be an orator or a lecturer—few teachers could make a living on the lecture platform—but he should have a satisfactory voice and the ability to express his thoughts clearly and pleasingly. He should occasionally hear recordings of his speech and try to correct whatever deficiencies he discovers.

An occupational hazard of teaching is that it tends to create objectionable speech habits. Three of these are common enough to merit consideration: unnaturally precise enunciation, rising inflection, and a "know-it-all" tone. In the effort to serve as a model and to wean students away from sloppy enunciation, "Cher turn tspell, 'enry," teachers tend to pronounce each syllable with unnecessary distinctness: "It is your turn to spell, Henry." The happy medium is that of a capable radio or TV announcer, who would say something like this: "It's your turn tuh spell, Henry." The excessively correct enunciator tries to give each word its dictionary pronunciation regardless of context; however, in such a sentence as "He said that that was a mistake," the two "thats" should not really be pronounced in the same way. The second fault, that of ending a sentence with a rising inflection, is probably attributable to the fact that teachers ask so many questions that the rising inflection becomes habitual; then, even when they are making a statement, they make it sound interrogative. The third fault, the particularly obnoxious "know-it-all" tone, sometimes develops in teachers who have taught the same thing in the same way for a half-dozen years; the tone leaves the impression, "I am Sir Oracle; when I ope my lips, let no dog bark." When this tone is used, students are likely to speak with hesitation.

Sir Oracle is unlikely to be a successful teacher, because he unintentionally discourages class participation. It should be the teacher's role to help each student make his best contribution to the class. That means that the teacher must be a leader and a guide, but not a dictator. It means that the class atmosphere must be such that each student knows that what he has to offer will be welcome, that he has a share in making the class a success. A class is like an automobile: The teacher provides both lubrication to reduce friction and water for cooling, but the students supply much of the fuel that results in forward movement.

Some Teaching Techniques

Some techniques that have been employed successfully in teaching each of the oral activities listed on page 423 are the following:

Group I

Conversation. The small-group technique lends itself most readily to conversation, but one warning is in order: Each group should have a fairly definite subject to discuss. Before the first such conversation, there might well be a class discussion of the characteristics of good conversation: alertness of each speaker and listener, tactfulness, courtesy, attempting to make real contributions, avoidance of showing off or talking too much, avoidance of interrupting, the asking of leading questions, and so on.

To illustrate how conversation via the small-group method may grow out of literature, let us assume that a freshman class has read the first twelve chapters of *Treasure Island.* The students may be divided into five or six groups; one group may talk about which character is the most fascinating; another, what it has learned about eighteenth-century customs; another, what sea terms it has added to its vocabularies; another, what its members would have done if they had been in Jim's place in the apple barrel; another, what kinds of treasure hunting are carried on today; and another, the life and customs of buccaneers. The teacher may move from group to group, putting in a word here and there. If teacher and class wish, the results of each conversation may be summarized for the rest of the class by a member of each group.

Some classes may profit from role-playing conversations. A boy, for instance, wants to go to a summer camp, but his parents have some practical objections. Students act out the conversation. A tape recorder plays it back, being stopped at any points where something should be discussed, such as what should have been left unsaid or what added arguments could have been offered or how a statement could have been made more tactfully.

Telephoning. A junior high school class may spend a profitable hour in discussing telephone ethics and courtesy, telephone pests, and the qualities of a pleasing voice, as well as in dramatizing certain familiar instances when the telephone may cause friction within the family. Dramatization of good and bad telephone habits is also helpful.

Making Introductions. Unless he has observed the right people very carefully, the student is likely to have difficulty in introducing one person to another. Class discussion should cover the topics of when introductions are in order, who should be presented to whom, what the acceptable phrases are, what should be included besides the exchange of names, and how introductions should be acknowledged. The discussion should be followed with demonstrations and practice. Groups of three students may work together effectively, taking turns in acting as various imaginary persons both old and young.

Giving Directions.   Almost any student can relate instances in which he was given unclear directions concerning the location of the post office or some other place he wanted to find. The reason for the lack of clarity may have been the director's ignorance, inability to visualize, or poor speech habits. Junior high school students, working in small groups, may take turns being complete strangers in town and asking for assistance. Those giving the directions must remember that the "strangers" do not know any of the landmarks and may not even know the points of the compass. Giving directions in a rural area—for instance, how to find a spring or a certain tree—may pose a still more difficult problem.

Telling Stories.   Since nearly everyone enjoys stories, it is unfortunate that most persons do not tell them well. There is a tendency to bring in irrelevant statements, add unnecessary "see's" and "you know's," relate events in illogical order, laugh before the hearers know what is funny, leave out important details, and spoil the climax. The best cure is discussion of the characteristics of effective storytelling, plus plenty of opportunity to practice. A teacher should encourage students to include pointed anecdotes in their reports on authors, to relate to the class stories or parts of stories that they have found interesting, and to bring into class discussion pertinent illustrative stories, funny or otherwise. For years a storytelling unit has been included in many English classes of Pontiac, Michigan, on the ground that the ability to tell stories well is useful in camp life, church schools, law, acting, broadcasting, medicine, teaching, ministry, clerking, and parenthood.

Reading Aloud.   In the past few decades the elementary schools have stressed silent reading to the near exclusion of reading aloud, although good modern programs have corrected that tendency. If the secondary schools likewise ignore oral reading, students will receive no assistance in mastering an activity that has at least the following values: meeting the adult needs for reading newspaper items, announcements, letters, reports, and prepared papers; reading to children or others for pleasure; reading in order to increase enjoyment of literature; providing incidental help on speech; and giving opportunity, through reading announcements and the like, to make students feel that they "count."

Often the understanding and appreciation of literature may be improved by oral reading. The teacher will need to help the students improve their phrasing, their emphasis, and their tempo. On the matter of phrasing, Harlen Adams has commented,

> By a certain cadenced silence the reader marks his period; by a half silence, his comma; by a certain accent, an interrogation; by a certain tone, an exclamation. And I must assure you that it is exclusively on the skillful distribution of these insensible points that not only the interest of the story, but actually its clearness, its comprehensibility, altogether depend.[1]

The importance of emphasis may be shown by having members of the class pronounce a monosyllable like "Oh," "Yes," or "No," or a sentence like "John didn't say that" to indicate different meanings. By changing the place of emphasis in "John didn't say that," the speaker may indicate (1) that someone else said it, (2) that the speaker is denying that John said it or is astonished that he did, (3) that John implied it even though he didn't say it, or (4) that John said something else. In connection with literature, classes may often discuss how a given speech should be interpreted. Perhaps the most famous example is Lady Macbeth's "We fail" (Act I, scene vii). Does Lady Macbeth say matter-of-factly, "We fail," or does she pause after "We" and say, "fail" in a tone of disbelief, as if failure is impossible?

Tempo likewise should be appropriate. Teacher and class ought to see, for instance, that the movement in humorous selections should be brisk and sometimes even breathless, that the reading of "How They Brought the Good News from Ghent to Aix" or "The Ballad of East and West" should suggest the rapid hoofbeats of the horses, that "Thanatopsis" demands a slow, thoughtful reading.

Oral reading, then, provides much opportunity for developing flexibility—a flexibility that may be carried over into other speech activities. It permits also a study of meaning, and the clarification of meaning through effective use of the voice.

Informal Discussions. In school, students need to participate in numerous class discussions; in later life, most of them will take part in business conferences, club and political meetings, and family discus-

[1] "Speech Activities in the Secondary School," *English Journal*, XXXV (March, 1946), 129.

sions. The principles underlying good conversation are also basic to these discussions involving larger groups.

A satisfactory discussion requires progress toward a recognized goal and involves contributions of all, or nearly all, the members of the group. As aimless discussion is of little value, a topic of discussion should usually be phrased as a problem to be solved. Perhaps no unquestionable solution exists, but at least tentative conclusions may often be drawn.

Getting all students to take part is sometimes a problem. However, if the teacher remembers the particular strong points of each student, he may occasionally supply a lead or a question that will bring in some of the silent ones. The attitude that each person has something worthwhile to offer usually brings results, and a few words of praise sometimes can transform a violet into a rose, or at least into a carnation. Some teachers like to have a discussion topic determined in advance, with each student responsible for preparing and being ready to present three reasons for believing as he does.

Group II

The Interview. Although most students will take part in only a few interviews during their lifetimes, those few may be of major importance. Their chances of employment in their chosen work will sometimes depend upon the success of one interview. Some colleges also require interviews with their prospective students. Yet many employers and college interviewers complain that young people are often careless in appearance and manners, that they slouch and sprawl, that their answers to questions are delivered in a slovenly fashion, and that they have nothing positive to contribute. These complaints suggest that a valuable project for the junior or senior year is a short study of techniques of the interview, and dramatizations of good and bad techniques. Then the small-group plan can be employed to allow each student practice in interviewing and being interviewed for mythical positions. Students who have had such training, artificial though the situation is, are often loud in its praise.[2]

Making Announcements. The good announcement is not unlike the lead of a news story, in that it usually answers the questions who, what, where, and when, and sometimes why and how. In school many announcements must be made, and conscientious teachers see to it that

---

[2] The technique of a quite different kind of interview, that of a speaker or other personage who visits the school, may well be left for the journalism class, since it has value for comparatively few students.

each student occasionally has such responsibility. It is desirable to have committees in charge of bulletin boards, the radio, the classroom library, special occasions, and the like; with such committees, the need for announcements often appears. Homerooms and assembly programs also frequently necessitate announcements. Since in adult life almost everyone is occasionally expected to announce something to a group, practice in giving announcements based on the "five W's" is desirable.

Introducing a Speaker. Although opportunities for introducing outside speakers are rather rare, one student may sometimes present another to a school group. The chairman of a discussion panel, for instance, may remind his classmates of some pertinent qualification of the next speaker. Or, in those schools where students sometimes appear before other classes to talk about their specialties, someone, preferably a student, must introduce them.

Giving Reports. Reports in English and other classes are frequent and may be valuable. Too often, though, a report is dull and almost worthless because the student chooses too big a subject (e.g., The Publishing Business), fails to narrow it, takes notes on only an encyclopedia article, and for his report simply summarizes what the encyclopedia says. Guided, the same student will cut the subject down to workable size, consult more than one source, and employ his own plan of organization for the material.

The report subjects should grow from the classwork and not be chosen merely for the sake of having reports. Second, students should usually be given some degree of freedom in choosing the subjects of their reports, because they are more likely to make interesting whatever they themselves find interesting. Third, ordinarily, not many reports should be given on the same day.

As an illustration, suppose that a senior class is studying eighteenth-century English literature. The teacher suggests that certain reports will enlighten and enliven much of the study. He invites the students to be on the alert for subjects that they would like to investigate, and in addition he lists a rather large number of topics including such subjects as Whigs vs. Tories, eighteenth-century etiquette or dress or amusements, Fielding's *Tom Jones,* the story of Johnson's dictionary, etc. Each student should choose the topic that interests him most and should talk with the teacher concerning sources of information and the most appropriate time for his report. The subject of etiquette should probably be discussed when the class is reading Addison and Steele, Johnson's dictionary when the class is reading from the

Rambler essays, and so on. In other words, the reports are interspersed within the rest of the work, and each student makes his contribution when it is most meaningful.

The principles of organization discussed in Chapter 8 are as important in oral as in written English. Time should be taken occasionally to refresh students' memories concerning the possible types of organization and how to employ them. The usefulness of outlines—at least topic outlines—can be more easily demonstrated for oral work than for written compositions.

Some shy students are extremely hesitant about giving reports; the thought of standing before the class terrifies them so much that they will even feign illness to escape. Sympathy for these students is better than scorn. Also, a gradual building up to reports is better than a sudden assignment. If a teacher is aware that some students are excessively shy, he may first encourage participation while the students are seated, later have them place written work on the board and explain it, and then allow them to use notes freely in their reports. A friendly, cooperative atmosphere within the classroom is desirable and may be encouraged by the teacher's frequent praise of the student audience.

One teacher anticipates the most common troubles in oral reports by dramatizing the types of difficulties. She herself, before students have given any reports, presents a little talk as it would be given by a "mouse," a bashful boy, Miss And-uh, Mr. Bored Sophisticate, Mr. Unprepared, Miss Phonograph, and, finally, Mr. Average Student, whose tone is pleasant and enthusiastic.

Sometimes the teacher may remark that he himself has had to overcome stage fright, and may refer to famous stage actors and actresses who feel frightened or even nauseated before each performance.

Following Parliamentary Procedure. Since parliamentary procedure is of marked importance in our life (business, church, and club meetings, as well as local, state, and federal government), students should become familiar with the order of business and should be able to trace a motion, with amendments, from origin to disposal. In addition, they should know such technicalities as the procedure in electing officers, the method of addressing the chair, and the order of precedence of motions.

Class following of parliamentary procedure, however, need not be mere routine. In some classes, discussion of controversial issues is a more or less regular practice. A chairman and a secretary are elected, the topic is explained and then discussed, and the opposing points of view are summarized at the end of the hour. Students must be recognized by the chair before speaking. Discussion must be kept free of personalities. Courtesy should be the rule, with frequent use of such remarks as "Mr. Chairman, I believe that Jim is partly right, but I should like to disagree with one statement." Opinion should be supported by as much factual evidence as is available.

A value inherent in such a plan of discussion is that it helps students to think about issues of importance to them. It is important for all students to develop the ability

1. To employ a reflective and analytical technique rather than the argumentative technique in approach to controversial problems
2. To display competence in, and inclination toward, defining key words and phrases used in discussion
3. To display competence in reinforcing general or abstract concepts with appropriate concrete details
4. To master and to apply the principle that the truth of a solution depends upon the degree to which it corresponds with the basic assumptions

The types of subjects that may be considered in parliamentary discussions vary widely. Some teachers prefer national and international issues. Others advocate consideration of problems nearer the students: home difficulties, cheating, athletics, courtesy, movies, etc. Community issues (generally non-political ones) may be discussed; class consideration of such an issue as school-district reorganization has even been known to affect a community's decision on an important problem. It would seem advisable to begin with subjects in which students have an immediate personal interest and gradually to branch out into topics with wider implications.

Defining.   Perhaps defining should not be listed as a special speech activity, since it is needed frequently in reports and discussions, but it provides enough pitfalls to seem to require separate treatment. Much disagreement or confusion may be avoided if terms are carefully defined. Therefore, when Ray is talking about a "good football team," he should be expected to define "good"; when Katherine is talking about the education of Indians, both "education" and "Indians" need definition; when any student uses a technical term that may be unfamiliar to the class, he should pause to explain it.

Every good definition, students should learn, does two things: It places the thing being defined in a general category and then distinguishes that thing from others in the same category. For instance, if one is defining "psychiatry," one says first that it is a science (the general category); then one distinguishes it from other sciences by saying that it involves the treatment of mental diseases.

Panel Discussions. In many ways the panel discussion is preferable to debate. It is less formal and more natural; it permits audience participation; and, as has often been said, unlike debate it searches for truth rather than victory.

Careful preparation is essential to success in panel discussion. Students must be familiarized with the usual pattern: opening remarks by the chairman; introduction of speakers; rather formal presentation of differing points of view by members of the panel; informal exchange of comments, additions, and rebuttals; and audience participation. (There are, of course, many possible variations of this pattern; in a less formal panel, there may be no set order for the speakers.) If the topic is a controversial one, care must be taken to have approximately an equal number of speakers for each side. The members of the panel must know exactly what issue or issues are involved, and who is to present which points of view. Material must be sought and organized as carefully as it would be for a debate.

Loren Reid suggests an ingenious method of appraising individuals' contributions to discussions of almost any type. He suggests that the teacher mark a tally each time a student speaks, even only a sentence or two. A *plus* indicates a helpful contribution, a *zero* a neutral one, and a *minus* a contribution that is "digressing, sidetracking, blocking or overly-aggressive." Thus, some students may be marked like this:

```
Crews   0 + + 0 0 0 0 0 0 0 0 0
Goold   + + + +
Mutti   0 0 − 0 − 0 0 − 0 − 0
Page    0 0 0 0 + 0 3
```

It should be useful, too, for students to employ this device occasionally in evaluating their classmates' contributions: It should lead to good listening and to critical thinking.

Group III

The types of speaking listed under Group III—book reviews, dramatizing, debating, platform speaking, after-dinner speaking, choral reading, reciting of memorized passages, and participation in radio programs—are of varying value as class activities. Dramatization and choral reading have considerable worth in aiding literary appreciation

---

[3] *Teaching Speech* (Columbia, Mo.: Artcraft Press, 1960), p. 188.

and, therefore, deserve class time; book reviewing (which is not necessarily the same as book reporting) may likewise possess merit for some students. It is doubtful, though, that class hours, limited as they are, should be spent on debating, after-dinner speaking, and principles of microphone technique.[4] The old practice of reciting long memorized passages—to which the rest of the class paid scant attention—was wasteful of time.

In general, the activities in Group III demand little class attention, except where dramatizing and choral reading seem advisable.

Group IV

Teaching the types of speaking needed for professional work is primarily the responsibility of the college, not of the high school. The foundations for a salesman's speaking habits, a minister's speaking habits, and so on, are laid in the elementary and secondary schools, but detailed work is possible only on a more specialized level.

THE IMPROVEMENT OF THE INDIVIDUAL'S SPEECH

The class activities that have been described should lead to improvement of speech habits by giving class members practice in numerous situations requiring speech. But there is still something more that the teacher can do to help individuals better their oral English. This is remedial and developmental work aimed at reduction or elimination of faults in speech.

It must be stressed that the teacher who is not a trained speech correctionist should never try to remedy faults that may be organic. Some persons have serious nervous maladjustments or malformed speech organs; for anyone but a specialist to attempt to apply treatment for these persons may be dangerous.

The majority of students, however, have speech defects that can be corrected by the non-specialist. Some of these flaws appear in what is said; others, in how it is said.

Improving Content and Organization

In most speech activities, class and teacher should focus attention upon what is said. The delivery is, after all, only the vehicle for conveying thought; the thought itself is the important thing.

[4] Radio or TV work, of course, does have value if a class is fortunate enough to be granted air time occasionally. Also, a class may sometimes happily prepare a radio script and present it over a public-address system or closed-circuit TV— or even with just a dummy microphone.

In class discussions the teacher may do much to encourage attention to facts. When George glibly condemns Congress as incompetent, he should be pinned down to specific accusations and asked for definite evidence to prove his statements. When Margaret says, "All French people are frivolous. I knew a French girl and she . . . ," there is the opportunity to demonstrate that an assuredly valid conclusion cannot be drawn from only one or two instances. When Clarence, whose family has voted Republican for seventy-five years, remarks bitterly that wars usually start during Democratic administrations, he not only is revealing personal prejudice but also is guilty of *post hoc, ergo propter hoc.* Whenever a student shifts from issues to personalities (a favorite trick of politicians), he is ignoring the question. Louise's remark, "Everybody's wearing whozits now, so we ought to get some," has the hidden premise that we should do what "everybody" is doing. Examples could be multiplied, but the point is simply that the teacher should be constantly alert for weaknesses in reasoning and lack of evidence; he should encourage the class to challenge demonstrable fallacies. The intent is not to make a class argumentative but, rather, to make it a mentally awake one that thinks about what it hears.

The teacher should also remove some of the snags of content and organization before the students come to them. Unaided, most students will find little material for reports and discussions, and will not organize what they do find. With the teacher's help, however, they will uncover information in addition to that offered by the old stand-by, the encyclopedia. They will see how examples add to the interest and clarity. The teacher also is responsible for showing the students how they can apply to their more formal talks the principles of organization they use in written composition. For a report, they learn, a good plan is to have an interest-rousing opening, a body with not more than four well-illustrated main points (the most important usually last), and an ending that summarizes or restates in memorable fashion what has previously been said.

On the matter of permitting notes for rather long presentations, opinions differ. Students seem usually to do their best work if they are allowed to have notes on small cards—notes that will remind them of the steps in their talks. These notes should consist only of words or phrases, not complete sentences, because students tend merely to read anything written in sentence form. The little cards provide comfort, if nothing else; the students know that they cannot become completely lost when they have a few scribblings to which they may refer. There is nothing disgraceful about consulting notes; college professors who have given the same lecture a dozen or more times make extensive use of them. And one cannot help wondering how a teacher can conscientiously forbid his students to use any notes when he himself refers frequently to a bundle of cards as he addresses the PTA.

In the follow-up after rather formal work in oral English, most of the remarks should concern the content and organization. Although the class must be kept constantly aware of the importance of good enunciation, accepted pronunciation, and so on, the comments should be more meaningful than "He said, 'and-uh' " or "He mispronounced 'Italian'." Judicious praise of what was said is superior to random criticism of the method of saying it. Additions to the content are in order, as are questions addressed to the speaker to elicit further information. Sometimes the teacher may speak favorably of the careful way in which Sally or Pete organized a presentation, or may pause to comment approvingly on an especially happy illustration. Adverse criticisms should, as a rule, be given following a number of presentations, and ought to refer to weaknesses observed in several of the talks. If one of the speakers has a unique fault in content or organization, it may be mentioned to him in privacy, unless some of the questions and comments bring it out incidentally.

Improving Vocal Quality

Almost certainly among your students there will be a fairly large number whose vocal quality is poor. The three defects you will find are throatiness, thinness, and either nasality or denasality.

The throaty voice is unpleasantly deep and husky; the sound seems lost in the throat or even in the chest. The prevalence of throatiness, which results in making words hard to understand, accounts in large part for the fact that "Whadja say?" is the sentence most frequently spoken in the United States.[5]

Exercises in throat relaxation and in clear articulation may be recommended to throaty-voiced students. If several in one class have the same handicap, they may perform some of the exercises as a group, while other groups are working on faulty pronunciation or on overcoming other defects. A good exercise for throat relaxation is to sit upright, drop the head forward until the chin touches the chest, turn the head slowly to the right until the chin touches the right shoulder, then turn to the left, and repeat several times. Another is to take an

[5] Some years ago researchers for Funk and Wagnalls made this interesting but disconcerting discovery.

imaginary drink of water and say "Oh" as the throat is open, a second drink and "Ah," and other imaginary drinks for the other vowel sounds. Still another exercise is to open the jaws wide and say the vowel sounds, to be followed later by words in which each vowel sound appears.

In all such exercises, it is perhaps needless to say, no individual should be made to feel ashamed or self-conscious. A teacher sometimes has an entire class perform certain exercises when he knows that only two or three students need them. The small-group plan, though, with each group working on something that it needs, is less wasteful of time.

The thin voice lacks resonance, is usually high in pitch, and sometimes degenerates into an unpleasant whine. Humming is often mentioned to students as a means of increasing resonance. Long practice in sustaining the *m, n,* and *ng* sounds is also beneficial; these sounds may later be combined with vowels, as *am, em,* etc., and, still later, sentences with many *m's, n's* and *ng's* may be used. Elizabeth von Hesse, in *So To Speak* (Philadelphia: Frederick A. Stokes Co., 1941), advises, "Hang-ng on-n to your sing-nging-ng soun-nds."

Only the sounds of *m, n,* and *ng* should be allowed to pass through the nose. If any others do so, speech is described as nasal. The reverse of nasality, called denasality, occurs when the sounds of *m, n,* and *ng* do not pass through the nose. A speaker then sounds as if he has a cold; he says "ted tidy Idiads" instead of "ten tiny Indians."

A student may test his nasality by placing his finger beside his nose as, with his mouth open, he prolongs the sounds of *m, n,* and *ng,* and then of other consonants and the vowels. If he can feel distinct vibration for the *m, n,* and *ng* sounds, and not for the others, his nasal resonance is normal. If, however, he feels much vibration when he pronounces vowels, he should practice making the sound issue from his mouth instead of his nose; unless there is something organically wrong, he should be able to overcome his difficulty. Denasality, though, is often due to stoppages and perhaps can be corrected only by a speech pathologist.

Improving Pitch

Most persons are unaware of their own vocal shortcomings, because they have never actually heard themselves speak. If your school has facilities for making recordings, let each of your students hear himself. More than likely he will say, or at least think, "Do I really sound that bad?"

One of the causes of "sounding that bad" is defective pitch. Very high-pitched voices are offensive, and very low-pitched ones are often monotonous. Frequently the only step needed for a cure is a conscious attempt to vary the pitch—for the low-pitched near monotone to reach toward higher levels and for the person with high pitch to try to bring the voice down. The vocal apparatus in most persons can be used flexibly if it is given a chance, but nearly everyone tends to use it in the easiest way, regardless of whether that way is pleasant to his hearers. Throat-relaxation exercises, like those described on page 435, are helpful, but primarily the treatment for most students is simply to make them aware of the deficiency and to suggest reasons for doing something about it.

Improving Enunciation

Americans are breath-lazy, throat-lazy, jaw-lazy, tongue-lazy, and lip-lazy. As George Arliss declared, the chief defect of British speech is snippiness, and the chief defect of American speech is sloppiness. As a result of our lazy habits, we say "Uh dunno," "Whurya gawn?" "Whuh timezut?" etc. Although overprecise articulation seems affected, there is a happy medium in enunciation as in all things else.

Unless there is something wrong physiologically, anyone can improve his enunciation if he wishes. That fact implies that the teacher, or someone else, must supply motivation if enunciation is to be improved. One clever but possibly not very humane teacher told her class that she was going to read to them the questions that would be asked on the examination the next day, but that she would read as she had heard some of them talk. She proceeded to mumble through the questions so that only a word here and there was distinct. Most of the students understood what she was trying to do! Other teachers have had their students note the enunciation of favorite TV stars and movie actors, and a few have skilfully led students to a realization that recognized leaders in almost all spheres of activity enunciate clearly. Still other teachers have used friendly ridicule—not of individual students but of people who habitually sound as if their mouths are filled with mush.

Poor enunciators tend to mumble, to insert extra syllables into words, or to omit syllables. The mumblers habitually speak indistinctly. Mouthers say, "abaout" for "about," "baud" for "bad." The omitters tend to ignore middle syllables: "telscope" for "telescope," "connent" for "continent." All three defects, unless they are cured early, seem to increase with age. So, if you can motivate your students to struggle effectually against them, you can save many people hundreds of hours of unpleasant listening.

Improving Pronunciation

It is not a criminal offense to mispronounce a word; in fact, if one could go back far enough into the past, one might find a time with the mispronunciation regarded as correct. Pronunciations do change; Alexander Pope and his contemporaries, for instance, said "tay" for "tea" and "jine" for "join."

Right there is your entering wedge for correcting errors in pronunciation. Your students are modern—aggressively so. They want to do almost everything the way it is done today—none of this old-fashioned stuff for them. Encourage them to be as modern in their pronunciations as they are in their clothes or their music. Certainly, Grandpa said, "crick," but we say "creek" today; Mark Twain's friends said, "genuwine," but we don't.

Let them know, too, how dictionary makers determine what is correct pronunciation. The diacritical marks do not reflect someone's opinion; rather, they are determined by a careful study of how each word is pronounced by the majority of the educated people who use it. When one keeps up with the dictionary, one is keeping up with the Joneses—as well as with the Smiths and the Smythes.

If you use pronunciation drills, be sure to concentrate on words that you have heard your students mispronounce. Such drills are usually better than stopping each student whenever he mispronounces a word; you should make a mental note of his error and include the word later in a list. Thus, you will save yourself the fate of the wife who always corrected her husband's mistakes:

> I whammed her on the cerebellum
> Her beating brain to overwhelm;
> I hung her body on an elm—
> And as she died, she whispered, "Elm." [6]

You will also save your students from embarrassment and dislike of speaking. Your list will probably consist mostly of common words: "asked," "column," "February," "government," "get," "idea," "just," "library," and so on.

Some teachers devote two or three minutes per class hour on pronunciation demons. For instance, the class each day for a week

[6] By Morris Bishop, quoted in *Word Study*, April, 1943.

may pronounce the same five or ten words, printed on large cards. New cards are introduced the following week, with some of the older ones brought back for review.

A less time-devouring method is to have daily class drills on 10 words, changed each day for 20 days, with occasional reviews. Then comes a test in which each student is given, entirely at random, 10 of the 200 words. He gets 100 per cent if he pronounces all 10 correctly, barely passing if he misses 1, and zero if he misses 2 or more. The weakness of this plan is its excessive emphassis on grades.

One caution: Be sure that the pronunciations you attack are actually unaccepted. Some teachers have been surprised to learn that their own favorite pronunciations of such words as "bouquet," "gratis," "isolated," "menu," and "panorama" are not the only ones listed in reputable dictionaries.

Improving Body Control

Bernard shuffles up to the front of the class, glances in final desperation at the teacher, sways a little, puts both feet close together and sways some more, fidgets with his hands, and focuses his gaze on his toes as he begins to mumble at the floor. Bernard, with numerous variations, is in almost all classes. What can be done for him and his sister?

The importance of having a friendly class atmosphere has already been emphasized. That in itself will help Bernard and Bernardine, will give them confidence that their efforts will be received cordially, will contribute to the knowledge that they are before the class because they have something to offer and not because teacher wants to criticize them. But there is something more that the teacher can do, something too rarely done in English classes. The teacher can give all the students practice in walking, in pantomiming, and in using the hands.

Here is how one teacher accomplishes this. In connection with vocabulary work, she and the class list as many synonyms as possible for "say" and "walk." The ostensible purpose is to add words like "orate" and "saunter" to students' vocabularies. Then she asks for volunteers to act out some of the words in front of the class: Doris shouts, Jimmy strolls, and so forth. When the volunteers have performed, words are still left; the teacher asks the non-volunteers, in pairs, to act out some of the words in order to demonstrate the contrast: Bernard skips while Roy totters. Having the shy ones work in pairs makes each less self-conscious.

Then, when all the words have been pantomimed, the teacher temporarily abandons vocabulary work and casually inquires what are the characteristics of an attractive style of walking. "How do movie stars usually walk?" Gradually she elicits the information that graceful walkers carry the weight on the balls of the feet, keep the abdomen flat, have the shoulders relaxed, and lead with the chest. She emphasizes leading with the chest, because that is perhaps the most important essential. "Let's try it," she says to the class. "We'll have a little parade around the room, with everybody walking the way we have described. Bernard, you lead, and we'll all fall in behind you." Later, she frequently reminds the class of the principles of graceful walking, asks for more illustrations, and tactfully suggests that it is worth their while to walk well, in class and out.

She makes more use of pantomime on other occasions. She also has her students make many explanations at the blackboard and give a chalk talk now and then. In the students' minds, the purpose is only to explain something to the class, but the teacher knows that, when people use their hands in public, they think less about them.

This teacher says little about gestures, because she believes that no gesture is worthwhile unless it is a natural accompaniment of the thought; the arm waving of the elocutionists she deplores. She says more about looking at the audience, and herself puts on a little act in which she alternately addresses the floor, the ceiling, the window, the door, and the portrait of Longfellow.

Perhaps the methods of this teacher seem too unorthodox to you. However, they do get results—her students appear more happy and cooperative and less self-conscious than those of dozens of other teachers.

"Trippingly on the Tongue"

You recall Hamlet's famous advice:

Speak the speech, I pray you, as I pronounced it to you, trippingly on the tongue; but if you mouth it, as many of your players do, I had as lief the town-crier spoke my lines.

We teachers may not succeed in getting all our students to speak as well as Hamlet advised, but we should, in the years that we teach them, be able to help them to find something worth saying, plan how to say it, and say it reasonably well.

Speech is but the incorporation of thought.—JOSEPH JOUBERT
Let him be sure to leave other men their turn to speak.—FRANCIS BACON

As a vessel is known by the sound, whether it be cracked or not, so men are proved, by their speeches, whether they be wise or foolish.— DEMOSTHENES

The voice is a human sound which nothing inanimate can perfectly imitate. It has an authority and an insinuating property which writing lacks. It is not merely so much air, but air modulated and impregnated with life.—JOSEPH JOUBERT

THE IDEA BOX

GUIDING CLASS DISCUSSIONS

Examples of remarks that can improve discussions:
1. "What evidence is there for this belief?"
2. "This digression has been interesting, but let's get back on the subject."
3. "Should we bring out the facts before we attempt a solution?"
4. "Is it true that so far we have agreed on these points . . . ?"
5. "Let's hear now from those who haven't said anything."
6. "Could it be that we are letting personal prejudices sway us too much?"
7. "I don't understand. Can you think of an example?"
8. "Is a middle-of-the-road position more sensible than either extreme?"
9. "Can anyone think of circumstances in which this suggestion would not work?"

A TIP TO A DISCUSSION LEADER

A simple but effective opening for a youthful discussion leader is to ask, "Do all of you agree with George (or Lucille)?"

STUDENT CHECK LIST FOR DISCUSSION

Marian Zollinger and Mildred A. Dawson suggest fifteen questions by which students may evaluate their own contributions to class discussion. "Evaluation of Oral Communication," *English Journal*, XLVII (Nov., 1958), 500.

WHEN SHOULD ONE CRITICIZE?

Professor Loren Reid, a distinguished teacher of speech, says that students may justifiably be interrupted for quickly remediable flaws in delivery, such as insufficient volume, poor eye contact, or faulty vocal emphasis. "When teachers want to give their attention specifically to delivery, they assign brief speeches." But there should be no interruptions to consider content; such criticism may be delayed until the end. *Teaching Speech* (Columbia, Mo.: Artcraft Press, 1960), p. 159.

COMBATING STAGE FRIGHT: MORE SUGGESTIONS

1. Advise fearful students to start a talk with something funny. Doing so may relax them and the audience too.

2. Help students select topics that they are genuinely interested in, even concerned about. Thinking about the subject will leave less time to think about the self.

3. Advise rehearsing the talk but not memorizing it. Fear of forgetting contributes to fright.

OVERCOMING SHYNESS

1. "A good device for overcoming initial reticence is to introduce a subject which contains much controversial matter. As soon as the teacher sees that the subject matter has caught the fancy of the class, he allows students to select a chairman and plan their own talks." (Arigo La Tanzi, Braintree, Mass.)

2. Another teacher begins by having students make an announcement of a real or imaginary event, including time, place, purpose, cost, and any other needed information. Generally, the more imaginary the event, the livelier the announcement. Second step: a prepared (but not memorized) three-minute oral reading of anything the student likes.

GETTING THEM ALL TO TALK

Donald W. Hensel, Boulder, Colorado, pits class against class in a "discussion race." He notes the percentage who contribute to class discussion and announces it to the next class, who try to exceed it. Students urge their fellows to "Say *something*." The shy gradually become less shy, and slowly the quality of discussion also improves because of the general participation. (Probably not a useful device for more than a few weeks.)

ORGANIZING THE WORK IN SPEECH

In Atlantic City High School, a speech teacher takes over each of the ninth grade English classes for six weeks during the year, working with several classes the first six weeks, other classes the next six weeks, and so on. In the tenth, eleventh, and twelfth grade the English teachers build on these foundations, including activities according to a departmental plan. For details, and useful suggestions about organizing the whole speech program, see Ruth E. French, "Planning Speech Training for All Youth," *English Journal*, XLV (Sept., 1956), 328.

THE SPEECH CONSULTANT

West Canada Valley High School, Middleville, New York, employs for eighty half-days a year a speech consultant from a nearby college. He has worked out a specific schedule of speech teaching and gives instruction beyond the scope of most English teachers. For details, see "The Speech Consultant Teaches Speech in the English Classroom," *English Record*. XIII, No. 2 (1962), 30.

A SIMPLE SPEECH PLAN

In an extraordinarily compact but specific article, "Let Any Student Speak" (*Illinois English Bulletin,* Feb., 1961), Wilmer Lamar describes a highly successful program for teaching speech in the English classroom. One of the many techniques suggested is the following of a simple outline, especially useful for inexperienced teachers. The five divisions of a speech are (1) awakener (question, striking statement, narration, arousing of suspense, quotation, personal incident), (2) point (statement of what the speaker is driving at), (3) reason (why the point is important), (4) examples (the body of the talk), (5) conclusion (restatement, quotation, relevant question, or call to action).

MEASURING CHANGE OF OPINION

Before an argumentative or persuasive presentation or discussion, ask class members to indicate on slips of paper whether they favor or oppose the proposition or are undecided. After the presentation, have them indicate "more strongly favor," "favor to about same degree," "more strongly oppose," "oppose to about same degree," "still undecided," "shifted from favor to undecided," "shifted from oppose to undecided," etc. Have a pair of students tally the number and direction of opinion shifts.

BRAG SESSIONS

Kate Kitchen (*North Carolina English Teacher,* Dec., 1957) invites her seniors to keep their classmates informed of any honors or distinctions that come to the group during the year. A good speech activity, and splendid for morale, Mrs. Kitchen comments.

"PYGMALION TO THE RESCUE"

Alice B. Tolle, disturbed by her Illinois students' pronunciation of "pin" for "pen" and "arn" for "iron," etc., expresses indebtedness to Shaw or *Pygmalion* or *My Fair Lady* for her decision to spend class time on lively pronunciation drills; she supplemented Proofessor Higgins' tactics by using a tape recorder. *Illinois English Bulletin,* Nov., 1960.

AUDIO-VISUAL AIDS AND DEMONSTRATIONS

Encourage use of maps, charts, pictures, diagrams, and the like in talks and reports. These may be especially useful in how-it-works or how-to-do-it explanations.

Demonstrations, with actual objects, may help shy students forget themselves. For example, a basic dance step, artificial respiration, tuning a musical instrument.

BRAINSTORMING

As a problem-solving technique (to be used only in the face of a *genuine* problem) try a brief brainstorming session. The rules: (1) Allow no adverse criticism, even if a suggestion seems utterly ridiculous. (2) Welcome imaginative ideas. (3) Try for many and diverse ideas. (4) Combine and improve ideas (called "hitchhiking").

A recorder notes all suggestions. A day later, the group appraises the ideas to see whether any of them or any combination of them may afford a solution.

STUDENT RESPONSIBILITY

Let students conduct bees, vocabulary tests, and dictations, and carry messages, make announcements, etc. Put poor speakers in the back of the room so that they have to speak distinctly to be heard.

INDIVIDUAL DIFFERENCES

"Avoid 'blanket' assignments for themes and speeches. Present a long list of choices, or let the student choose his own within reasonable bounds. For example, in speaking, a typical assignment may be called a 'sales talk,' but the student may sell any thing or idea that he wishes." (Harold R. Hansen, Menomonie, Wis.)

PLANNING TO DO THINGS

In a class that really does things—dramatizes, takes field trips, interviews, etc.—discussions involving the planning for these things are usually lively.

IMPROVING REPORTS

A West Virginia ninth grade class taught by Anna Brochick made these decisions about ways to improve its reports: (1) Every oral report must show that the reporter "went out of his way" to make it good. (2) The beginning and ending should show some originality. (3) The reporter must try to use acceptable speech. (4) Material should be well organized. (5) The reporter should try to make himself easily heard. (6) Each report should be subject to group evaluation and to evaluation by the reporter.

ORAL ENGLISH IN COMMUNITY AFFAIRS

The Speech Department of Reno, Nevada, recommends: "The speech program can help to promote community affairs such as Red Cross and Community Chest campaigns. Student participants become more civic conscious. Presenting such programs before adults makes for excellent public relations because the citizens of the community have an opportunity to see one thing that the schools are doing." This department also recommends inviting guests to class periods when there are special oral presentations.

SPEAKER'S BUREAU

In Roosevelt High School, Chicago, a "Speaker's Bureau," with a faculty sponsor, is in charge of publicizing school activities. Members make announcements in homerooms, etc., and sometimes are sent to speak before civic organizations such as Kiwanis, Union League Club, etc. (Lynne Harford)

ORAL ENGLISH IN VOCATIONAL GUIDANCE

Students may write to trade schools or colleges in which they are interested. Then, in class, they present prepared talks on entrance requirements, courses and training offered, social life, and rating.

EXTEMPORANEOUS SPEAKING

"I use magazine articles as vehicles for training in an extemporaneous style of informal speaking. A student selects a magazine article, reads it, makes brief notes, and discusses the article in front of the class. I believe we destroy motivation by asking a student to stand before the class and discuss 'a day in the country' or 'my most embarrassing moment.' A magazine article, however, gives him solid ground upon which to stand and improves his oral English." (Frances Albright, Portales, N.M.)

SOUND OFF

At the University of Illinois High School, Robert E. Potter's seniors, at unannounced times, were asked to "sound off" for three minutes (no more) on any topic they wanted to talk about. The class was given ten minutes to prepare, and students were called on in random order. No criticisms were made until all had spoken, although Mr. Potter wrote on separate pages comments at which each student could look later. Good practice in impromptu speaking, Mr. Potter claims.

BREATHING

"To obtain clear, distinct speech, the most valuable technique is the regular practice of diaphragmatic breathing and vowel sounding in class, in chorus. This need only be done enough to educate pupils to the idea that speech is always more clear and forceful when supported by well-controlled breath." (John Ferrett, Braintree, Mass.)

TONGUE TWISTERS WITH A PURPOSE

Many students who are slovenly in enunciation do not distinguish clearly between the voiceless and voiced consonants: *f* and *v, t* and *d, p* and *b, k* and *g, s* and *z, ch* and *j, sh* and *zh, th* as in "thin" and *th* as in "this." Tongue twisters, written by teacher or students, will help. Examples from *Better English,* published by Ginn & Co. (Boston, 1959):

Face the fancy vase and find the fine vine, Vinnie.
Mat's satin hat had saddened Dad, hadn't it?
Proud papa babbled, played, bubbled, clapped, and boasted.
Come goat, come goat, come goat, come goat, come goat!
Chug—chug—jug—jug—chug—jug—chuck—chuck—junk—chuck—
    junk—junk—chunk—chuck.
Big black pigs bickered blatantly by papa's big pig pen, Ben.

GETTING OTHER TEACHERS TO HELP

1. If possible, get other teachers to encourage good speech habits in their classes.

2. The teaching of parliamentary procedure is sometimes allocated to the homeroom.

USING "WEEKS"

"Book Week," "Good Manners Week," etc., often supply excellent motivation for oral activities.

STANDARDS FOR ORAL READING

Positive Qualities	Negative Qualities
1. Correct pronunciation of every word	1. Carelessness
2. Distinctness and open tones	2. Tight jaw, closed mouth, lazy lips
3. Suitable speed	3. Too slow, too fast, jerky
4. Correct phrasing	4. Wrong pauses
5. Observance of punctuation marks	5. Not understanding the meaning
6. Variety of tone	6. Monotone
7. Smoothness	7. Repetition of syllables or words
8. Showing the reader's interest	8. Lack of preparation
9. Ability to glance away from the book for brief glances at the audience	9. Indifference to audience, hanging head, wrong position of book
10. Comfort while reading	10. Breathlessness
11. Good habits of speech	11. Adding syllables not in print (such as "uh, an")
12. Correct emphasis on words	12. Extra stress given to wrong syllables or words
13. Ability to read as if telling something	13. Singsong
14. Vitality in reading	14. Lack of vigor

(From *Minimum Essentials in the Mechanics of English Composition*, prepared for use in Albuquerque, New Mexico, schools.)

TO ELIMINATE SINGSONG READING

"Copying poetry in prose paragraphs is a valuable help in destroying the singsong so common with beginning readers of poetry." (Frances Albright, Portales, N.M.)

PUZZLES

An excellent way to make students aware of the need for clear presentation is to have them explain the solutions of certain puzzles. For example, two trains, each 1,000 feet long, meet. The only sidetrack is 500 feet long. How can they get past each other?

TALL STORIES

To make students forget themselves in their subjects, try a tall-story contest.

COMMEDIA DELL'ARTE

A useful device for overcoming shyness and teaching thinking on one's feet is a modification of the old *commedia dell'arte*. The teacher or a student briefly summarizes a simple story with few characters. Students then act it out, improvising the dialog. Once the students have become accustomed to making it up as they go along, they may be given a story with the ending omitted; the actors must then work out a reasonable solution by themselves *while* they are acting.

15

THE TEACHER WHO GROWS

THE PALACE OF ART

The teacher of English is not a creature apart. Despite what he knows that the majority in the community do not know, despite his travels in the realms of gold, he is still a human being, with human strength, human weakness, human need.

You remember Tennyson's "The Palace of Art." The poet says that his soul built a magnificent palace, "full of great rooms and small," splendidly decorated with tapestries depicting landscapes and myths, and adorned with portraits of Milton, Shakespeare, Dante, Homer, and others. There dwelt the poet's soul,

> Communing with herself: "All these are mine,
> And let the world have peace or wars,
> 'Tis one to me.
>
> "I take possession of men's minds and deeds,
> I live in all things great and small,
> I sit apart holding no forms or creeds,
> But contemplating all."

"Three years she throve, but on the fourth she fell," because in her lovely palace were excessive solitude, "uncertain shapes," and "dull stagnation." The air needed changing. Tapestries portraying homes and rivers and wood nymphs were inadequate substitutes for real homes, real rivers, real people; the tapestries would become more meaningful if they were not separated completely from actuality;

Milton and his "L'Allegro" would mean most to one who knew first-hand of upland hamlets and shepherds who tell stories "under the hawthorn in the dale." So, Tennyson says, his soul "threw her royal robes away."

> "Make me a cottage in the vale," she said . . .
> "Yet pull not down my palace towers, that are
> So lightly, beautifully built:
> Perchance I may return with others there."

Regardless of how much the teacher loves literature—and he must love it—he cannot afford to immerse himself in it and ignore reality. Literature is a reflection and interpretation of life, but it is not life itself. The teacher, like the poet, must not lose contact with life, must not climb into the tower of a Palace of Art. His students are alive; the people in the community are alive. The teacher of English is a living link between the life about him and the life depicted in literature, just as the teacher of music is a link between "pops" and Beethoven. To his students the English teacher brings something fine—an enrichment of knowledge concerning themselves and their heritage. If he is to succeed in effecting this enrichment, though, he must know people as they are, as they breathe, work, play, sweat, eat, drink, smoke, talk, and dream. A teacher who knew only literature would be like a physician who knew only medicine and was ignorant of the bodies he was to strengthen.

THE TREADMILL

So the successful teacher cannot isolate himself in the Palace of Art. No more, however, can he place himself on a treadmill. You have perhaps seen pictures of a treadmill: One or more persons move a large cylinder by climbing steps mounted upon it; as their weight pushes one step down, another takes its place. Over and over they repeat the process, hour after hour and day after day, climbing the same steps, looking always at the same monotonous fixtures, reaching no higher point, while the massive cylinder slowly turns. Those long on the treadmill lose their human qualities and become automatons or less—mere physical forces, part of a mechanical assemblage of weights and counterweights.

Almost any kind of work can become a treadmill. Teaching can, very readily, but it need not. The danger lies in the ease with which the teacher, after a few years, may fall into a routine.

Today I teach as I taught before;
Tomorrow I work as I wrought before;
Friday I cry as I cried before;
Monday I die as I died before.

———

Bowed by the weight of tediousness he stands
Behind his desk and glowers at the class,
The emptiness of ennui in his face,
And in his eyes dull hate of all he sees.

How can a teacher avoid the treadmill? Perhaps a minister gave
the clue. For more than fifty years he had followed the routine of his
calling: a sermon every Sunday, prayer meeting every Wednesday,
christenings, weddings, funerals—each week much like 3,000 others.
His hair had become white, his face was wrinkled, but his eyes were
still vivacious as he rose to speak at the banquet on the occasion of
his retirement. "I have been excited for fifty-five years," he began.
"People excite me. They interest me. During my fifty-five years in
the ministry I have learned much about people. I know how they
blunder, how they err, how they stumble and often fall. I know how
they need leadership both human and divine. But I am perpetually
excited by the sparks I find in them—sparks of goodness and kindness
and self-sacrifice, sparks of promise for the future. In my small way
I have spent my life fanning sparks."

He concluded with quotations from Kahlil Gibran and Elizabeth
Barrett Browning:

You have been told also that life is darkness, and in your weariness you
    echo what was said by the weary.
And I say that life is indeed darkness save when there is urge,
And all urge is blind save when there is knowledge,
And all knowledge is vain save when there is work,
And all work is empty save when there is love,
And when you work with love you bind yourself to yourself, and to one
    another, and to God.[1]

———

The world waits
For help. Beloved, let us love so well,
Our work shall still be better for our love,
And still our love be sweeter for our work.[2]

Need more be said about how to avoid the treadmill?

[1] Kahlil Gibran, from *The Prophet* (New York: Alfred A. Knopf, Inc., 1923).
[2] E. B. Browning, from "Aurora Leigh."

THE TEACHER AND THE STUDENT

"Should we try to be pals to our students?" an earnest young prospective teacher once asked the author of this book.

"Heavens, no!" was the reply. "You people are already old men and old women in the eyes of most high school students, and every year you'll become more ancient. You can hope to become an older friend; maybe, if you're so inclined and really prepared for the job, a respected counselor. But a pal—never. Pals have to have much in common including similarity in age. Thirty-two and twenty-two may be pals, but not twenty-two and fifteen.

"Despite what I've said about your antiquity, though, some of you are young and attractive enough that one or more of your students will dream of you in a quite unorthodox teacher-student relationship. In other words, some of them may get what used to be called a 'crush on you.' When you suspect it, ignore it if you can. Pretend that it doesn't exist. It will probably go away. If pretense becomes impossible, if there is an open avowal, be gentle. Say how flattered you are, but how impossible the situation is. Make the break gentle, but clean and complete. Leave no room for hope. The student's pain and bitterness will last no more than a week or so—about the time it lasts when a going-steady pair breaks up.

"While we're on the general subject of relationships with students, let me urge you to continue learning about young people. You'll never know enough. Take a graduate course in adolescent psychology. A bit of sociology and anthropology may answer a question or two. Some fiction for teen-agers is realistic and filled with insights. You'll learn most, of course, about young people from your own students, from their writing, from their class responses, from their participation and behavior in cocurricular activities. Try to meet them socially on some occasions. Dinner at a student's home can be both revealing and pleasant.

"All this is relevant to the original question about 'palship.' Give them your best efforts. You are a teacher. You can be a teacher-friend. That's the end of the line. Next year you're teacher-friend to another generation."

THE ENGLISH TEACHER AND HIS COLLEAGUES

The English teacher has an especially strong motive for cooperating with his fellows. Since English overlaps all other fields to some extent, working with other teachers will pay large dividends to any English instructor. As has been said earlier, the English teacher hopes that all teachers in the school will constantly illustrate the attitude that good English is important. Happy relationships with other members of the English department may help to translate that hope to reality.

In meetings of his own department, the young teacher may best be rather quiet in his first year or so. Maybe, fresh from his exhilarating college experience, he sees ways in which the department should be reformed. Let him postpone the reform for a little while. Let him try in his own classes as much as possible of the reformed program, but let him prove *himself* as a teacher before he reforms others (who have already proved themselves). If his teaching is outstandingly successful, if some of his new methods and materials work miracles, the other members will be more receptive when, dry behind the ears, he speaks up in meetings.

A small but important matter: A teacher should find out about channels of communication in his school. If, for example, supplies are needed or a recommendation of some kind is to be made, should the information be channeled through a course chairman, the department head, the business office, the assistant principal, or someone else? Sad to say, some teachers and administrators resent being by-passed; sometimes bypassing will, indeed, result in confusion. Following channels, then, is the most sensible procedure. Only if a clearly unnecessary block develops is another procedure justified.

THE ENGLISH TEACHER AND THE COMMUNITY

Although in most communities a teacher is not now required to be so straitlaced as formerly, he is (quite rightly) looked upon as a leader and to some extent a model for youth. In the not-so-old days teachers sometimes had to sign contracts containing some rather absurd provisions: that they would not leave town on more than four week ends during the school year, that they would teach a Sunday-school class, that they would not use makeup, that they would not dye their hair, and even—in at least one community—that they would not fall in love! Today such stipulations are rarely found, because teachers are becoming increasingly regarded as responsible adult citizens who are entitled to lead lives of their own.

Nevertheless, just as a doctor or a minister assumes certain professional obligations when he voluntarily chooses his profession, so does the teacher. The obligations are a part of the profession. The bricklayer may carouse nights and week ends and still do what he is paid for—lay so many bricks a day. The milliner's assistant may be guilty of some variety or varieties of turpitude without impairing her trimming of hats. But the teacher, as a leader of youth, cannot conscientiously set an example that he would not want young people to follow.

This does not mean that the teacher should be a prude—far from it. The teacher of English should be one of the most broad-minded persons in the community, because he knows the mainsprings of human action, and because he knows the weaknesses as well as the strengths of people. So he is not a prude, but he does try to live in such a way that young people would not find him an unwholesome example.

He chooses clothes that are reasonably conservative without being dull or hopelessly outmoded. Unless he receives advice to the contrary (this seldom happens today), he smokes if he wishes at times when he is not on duty. In most communities he will not be criticized if he drinks a cocktail in his own or someone else's home, though he should not be a habitué of the neighborhood tavern. He dances and plays cards and goes bowling if he likes and, in general, leads a normal social life.

It is encouraging to note the increasing amount of political freedom being given to teachers. Whereas in former years a teacher might lose his position if he went to a Republican rally in a Democratic town (or vice versa), today a teacher is expected to maintain as active an interest in politics—even local politics—as anyone else. That is, in this area also, he is being regarded more and more as a responsible adult citizen of a democracy. It is his duty, as a well-informed member of the community, to express himself on matters of political importance. This does not mean that he electioneers in his classroom, but it does mean that in public meetings he does not hesitate to speak his mind.

Another question that merits consideration is this: What does the community, especially the small one, expect of the English teacher as his special contribution to the life of the community?

The English teacher is usually thought of as a person who can speak and write reasonably well and who knows much about literature. If he can act or if he has musical ability or other talents, the small community will consider him an especially welcome addition and perhaps will overburden him with requests, some of which he may have to refuse. Even though he has no special talents, he will occasionally be asked to review a current book or play, give a talk at a meeting of the PTA, write a feature or a review for the local newspaper, or possibly give a talk over the air. Oral readings from literature, if well selected and well delivered, afford excellent entertainment and may win friends for himself and his school. If the teacher has a good subject and enough time, he may occasionally speak before men's luncheon clubs or women's gatherings.

Words are the English teacher's chief stock in trade, and his chief value to the community outside of school hours lies in what he does with words. He should not consider himself a missionary bringing sweetness and light to the uncultured heathen, but he may bring wholesome entertainment and worthwhile information to his community through what he writes and says. Although the welfare of students is his first responsibility, he may, if he has time and energy remaining, enjoy himself and give pleasure to others by using his skill with words.

THE ENGLISH TEACHER AND HIS BOOKS

The English teacher should be the most omnivorous reader among the faculty. Books are his specialty, and all learning is his province. Never, of course, can he catch up on his reading. The presses clatter and rumble ceaselessly.

Inevitably, much of his reading will be in Western classics that he has missed or largely forgotten: Homer, Aeschylus, Aristotle, Vergil, Ovid, Dante, Racine, and many more. Some reading is necessary to refresh his memory of the giants of English and American literature. He is aware of vast gaps, too: The literature of the Orient, of Australia, of Latin America may be almost unknown to him. Books for adolescents he should at least skim. Philosophy, sociology, the fine arts, science for laymen, good current magazines—the list goes on and on.

Then there is professional reading. The *English Journal* tops the list, but he has found that *College English, College Composition and Communication,* and even *Elementary English* have many relevant articles. *Abstracts of English Studies* gives him a glimpse of what is happening in literary scholarship. *The Reading Teacher* and *Educational Leadership,* the *NEA Journal*—he expands the list to suit his special interests. Important new books on teaching and on literary and linguistic scholarship appear every year.

A hopeless task? Yes, in a way, for the days and the nights and the summer are never long enough. Yet, in another way, it isn't hopeless and it isn't a task. There is always a book to look forward to, a magazine crying to be read, the pleasure of new knowledge to be savored. How can any English teacher's life be dull?

THE ENGLISH TEACHER AS EXPERIMENTER

There is an easy way to teach English in the second year and forever after. That way is simply to repeat whatever was done in the first year, to follow exactly the same outlines, the same lesson plans. So easy! But so deadening to teacher and students alike! So futile —for whose first year of teaching (or thirtieth) has ever been so nearly perfect as to deserve endless repetition?

The lively, exciting classroom is the one where something new is always being tried—new books, other new materials, new procedures. It is the classroom where the teacher isn't always sure how something will turn out, because part of what he is doing he has never done before. At least once a week, maybe even once a day, he conducts a little experiment. Some of the experiments fail; some succeed; but they all help to keep him alert.

No big experiments are needed—just a substitution of this poem for that; just a little more room for student initiative this hour, an unusual kind of test tomorrow, a filmstrip, a tryout of a programed textbook. Sometime, perhaps, there *will* be a big experiment—*Research* maybe—with all the trimmings of control groups and coefficients of correlation and a picture in the paper. But that isn't necessary. Lots of little experiments are enough to keep sap flowing.

THE ENGLISH TEACHER AS JOINER

In some schools it is made clear that every teacher is "expected" to join the National Educational Association (NEA) and the state association. Such associations have helped greatly in the fight to increase teachers' salaries and pensions; they have made some contributions to educational research; and occasionally an article useful to a classroom teacher appears in their publications. For these reasons, joining should be voluntary, before anybody needs to say "It's expected" or "We're always a hundred per cent."

The organization that addresses itself exclusively to English teachers is the National Council of Teachers of English. In addition to publishing half a dozen important magazines, the NCTE has sixty or so committees working on problems of the profession, publishes pamphlets and a few books on curricular and other matters, sponsors literary tours abroad, manages a talented-student competition that has helped many young people obtain college scholarships, works toward a reasonable teacher load, and makes available to its members, at reduced cost, large numbers of recordings, filmstrips, literary maps, and other teaching aids. Its conventions, held annually at Thanksgiving time, move to a different city each year in accordance with a set geographical pattern; the leaders of the profession are often at the speakers' tables there, but competent young persons—tomorrow's leaders—are constantly being sought. The NCTE is the one organization that an English teacher cannot afford not to join.

Most states and some communities or other areas within a state have English-teacher organizations, of which most are affiliated with the NCTE. Because these organizations concern themselves with state or area problems in English teaching, they are worth support. Some of them publish excellent small magazines or newsletters, and most of them hold one or more professional meetings each year.

For those especially interested in reading, the International Reading Association has a strong program and a good magazine. The Association for Supervision and Curriculum Development of the NEA appeals to those who do the things suggested by its title; it, too, has a good magazine, of which perhaps a fourth is pertinent to English teaching. Other special-interest associations exist and may appeal to individual teachers.

"Should I join a teachers' union?" The answer to that may best be left to your own conscience. Unions have effected considerable improvements in salaries and working conditions in a number of places. But, since strikes are a union's chief weapon, a basic question is whether it is ethical for members of any profession to strike. This question has arisen in the medical profession in countries that have government control over compensation for doctors, and has been a focus of discussion in teachers' strikes in the United States. It is not a question that permits an easy answer.

ADVANCEMENT IN THE PROFESSION

In several ways a devoted and hardworking teacher of English can advance professionally. Some school systems require earning of additional college credits, educational travel, in-service study, or contributions to curriculum development as a prerequisite to certain upgradings in salary. But aside from these rather obvious means, in what ways may a teacher move upward?

There is, of course, a chance to move to a "better" school. "Better" should not, however, be confused with "bigger." Some relatively small schools have English departments, English programs, and salary schedules superior to those of many larger schools.

Some English teachers become interested in part- or full-time work in guidance and counseling. A graduate degree in this field may be required. The penalty involved is likely to be abandonment of the classroom in favor of individual work with students and perhaps the conduct of a testing program.

Administration beckons some English teachers. This is most likely to take the form of a department headship, which in large schools generally involves an increase in salary and a reduction of teaching responsibilities. Administration may also mean a principalship or even a superintendency. For either of these posts, special graduate work is almost essential. Although the loss of able classroom teachers to administrative posts is in a way lamentable, it is good for a school to have administrators with strong academic interests and preparation.

College teaching offers another attraction, and, with the increasing shortage of college teachers, genteel raids on high school departments may be expected to increase. However, unless the teacher is willing to expend the time and effort to earn a Ph.D., he will almost inevitably never rise above the lower echelons in college teaching.

Some universities are now developing special Ph.D. programs in the teaching of English. These degrees, which are likely to require a major in English and a minor in education, and which have high school teaching as a prerequisite, prepare teachers to take over college methods courses and to counsel prospective teachers; they also prepare the candidates for headships in large high school English departments and for supervisory positions in city or county school systems, or in state departments of education.

Committee work and writing for local, state, and national organizations of teachers offer a different road for advancement and do not take the teacher from his classroom. Able people are always needed to help with research in these organizations, and their editors are always looking for excellent manuscripts. No money, as a rule, is paid for such work or such articles, but professional prestige may be sufficient remuneration. Some school districts recognize professional contributions in their salary schedules.

Individual research is a special means of advancement, open to a few persons who are patient and thorough. Such research may be in conjunction with work toward an advanced degree, but it need not be. If Congress makes it possible for Project English (in the U.S.

Office of Education) to broaden its scope, financial support may become available for a large number of needed research studies.

Writing is attractive to some English teachers. Good textbooks, which are usually developed cooperatively by teachers and by representatives of a publishing firm, are always needed.[3] Writing for children or adolescents also appeals to some teachers.[4] So do other kinds of writing: A fairly large number of today's novelists, poets, and writers of non-fiction were or are teachers of English.

Unfortunately, several of the roads to advancement tend to take the teacher partly or entirely out of the classroom. For most teachers the best route may be the one that keeps them in the classroom doing the job each day as well as they are able, experimenting on a small scale, working with children, spending most of a lifetime in the same community, growing old and honored in Littleville or in Bigg High. Perhaps no other road leads to greater satisfaction.

THE IDEA BOX

GETTING OFF TO A GOOD START

Maybe it's a cliché, but the best way to build for the future *is* to start with a solid foundation. Useful for this purpose is the NCTE portfolio of a dozen articles, "Helps for Beginning Teachers of English."

THE WIDENING CIRCLE

Can you use this in what must be your constant struggle, the fight against provincialism?

Each of us lives inside a small circle, the circumference of which is our own experience. Timidity or complacence restricts many of us to a never expanding circle; we live our one life and die in its narrow confines. Others of us are battering constantly against the rim, seeking new knowledge and new experiences, reaching out geographically, hunting for what those younger and those older know that we do not, searching backward through time; we bulge the circle here and there, and gradually it becomes a larger circle. The seekers, the bulgers, live a richer, more exciting life than do the provincials—maybe not a happier life but a more rewarding one. The provincials are vegetables; the seekers are Daniel Boones.

WORTH THINKING ABOUT

1. Maybe we English teachers try to do too many things. Maybe it is better to do a few well than to do many poorly. Maybe it is better to hit a clean single than to strike out trying for a home run.

[3] Some suggestions are available in the article "Textbook Writing" in J. N. Hook's *Hook's Guide to Good Writing: Grammar, Style, Usage* (New York: The Ronald Press Co., 1962), pp. 460–61.

[4] *Ibid.*, "Writing for Children," pp. 507–11.

2. Everybody has to have certain skills to make a living; besides, he has to know how to live with his fellow men. English contributes richly to the fulfilment of both needs.

GROWING DOWNWARD AND UPWARD

Is it possible to grow downward and upward at the same time? Beginning teachers may find that they can grow upward in their appreciation of literature by looking at it through the unspoiled eyes of high school students instead of the horn-rimmed, possibly pedantic eyes of their college professors. For an illustration of this enigmatic statement, read "Literature and the Beginning Teacher," by Georgia Christopher, *English Journal*, XLVIII (Sept., 1959), 321.

I'VE BEEN READING . . .

A few social evenings each year may provide both pleasure and profitable interchange, especially if elementary, junior high, senior high, and possibly college teachers participate. After dinner, instead of having a formal program, each person present may talk informally for no more than five minutes on "I've been reading . . ." Literature, professional books and articles, even popular magazine articles may be included.

"DOES ENGLISH HAVE A CHANCE?"

William H. Evans discusses three kinds of "barriers to the improvement of English instruction": community-made barriers, administration-made barriers, teacher-made barriers. In the last category he includes unnecessary repetition, reluctance to experiment, fostering ridiculous traditions, and too little participation in professional organizations. *English Journal*, LII (Jan., 1963), 22.

IF CONFERENCES ARE COMING

1. Little has been written about techniques of the conference with a student. Edgar Logan, of Detroit, makes these suggestions: (1) Make definite appointments. (2) Use no sarcasm. (3) Don't pry into the student's personal life. (4) Stick to the subject, for example, the compositions that the student has written recently. (5) Stress the things *this* student needs as an individual, not something the whole class will soon be taught. Mr. Logan comments that sometimes it is good to talk over a student's paper that the teacher has not yet graded or even read. "Composition Conference," *Clearing House*, XXXV (May, 1961), 524.

2. A detailed discussion of values and techniques of teacher-student conferences is in "We Are Trying Conferences," by Janet Emig, *English Journal*, XLIX (April, 1960), 223. Praise and individualized suggestions for improvement are the chief goals of each biweekly conference.

ENLISTING STUDENT AID

1. Often ask classes for ideas about procedure or content; doing so will increase their interest.

2. Assign routine tasks to students. The experience will be good for them, and the aid will be helpful to you.

MAKING THE CLASSROOM ATTRACTIVE

1. Ideally, each English teacher should have a classroom of his own.

2. Enlist student aid in improving the appearance of your classroom. Students' interest will carry over into their classwork.

3. For principles of bulletin board displays, see Hulda Fritzemuir's "An Effective Aid," *English Journal,* XLVI (Jan., 1957), 42.

INDIVIDUAL DIFFERENCES

1. Says a teacher in Enterprise, Oregon, "I honor outside work that is done by a poor student to raise a grade. I allow book reports that are adapted to the individual interest and reading ability. If a student cannot get the work regularly given, I give him work that will be of benefit to him individually."

2. In Norman, Oklahoma, a forty-minute period is provided daily for conferences with students. In Deering High School, Portland, Maine, the last part of each day is used for this purpose.

3. An occasional period of supervised study gives the teacher the opportunity to help each student with what he needs most.

4. It is desirable that each student keep a notebook specifically for his English. Brother Linus Urban, of Christian Brothers College, Memphis, recommends that for high school sophomores the notebook have separate divisions for minimum essentials, important rules, vocabulary list, individual spelling list, individual notes and quotations, and dictation exercises. Other teachers prefer to have more space devoted to literature, assignments, etc.

TO ENCOURAGE STUDENTS

1. Let them redeem themselves. If a student says "I don't know," give him another chance later, and another, and another. If there is anything right in an answer, accept it even though the rest of the answer needs emending.

2. On the bulletin board each week, list the authors and titles of the best pieces of student writing prepared during the preceding week. Give similar recognition for other "bests." Irvin C. Poley recommends checking the class roll weekly to see that each member has had the opportunity to "distinguish" himself in some way.

THOUGHTS ON DISCIPLINE

1. If the teacher knows his subject and is truly courteous (not merely polite), troubles with discipline seldom arise.

2. Troublemakers are often students who have too little to do or who cannot do what has been assigned. The cures should be obvious.

3. The potential "bad boys" may be given special positions with high-sounding titles: Chairman of the Classroom Library Committee, etc. They may also be won over by having them do special favors for the teacher (not vice versa).

4. Probably a student should never be scolded before the class. A friendly private conference, with an attempt to get at the cause of the difficulty, brings much better results.

TO KEEP THINGS IN ORDER

1. Have a file for pictures, maps, notes, and other supplementary aids.
2. Keep an assignment book.
3. Keep your grade book up to date.
4. Return papers promptly.
5. Use the NCTE Cumulative Reading Record for book reports.
6. Follow a set procedure in recording absences.

FREE AND INEXPENSIVE MATERIALS

In each September issue of the *English Journal* for a number of years, John Searles has listed useful free and inexpensive materials newly developed for secondary English.

KEEPING THE PUBLIC INFORMED

An NCTE pamphlet, "Informing the Public about the English Language Arts," "has been prepared particularly for teachers of English in the elementary and secondary school to help them inform the public about the teaching of English."

GOOD-BY, QUILL PEN

Dr. Joseph Mersand, a past president of the NCTE, asserts, "We shall have to become acquainted with many new materials of instruction, with newer methods of utilizing them, with better ways to understand our students, and devices for evaluating our instruction. The English teacher, armed with a grammar, a literature anthology, and a piece of chalk, may have been acceptable in my high school days, though he was rarely popular; but in the demanding days ahead, he will be as out of date as the quill pen." *SRA Insight,* Winter, 1963, p. 6.

ON FREEDOM

" 'They'—the public, the administrators, the critics—have no right to take freedom from us, the teachers; but freedom is not something one wins and then possesses; freedom is something we rewin every day, as much a quality of ourselves as it is a concession from others. Speaking and writing and exploring the books of the world are prime fields of freedom." When you need inspiration, look up Lou La Brant's "The Rights and the Responsibilities of the Teacher of English," *English Journal,* L (Sept., 1961), 379.

A TEACHER'S HAPPINESS

Happiness, according to Lin Yutang, consists of moments. A teacher cannot expect an endless series of joy-filled hours, success after success. A reasonable goal may be one or two moments a day—on the average. They will make an impressive array by retirement age.

NAME INDEX

Abbott, Allan, 291
Adams, Daniel, 345
Adams, Harlen M., 221, 427
Addison, Joseph, 28, 29, 65, 124, 214
Aeschylus, 154
Albright, Frances, 445
Allen, Frederick L., 156–57
Allen, Harold B., 270
Allingham, Margery, 259
Alm, Richard S., 78
Alva, Charles, 271
Alwin, Virginia, 78
Amory, Cleveland, 122
Anderson, Lorena A., 57, 263
Anderson, Maxwell, 154, 174
Anderson, Robert H., 59
Anderson, Sherwood, 369
Anker, Lieber, 204n
Arends, Robert, 263
Arliss, George, 437
Arnold, Elizabeth, 180
Arnold, Matthew, 215, 223
Assuma, Donald J., 117
Austen, Jane, 156, 395
Ayer, Fred C., 356

Bacon, Francis, 215
Ballet, Arthur H., 181
Baloyan, Mary, 148
Barrett, John, 352
Barrie, Sir James M., 154, 174
Barton, Elizabeth B., 223, 394
Battista, Thomas, 109
Baugh, Albert C., 274
Baxter, Frederic, 394
Becker, Carl, 196–97
Benardete, Doris, 261
Benét, Stephen Vincent, 47
Bennett, Robert A., 78
Benson, Eunice P., 57
Bernard, Kenneth, 184

Besier, Rudolph, 154
Bing, Ada M., 117
Bishop, Morris, 438
Bishop, Selma, 268–69
Blake, Howard, 363
Blake, William, 223
Bloch, Bernard, 271
Bloomfield, Leonard, 271
Boas, Ralph, 44
Boggs, W. Arthur, 260
Booth, Wayne, 175
Botel, Morton, 368
Boutelle, Margaret, 116
Boyd, Gertrude A., 356
Braddock, Richard, 265
Bratton, Dorothy, 144
Bressler, Leo A., 225
Britain, James C., 256
Brochick, Anna, 444
Brontë, Charlotte, 156
Brown, Don, 419
Brown, Eleanor, 267
Brown, Mrs. Maurice C., 24
Browning, Elizabeth Barrett, 195–96,
    450
Browning, Robert, 130, 195, 196, 294
Brumback, Doris A., 185
Bruner, Jerome, 38–39
Brunstein, James J., 420
Bryant, William Cullen, 188–89
Buck, Gwen, 179
Buck, Pearl, 167
Budinger, Jean Paul, 56
Buffon, Georges, 173
Bullock, Marie, 266
Burge, Armand, 317
Burke, Edmund, 32, 126, 128
Burke, Virginia M., 263
Burns, Robert, 28, 195, 223
Burton, Dwight L., 115, 142, 185
Burton, Katherine, 261

SUBJECT INDEX